TIME
LINES

WORLD HISTORY
YEAR BY YEAR SINCE 1492

TIME LINES

WORLD HISTORY
YEAR BY YEAR SINCE 1492

ILLUSTRATED BY JIM ROBINS

CRESCENT BOOKS
New York

TIME LINES was edited and designed by Mitchell Beazley International Limited, Artists House, 14-15 Manette Street, London W1V 5LB.

This 1991 edition published by
CRESCENT BOOKS
distributed by
Outlet Book Company, Inc.,
a Random House Company,
225 Park Avenue South,
New York, New York 10003.

ISBN 0-517-05146-X

8 7 6 5 4 3 2 1

Editor	Frank Wallis
Art Editor	Eljay Crompton
Assistant Designers	Stuart Eade, Stephen Buchanan
Picture Researcher	Kate Poole
Contributors	Arthur Butterfield, Sarah Polden, James McCarter, Michael Carter, Richard Dawes, Robert Stewart US national events: Sachem Publishing Associates, Guildford, Conn.
Illustrator	Jim Robbins
Production	Ted Timberlake

Photoset in Great Britain by Bookworm Typesetting, Manchester
Reproduction by Fotographicas Limited, London, Hong Kong
Printed in Spain by Graficas Estella, S.A., Navarra

Mitchell Beazley — 13081 — 6.12.90
Creative Text — 33408-2 — 2nd — 365

C O N T E N T S

INTRODUCTION

The year 1492 was an eventful one. In Spain, Ferdinand and Isabella expelled the Moors from Granada, their last outpost in Europe. In France, Charles VIII took control, annexed Brittany, and found his country invaded by Henry VII of England, intent on freeing Brittany and forcing the expulsion of Perkin Warbeck, a pretender to the English throne. In Italy, Pope Innocent VIII died and Leonardo da Vinci sketched a flying machine. In Nuremberg, the first terrestrial globe was constructed by Martin Behaim.

Meanwhile, Christopher Columbus was discovering America.

The exact science of hindsight permits us to see that this remarkable navigator's accidental discovery (for Columbus was hoping to reach the East Indies, and believed he had) set in motion economic and cultural changes that hastened the end of the medieval world and would shape modern history. Within 400 or so years, a land roamed and farmed by scattered Amerindian tribes at the time of Columbus was to take over the leadership of the "free" world and confront another great power that in 1492 was only just beginning to coalesce around its principal city, Moscow.

The remaining years of the 15th century saw Warbeck executed, the Jews expelled from Portugal and Spain, an attempt by Charles VIII to claim his inheritance of Naples, Vasco de Gama's voyage to India, reorganization of the Holy Roman Empire, and a war between Venice and the Ottoman Empire. It is at the beginning of the 16th century that this book opens. Europe was on the verge of the High Renaissance, the Reformation and the great age of discovery that would open Latin America and the Far East. From 1500 on the pace of life increased, as the orthodoxy of the medieval age gave way to the questioning spirit of modern times. In a little more than 450 years, human beings would stand on the Moon.

Ribbons of Time charts that progress. Some will find fascination in following a particular "ribbon" – art, or science, say – through the centuries. Others may be more intrigued by reading down a year, to discover what happened in the various fields of literature, art, music, science and so on at the same time. However the book is approached and used, its pattern of repeated motifs provide a fascinating commentary on the strengths and weaknesses, the glories and follies, of our ancestors – and of us.

THE

16th

CENTURY

	1500	**1501**	**1502**	**1503**	**1504**
World Events	**King Louis XII** of France captured Milan in the Italian Wars. **The Diet of Augsberg** established a Council of Regency to administer the Holy Roman Empire. **Brazil** was discovered and claimed for Portugal by the Portuguese navigator, Pedro Alvarez Cabral.	**France and Spain** occupied Naples, and French troops entered Rome. Louis XII was declared King of Naples by the Pope. **The Peace of Trent** brought recognition by German Emperor Maximilian I of French conquests in northern Italy. **The Turks** took Durazzo from Venice. **Russia,** under Ivan III, invaded Lithuania. **Gaspar de Corte-Real,** a Portuguese navigator, made the first authenticated European landing on the northern continent of the Western Hemisphere since the 1000s. **Amerigo Vespucci,** Florentine navigator, explored the coast of Brazil on his second voyage to the New World.	**The Safarid dynasty** in Persia was founded by Shah Ismail. **The last Moors** were expelled from Castile. **Vasco da Gama** founded a Portuguese colony at Cochin, in China. **St Helena** was discovered by the Portuguese explorer João de Nova. **Christopher Columbus,** on his fourth and last voyage to the New World, explored Central America, discovering St Lucia, the Isthmus of Panama, Honduras, and Costa Rica. **Montezuma II** ascended the throne of the Aztec Empire.	**The French in Italy** were defeated by the Spaniards in the battles of Cerignola and Garigliano, and Spanish forces temporarily entered Naples. **The War of Succession** between Albert IV of Bavaria and Rupert of the Palatinate (a state of the Holy Roman Empire), broke out. It was one of the last internal disputes in a 250-year history of family feuds. **Zanzibar** became a Portuguese colony.	**The Treaty of Lyons** force[d] Louis XII of France to ce[d]e Naples to Ferdinand II of Ara[g]on, and Naples remaine[d] under Spanish control for th[e] next 200 years. **Bâbur,** founder of the Mugha[l] dynasty in India, capture[d] Kabul, in Afghanistan.
Literature Religion Philosophy	**A Year of Jubilee** was proclaimed by Pope Alexander VI with a call for a crusade against the Turks. **Desiderius Erasmus,** Dutch humanist scholar, published his *Adagia.* **Valencia University** was founded.		**Wittenberg University** was founded.	**Thomas à Kempis's Imitation of Christ,** a book that has had more religious influence than any except the Bible, appeared in its first English translation. **Julius II** became Pope.	**Raphael** painted *The Marriag[e] of the Virgin,* which exem[p]lifies some major principle of High Renaissance art. **Giorgione,** about this date painted *The Tempest,* which marked a turning point in the history of art.
Art and Architecture	**Aldus Manutius,** an Italian printer, founded the Venice Academy for the study of Greek classics, and invented italic type. **Antwerp Cathedral** was completed after 148 years. **By 1500,** when he painted *Mystic Nativity,* Sandro Botticelli was out of key with public taste, his reputation was only restored in the 19th century.	**Michelangelo** returned to his native Florence after a five-year stay in Rome to begin work on his statue of *David,* completed in 1504, which would become the most famous piece of heroic sculpture in the world.	**Donato Bramante** began the Tempietto of S Pietro in Montorio, Rome. **Vittore Carpaccio** began his fresco cycle *Scenes from the lives of SS George and Jerome.* Full of light and detail, it is typical of the Venetian manner. **Lucas Cranch,** German painter and etcher, began his career in Vienna. In 1521 he painted the most famous portrait of Martin Luther.	**Canterbury Cathedral** was finished after 433 years. **Heny VII's chapel,** the final stage of English Gothic art, was begun in Westminster Abbey. **Leonardo da Vinci** began painting the *Mona Lisa.*	**The construction of a Sue[z] Canal** was proposed to Turke[y] by Venetian ambassadors. **Coins** appeared bearing a[n] accurate likeness of Henr[y] Tudor, the reigning Englis[h] monarch.
Performing Arts					
Science and Technology		**The Anglo-Portuguese Syndicate** completed the first of five voyages to Newfoundland.		**The pocket handkerchief** came into general use in polite European society.	
America			**Hispaniola** received 2,500 new colonists. **Amerigo Vespucci,** after his second voyage, claimed that South America was a separate continent.	**Christopher Columbus** spent a year shipwrecked and marooned in Jamaica before returning to Spain.	

CABRALS' CARAVAL

DOVASCODAGAMA· VISOREÏE COMDE·

VASCO DE GAMA

CANTERBURY CATHEDRAL

1505

Portuguese explorers discovered Ceylon (Sri Lanka), and established factories on the east coast of Africa.
Ivan III ("the Great"), ruler of Russia, died and was succeeded by his son Basil III.
Maximilian I began a reformation of the Holy Roman Empire.
Christopher Columbus died in poverty in Spain, still under the impression that he had discovered new parts of Asia.

Christ's College, Cambridge, was founded.
The first history of Germany *Epitome Rerum Germanicarum*, by Wimpfeling, was published.

Michelangelo was called to Rome by Pope Julius II.
Heironymus Bosch began *The Garden of Earthly Delights*, at about this time, a huge triptych that marked the last fling of the Gothic Middle Ages.
Giovanni Bellini painted *The Virgin and Child with saints*, the most perfect realization of the "holy conversation" theme in all Western painting.

1506

Machiavelli, the Italian diplomat, created the Florentine militia, the first Italian national troops.
Mozambique, in Africa, was colonized by the Portuguese.
Philip I of Castile died and was succeeded by a Council of Regency because of the insanity of his widow.
Riots in Lisbon led to the slaughter of between 2,000 and 4,000 converted Jews.

The University of Frankfurt-on-the-Öder was founded.

Bramante began to rebuild St Peter's Cathedral in Rome, which had been neglected in the 14th century when the popes resided at Avignon. It was one of the most ambitious building projects ever undertaken and took 120 years to complete.
The Laocoön sculpture, which was to serve as a peg for Goethe's aesthetic theories, was unearthed in Rome.

Spices from the East Indies were imported into Europe by the Augsburg merchant, Jakob Fugger.
Sugar cane was grown for the first time by the Spaniards in the West Indies.

1507

The States-General (parliament) of The Netherlands appointed Margaret of Austria as Regent until the Archduke Charles should come of age.
The Diet of Constance recognized the unity of the Holy Roman Empire and founded the Imperial Chamber, the empire's supreme judicial court.
Genoa was annexed by the French.

Martin Luther, was ordained.
Pope Julius II proclaimed an indulgence for the re-building of St Peter's.
Martin Waldseemuller, a German geographer, labelled the New World "America", for the first time, in his book, *Cosmographiae introductio,* and gave Amerigo Vespucci credit for discovering it.

Glass mirrors were greatly improved by a new Venetian manufacturing technique.

1508

King Maximilian I assumed the title of Emperor without being crowned.
The League of Cambrai was formed against Venice by Ferdinand of Aragon, Emperor Maximilian, Louis XII of France, and the Pope as part of the ongoing dispute over sovereignty in Italy.
Cuba was explored by the Spanish navigator Sebastián de Ocampo.
Puerto Rico was explored by the Spanish navigator Juan Ponce de León.

Michelangelo began painting the ceiling of the Sistine Chapel in Rome.
Raphael, at the age of 26, entered the service of Pope Julius II and was entrusted with the decoration of the new papal apartments.

1509

The Battle of Diu, in which the Egyptian and Gujarat fleets were routed by the Portuguese, left the latter in control of the Indian seas and the spice trade.
Spanish armies invaded North Africa in a crusade against the Muslim rulers of Tripoli, Oran, and Bougie.
The Venetian defeat at Agnadello led to the annexation of Faenza, Rimini, and Ravenna by Pope Julius II, and Otranto and Brindisi by Ferdinand of Aragon.

Erasmus lectured at Cambridge and dedicated his *Encomium moriae* ("In Praise of Folly"), a witty satire on church corruption and scholastic philosophy, to Thomas More.
Sebastian Brant's *Ship of Fools,* a German satire first published in 1494, appeared in an English version by Alexander Barclay.
Persecution of the Jews in Germany was led by the converted Jew, Johann Pfefferkorn, under Maximilian I.
Brasenose College, Oxford, and **St John's College,** Cambridge, were founded.

Peter Henlein, of Nuremberg, invented the watch (nicknamed the "Nuremberg egg").

Spanish conquistadores founded a colony at Darien on the Isthmus of Panama.

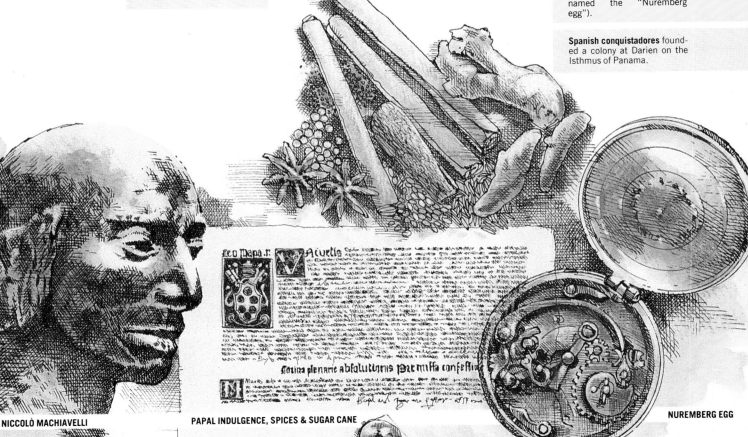

NICCOLÒ MACHIAVELLI   **PAPAL INDULGENCE, SPICES & SUGAR CANE**   **NUREMBERG EGG**

	1510	**1511**	**1512**	**1513**	**1514**

World Events

1510
War broke out between Denmark and the Hanseatic League.
Goa was captured by the Portuguese, becoming Western Europe's first possession in India.
The east coast of North America was explored by Europeans.
The slave trade began with a consignment of African slaves who were ferried across the Atlantic to work on Portuguese sugar plantations in Brazil.

1511
Pope Julius II joined the Holy League with Aragon and Venice against the French in Italy. Papal forces captured Modena and Mirandola from the French.
Vasily III became the new patriarch of Moscow.
Poland established serfdom.
Malacca, centre of the East India spice trade, was captured by the Portuguese.

1512
French armies defeated the forces of the Holy League in the Battle of Ravenna.
Navarre was conquered by the Spaniards, who annexed it to Castile.
Henry VIII of England claimed the throne of France and sent troops unsuccessfully into Spain.
Selim I deposed his father, Bayazid II, and became Sultan of Turkey.
Portuguese explorers discovered the Celebes, and found nutmeg trees in the Moluccas, thereby starting an 84-year monopoly of the nutmeg and mace trades.

1513
French forces were defeated in Italy by Henry VIII and Holy Roman Emperor Maximilian. Louis XII gave up Milan.
The Battle of Flodden Field saw the English defeat the Scots, and James IV of Scotland killed. The Scottish navy was sold to France.
Christian II became King of Denmark and Norway. He later asserted his right to the Swedish throne by force of arms.
A Portuguese expedition under Jorge Alvarez reached Canton.
The Pacific Ocean was discovered by the Spanish explorer Vasco Núñez de Balboa, who crossed the Isthmus of Panama and claimed the ocean for Spain.

1514
Selim I, Sultan of Turkey declared war on Persia.
England and France declared truce in their warfare. Mary Tudor, sister of Henry VIII married Louis XII.
Vasily III, ruler of Moscow captured Smolensk from Poland.
A peasants' revolt in Hungary was instigated by George Dozsa, a soldier of fortune, who was later captured and grilled alive.

Literature Religion Philosophy

1510
Erasmus became Professor of Greek at Cambridge University.
John Colet, English churchman and humanist, founded St Paul's School in London.
Everyman, the first English morality play, was performed.

1511
Raphael completed his great decorative commission, the frescoes in the Stanza della Segnatura in the Vatican, for Pope Julius II.
Fra Bartolommeo painted *The Mystic Marriage of St Catherine*, emphasizing his mastery particularly in the display of draperies.

1512
The Lateran Council was convened by Pope Julius II to try for the first time to reform abuses within the Church of Rome.
Shi'ism became the state religion of Persia.
"Masque" was used for the first time to describe a poetic drama.

1513
Niccolò Machiavelli wrote *The Prince* (published in 1532), in which he gave reasons for the rise and fall of states.
The Inquisition was introduced into Sicily.

1514
Thomas Wolsey was made Archbishop of York.
A papal bull was issued by Pope Leo X against slavery.

Art and Architecture

1510
Raphael painted *The Triumph of Galatea*, a fresco on the wall of the Farnesina, the villa of Agostino Chigi.

1511
In Germany, Sebastian Virdung published the earliest extant manual for playing musical instruments.

1512
Michelangelo completed his painting of the Sistine Chapel.
Raphael completed the *Sistine Madonna*, a visual expression of Renaissance humanism.

1513
Chartres Cathedral, near Paris, was completed after 400 years.
Michelangelo began work on his *Moses,* the awesome central figure of the statues surrounding the tomb of Julius II.
The Palazzo Farnese, designed by Antonio de Sangallo the younger and Michelangelo, was begun. It is the largest and one of the most magnificent Renaissance palaces in Rome.

1514
Hampton Court Palace, near London, was begun for Wolsey.

Performing Arts

Science and Technology

1510
The wheel-lock firearm was introduced in Nürnberg, Germany.
Leonardo da Vinci designed a horizontal water wheel that was a forerunner of the modern water turbine.
Sunflowers from the Americas were introduced by Spaniards into Europe to start an important oil seed crop.

1511
Cuba was occupied by the Spanish commander, Diego de Velázquez de Cuellar.

America

1512
Double-decked warships began to be used by England's Royal Navy. They displaced 1,000 tons and were armed with 70 guns.

Black slaves were imported into Hispaniola by Spain to replace moribund Indian laborers.
Newfoundland cod banks were exploited by fishermen from England, France, Portugal, and Holland, who sent the dried catch back to Europe.

1513
Florida was discovered by the Spanish explorer Juan Ponce de León, who planted orange and lemon trees there.

1514
The natives of Cuba were conquered by Spanish soldiers.
Panama received 1,500 Spanish settlers.

SLAVE TRADE

SUNFLOWER & NUTMEG

CHARTRES CATHEDRAL

1515

Louis XII, King of France, died and was succeeded by Francis I; Francis went on to conquer Lombardy in northern Italy. French armies defeated the Swiss and Venetians at the Battle of Marignano. Milan fell to Francis I.

The capture of Hormuz by Afonso d'Albuquerque, Viceroy of the Portuguese Indies, forced all other traders to round the Cape of Good Hope and established Portugal's supremacy in trade with the Far East.

Juan Díaz de Solís, a Spanish navigator and discoverer, reached the Río de la Plata in South America and discovered Argentina.

Alexander Barclay began composing his *Eclogues,* the ealiest pastoral poems in English.

Raphael was appointed chief architect of St Peter's in Rome to succeed Bramante.

Matthias Grünewald completed the enormous altarpiece for the Antonites of Isenheim.

Magnyficence by John Skelton became one of the best-known morality plays.

The first nationalized French factories (manufacturing tapestries and arms) were established.

Havana, later the capital of Cuba, was founded by Spanish conquistadores.

1516

Archduke Charles, who later became Emperor Charles V, succeeded his late grandfather, King Ferdinand II of Spain and founded the Hapsburg dynasty.

The Treaty of Noyon brought peace between France and Spain.

Seliman I, the Ottoman Sultan, supported by artillery, routed the Mamelukes at the Battle of Markdabik, north of Aleppo, capturing Aleppo and Damascus.

Thomas More, English author, wrote *Utopia,* a work of fiction describing an island governed entirely by reason.

Erasmus edited a version of the New Testament in Greek and Latin.

Corpus Christi College, Oxford, and **Seville University** were founded.

The first published account of the discovery of North America appeared in *De Rebus Oceanicus et Novo Orbe* by Italian historian Peter Martyr.

Titian began *The Assumption of the Virgin,* a monumental altarpiece in the Church of the Frari, Venice.

Music printed from engraved plates was used for the first time in Italy.

Indigo dye was introduced into Europe.

Juan Díaz de Solís, a Spanish explorer, was killed on the coast of Argentina.

1517

Archduke Charles left The Netherlands for Spain, entering Valladolid in triumph.

Cairo and Mecca were captured by the Turks. Arabia came under Turkish control.

A monopoly in the African slave trade was granted to Florentine merchants by Archduke Charles.

A Mayan civilization in Yucatán, a peninsula to the southeast of Mexico, was discovered by Spanish explorer Francisco Fernández de Córdoba.

Martin Luther nailed to the door of Wittenberg Cathedral 95 theses detailing abuses within the Church of Rome. The act marked the start of the Reformation in Germany.

Seville Cathedral was completed after 115 years.

Bartolomeo de las Casas, the first Spanish priest to be ordained in the New World, pleaded the case of the oppressed and enslaved American Indians.

1518

Portugal and the Kingdom of Kotte, Ceylon, signed a peace treaty.

The Peace of London was arranged by Cardinal Wolsey between England, France, the Pope, Maximilian I, and Spain.

Algiers and Tunis, Barbary states in North Africa, were founded.

Ulrich Zwingli, a Swiss clergyman, supported Martin Luther's Reformation. Luther was summoned to the Diet of Augsburg, where he refused to recant.

Gil Vicente, founder of Portuguese drama, wrote the farce *The Ship of Purgatory.*

Forks were used for the first time at a banquet in Venice.

A college of physicians, authorized by Henry VIII, was founded by Oxford physician Thomas Linacre.

Porcelain from Asia was imported into Europe for the first time.

Spectacles with concave lenses for the short-sighted were first shown in a portrait of Pope Leo X by Raphael.

The first fire-engine, built by German goldsmith Anthony Blatner, rolled through the streets of Augsburg.

New Spain was the name given by Spanish explorer Juan de Grijalva to the Spanish viceroyalty comprising Mexico, Central America north of Panama, the Spanish West Indies, and southwestern North America. Grijalva was also the first European to smoke tobacco, introduced to him by a native chief.

A licence to import 4,000 African slaves into the New World colonies was granted to Lorens de Gominot.

1519

Charles I of Spain became Holy Roman Emperor as Charles V, on the death of Maximilian I.

Ferdinand Magellan a Portuguese navigator working for Spain, left Europe on his journey to circumnavigate the world.

Hernán Cortés, a Spanish conquistador, entered Tenochtitlan, capital of Mexico, and met the Aztec ruler Montezuma.

Sikhism, a combination of Hinduism and Islam, was founded by Nanak, who was born near Lahore, Pakistan.

Ulrich Zwingli initiated the Swiss Reformation with his preaching in Zurich.

Martin Luther questioned the infallibility of the Pope in his Leipzig Disputation with Johann Eck.

Gil Vicente wrote a second farce, *The Ship of Heaven.*

Leonardo da Vinci, the greatest artistic and inventive genius of the Italian Renaissance, died.

St George's Chapel, Windsor, was completed after 46 years.

The Château of Chambord was begun in France, taking some 30 years to complete.

A mass-production technique for casting brass objects was being practised in Italy.

The Gulf of Mexico was explored by the Spanish navigator Domenico de Pineda.

MARTIN LUTHER   **MAYAN CIVILIZATION**   **LEONARDO DA VINCI**

	1520	1521	1522	1523	1524
World Events	**King Christian II** of Denmark and Norway defeated a Swedish army at Lake Asunden and was crowned King of Sweden. He then treacherously renounced his offer of an amnesty and massacred most of the Swedish leaders. **Emperor Charles V's** meeting with Henry VIII at Dover and Canterbury resulted in an Anglo-French commercial treaty. **Suleiman I** ("The Magnificent") became Sultan of Turkey on the death of his father, Selim I. **Ferdinand Magellan** sailed round the southern tip of South America into the South Sea, which he renamed the Pacific Ocean.	**Pope Leo X** conferred the title of "Defender of the Faith" on England's Henry VIII. **Suleiman I,** the Ottoman Sultan, conquered Belgrade and invaded Hungary. **French support for rebels in Spain** started an eight-year war between France and Holy Roman Emperor Charles V. **Ferdinand Magellan** discovered and claimed the Mariana Islands in the Pacific, named by him Islas de los Ladrones (Islands of Thieves). Magellan was killed by natives on Cebu 10 days later. **Hernán Cortés** conquered the Mexican city of Tenochtitlan (now Mexico City) after an 85-day battle.	**Gustavus Vasa** became administrator of Sweden, pledging himself to free his country from Danish control. **England declared war** on France and Scotland. Holy Roman Emperor Charles V visited Henry VIII in England and signed the Treaty of Windsor, both monarchs agreeing to invade France. **Suleiman I** captured Rhodes from the Knights of St John, who were resettled on Malta by Charles V. **The first circumnavigation of the world** was completed by the 18 survivors of the original Magellan expedition, under Sebastián del Cano. **Pascual de Andagoya,** Spanish explorer, became the first European to set foot in Peru.	**After civil war in Denmark,** Christian II was deposed and exiled. His uncle became King Frederick I of Denmark and Norway. **Gustavus Vasa** was elected Gustavus I of Sweden. **The Portuguese settlers** were expelled from China. **Pope Adrian VI** died and was succeeded by Pope Clement VII.	**The Peasants' War,** in which Protestants fought against Catholics and demanded an end to feudal services and oppression by the landed nobility, broke out in Germany. **French armies were defeated** and driven from Lombardy, when their commander, the Chevalier Bayard, was killed. **The Treaty of Malmö,** by which Denmark confirmed Swedish independence under Gustavus Vasa, was signed. **Aden** became a tributary of Portugal. Vasco da Gama became Viceroy in India. **Six Swiss cantons** sided against Zurich and the Reformation movement.
Literature Religion Philosophy	**The Royal Library of France** was founded at Fontainebleau by King Francis. **The Anabaptist movement** began to take shape in Switzerland, Germany, and The Netherlands. Anabaptists were Protestants who baptized believers only, and not infants.	**Martin Luther** appeared before the Diet of Worms and refused to recant his "heretical" principles. German princes supported him, and he proceeded to translate the Bible in defiance of the Diet.	**Martin Luther** returned to Wittenberg, having completed his translation of the New Testament, and inaugurated public worship with the liturgy in German. His supporter, Ulrich Zwingli, condemned Lenten fasting and celibacy. **Adrian VI, the last non-Italian pope** until John Paul II, was elected. **A polyglot Bible,** printed in Hebrew, Greek, Latin, and Aramaic, was published in Alcalá, Spain.	**Titian's** *Bacchus and Ariadne,* a heroic mythological composition painted for Alfonso d'Este, Duke of Ferrara, demonstrated the artist's control and inventiveness, and a new awareness in the handling of colour. **Hans Holbein** completed the first of several portraits of Erasmus, which faithfully capture the sitter's ascetic nature. He also began designs for 51 plates on the *Dance of Death* which reflected Reformation ideas.	**Ulrich Zwingli** abolished Catholic mass in Zurich.
Art and Architecture	**Joachim Patenier** painted one of the earliest industrial pictures showing a blast-furnace.	**The Château de Chenonceaux,** in France's Loire Valley, built for the royal tax collector Thomas Bohier, was completed after eight years.		**The first manual of lute playing** was published in Vienna by Hans Judenkünig.	**Italic type** was used for the first time in English typography in Robert Wakefield's *Oratio,* printed in London by Jan Wynken de Worde. **A German hymnal,** *Geistliche Lieder,* was produced jointly by Martin Luther and Johann Walther.
Performing Arts					
Science and Technology	**Cubic equations** were solved for the first time by the Italian mathematician Scipione del Ferro.	**The manufacture of silk** was introduced into France. Silk cloth had been made in Sicily since the 1100s.	**A flying machine,** for use in war, was designed by German artist and engraver Albrecht Dürer.	**The first English manual of agriculture,** *Book of Husbandry* by Anthony Fitzherbert, was published. **The first marine insurance policies** were issued at Florence.	**The first textbook on theoretical geography,** *Cosmographia,* was produced by Peter Bennewitz, German professor of mathematics.
America	**Chocolate** was brought to Spain from Mexico for the first time. **A smallpox epidemic** raged in Vera Cruz, Mexico.	**San Juan,** Puerto Rico, was founded by Spanish conquistadores. **The American Atlantic coast** was explored by Spanish explorer Francisco de Gordillo as far north as South Carolina.	**Guatemala** was conquered by Spanish armies. **A massive slave rebellion,** the first of dozens, was crushed in Hispaniola.	**The first turkeys** were introduced into Spain from America. **Sugar** was grown in Cuba for the first time.	**New York Bay** and the **Hudson River** were discovered by the Florentine navigator Giovanni da Verrazano on a coastal exploration from Cape Fear northward to Newfoundland.

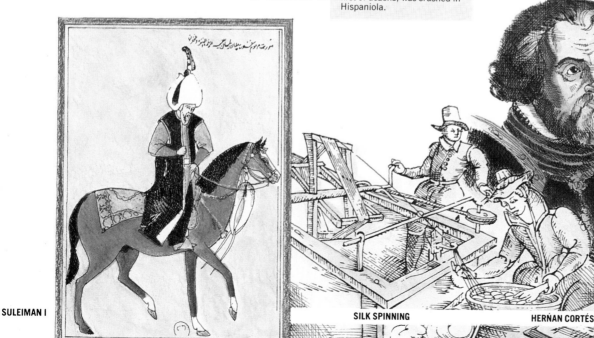

SULEIMAN I   SILK SPINNING   HERŃAN CORTÉS   LUTE

1525

The Battle of Pavia made Charles V master of Italy with the rout of the French and Swiss by German and Spanish forces. Francis I was captured and taken to Spain.
Catholic princes formed a Catholic League at Dessau.
Turkey and Hungary signed a seven-year truce.

Thomas Münzer, German Anabaptist, set up a communistic theocracy at Muhlhausen in Germany.
The Mennonites, a Protestant branch of the Anabaptists, were formed in Zurich.
The Capuchin order of friars was founded in Italy. Capuchins were to become among the most effective Roman Catholic preachers and missionaries in the Counter-Reformation.
William Tyndale's translation of the New Testament was published at Worms.

The gateway of the University of Salamanca is a supreme example of the profuse, lively decoration favoured by Spanish architects at this time, a style described as "Plateresque".
Hampton Court Palace was presented to Henry VIII by Cardinal Wolsey.

The first German manual on geometry was compiled by the German engraver Albrecht Dürer.
Hops were introduced into England from Artois in France.

Francisco Pizarro, Spanish conquistador, sailed from Panama to explore Peru.

1526

The Peace of Madrid was signed by Francis I of France and Emperor Charles V. Francis renounced claims to much Italian territory.
The Battle of Mohács resulted in the death of Hungary's Louis II and the defeat of the Hungarian armies by the Turkish forces of Suleiman I.
Ferdinand of Austria was elected King of Bohemia, thus inaugurating the Austro-Hungarian state.
The League of Cognac was formed by Pope Clement VII against Emperor Charles V.
Peace between Russia and Poland was concluded.
Bâbur, Mughal Emperor of India, established the Mughal dynasty in Delhi.

The Teutonic Knights, a German military and religious order of knights and priests, broke away from the Roman Catholic Church to become Lutherans.

Albrecht Dürer painted *The Four Apostles*, his last great religious painting, which he presented to the city of Nuremberg.
Adam and Eve by Lucas Cranach the Elder is typical of the artist's style, Gothic and northern as opposed to the "decadent" Italian.

John Taverner, organist and composer, was appointed Master of Choristers at Oxford University.

1527

Rome was sacked by German and Spanish mercenaries in the pay of Charles V. The event, which left 4,000 dead, is seen by some as the end of the Renaissance.
Florence reverted to a republic after the Medici nephews of the Pope were expelled from the city.
Ethiopians faced firearms for the first time when they were invaded by Muslim Somali Chief Ahmed Gran.
England and Russia established regular trade links for the first time.

Henry VIII appealed to the Pope for permission to divorce Catherine of Aragon.

Adrian Willaert, Flemish composer, was made *maestro di capella* at St Mark's, Venice.

Chemotherapy and the modern school of medical thinking was established by Theophrastus von Hohenheim at the University of Basel, in Switzerland.

Hernán Cortés completed the conquest of New Spain. Conquistadores carried tomatoes, avocados, papayas, and vanilla back to Spain.

1528

England and France declared war on Emperor Charles V. The French army was later expelled from Naples and Genoa.
The Scottish Reformation began.
Philipp Melanchthon, Protestant reformer, proposed German educational reforms.
A typhus epidemic swept through Italy killing tens of thousands.

Baldassare Castiglione's *Il Libro del Cortegiano* was published. An exhaustive study of etiquette and court life, it was a literary masterpiece, read and copied throughout Europe.
Jacob Hutter, an Austrian evangelist, founded a "community of love", whose members shared everything.
The dissolution of 22 religious houses by Cardinal Wolsey provided funds for the founding of several colleges.

Hans Holbein painted *The Artist's Family*. He returned temporarily to Basel after meeting Sir Thomas More in England.

The first manual of surgery, *Die kleine Chirurgia*, was written by Paracelsus (Theophrastus von Hohenheim), a Swiss physician and alchemist.

The Welser family, Augsburg merchants, received from Charles V the rights to colonize most of north-eastern South America.
Wheat was introduced into New Spain.
Herná Cortés was recalled to Spain, bringing with him haricot beans.

1529

Civil war in Switzerland raged between Reformed and Catholic cantons, with the Catholics eventually being defeated.
The Ottoman Empire reached its peak; the Turks settled in Buda, on the left bank of the Danube, after failing in their siege of Vienna.
Spanish rights in the Spice Islands were ceded to Portugal by Emperor Charles V.

The term "Protestants" was applied for the first time to the Lutheran minority at the second Diet of Speyer when Martin Luther's followers protested against restrictions on their teachings.
Luther published two hymns destined to become famous: *Away in a Manger* and *A Mighty Fortress Is Our God*.

Francisco Pizarro was made governor for life and captain-general in New Spain. He returned to Peru in a fleet of three ships.
Paprika from the New World was planted by the Turks at Buda.
Maize from America, grown in Turkey, was introduced into England as "turkey corn".

HAMPTON COURT   FRANCISCO PIZARRO   ANNE BOLEYN   CATHERINE OF ARAGON

World Events

Charles V was crowned Holy Roman Emperor by Pope Clement VII. He captured Florence, restoring the Medici family to power, and ceded Malta to the defeated and landless religious order the Knights of St John of Jerusalem.
The Antwerp Exchange was founded.

Francisco Pizarro left Panama with about 180 men to begin the conquest of Peru.
Halley's comet, believed to be a random omen of disaster, caused panic in many parts of the world. It was later named after the English astronomer Edmund Halley, who calculated its orbit and correctly foretold the date of its return.
Ferdinand I was elected King of the Romans, some 27 years before succeeding his brother, Charles V, as Holy Roman Emperor.
The Schmalkaldic League was formed by the early German Protestants to defend themselves against Charles V and the Roman Catholic states.

John Calvin, the French theologian, started the Protestant Reformation in France.
Suleiman I, Sultan of the Ottoman Empire, invaded Hungary.

Ivan IV ("Ivan the Terrible") succeeded to the Russian throne at the age of three. He ruled under the regency of his mother and later of powerful nobles until 1544.
Suleiman I concluded a treaty with Austria to give him time to deal with dissident elements in Anatolia.
Francisco Pizarro captured Cuzco, imprisoned and murdered Atahualpa, ruler of the Inca Empire, and completed his conquest of Peru.

The Ottoman Empire began to reach its greatest extent under Suleiman I, who conquered most of Hungary, captured Tunis and Mesopotamia, and took Baghdad from the Persians.
Jacques Cartier, the French sailor whose discoveries were the basis of later French claims to Canada, reached Labrador in his attempts to find a north-west passage.

Literature Religion Philosophy

The Augsburg Confessions, documents of faith drawn up by the Lutheran leaders Martin Luther and Philipp Melanchthon, were presented unsuccessfully to the German Diet at Augsburg, convoked by Emperor Charles V.

Ludovico Ariosto, one of the leading poets of the Italian Renaissance, published the third and last edition in his lifetime of his long epic poem, *Orlando Furioso*. This sceptical, humorous work about legendary chivalry had a marked effect on the writing of later authors such as Edmund Spenser and Miguel de Cervantes.
François Rabelais, the French satirist, published *Pantagruel*. The book is a grotesque and humorous satire on almost every aspect of contemporary religion and culture.

Ignatius Loyola, a Spanish ecclesiastic, founded the Society of Jesus (Jesuits) in Paris, with the aim of defending Catholicism against heresy and undertaking missionary work.

Art and Architecture

The Italian artist Antonio Allegri de Correggio painted *Adoration of the Shepherds*, his supreme altarpiece.
Titian, Italian artist and chief master of the Venetian school, painted *Cardinal Ippolito de' Medici*.

Ulrich Zwingli, the Swiss Protestant reformer, was killed in action in the Swiss civil war between the Protestant and Catholic cantons.
The Inquisition in Portugal became notably assiduous, in reaction to the spread of Protestantism damaging the cultural and commercal development of the country.
Desiderius Erasmus, the Dutch humanist and scholar, published the first complete edition of Aristotle's works.
Emblemata by Andrea Alciati was published, the first and most influential emblem book.

Hans Holbein the Younger painted *The Ambassadors*, a brilliant portrait of two French ambassadors to the English court. After arriving from Germany to settle in England, Holbein became court painter to Henry VIII. **Titian** painted Charles V. Titian had become his court painter in Bologna in 1530, an association of major significance in his career.

Michelangelo settled in Rome and, until 1541, painted the immense *Last Judgement* on the altar wall of the Sistine Chapel.
Mannerism, influenced by Michelangelo, developed in painting and architecture. Francesco Parmigianino, who painted *Madonna with the Long Neck,* was a leading exponent.
The church of St Basil was begun in what is today Red Square, Moscow.
Regensburg Cathedral, in what is now West Germany, was finally completed, after 259 years in the building.

Performing Arts

The earliest-known French contract for *commedia dell' arte* players was drawn up.
Etienne Briard introduced round characters in music engraving.

The first madrigals, which developed chiefly in Italy and England, were printed in Rome.

Science and Technology

Bottle corks were first mentioned in Palsgrave's English-French Dictionary.
The carpenter's bench and vice first came into use.
Georgius Agricola, a German mineralogist and scholar, published *De Re Metallica,* the first systematic mineralogy.

De Architecture by Vitruvius (70—15BC) was translated into Italian.

The first stage theatre of a permanent and public kind was established at Ferrara, in Italy.

Sugarcane was first cultivated in Brazil, having spread there from Central America. Christopher Columbus had carried cuttings of the plant on his second voyage across the Atlantic, and established a plantation on Santo Domingo.

America

HALLEY'S COMET   CONQUEST OF PERU   MADRIGALS

The Spaniards founded a temporary settlement on the banks of the Río de la Plata, which 45 years later became established as the city of Buenos Aires. On the west coast of South America, Diego de Almagro explored Chile and Francisco Pizarro founded Lima.
The Anabaptists formed a communist state at Munster. Their leader, John of Leiden, was tortured to death after the city was recaptured.
Tunis was occupied by the Spaniards.

Rabelais published the second edition of *Gargantua*. The book was published after *Pantagruel*, although it formed the first part of the two-part work.
Miles Coverdale's translation of the Bible into English, "out of Dutch and Latin", was published with a dedication to Henry VIII. It was the first complete Bible to be printed in England.
Sir Thomas More, after refusing to sanction Henry VIII of England's divorce from Catherine of Aragon, was sentenced to death by hanging. This was commuted to beheading.

The Belvedere was begun, summer palace of Prague Castle. The design derives from Brunelleschi's foundling hospital in Florence.

Savoy and Piedmont were conquered by France.
Provence was invaded by Charles V.
The St Lawrence River was discovered by Jacques Cartier and explored as far as the site of Montreal.

Suppression of the smaller monasteries in England, under Thomas Cromwell, was completed.
John Calvin published *The Institutes of the Christian Religion*, which was to spread Calvinist ideas across Europe.
The Pilgrimage of Grace, an uprising of some 30,000 people led by Robert Aske in protest against the dissolution of the monasteries, affected all the northern counties of England. It ended the following year with the arrest and hanging of Aske.
William Tyndale, an English Protestant and humanist famous for his translation of the New Testament from Greek into English, was burnt at the stake as a heretic.

Holbein was made court painter to Henry VIII of England.

The first song book with lute accompaniment was published in Spain.

Asunción, capital of Paraguay, was founded by Spanish pioneer Juan de Salazar.

The first Catholic hymnal was published. The complete works of *Cicero, Opera omnia,* were published in Venice in four volumes.

Sebastiano Serlio, Italian architect at the palace of Fontainebleau, published the first of six volumes of *Trattato di Architettura.*
Jacopo Sansovino began building the famous Old Library of St Mark's, Venice.
Holbein's masterpiece as court artist was his life-size Tudor dynastic portrait in Whitehall Palace.

The first conservatories of music were founded: for girls in Venice, for boys in Naples.
Costanzo Festa published his first book of madrigals, in Rome, a landmark in the development of the form.

Niccolo Fontana founded the science of ballistics.
Gerhardus Mercator, the Flemish geographer who invented the Mercator system of map projection, surveyed and drew a map of Flanders which was so accurate that Charles V made him his geographer.
Paracelsus, Philippus Aureolus, a Swiss physician and alchemist, published his *Grosse Astronomie,* a manual of astrology.
Andreas Vesalius the Belgian "father of anatomy", accepted the chair of anatomy in Padua. Six years later, his book *Fabrica (Concerning the Fabric of the Human Body)* contained the first complete description of the human body.

The Truce of Nice was arranged between Charles V and Francis I King of France. It lasted just 10 months.
Calvin was exiled from Geneva for three years and lived in Strasbourg.
Bogotá, which, in 1819, became the capital of Colombia, was founded by Gonzalo Jiménez de Quesada, a Spanish conquistador.

The feast of Corpus Christi first saw the performance of religious plays in Mexico.

Titian demonstrated his technical skill and magnificent colouring in *The Urbino Venus.*

Mercator used the name "America" for the first time.
The earliest reference to a diving bell was made at Toledo, in Spain.

Hernando de Soto, a Spanish explorer, landed at Tampa Bay, Florida. The next year he discovered and crossed the Mississippi River.

The Six Articles, the name given to a religious statute, was passed at the instance of Henry VIII. It set forth the position of the English Church on six fundamental points in an effort to stem the growth and influence of the English Protestants.

Michelangelo began to redesign the Capitol in Rome.

Jacques Arcadett, a Dutchman, was appointed master of music at the Julian Chapel, Rome. His first book of four-part madrigals was published at about this time and reprinted for more than a century.
The wedding of Cosimo I de Medici of Florence and Eleanora of Toledo included a musical *intermedi,* one of the first such interludes for which music survives.

Olaus Magnus, a Swedish ecclesiastic and historian, produced a map of the world.
The earliest form of flintlock was first recorded in Sweden.

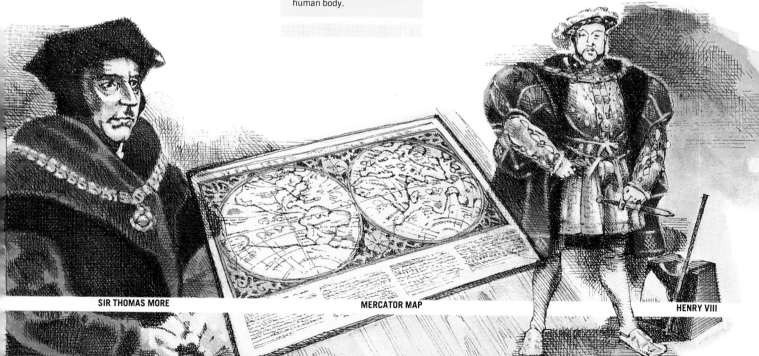

SIR THOMAS MORE   **MERCATOR MAP**   **HENRY VIII**

World Events

1540
Venice and Turkey signed a treaty at Constantinople.
Sher Shah, Afghan rebel, became Emperor of Delhi.
The united companies of barbers and surgeons were incorporated in London.
The first potato from South America reached Pope Paul III. It was then taken to France and grown as an ornamental plant.

1541
Ethiopia was invaded by the Portuguese.
Suleiman I annexed southern and central Hungary.
Francisco de Orellana, Spanish soldier and explorer, descended the River Amazon from the Andes to its mouth in the Atlantic Ocean.
Jacques Cartier, a French explorer, established a short-lived community at Quebec.

1542
War was renewed between the Holy Roman Empire and France.
Antonio da Mota, a Portuguese explorer, became the first European to enter Japan.
Hernando de Soto, died and was buried in the Mississippi, the river he had earlier discovered.

1543
Filipino natives expelled Spanish conquistador Ruy López de Villalobos from their islands a year after he had discovered and named them.
Philip of Spain married Maria of Portugal.
Henry VIII of England and Emperor Charles V formed an alliance against France.
King Francis I of France invaded Luxembourg; a combined French and Turkish fleet captured Nice.
The first European visitors to Japan introduced muskets and baked bread.

1544
Henry VIII of England crossed to Calais to campaign with Emperor Charles V against Francis I of France.
The Turks invaded Hungary for the third time and seized the Hungarian crown jewels.
The Peace of Crépy ended the fighting between Charles V and Francis I. Henry VIII was not consulted. France surrendered much territory; Charles gave up his claim to Burgundy.
Gustavus I of Sweden signed an alliance with France.

Literature Religion Philosophy

1540
The Jesuits were recognized by Pope Paul III. They were to become the chief agents of the Church of Rome in spreading the Counter-Reformation.

1541
John Knox, a Scottish theologian and historian, led the Calvinist Reformation in Scotland.
John Calvin, a French theologian, set up a theocratic government in Geneva.
Ignatius Loyola, a Spanish ecclesiastic, was elected first general of the Jesuits.

1542
The Inquisition, established by Pope Paul III in Rome, tried and tortured alleged heretics in an effort to stem the spread of the Reformation.
Magdalen College, Cambridge, was founded.
The University of Zaragoza was founded.

1543
Protestants were burnt at the stake for the first time by the Spanish Inquisition. Pope Paul III issued an Index of prohibited books.

1544
The University of Königsberg was founded.
The first herbarium was published by Italian botanist Luca Ghini.

Art & Architecture

Performing Arts

1542
The Medici tapestry factory was founded in Florence at about this time.

1543
Benvenuto Cellini, the Italian goldsmith, produced a magnificent salt cellar for Francis I, which still survives.
Hans Holbein, one of the greatest artists of the German Renaissance, died in England.

Science and Technology

1540
Ether was produced from alcohol and sulphuric acid.
The pulmonary circulaton of the blood was discovered by Michael Servetus, a Spanish theologian and physician, who was later burnt at the stake for heresy.

1541
Michelangelo completed *The Last Judgement* on the altar wall of the Sistine Chapel at Rome. It is one of the largest paintings in the world.

1542
The coast of California was investigated by Spanish explorer Juan Rodriguez Cabrillo.
Asunción, capital of Paraguay, was settled by 150 Spanish colonists.

1543
A Sun-centred planetary system was proposed in the book *De Revolutionibus Orbium Caelestium* by the Polish astronomer Nicolas Copernicus, published in the year of his death.

America

1540
Hernando de Alarcón, a Spanish explorer, discovered the Colorado River.
Francisco Vázquez de Coronado, a Spanish explorer, introduced horses, mules, pigs, cattle, and sheep into the American south-west.
García López de Cárdenas, a Spanish explorer, penetrated to the Grand Canyon of the Colorado River.

1541
Francisco Vázquez de Coronado continued his exploration of the American south-west by leaving New Mexico and crossing Texas, Oklahoma, and east Kansas.
Jacques Cartier, a French explorer, established a short-lived community at Quebec.

1543
New Spain received European vegetables and grains such as broad beans, chickpeas, barley, and wheat, transported there by a new viceroy from Spain.

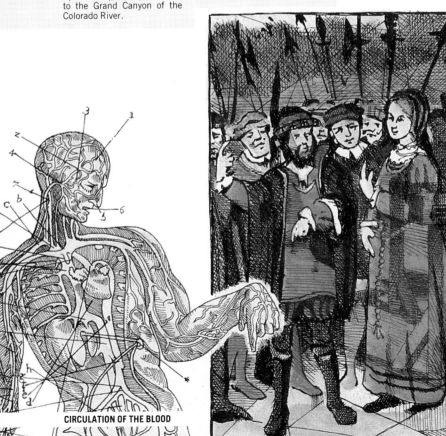

CIRCULATION OF THE BLOOD

JACQUES CARTIER   **THE INQUISITION**

A French fleet entered the Solent; the *Mary Rose*, the pride of England's fleet, capsized with heavy loss of life in Portsmouth harbour. French troops landed on the Isle of Wight.
Tréport, in Normandy, was set ablaze by an English fleet commanded by Lord Lisle.

Decrees issued by the Council of Trent initiated the Catholic, or Counter, Reformation.
Konrad von Gesner, Swiss naturalist, published the first volume of his *Bibliotheca universalis*, a catalogue of all the writers who ever lived.
Benvenuto Cellini wrote his *Autobiography*.

The Florentine painter Agnolo Bronzino produced his best-known work at about this time: *Venus, Cupid, Folly and Time*.

Claude Garamond, a French typographer, cut a Greek type that remained in use until the early 19th century. There are modern typefaces that bear his name.
The first European botanical garden was established at Padua.

A typhus epidemic killed hundreds of thousands of natives and colonists in Cuba and New Spain.

Anglo-French hostilities ended with the Peace of Ardres.
The Catholic Counter-Reformation inspired Charles V to conduct the Schmalkaldic War against the Protestant princes.
The Turks occupied Moldavia, an eastern European principality.

Martin Luther, "the father of Protestant civilization", died after some years of comparative privacy.
The first Welsh book, *Yny Lhyvyr Mwnn*, was printed.

The building of the Louvre was begun in Paris by French architect Pierre Lescot.
Michelangelo designed the dome of St Peter's in Rome.
Titian painted his great family portrait *Paul III and his Grandsons Ottavio and Cardinal Alessandro Farnese*.

Gerardus Mercator, Flemish geographer, affirmed that the Earth had a magnetic pole.
The first description of typhus and the nature of contagion were given by Italian physician Girolamo Fracastoro in his work *De contagione et contagiosis morbis*. He had earlier described and named syphilis.

A major Mayan rebellion in New Spain was brutally crushed by the Spanish conquistadores.

Ivan IV ("The Terrible") was crowned Tsar of Russia, the first Russian ruler formally to assume that title.
Francis I of France died and was succeeded by his son, Henry II. The new king was to be dominated by his mistress, Diane de Poitiers, during his 12-year reign.
Moscow was destroyed by fire.
The Battle of Muhlberg resulted in the capture of the Elector of Saxony by the forces of Charles V.
The Truce of Adrianople was concluded between Charles V and Ferdinand I of Hungary, and Suleiman I, Sultan of Turkey.

French became the official language of France, displacing Latin.
Nostradamus, the French astrologer, made his first predictions.
The Statute of the Six Articles, defining heresy, was repealed by the English parliament.

Henricus Glareanus, Swiss music theorist, published his *Dodekachordon*, on the 12 church modes.

Charles V annexed the 17 provinces of The Netherlands to the Burgundian Circle of the Empire.
King Sigismund I of Poland died.
Mary Queen of Scots, who was engaged to the Dauphin, landed in France, aged six.
The Battle of Xaquixaguane, in Peru, saw Gonzalo Pizarro, son of the conqueror of Peru, defeated and executed by Pedro de la Gasca.

Francis Xavier founded a Jesuit mission in Japan.
The University of Messina was founded.

Tintoretto, a leading artist of the late Renaissance, established his reputation with *St Mark Rescuing the Slave*.
Titian painted his monumental portrait of *Charles V at Muhlberg*.

The first historical drama in English literature, John Bale's *Kynge Johan*, appeared.
The first theatre in Paris, the Hôtel de Bourgogne (a roofed building), was opened.

Silver mines in Mexico were exploited by the Spaniards.

The 17 provinces of The Netherlands became independent of the Holy Roman Empire.
France declared war on England.
The first national assembly in Russia was called by Tsar Ivan IV.

Pope Paul III died, to be succeeded by Julius III.
Thomas Cranmer, Archbishop of Canterbury, issued the *Book of Common Prayer*. Other prayer books were forbidden by the Act of Uniformity.
La Pléiade, a group of seven French poets, of whom the greatest was Pierre de Ronsard, established the Alexandrine metre of a 12-syllable line.

The Villa d'Este, at Tivoli, was designed for the Cardinal d'Este Ippolito II by Pirro Ligorio.

Court jesters, mainly dwarfs and cripples, appeared in Europe.

Jesuit missionaries arrived in South America.
São Salvador (later Bahía), in Brazil, was founded by Portugal's first governor of Brazil, Thomé de Souza.

THE *MARY ROSE*   IVAN THE TERRIBLE   A JESTER

	1550	1551	1552	1553	1554
World Events	**The Peace of Boulogne** ended the war of England with Scotland and France. France bought back Boulogne for 400,000 crowns. **Anton Fugger,** an Augsburg banker, went bankrupt, causing bankruptcies and financial chaos throughout Europe. **Helsinki** was founded.	**French forces,** under Henry II, began campaigning against Charles V in Italy. **Turkish forces** failed to take Malta but captured Tripoli. **Don Philip** was recognized as the sole heir of Charles V.	**The Treaty of Friedewalde** confirmed an alliance between Henry II of France and the Protestant princes of Germany against Charles V. **The Turks** invaded Hungary again, with a victory at the Battle of Szegedin. **Ivan IV** of Russia began his conquest of Kazan and Astrakhan.	**Suleiman I** of Turkey made peace with Persia. **The League of Heidelberg** was formed by German Catholic and Protestant princes to stop Philip of Spain becoming Holy Roman Emperor. **The Mediterranean** was ravaged by Turkish warships. **Seeking a north-east passage to China,** English explorers Hugh Willoughby and Richard Chancellor voyaged to Russia via Archangel. Willoughby discovered Novaya Zemlya and died on the Kola Peninsula.	**Henry II of France** invaded The Netherlands. **Queen Mary I** married Philip of Spain, son of Emperor Charles V. **Reconciliation was effected** between England and the Pope. **Dragut,** leader of the Mediterranean pirates, recaptured Mehedia, in Tunisia, from the Spaniards.
Literature Religion Philosophy	**A concordance** of the entire English Bible was published by the English theologian John Marbeck. **The earliest known English comedy,** *Ralph Roister Doister,* was written by Nicholas Udall.	**Cranmer's 42 Articles,** the basis of Anglican Protestantism, were published. **The National University of Mexico** was founded. **The University of Lima** was founded. **The papal university** in Rome was founded by the Jesuits. **Persecution of the Jews** became widespread in Bavaria.	**The Augsburg Interim** was annulled. Lutherans were allowed freedom of worship in Germany. **Christ's Hospital,** in London, was founded by Edward VI. **The Second Prayer Book of Edward VI,** more radical than the first, was authorized by a second Uniformity Act.	**Protestants,** fearing persecution, began to leave England for Switzerland. **Virgil's** *Aeneid,* was translated into English, the first translation of a Latin poet published in England.	**John Knox** fled to Geneva, where he met Jean Calvin. **The first German romance novel,** *Der Goldfaden,* was written by Jörg Wickram. **Palladio** wrote *L'Antichita di Roma,* a guidebook to Roman antiquities.
Art and Architecture	**Giorgio Vasari,** an Italian architect-painter, published his definitive *Lives of the Artists* and founded the Fine Arts Academy in Florence. **Michelangelo** began *The Deposition from the Cross,* which included a self-portrait (as Nicodemus). **Japanese "Ukiyoe" painting,** taking subjects from everyday life, had its beginnings. **Palladio,** the Italian architect, designed the Villa Rotunda, Vicenza. With its four porticoes and symmetrical plan, it is an example of his search for harmonious proportions.	**Palestrina,** an Italian composer, was appointed director of music at St Peter's in Rome.	**Cleopâtre Captive** by Etienne Jodelle, the first French Neoclassical tragedy, was completed. It was presented before the court in Paris the next year.	**Christopher Tye** composed *The Acts of the Apostles.*	**Benvenuto Cellini** completed the bronze *Perseus,* his masterpiece. **Palestrina** composed his first book of Masses.
Performing Arts	**The first musical setting** of the English liturgy was produced by John Marbeck.				
Science and Technology	**Trigonometry tables** were published by Rhäticus, a German mathematician.	**Printing** was introduced into Ireland. **Astronomical tables,** based on numerical values provided by Nicolas Copernicus, were published by the German astronomer Erasmus Reinhold. **The first modern zoology,** *Historia animalium,* was written by Konrad von Gesner. **The theodolite** was described by its English inventor, Leonard Digges, in his posthumously published *Pantometria.*	**Books on geography and astronomy** were burnt in England because of fears of magic. **Bartolommeo Eustachio,** an Italian anatomist, described the Eustachian tube of the ear and the Eustachian valve in the heart.	**The camera obscura** was improved by Italian inventor Giambattista della Porta. **Michael Servetus** discovered the pulmonary circulation of the blood. He was later burnt at the stake for heresy.	**The medicine of the Renaissance** was codified by French physician Fernelius. **Flemish hop growers** emigrated to England.
America	**Mercury** was discovered in Peru.				**São Paulo,** in Brazil, was founded.

VILLA ROTUNDA   THE THEODOLITE   MARY I

The Holy Roman Empire acknowledged Lutheranism in the Peace of Augsburg.
The Ottoman Empire was undertaking its conquest of the North African coast, which it was to complete in 1556.
Japanese pirates besieged Nanking.

The first comprehensive study of birds, *L'Histoire de la nature des oyseaux*, was published by French naturalist Pierre Belon.
The first Aztec dictionary was published.
Pope Julius III died. He was succeeded briefly by Marcellus II and then by Paul IV.
The first Jesuit play was performed in Vienna.

Michelangelo's *Rondanini Pietà*, left unfinished at his death, has a modern, Impressionistic quality.

The beginning of peace in Europe that was to last for several years began when Charles V resigned and ended his days in a Spanish monastery. He bequeathed Spain to his son Philip II, and the Holy Roman Empire to his own brother, Ferdinand I.
Akbar the Great became Mogul Emperor of India, defeated the Afghans at the Battle of Panipat in the Punjab and began a 49-year reign.
The worst earthquake in history devastated China's Shansi Province, killing 830,000.
The first tobacco seeds, ready for sowing, reached Europe from Brazil, brought by a returning Franciscan monk.

The Jesuit Order was established in Prague.

Suleiman's mosque in Constantinople was completed after six years' work.

Orlando di Lasso, Belgian composer, composed his first book of motets, among the earliest of more than 2,000 compositions.

A navigational guide for voyagers to China, *The Castle of Knowledge*, was written by English mathematician Robert Recorde, who also was the first to use the equal (=) sign.
George Bauer (Agricola), a German doctor, gave a full description of mining, smelting, and chemistry in *De Re Metallica*, published at Basel. It is still the major source on the state of technology in the later Middle Ages.

England, allied to Spain, declared war on France. The French were defeated by Spanish and English troops at the Battle of St Quentin.
The Russians invaded Poland to start the 14-year Livonian War of succession in the Baltic lands held by Teutonic Knights.
John III (the Pious) of Portugal, who began the Inquisition, died, and was succeeded by his three-year-old grandson Sebastian.
The influx of American silver brought about bankruptcies in France and Spain.
The Portuguese settled in Macao, on the coast of southern China, and established trading factories there.

Catholics and Protestants met at Worms in a final effort to achieve conciliation.
The first English play to be censored, *The Sack-Full of Newes*, was produced at Aldgate, in London, and promptly suppressed.
The Geneva Testament, translated by William Whittingham, was the first English *Testament* to be divided into verses and printed in Roman type.

The first English treatise on algebra, *Whetstone of Witte*, was published by Robert Recorde.

Mary Queen of Scots married the Dauphin, who was later to become Francis II of France.
Charles V, former Holy Roman Emperor, died three weeks after eating an eel pie.
Ferdinand I became Holy Roman Emperor without being crowned by the Pope.
The Hamburg Exchange was founded.

English Protestants began to flock back to their homeland from Geneva and Zurich under the favourable religious climate.
John Knox fired a chauvinistic broadside with the publication of his *The First Blast of the Trumpet against the Monstrous Regiment of Women*.
The University of Jena was founded.

Natural Magic, the first published account of the use of the *camera obscura* as an aid to artists, was published in Italy by Giovanni Battista della Porta.

Thomas Gresham, English financier, put forward proposals for reforming the English currency in the course of which he formulated "Gresham's Law", a hypothesis that bad money drives good money out of circulation.
Two compasses for master pilots were invented by the English mathematician John Dee.

King Christian III of Denmark and Norway died after almost 24 years on the throne, to be succeeded by his son, Frederick II.
The Treaty of Cateau-Cambresis ended the war between the late Holy Roman Emperor and France, and between England and France. Calais was to remain French for eight years and then be restored to England.
Henry II, King of France, died after being struck in the head by a tournament lance, thus fulfilling a prophecy by Nostradamus.
Queen Elizabeth I of England was crowned. Lord Dudley quickly became her favourite.

Pope Paul IV died and was succeeded by Pius IV.
Geneva Academy was founded (it became a university in 1873).
John Knox preached an inflammatory sermon at Perth, inciting the Protestant lords to rise. They captured Edinburgh and sacked religious houses in other cities.
The Elizabethan Prayer Book was used for the first time.

The Escorial, the enormous and highly influential palace built on a grid plan for Philip II, was begun in Madrid.

The understanding of human blood circulation was advanced by the work of Italian anatomist Realdo Columbus.

A party of 1,500 Spanish settlers sailed from Vera Cruz to found a settlement on Pensacola Bay, in Florida. They were repulsed by hostile Indians.

PERSEUS   AKBAR   ELIZABETH I

World Events

1560

The Huguenot conspiracy of Amboise attempted unsuccessfully to overthrow the Guises (a powerful French ducal line that championed the Catholic cause).
Turkish galleys routed a Spanish fleet off Tripoli.
King Francis II of France died and was succeeded by Charles IX. Francis's widow, Mary Queen of Scots, decided to return to Scotland.
King Gustavus I of Sweden died and was succeeded by Eric XIV, who courted Queen Elizabeth I.

1561

Madrid became the capital of Spain by order of Philip II.
The Order of the Teutonic Knights in the Baltic states was secularized.

1562

The Wars of Religion in France were sparked off by the massacre of more than 60 Huguenots by the Guises during a Protestant church service at Vassy.
The Treaty of Hampton Court, signed by Elizabeth and Louis I de Bourbon, the Huguenot leader, called for English troops to occupy Dieppe and Le Havre.
An eight-year truce was signed by Emperor Ferdinand I and Suleiman I, Sultan of Turkey.
Maximilian, son of Ferdinand I, became King of Bohemia.
John Hawkins, English naval commander, removed 300 African slaves from a Portuguese ship bound for Brazil. This marked the start of English participation in the slave trade.

1563

The Seven Years' War with Sweden was started by Frederick II of Denmark, allied to Poland, Lubeck, and Saxony.
The Peace of Amboise ended the First War of Religion in France. Huguenots (Protestants) gained limited toleration. The French, united, regained Le Havre from the English.
Maximilian II was elected King of Hungary.

1564

The Peace of Troyes ended the war between England and France, with England renouncing its claim to Calais for a substantial payment.
Holy Roman Emperor Ferdinand I died and was succeeded by his son Maximilian II.
Ivan IV of Russia was forced by the boyars (Russian nobles) to withdraw from Moscow.
The Philippines were occupied by the Spaniards, who built Manila.

Literature Religion Philosophy

1560

The Church of Scotland was founded.
The beginnings of Puritanism appeared in England.
The first classic Chinese novel, *Ching P'ing Mei,* was written by Hsu Wei.

1561

Ruy López wrote the first manual of chess instruction.
The first Calvinist refugees from Flanders, clothworkers, settled in Sandwich, England.
The Edict of Orleans suspended the persecution of Huguenots.

1563

The adoption of the 39 Articles, combining Protestant doctrine with Catholic church organization, finally established the Church of England. Dissenting groups included Puritans, Separatists, and Presbyterians.
The Counter-Reformation, led by the Jesuits, began in Bavaria.
The first English edition of *Foxe's Book of Martyrs,* illustrated, appeared.

1564

The Council of Trent ended with the Pope promulgating *professio fidei,* the final definition of Roman Catholicism.
The Counter Reformation began in Poland.
John Calvin, one of the great leaders of the Protestant Reformation, died in Geneva.

Art and Architecture

1560

The Uffizi Palace (later Gallery), Giorgio Vasari's most important commission, was begun in Florence.

1561

The basilica of St Basil, in Moscow, was completed after 26 years.

1562

The University of Lille was founded.

1564

Michelangelo, one of the greatest painters and sculptors of all time, died in Rome.

Performing Arts

1561

The earliest known English tragedy, *Gorboduc, or Ferrex and Porrex,* by English dramatists Thomas Sackville and Thomas Norton, marked the first use of blank verse in the English theatre.

1562

The Rape of Europa, painted for Philip II of Spain, was the most celebrated of Titian's erotic mythologies.
The Council of Trent demanded that clarity replace embellishment and display in church music.
The first great Italian violinmaker, Gasparo Bartolotti, began his career.

1563

Pieter Bruegel the Elder, the greatest Flemish artist of the 16th century, painted *The Tower of Babel.*
The English composer William Byrd was appointed organist at Lincoln Cathedral.

1564

Andrea Amati made one of the first of his famous violins, which survives to this day.

Science and Technology

1560

The first scientific society was founded in Naples by Giovanni Battista della Porta.

1561

Printing was introduced into India by Portuguese monks at Goa.
One of the first studies in anatomy appeared in *Observationes anatomicae,* by Gabriel Fallopius.
Tobacco seeds and powdered leaves were sent to France by the French ambassador to Lisbon, Jean Nicot. The French used them for medicinal purposes. "Nicotine" is derived from the ambassador's name.

1563

Gerardus Mercator, the Flemish geographer, produced the first detailed map of Lorraine.

1564

Andreas Vesalius, "the father of modern anatomy", was forced by the Inquisition to make a pilgrimage to the Holy Land and disappeared on the voyage.
The horse-drawn coach was introduced into England from Holland.

America

1561

King Philip II of Spain forbade any more attempts by Spaniards to settle the Florida region. The French seized the opportunity to step into the vacuum.

1562

Milled coins were first introduced into England.
A survey of spas in Europe was published by William Turner.
The first conservatory in England was built by William Cecil, to protect his subtropical plants and trees.

THE BASILICA OF ST BASIL   CHESS   TOBACCO

The Turks besieged Malta, which was defended by the Knights of St John.
A Spanish expedition led by Pedro Menéndez de Avilés settled in St Augustine, Florida, and founded the first permanent European colony in North America.
Mary Queen of Scots married Henry, Lord Darnley.
Pope Pius IV died.

Pieter Bruegel the Elder received the commission for his most celebrated works, a series of paintings of *The Months*. Five survive, including *Hunters in the Snow*.
Palladio finished S Giorgio Maggiore Church in Venice.
Indian Mughal art assimilated the Persian tradition of miniature painting.

The bourrée, derived from a traditional French clog dance, was introduced at the French court of Catherine de' Medici.

The Royal College of Physicians in London was officially permitted to carry out human dissections.
Pencils were first manufactured in England.

Rio de Janeiro was founded by the Portuguese, who destroyed the existing French colony.

The Turko-Hungarian War restarted, in spite of the truce of 1562.
Religious riots in The Netherlands were instigated by fanatical Calvinists. Regent Margaret abolished the Inquisition.
Suleiman I ("The Magnificent") died, and his great empire was to begin a gradual decline under his slothful son, Selim II, who succeeded him.

Calvinism was combined with Zwinglianism by Swiss theologian Heinrich Bullinger in his *Helvetian Confession*.
Cardinal Michaele Ghislieri was elected Pope Pius V.

Peasant Wedding Dance by Pieter Bruegel the Elder revealed his skill at depicting rustic festivities.

Japanese music began to win its individual character with the popularization of national forms of vertical bamboo pipe (*shakuhachi*), three-stringed guitar (*samisen*), and zither (*koto*).

A pioneer manual of veterinary science appeared when G. Blundeville published his *Foure Chiefest Offices Belonging to Horsemanship*.
One of the world's first newspapers, *Notizie Scritte*, appeared in Venice.

The Second War of Religion in France began as a result of the Conspiracy of Meaux by the Huguenots.
The Duke of Alva, one of Philip II of Spain's military commanders, arrived in The Netherlands as military governor and began a reign of terror. Margaret of Parma resigned the regency.
The Solomon Islands in the Pacific were discovered by Spanish explorer Álvaro Mendaña de Neyra.

A monastery council to superintend the clergy was established by Maximilian II.
Rugby School in England, where the first game of rugby was played, was founded by Laurence Sheriff.

Longleat House was begun. It shows the impetus given to English domestic architecture by the Reformation.

Typhoid fever swept through parts of South America, killing more than two million Indians.

Sultan Selim II and Emperor Maximilian II made peace, with the Sultan receiving a large annual payment.
The Swedes declared Eric XIV unfit to reign and proclaimed John III king.
Leaders of the Flemish opposition to the Spanish Inquisition were beheaded as traitors at Brussels. An 80-year war of independence from Spain carried on by the Calvinist and predominantly mercantile Dutch provinces.
General Oda Nobunaga, Japanese leader who siezed Kyoto and destroyed the power of the feudal lords, introduced a dynamic period of centralization and expansion.

The Bishops' Bible, supervised by Archbishop Matthew Parker, was published in opposition to the popular Geneva (Calvinistic) Bible.
Jesuit missionaries were warmly welcomed in Japan.

Il Gesù, the mother church of the Jesuit order, was begun in Rome.

Gasparo da Salò began making violins at Brescia.

Italian anatomist Constanzo Varoli studied the anatomy of the human brain.
Bottled beer was invented by Alexander Nowell, Dean of St Paul's in London.

The Union of Lublin saw Lithuania merged with Poland and Lublin by Sigismund II of Poland.
A Morisco rebellion in Granada was put down by Don John of Austria.

The first part of a Spanish epic on the conquest of Chile, *La Araucana*, was published at about this time by Alfonso de Ercilla y Zúñiga.

Tycho Brahe, the Danish astronomer, built a quadrant measuring 5.8 metres, and a celestial globe with a diameter of 1.5 metres, at Augsburg.
Gerhardus Mercator, the Flemish geographer, produced his Map of the World, for the use of navigators, on the projection that bears his name to this day. He was also the first to use the name "atlas" for a collection of maps.

MARY QUEEN OF SCOTS   ANATOMICAL STUDIES   OPPOSING THE INQUISITION

	1570	1571	1572	1573	1574
World Events	The Turks declared war on Venice, which refused to surrender Cyprus. The Turks sacked Nicosia. The Peace of St Germain-en-Laye ended the third civil war in France. The Peace of Stettin marked Denmark's recognition of the independence of Sweden. Sweden gave up its claim to Norway. The port of Nagasaki was opened to overseas trade by the Japanese. Ivan the Terrible, Tsar of Muscovy, sacked the city of Great Novgorod, massacring most of its inhabitants during a five-week reign of terror.	Pope Pius V signed an alliance with Venice and Spain to fight the Turks. The Battle of Lepanto resulted in a complete victory by the Spanish and Venetian ships under Don John of Austria over a huge Turkish fleet. 117 Turkish ships were sunk. Moscow was sacked by Tartars from Crimea. A reconciliation took place between Charles IX of France and the Huguenots.	The Massacre of St Bartholomew's Day, in which 50,000 Huguenots and their leader, Admiral Gaspard de Coligny, were killed in and around Paris, resulted in France's Fourth War of Religion. Dutch warships, "Beggars of the Sea", effectively harried Spanish shipping in the English Channel fuelling the Dutch War of Independence. A refurbished Turkish fleet captured Cyprus. The Polish monarchy became elective on the death of Sigismund II.	The Peace of Constantinople ended the war between Turkey and Venice. Venice surrendered Cyprus and paid Turkey a large indemnity. The Pacification of Boulogne marked the end of France's Fourth War of Religion. The Huguenots gained an amnesty and were promised freedom of conscience. Don John of Austria captured Tunis from the Turks. Shogun Yoshiake in Japan was routed in his challenge of ruler Nobunaga Oda, thus bringing to an end the Ashikaga shogunate after 237 years. Wan Li, of China, began a 47-year reign as emperor of the Ming dynasty.	The Fifth War of Religion began in France. The French king, Charles IX, died and was succeeded by his brother, Henry of Valois (Henry III). Selim II, Sultan of Turkey, died and was succeeded by his son, Murad III. Spanish forces in The Netherlands besieged Leyden, but William the Silent breached the dykes to flood the land and allow his ships to sail up to the walls and lift the siege. Turkish troops captured Tunis from the Spaniards. The Portuguese began to settle Angola.
Literature Religion Philosophy	The Consensus of Sendomir united Lutherans, Calvinists, and Moravian Brethren against the Jesuits in Poland. Pope Pius V excommunicated Queen Elizabeth I of England. A treatise on education, The Scholemaster, by the English scholar Roger Ascham, was published posthumously.	Delft ware was introduced to England at about this time by potters from Antwerp. Harrow School in England was founded by John Lyon. Jesus College, Oxford, was founded by Hugh Price.	Pope Pius V died; succeeded by Pope Gregory XIII. The Society of Antiquaries was founded in London. Luis Vaz de Camões, Portuguese poet, published Os Lusíadas, an epic poem about Vasco da Gama's voyages. The first book privately printed in England, De Antiquitate Britannicae Ecclesiae, by Matthew Parker, was published.	Paolo Veronese, was hauled before the Inquisition and accused of painting profanities.	The University of Berlin was founded. An auto-da-fé took place in Mexico for the first time. Justus Lipsius, Flemish scholar, edited The Histories and The Annals of Tacitus.
Art and Architecture	Palladio published I quattro libri dell'architettura, a summary of classical architecture. Nicholas Hilliard painted his famous portrait of Elizabeth I.				Giorgio Vasari completed Florence's Uffizi Palace after 14 years of building.
Performing Arts			One of the earliest cellos was made by Andrea Amati in Cremona.	The first German cane-sugar refinery was established at Augsburg.	Juan Fernández, a Spanish navigator, discovered a group of islands, to be named after him, nearly 400 miles off the west coast of South America.
Science and Technology	Abraham Ortelius, of Amsterdam, published Theatrum orbis terrarum, the first modern atlas.		Ambroise Paré, French surgeon, brought more humane treatment for battlefield wounds. He substituted egg yolks and turpentine for boiling oil, and introduced arterial ligature instead of cauterization.	Sir Francis Drake, captured a huge shipment of Spanish silver as it was being transported across the Isthmus of Panama.	
America	Fray Batista Segura led a group of Spanish Jesuits into the Chesapeake Bay region to convert the Indians.	The Jesuits in Chesapeake Bay were wiped out by the Indians, resulting in the complete withdrawal of all Jesuits from Florida.			

HILLIARD'S MINIATURE   THE BATTLE OF LEPANTO   POPE PIUS V   CELLO

Stephen Báthory was elected King of Poland, after the defection of Henry, who became King of France.
The sovereignty of the Netherlands was offered to Queen Elizabeth by William of Orange, who faced defeat. Elizabeth declined the offer.
Bengal was conquered by Mughal Emperor Akbar.
Spain faced bankruptcy, and its troops in The Netherlands could not be paid.
Plague swept through Sicily and Italy.

Leyden University was founded to commemorate the siege.
Torquato Tasso, Italian poet, wrote *Jerusalem Liberated,* an epic of the First Crusade.

English organists and composers Thomas Tallis and William Byrd published their *Cantiones,* a collection of 34 much-loved motets, after being granted a royal licence to print and sell music.

The first European porcelain was produced at Florence, but was much inferior to the Chinese original.

Maximilian II, Holy Roman Emperor, died, and was succeeded by his eldest surviving son, Rudolf II.
The Peace of Monsieur ended the Fifth War of Religion in France. Huguenots were granted freedom of worship in all places except Paris.
In "the Spanish Fury", Antwerp was sacked by mutinous Spanish forces.
The Pacification of Ghent united all 17 provinces of The Netherlands in the face of Spanish occupation.
Martin Frobisher, the English navigator, discovered Frobisher Bay in Canada.

Jean Bodin, a major French political theorist, published his *Six Books of the Commonwealth,* arguing that the basis of any society was the family.

The first purpose-built theatre in Britain was The Theatre in Shoreditch, London.

Carolus Clusius, a French botanist, published his treatise on the flowers of Spain and Portugal, the first modern botany.
François Viète, the French mathematician, introduced the use of letters for quantities in algebra.

The Sixth War of Religion erupted in France. It ended five months later with the Peace of Bergerac, under which the Huguenots gained more important concessions.
Don John of Austria, Governor of The Netherlands, issued his Perpetual Edict by which all Spanish troops were to be withdrawn from The Netherlands and ancient liberties restored.
Danzig surrendered to Stephen Báthory, King of Poland.
Francis Drake set out to circumnavigate the world.

Raphael Holinshed published his *Chronicles of England, Scotland and Ireland.*

El Greco (Doménikos Theotokópoulos) went to Spain at about this time and settled permanently.

London's second playhouse, The Curtain, opened in Finsbury.
Javanese fleeing the spread of Islam reached Bali and kept early traditions of Indonesian music alive.

Don John of Austria died of fever. He was succeeded as Governor of The Netherlands by Alessandro Farnese, Duke of Parma.
Sebastian, King of Portugal, invaded Morocco and was killed, along with the King of Fez and the Moorish Pretender, in the Battle of Alcazar. He was succeeded by Cardinal Henry.
The Catacombs of Rome (underground tunnels and tombs) were discovered by accident.

John Lely, English dramatist and novelist, began *Euphues, the Anatomy of Wit,* an early novel of manners.

Faience, a tin-glazed earthenware, was manufactured at Nevers, in France, by the Conrade brothers.

Chinese pharmacology was summed up by Li Shih-Chen in his *Great Pharmacopoeia.* Chinese medicine was completely conservative and few new treatments were reported.

Sir Francis Drake, on his way round the world, ravaged the coasts of Chile and Peru, renaming the *Pelican* (his flagship) the *Golden Hind.*

The Union of Utrecht brought seven northern (Protestant) Netherlands provinces together, united against Catholics. They were known as the "United Provinces" and became the foundation of the Dutch Republic.
The Peace of Arras ensured that the southern provinces of The Netherlands were reconciled to Philip II.
Portuguese merchants set up trading stations in Bengal.

Plutarch's Lives, biographies of noble Greeks and Romans of the first and second centuries AD, was translated into English from the French.
English poet Edmund Spenser wrote *The Shepheardes Calender,* an eclogue (pastoral or idyllic poem) for each month of the year.

Giambologna began *The rape of the Sabine,* a remarkable example of Mannerist sculpture.

Sir Francis Drake sailed into San Francisco Bay and proclaimed English sovereignty over New Albion (California).

UFFIZI PALACE MARTIN FROBISHERS FAIENCE

World Events

1580

Philip I, King of Portugal, died, and Portugal came under Spanish rule when it was invaded by Spanish forces under the Duke of Alba. Philip II was proclaimed king and united the colonial empires of Spain and Portugal.
France's Seventh War of Religion broke out, ending with the Peace of Felix.
Ivan IV (The Terrible) of Russia killed his son and heir with his own hands.
Francis Drake returned to England after circumnavigating the world.

1581

The seven northern provinces of The Netherlands renounced their allegiance to Philip II.
The Portuguese Cortes (national assembly) submitted to Philip II of Spain.
Akbar, Mughal Emperor of India, conquered Afghanistan.
Stephen Báthory, King of Poland, invaded Russia. Russia began the conquest of Siberia.
Sweden and Poland overran Livonia.

1582

The Peace of Jam-Zapolski was concluded between Russia and Poland, under which Russia lost access to the Baltic and surrendered Livonia and Estonia to Poland.
The Gregorian Calendar was instituted by Pope Gregory XIII because the old Julian calendar had an error of one day in every 128 years. Roman Catholic countries adopted the new calendar, but Protestant countries did not fall into line until 1700 or later.
Nobunaga, ruler of Japan, was assassinated by Akechi Mitsuhide. He was succeeded by Hideyoshi, who killed Mitsuhide and carried on the work of breaking feudal power.
William of Orange escaped an assassination attempt.

1583

The Duke of Anjou sacked Antwerp (the "French Fury") but, failing to capture it, retired from The Netherlands to France.

1584

Ivan IV (The Terrible), Tsar of Russia, died and was succeeded by his weak-minded son, Fyodor I. Boris Godunov, Fyodor's brother-in-law, assumed general control.
William of Orange was assassinated by Burgundian Balthasar Gérard, on the orders of Philip II. He was succeeded by his 17-year-old son, Maurice of Nassau.
A Dutch trading post was established at the Russian port of Archangel.
Brazilian sugar was sold to the rest of Europe by Portugal, which dominated the world's sugar trade.

Literature Religion Philosophy

1580

A Jesuit mission in England was begun by Edmund Campion and Robert Parsons.
The first Sunday Schools were established in Milan by Carlo Borromeo, Archbishop of Milan.
Michel de Montaigne, French scholar and nobleman, wrote his personal essays, entitled *Essais.*

1581

Converts to Roman Catholicism in England were subject by law to the penalties of high treason.
Pope Gregory XIII attempted in vain to reconcile the Roman and Orthodox churches.
English Jesuit Edmund Campion was executed for treason.

1582

A Jesuit mission was founded in China.
The University of Edinburgh was founded.
Richard Hakluyt, English clergyman and geographer, wrote *Divers Voyages Touching the Discovery of America.*

1583

Giovanni da Bologna completed the sculpture *The Rape of the Sabine Women* for the court of the Medicis in Florence.
The Queen's Company of Players was formed in London by Sir Edmund Tilney, Master of the Revels.

1584

Sir Philip Sidney began a radical revision of his pastoral romance *Arcadia.*

Art and Architecture

1580

Longleat was built in Wiltshire, England, by Robert Smythson.

1583

Italian botanist Andrea Cesalpino published *De Plantis,* the first modern classification of plants.
Galileo discovered the parabolic nature of trajectories.
The first known life insurance policy was issued in England on the life of Londoner William Gibbons. His life was insured for £383 6s 8d at a premium of eight per cent per annum.

1584

The oldest surviving lighthouse (wave-swept) was begun at Cordonau, by the mouth of the Gironde River in France.
A European public banking system was begun with the establishment of the Banco di Rialto in Venice.

Performing Arts

1580

The English folk tune *Greensleeves* was mentioned for the first time.

1581

The first dramatic ballet, *Ballet Comique de la Reyne,* was performed at Versailles.

Science

1581

Galileo Galilei, the great Italian scientist, discovered the isochronous (equal time) swing of the pendulum by observing a swinging lamp in Pisa Cathedral.
The flageolet was invented by Sieur Juvigny.

1582

Sir Philip Sidney completed his collection of sonnets on one theme, *Astrophil and Stella.* At about this time he also wrote his *Defense of Poesy.*

1583

English explorer Humphrey Gilbert annexed Newfoundland in the name of Queen Elizabeth and founded the first English settlement in the New World. He was later drowned at sea and the colony disappeared.

America

1584

Walter Raleigh, English explorer, courtier, and writer, settled the Virginia colony on Roanoke Island, naming it after the virgin queen.

GALILEO   LONGLEAT   GREGORIAN CALENDAR   *RAPE OF THE SABINE WOMEN*

The War of the Three Henries (Henry III, Henry of Guise, and Henry of Navarre) began when Henry of Navarre, a Huguenot, became heir to the French throne.

To avenge the murder of William of Orange, Elizabeth extended her protection to The Netherlands against Spain.

Antwerp was sacked by the Duke of Parma, resulting in a serious and long-lasting loss of trade for that port.

Francis Drake attacked the Spanish ports of Vigo and Santo Domingo. English shipping in Spanish ports was then confiscated, this being a virtual declaration of war by Spain.

A dictatorship in Japan was set up by Hideyoshi.

A Jesuit university was founded in Graz, Austria.

Decimals were introduced into mathematical calculations in physics by Dutch mathematician and military and civil engineer Simon Stevin in his *Die Thiende.*

The first time-bombs were floating mines, actuated by clockwork, and used by the Dutch at the siege of Antwerp.

Bartholomew Newsam built the earliest surviving English spring-driven clocks.

John Davis, English explorer, discovered the strait, named after him, between Greenland and Canada.

Abbas I became Shah of Persia, succeeding Shah Mohammed.

Stephen Báthory, King of Poland, died and was succeeded by Sigismund III.

Akbar, the greatest Mughal Emperor of India, attempted to establish "Din Illahl" as a universal religion acceptable to his many Hindu subjects. The movement eventually collapsed under the 18th-century Muslim revival.

El Greco painted *The Burial of Count Orgaz.* This depicted the miracle of the saintly count's funeral, when St Augustine and St Stephen had personally descended from heaven to bury the corpse with their own hands.

The Lateran Church of St John, Rome, was rebuilt on the orders of Pope Sixtus V, who had succeeded the late Gregory XIII.

Pope Sixtus V proclaimed a Catholic crusade for the invasion of England. Philip II prepared an invasion fleet but was interrupted by Francis Drake, who "singed the king's beard" by burning 10,000 tons of shipping in Cadiz harbour.

Portuguese missionaries were banned from Japan by Hideyoshi.

Christopher Marlowe's *Tamburlaine the Great* was first produced and published three years later. Marlowe established blank verse as a dramatic form.

Johann Spies completed the *Historia von D. Johann Fausten,* the first published version of the Faust legend.

Osaka Castle, in Japan, whose foundation had been laid by Hideyoshi four years earlier, was completed with the help of 30,000 workers.

The Rialto Bridge, in Venice, was begun by Italian architect Antonio da Ponte.

Inigo Jones, English architect and theatrical designer, began building Cobham Hall, in Kent. It was finished by the Adam brothers.

Claudio Monteverdi, Italian composer, published his first book of madrigals.

An early collection of Jewish songs was published in *Zeminoth Israel.*

The first English child to be born in North America was Virginia Dare, daughter of John White, who established Walter Raleigh's second settlement in Roanoke, Virginia.

The "invincible" Spanish Armada sailed from Lisbon against England, led by the Duke of Medina Sidonia. It was shattered around the coasts of the British Isles by an English fleet under the command of Lord Howard of Effingham, with the help of Sir Francis Drake, Sir John Hawkins, and a violent storm. The victory opened the world to English trade and colonization.

The people of Paris rose against Henry III, who fled to Chartres. Seven months later he had Henry of Guise and his brother, Cardinal de Guise, assassinated.

Frederick II of Denmark died and was succeeded by his 10-year-old son Christian IV.

Christopher Marlowe's blank verse drama *Dr Faustus* was fully representative of the great period of English drama that was just beginning.

The Bible was translated into Welsh by Bishop William Morgan.

The Vatican library, built by Italian architect and engineer Domenico Fontana, was opened in Rome. Fontana also completed the cupola and lantern of St Peter's in Rome.

The first shorthand manual, *An Arte of Shorte, Swifte, and Secrete Writing by Character,* was published by English clergyman Timothy Bright.

An eye-witness account of the New World was provided by *A Briefe and True Account of the New Found Land of Virginia,* written by Thomas Harriot. It encouraged further settlement and investment.

Francis Drake, commanding 150 ships and 18,000 men, failed in his attempt to capture Lisbon.

Henry III, King of France, was assassinated by a Jacobin monk, Jacques Clément. Last of the House of Valois, he named Henry, King of Navarre, to succeed him. The new monarch, as Henry IV, became the first Bourbon king of France.

Catherine de' Medici, Queen Mother of France, died.

Boris Godunov asserted Moscow's religious independence from Constantinople.

Thomas Nashe, English satirical pamphleteer and dramatist, wrote *Anatomie of Absurdities,* a criticism of contemporary literature.

Richard Hakluyt wrote *The Principal Navigations, Voyages and Discoveries of the English Nation,* an account of the voyages of contemporary explorers.

Thomas Kyd's *Spanish Tragedy* was written at about this time.

Italian artist Caravaggio, leader of the Naturist movement, made skilful use of light in his *Bacchus* to bring into focus many details of suggestive power.

Thoinot Arbeau published *Orchésographie,* an early treatise on dancing, with tunes.

The stocking frame (the first knitting machine) was invented by the English clergyman William Lee.

The first water closet was designed by Elizabethan poet Sir John Harington and installed in his country house near Bath.

FRANCIS DRAKE   OSAKA CASTLE   CLAUDIO MONTEVERDI   THE ARMADA   HENRY IV

World Events

1590
The Cardinal of Bourbon was proclaimed King Charles X of France by the Catholic League. He died within five months.
The siege of Paris was laid by Henry IV, causing famine. It was raised by the Duke of Parma.
Shah Abbas I of Persia made peace with Turkey, abandoning Georgia, Shirva, and Tabriz.
The Emperor of Morocco annexed Timbuktu and Upper Niger.

1591
Dmitri, the son of Ivan the Terrible, was assassinated on the orders of Boris Godunov.
Christian I of Saxony died. He was succeeded by his eight-year-old son, Christian II.
Sir James Lancaster, an English navigator, became the first Englishman to reach the East Indies, sailing via the Cape of Good Hope with three ships.
The League of Torgau was formed by German Protestants.
The running of the bulls through the streets of the town was begun in Pamplona in northern Spain.

1592
King John III of Sweden died and was succeeded by his son, Sigismund III of Poland.
Emperor Rudolf II made peace with Poland.
Mombasa was settled by the Portuguese.
Emperor Akbar conquered Sind.
The Japanese invaded Korea but were later expelled by the Chinese.

1593
Emperor Rudolf II renewed his war against Turkey.
Sigismund III failed in his attempts to restore Roman Catholicism in Sweden.
Henry IV of France formally joined the Roman Catholic Church.

1594
Henry IV of France captured Paris and was crowned at Chartres.
Philip II of Spain closed the port of Lisbon to Dutch shipping.
English navigator James Lancaster broke the Portuguese trading monopoly in India.
Akbar the Great captured Kandahar in Afghanistan.
Martin Frobisher, an English explorer, was killed in helping an Anglo-French force to recapture Brest from the Spaniards.

Literature Religion Philosophy

1590
Edmund Spenser, the English poet, began *The Faerie Queene* (Books 1–3), an allegorical romance of chivalry at court.
Pope Sixtus V died, to be succeeded by Urban VII, who himself died 12 days later. He was succeeded by Gregory XIV.
William Shakespeare, began to produce a stream of historical dramas and comedies. By 1600 he had written some 20 plays, including *As You Like It, A Midsummer Night's Dream, Romeo and Juliet.*

1591
Henry IV of France was excommunicated by the Pope.
Pope Gregory XIV died and was succeeded by Innocent IX.
Trinity College, Dublin, was founded by Queen Elizabeth.

1592
The Presbyterian Order of the Church of Scotland was ratified by the Scottish parliament.
Pope Innocent IX died and was succeeded by Clement VIII.
The Latin translation of the Bible, *The Vulgate,* was issued in a definitive text.

1593
Christopher Marlowe, the great English dramatist and poet, was killed in a tavern brawl at Deptford, near London.

1594
By the Edict of St Germain-en-Laye, Huguenots were granted freedom of worship.
An early English picaresque novel, *The Unfortunate Traveller, or The Life of Jack Wilton,* was published by novelist-dramatist Thomas Nashe.

Art & Architecture

1592
The Last Supper, one of Tintoretto's last paintings, was possibly his finest work.

1593
The building of the Escorial palace near Madrid was completed after 30 years.
The Purana Pul bridge in Hyderabad, with 23 arches, was built across the River Musi.

Performing Arts

1593
Thomas Morley, the organist at St Paul's Cathedral in London, wrote five books of madrigals.
Chu-tsai-ya, of China, developed the 12 equal temperament semitones in an octave.
London theatres closed down for a year because of the plague.

1594
London theatres reopened.

Science and Technology

1590
Coalmining began in the Ruhr.
The first English paper mill was established at Dartford in Kent.
The compound microscope was invented by Dutch spectacles maker Zacharias Janssen.

1591
The first fire insurance originated in Hamburg. It was a municipal enterprise, signed by 101 persons, mostly brewers. No premiums were required.

1592
Windmills in Holland were used to drive mechanical saws.
The ruins of the Roman city of Pompeii were discovered.
Galileo moved to the University of Padua. In his *Della scienza mechanica* he dealt with the problem of raising weights.

1593
The first French botanical gardens were established by the University of Montpelier.
An account of binocular vision was included in *De refractione, optices parte* by Giambattista della Porta.
Orange and lemon juices were recommended as antiscorbutics by Admiral Sir Richard Hawkins, an English naval commander, who reported that 10,000 naval personnel under his command had died of scurvy.

1594
Sir Richard Hawkins rounded Cape Horn, ransacked Valparaíso, and was then defeated and captured by the Spaniards.
The Portuguese colony of Pernambuco in Brazil was ransacked by an English fleet.

America

1592
Juan de Fuca, a Spanish explorer, explored North America's Pacific coast and discovered British Columbia.

TO THE MOST MIGH-TIE AND MAGNIFI-CENT EMPRESSE ELI-ZABETH BY THE GRACE OF GOD QVEENE OF ENGLAND, FRANCE AND IRELAND DE-FENDER OF THE FAITH &c.

Her moft humble

Servant:
THE FAERIE QUEENE

Ed. Spenfer.

The firft Booke of the Faerie Queene.
Contayning
The Legend of the Knight of the Red Croffe OR Of Holineffe.

A 2

THE FAERIE QUEENE | **SHAKESPEARE** | **RICHARD HAWKINS**

Henry IV of France declared war on Spain.
Philip II of Spain promised to help the Earl of Tyrone's Irish rebels against England.
A Spanish expeditionary force landed in Cornwall, burning Penzance and Mousehole before retiring.
The Dutch East India Company sent its first ships to the Orient. The Dutch began to colonize the East Indies, taking much trade off the Portuguese.
Sultan Murad III of Turkey died, and was succeeded by Muhammed III, who promptly had 19 of his brothers murdered.
A peasant revolt broke out in Upper Austria.
Warsaw became the capital of Poland.
Walter Raleigh explored 300 miles of the River Orinoco in South America with four ships and 100 men.

Pope Clement VIII absolved Henry IV, recognizing him as King of France.
Robert Southwell, an English Jesuit poet, was found guilty of treason and hanged at Tyburn, after imprisonment and torture.

The bow was finally abandoned by the English army as a weapon of war.

A successful missionary effort in Florida was launched by Spain, where some 1,500 Indians were converted to Christianity, despite overt hostility.

The Decrees of Folembray ended the War of the Catholic League in France.
The Pacification of Ireland was signed, but the Earl of Tyrone refused to abide by it. A Spanish fleet sailing to help him was scattered by storms.
Cadiz was sacked by the English. The Spaniards captured Calais.
The Battle of Keresztes in northern Hungary ended in victory for the Turks over the Austrians.
Dutch navigator Willem Barents discovered Spitzbergen and the Barents Sea.
Sir Francis Drake, the greatest seaman of the Elizabethan age, died at sea on an expedition to the Spanish Main.

Edmund Spenser completed Books 4–6 of *The Faerie Queene*.

Blackfriars Theatre opened in London.

Galileo invented the thermometer.
Tomatoes were introduced into England, where they were grown as ornamental plants.
The trigonometrical tables of Georg Joachim Rheticus, containing all six ratios, were published posthumously.
Ludolph van Ceulen, in his *Van den Circkel,* gave the ratio of the diameter to the circumference of a circle to 20 places.

A second Spanish Armada left for England but was scattered by storms.
William V, Duke of Bavaria, abdicated in favour of his son Maximilian I.
The Dutch founded Batavia, in Java.
Japan's Toyotomi Hideyoshi ordered all missionaries to leave the country.

The Aldine Press, in Venice (founded in 1494), ceased after publishing 908 works.

In his ceiling painting *The loves of the gods,* Annibale Carracci revived the classical values of the High Renaissance.

The first opera, *Dafne,* was performed in Florence.
John Dowland, an English lutenist and composer, wrote his *First Booke of Songs.*
Italian musician Giovanni Gabrielli composed *Sonata Pian'e Forte* for two consorts, the first ensemble piece in which instrumentation was specified.

Hammocks on Royal Naval vessels were authorized by the English Admiralty.
The sector was invented by Galileo. It was used to solve algebraical problems mechanically.
Mount Hekla, an Icelandic volcano, erupted after 443 years.

Fyodor I of Russia died. Boris Godunov siezed the throne and was formally elected Tsar.
Henry IV ended the French Wars of Religion and granted equal rights to Catholics and Huguenots in the Edict of Nantes.
After the death of Duke Alfonso II, the last of the House of Este, Pope Clement VIII siezed the Duchy of Ferrara.
By the Peace of Vervins Philip II resigned all claims to the French crown. The country was united under Henry IV.
King Philip II of Spain died and was succeeded by Philip III.
Hideyoshi, the dictator of Japan, died and was succeeded by Ieyasu Tokugawa, who restored the shogunate.
Mauritius was captured by the Dutch.

Lope de Vega, the Spanish novelist-poet, wrote *La Dragontea,* an epic poem describing the fanciful adventures of Sir Francis Drake.
Ben Jonson, the English playwright-poet, wrote *Every Man in His Humour.*

Tycho Brahe wrote *Astronomicae Instauratae Mechanica* in which he gave an account of his discoveries and a description of his instruments.
Ironclad warships were invented by Korean Admiral Visunsin.

The Duke of Sully, the French superintendent of finances, reformed his country's taxation and economic policy, agriculture, and overseas trade.
The Swedish Diet deposed Sigismund III and proclaimed Charles of Södermanland ruler as Charles IX.
The first chamber of commerce was founded at Marseilles.
The plague swept through Spain.
Postal rates were fixed in Germany.
The first recorded auction sale took place when the library of Philip von Marnix was sold in The Netherlands.

Caravaggio's three paintings on *The life of St Matthew* were revolutionary in their dramatic realism and use of light.

The Globe Theatre, where Shakespeare's plays were performed, was opened in Southwark, London. It was owned by the actors themselves.

Copper coinage was introduced into Spain.
Studies in ornithology were published by the Italian naturalist Ulissi Aldrovandi.
Richard Hakluyt published the first authentic map of North America.

JAVANESE SETTLEMENT   WALTER RALEIGH   THE GLOBE THEATRE

CROSSING THE GREAT DIVIDE

The ocean between America and Europe carries more shipping than any other sealane in the world and is one of the world's busiest air routes. Today, the process of getting from one side to the other is so simple that the emphasis is on not whether it can be done but on how quickly it can be done. The mark was set by Columbus. Although Vikings led by Eric the Red made the journey to Greenland around 982, and his son, Leif, reached the North American coast by 1000, it was not until Columbus reached the West Indies in 1492, 35 days after quitting the Canaries, that there was a record to aim at.

To the businessman – whether a 17th tobacco merchant, a 19th century slaver with a perishable cargo, or a modern salesman with a portable computer – time has always equalled money. Each age has pushed its transport technology to the limit. Clipper ships were the swiftest the age of sailing ships could achieve; the *Scotia* the best of the age of paddle steamers. The *United States* set the standard for big screw-driven liners – and perhaps Concorde marks the peak of the jet age.

The Atlantic is some 3,000 miles wide between England and the United States. It took the Pilgrim Fathers, in the *Mayflower,* 66 days to make the journey in 1620, 130 years after Columbus. A 19th century slaver rarely took less than three months to get from West Africa to Florida. But by the middle of the 19th century the *Scotia* had made its fastest crossing in eight

days and three hours and 50 years later the Cunard liner *Mauretania* had cut that to four days, 10 hours and 41 minutes.

Humankind had been using powered aircraft for barely 16 years when John Alcock and Arthur Brown became the first to fly the Atlantic non-stop. It took them 28 hours and 27 minutes. Eight years later Charles Lindbergh made the first solo flight, in 33 hours and 39 minutes. Between 1932 and 1937 the German airships *Graf Zeppelin* and *Hindenburg* carried passengers on transatlantic flights, but the loss of the *Hindenburg* by fire as it was mooring at Lakehurst, New Jersey, in 1937 effectively ended the brief age of the airship. Flying boats operated for a year or two before World War II, but were replaced by propeller-driven land aircraft such as the DC–4 and the Constellation by 1946. The first turbojet transatlantic service began in 1958, with a De Havilland Comet 4S, which took six hours and 11 minutes from London to New York.

The current record for the fastest transatlantic flight is held by a SR71A "Blackbird" spy plane, which in 1974 did the trip in one hour, 54 minutes and 56.4 seconds. Concorde's best-ever is currently two hours, 55 minutes and 15 seconds, a record set on February 7 1988. It was assisted by a jet stream of up to 200 knots.

There are a handful of miscellaneous records, all from this century. The direction taken – east to west or west to east – can make a difference: the fastest west-east solo rowing record, set

in 1980, from Chatham, Massachusetts to Ushant, France, is 71 days and 23 hours; the fastest east-west row, from Penzance in England to Miami, set in 1970, is 160 days and eight hours. The fastest solo sailing, made in 1922, is 16 days; and the fastest solo balloon crossing, from Caribou, Maine, to Montenotte, Italy, is three days and 14 hours.

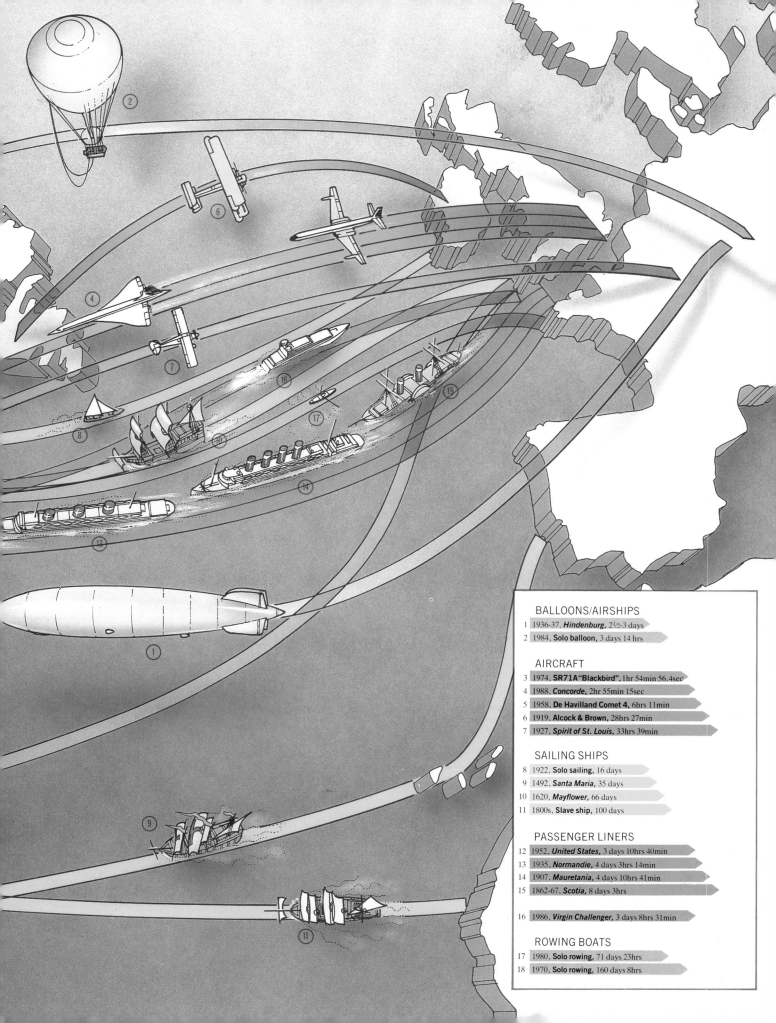

BALLOONS/AIRSHIPS

1 1936-37, *Hindenburg,* 2½-3 days
2 1984, *Solo balloon,* 3 days 14 hrs

AIRCRAFT

3 1974, **SR71A "Blackbird",** 1hr 54min 56.4sec
4 1988, *Concorde,* 2hr 55min 15sec
5 1958, **De Havilland Comet 4,** 6hrs 11min
6 1919, **Alcock & Brown,** 28hrs 27min
7 1927, *Spirit of St. Louis,* 33hrs 39min

SAILING SHIPS

8 1922, **Solo sailing,** 16 days
9 1492, *Santa Maria,* 35 days
10 1620, *Mayflower,* 66 days
11 1800s, **Slave ship,** 100 days

PASSENGER LINERS

12 1952, *United States,* 3 days 10hrs 40min
13 1935, *Normandie,* 4 days 3hrs 14min
14 1907, *Mauretania,* 4 days 10hrs 41min
15 1862-67, *Scotia,* 8 days 3hrs

16 1986, *Virgin Challenger,* 3 days 8hrs 31min

ROWING BOATS

17 1980, **Solo rowing,** 71 days 23hrs
18 1970, **Solo rowing,** 160 days 8hrs

EASY RIDING
the triumph of the automobile

The 20th century has been marked by a rate of technological advance greater than any previously known. Much of that progress has brought social and economic change in its wake. But if one single thing has wrought a revolution, it is the automobile.

Today's principal form of transport covers the ground on a sophisticated version of the wheel that was invented about 5,500 years ago. Another 1,500 years were to pass before spoked wheels were developed and it was not until the 16th century that some degree of comfort was introduced into passenger vehicles by the addition of primitive suspension – straps that suspended the body from the chassis. Springs were introduced about 1665.

There followed a curious period in which horse-drawn coaches, steam-propelled "automobiles" and steam trains

Stage coach (1700s)

were all carrying passengers. There is considerable argument over who first invented the automobile, but the British and the French agree that it was Nicolas-Joseph Cugnot, of Lorraine, whose steam-powered tricycle ran in 1769. By 1800, steam buses were being used in Paris and in the 1830s in England steam coaches had advanced to the point where a service ran from London to Cambridge, a distance of 48 miles. However, they encountered public opposition, eventually embodied in the Red Flag Act that required each carriage to have a crew of three, one of whom had to walk in front with a red warning flag. The Act was not repealed until 1896.

Most countries developed light steam cars in the 1860s: in the United States they were used well into the 20th century, with the Stanley "steamer" taking the world speed record at 127.66mph

in 1906.

At the same time as these early automobiles were being developed, stagecoach transportation reached a peak with the inauguration, in 1858, of

US locomotive (1860s)

the Butterfield Overland Express, the first transcontinental stagecoach service, which ran from Tipton, Missouri, to San Francisco. The journey of 2,800 miles took 25 days and was the fastest and longest sustained coach journey in the world.

But by the time of this achievement, the stagecoach was being challenged by yet another way of moving people from A to B. By 1812 steam locomotives had become practical propositions and in 1825 the first railroad – the Stockton and Darlington Railway – was opened. Five years later a line was opened between Liverpool and Manchester. The success of these lines spurred interest in the United States and in 1827 the Baltimore and Ohio Railroad received its charter. By 1865 the United States had 30,000 miles of railroad track and in 1869 the driving of a golden spike marked the linking of the Union Pacific and Central Pacific Railroads across the country. England had already laid some 13,000 miles of

railroad track and in 1885 Canada was crossed by the Canadian Pacific.

It seemed that hardly had the railroads got into their stride than they in turn faced a challenge.

Benz tricycle (1886)

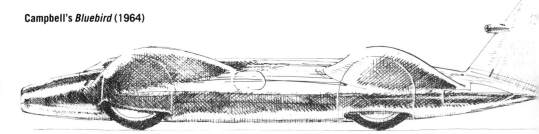

The internal combustion engine dated back to 1862, the year in which Jean-Joseph-Etienne Lenoir made a six-mile trip in the first automobile with such an engine. Carl Benz, who with Gottlieb Daimler, was to become the most important pioneer in the new form of transport, patented

his first car in 1886, a year after it first ran. His company produced its first four-wheeled cars in 1893 and by 1899 was making racing cars. The first motor race was held in 1905, from Paris to Bordeaux; the winner averaged 15mph. The current world record for a wheel-driven car, set by Donald Campbell's *Bluebird* in 1964, is 429.323mph.

In 1908 Henry Ford produced the first car designed for a mass market, the Model T. That single act of making the automobile available to almost everyone produced a revolution. Roads extended to take an increasing volume of traffic and, ultimately, the railroads felt the pinch and were forced to close uneconomic lines: today the United States has about 3,850,000 miles of roads and only a fifth of that amount in railroad track. The ratio of road to rail in Great Britain is about 1:10. One consequence of increasing dependence on roads was traffic jams: the French hold the world record, with a 109.3 mile-tailback recorded outside Lyon in 1980.

Today, the automobile is a mixed blessing. The pollution it causes is the target of attack by environmentalists and it is seen as congesting city centers – though there are people still alive who can testify that the condition of city streets when horse-drawn carriages and cabs were in vogue 80 years ago was not much better.

Campbell's *Bluebird* (1964)

THE 17th CENTURY

	1600	1601	1602	1603	1604
World Events	Ieyasu became absolute ruler of Japan after disposing of his rivals in the Battle of Sekigahara. **Maurice of Nassau** defeated the Spaniards at Nieuport. **Catholics in Sweden** were persecuted by Charles IX, and Swedish nobles in opposition were executed. **A Spanish army,** sent to support the Earl of Tyrone's Irish rebellion, landed at Kinsale.	**Ostend** was besieged by Archduke Albert of Austria. **Michael, Prince of Moldavia,** was murdered by Hungarians. **Dutch forces** removed the Portuguese from Malacca. **The "false Dmitri,"** who claimed to be a son of Ivan IV, raised support in Poland for a proposed invasion of Russia. **Dutch navigator Olivier van Noort** completed the fourth circumnavigation of the world.	**Persia and Turkey** went to war. **The first modern public company,** the Dutch East India Company, was founded in Batavia with a capital of £540,000. **Spanish merchants** were allowed into Japan.	**Queen Elizabeth I of England** died and was succeeded by her cousin James VI of Scotland, who ruled as James I of England, Scotland and Ireland. **Jesuits were recalled** to France by Henry IV. **Emperor Rudolf II** faced a revolt in Transylvania. **Power struggles in Japan** resulted in the Tokugawa (Edo) period, which advanced education and economic growth.	**James I of England** ended the war with Spain. **Sigismund III of Sweden** was deposed by his uncle, Charles IX, thus ensuring Protestantism for the country. **The Turks lost Tabriz** to Shah Abbas I of Persia. **Czar Boris Godunov** routed "False Dmitri," claimant to the Russian throne. **The Dutch lost Ostend** to Spanish forces after a siege that lasted three and a half years. **Russian Cossacks** founded Tomsk.
Literature Religion Philosophy	**François de Malherbe,** exponent of the classic alexandrine poetical measure, wrote his greatest work, *Ode au Roi Henri le Grande.*	**The most important** Dutch writer of the 17th century, Pieter Cornelisz Hooft, composed his love lyrics until 1610. They revealed the influence of his Italian travels. **John Donne** wrote *The Progress of the Soule.* **In Poland,** Faustus Socinus was the inspiration behind the Unitarian movement, which denied the existence of the Holy Trinity.	**Domenichino,** later to become the leading painter of the Bologna school, assisted Annibale Carracci with the decorative scheme of the Farnese Palace in Rome.	**Monteverdi** published his *Fourth Book of Madrigals.*	
Art and Architecture	**El Greco's** few, small landscapes are unique; the eerie lighting of a *View of Toledo* gives it a modern quality.		**A collection of German Lieder** was published in *Lustgarten,* by Hans Leo Hassler.	**L'Ecossaise** by Antoine de Montchretien, about Mary Queen of Scots, was one of the first plays to deal with near-contemporary events.	**Peter Paul Rubens,** who would become the greatest Flemish painter in the Baroque style, studied for four years in Italy the work of Renaissance masters and antique forms.
Performing Arts	**The first oratorio,** *La Rappresentazione di Anima e di Corpa,* by Emilio del Cavaliere, was performed in Rome. **Harps** were introduced into orchestras. **Will Kemp** danced in Morris steps from London to Norwich, recorded in Kemp's *Nine Daies Wonder.*	**Johann Kepler,** German astronomer, was appointed astronomer and astrologer to Emperor Rudolf II.	**The first successful abdominal surgery** was carried out in Prague by Florian Mathis, who removed a dagger from the stomach of a sword-swallower. **Barium sulfide** was discovered by Italian chemist Vincenzio Cascarido. **Laws of gravitation and oscillation** were studied by Galileo.	**A catalog of the stars** was published by Johann Bayer. **Valves in the vein** were discovered and accurately portrayed by Italian physician Fabricio di Acquapendente.	**The manufacture of silk** began in England. **Johann Kepler** published *Astronomiae pars optica,* in which he explained that the crystalline center of the eye was a lens that projected an inverted image onto the retina.
Science and Technology	**De Magnete,** a study of magnetism and electricity, was published by Englishman William Gilbert. He suggested that the Earth was a giant magnet with its own magnetic field.		**Raleigh sent** a last expedition from England to look for survivors of the ill-fated Roanoke colony. It found none.	**Samuel de Champlain** made his first voyage to New World, exploring the upper St. Lawrence River for France.	**A settlement was established** at Port Royal, Nova Scotia. **Champlain's second voyage** (1604—1606) to Canada and New England coast began.
America	**Spanish in Florida** regrouped after retreats in previous years and defeated the Indians; missions were subsequently established north and west of St. Augustine.				

JOHANN KEPLER   DUTCH EAST INDIAMAN   JAMES I   PETER PAUL RUBEN

Guy Fawkes, an English conspirator, was arrested in the cellars of Parliament, and accused of trying to blow up the House of Lords during the state opening of Parliament by James I.
Czar Boris Godunov died and was succeeded by his son, Fyodor II. "False Dmitri" entered Moscow, Fyodor was assassinated, and Dmitri was crowned Czar of Russia.
Ieyasu, ruler of Japan, died and was succeeded by his son, Hidetada.
Port Royal, in the West Indies, was founded by the French.

The first and one of the greatest of modern novels, *Don Quixote,* by the Spanish writer Miguel de Cervantes Saavedra, was published in two parts. The book has been translated more widely than any except the Bible.

A pioneer of modern anatomy, the Swiss anatomist Gaspard Bauhin, published his *Theatrum anatomicum.*

Discrimination against Roman Catholics in England inspired a voyage to find a site for a Catholic colony in North America. The account of the trip (1605–1606) excited interest in England in starting colonies in North America.

Guy Fawkes and his associates were sentenced to death and executed.
Boyar Vasili Shuisky was elected Czar of Russia after assassinating "False Dmitri."
The Turks and Austrians signed a treaty at Zsitva-Torok that brought peace for 50 years.
A Dutch fleet routed a combined Spanish and Portuguese fleet in the East Indies.
Spanish navigator Luis Vaez de Torres discovered the strait between Australia and New Guinea that bears his name.
A Royal Charter was granted to the Virginia Company in London, which dispatched 120 colonists to Virginia.
James I proclaimed a flag for England and Scotland.

A pioneer atlas of the world, the *Mercator-Hondius Atlas,* was published by Flemish engraver Jodocus Hondius.

Caravaggio fled Rome after killing a man, unable to settle anywhere thereafter.

Macbeth, one of Shakespeare's four great tragedies, was performed for the first time.
Ben Jonson completed *Volpone.*

The Plymouth Co. and the London Co., which sent three ships to the New World on 20 December. Land grants of the two companies in Virginia were separated by 100-mile buffer zone.

The proposed union of England and Scotland was rejected by the English Parliament.
Charles IX was crowned King of Sweden. War broke out between Sweden and Poland.
A Dutch fleet defeated a Spanish fleet off Gibraltar.
National bankruptcy was announced in Spain. The bank of Genoa failed.
Jamestown, Virginia, became the first permanent English settlement to be founded on the American mainland.

The Knight of the Burning Pestle, a play by Francis Beaumont and John Fletcher, ridiculed the middle classes.

A French school of tapestry was established in Paris with the help of Flemish weavers.

The earliest European opera extant, Monteverdi's *La Favola d'Orfeo,* was performed in Mantua, Italy.

Severe hardships marked the first months of the Virginia colony, and many settlers died. Captain John Smith was captured by Indians.

Czar Vasili Shuisky was threatened by a second "False Dmitri," who joined by a number of boyars including the Romanovs, advanced to the outskirts of Moscow.
Hungary, Austria, and Moravia were ceded by Rudolf II to his brother, Matthias.
A Protestant Union was formed by the Protestant States of Rhineland under Frederick IV of the Palatinate and Christian of Anhalt.

John Webster produced *The White Devil,* a revenge tragedy of cumulative cruelty and destructiveness.

Girolamo Frescobaldi was appointed organist at St Peter's in Rome.

Checks, called "cash letters," were first used in The Netherlands.
The telescope was invented by Dutch scientist Johann Lippershey and demonstrated before The Netherlands States-General.

John Smith, saved from death by the Indian girl Pocahontas, returned to Jamestown, explored Chesapeake Bay, and after confrontations with opponents was elected to govern Virginia (1608–1609).
Champlain founded Quebec City.

The Catholic League of German Princes was established in Munich in response to the formation of the Protestant Union the previous year.
Polish troops invaded Russian and besieged Smolensk. "False Dmitri" withdrew from Moscow.
A 12-year truce began between Holland and Spain.
Dutch traders arrived in Japan, rivalling the Spanish and Portuguese in the Far East.
The Bank of Amsterdam was founded.

Ben Jonson wrote his *Masque of Queens.*
Shakespeare completed his sonnet sequence of 154 poems dedicated to WH.

A collection of catches and rounds, called *Pammelia,* was published by Thomas Ravenscroft.
The first example of engraved music in England, *Fantazies of Three Parts,* was published by Orlando Gibbons.

Tin-enameled ware was manufactured at Delft.
Tea from China, sent by the Dutch East India Company, reached European ports.
The thermostat was invented by Dutch physicist Cornelius Drebbel.

Henry Hudson ascended the Hudson River to Albany for Dutch East India Co.
Virginia colonists planted corn for the first time.
Champlain reached the lake named for him.

GUY FAWKES AND CONSPIRATORS UNION FLAG LIPPERSHEY'S TELESCOPE

1610

World Events

Henry IV formed an alliance with the German Protestant Union. He was subsequently assassinated by François Ravaillac, a fanatical Frenchman, and succeeded by Louis XIII, under the regency of his mother, Maria de' Medici.
The Poles occupied Moscow and Czar Shuisky was deposed by the boyars, who set up a provisional government. An insurgent army failed to dislodge the Poles.
Upper Austria was laid waste by Archduke Leopold's mercenaries.
Frederick V became Elector Palatine on the death of his father, Frederick IV.

Literature Religion Philosophy

Siderius Nuncius by Galileo, though scientific in content, stands as an important work of literature.

Art and Architecture

Rubens' reputation was established by his two triptychs *The Raising of the Cross* and *The Descent from the Cross*.
Monteverdi published his *Vespers* in Mantua.

Performing Arts

Science and Technology

The first textbook on chemistry, *Tyrocinium Chymicum,* was published by French scientist Jean Beguin.

America

"Starving time" ended in Virginia, and Thomas West, Lord De La Warr, after whom Delaware was named, arrived as governor.
Henry Hudson began his last voyage (1610–1611) and discovered Hudson Bay.

1611

Denmark declared war on Sweden.
Sweden's Charles IX died and was succeeded by Gustavus Adolphus.
Archduke Matthias, younger son of Maximilian II, was crowned King of Bohemia.
Japan permitted trade with the Dutch.

The work of the Spanish poet Luis Gongora y Argote greatly influenced style in the remainder of the century.
Ben Jonson and **Inigo Jones,** one of the greatest of English architects, collaborated on the masque *Oberon Farey Prince.*
The Tempest was presented at court for the first time.

Domenichino began *The Life of St Cecilia,* an influential classical fresco cycle in S Luigi dei Francesci, Rome.

An anthology of music for virginals, *Parthenia,* was published, containing works by Orlando Gibbons, John Bull, and William Byrd.

The rifle was adopted for service by a Danish army unit.

The ill Lord De La Warr returned to England to seek help for the colony and was succeeded by his deputy, Sir Thomas Dale, who enforced strict codes to prevent disorder.

1612

Rudolf II died and was succeeded by his brother, Matthias, as Holy Roman Emperor.
The Poles were ejected from Moscow and a call was issued for the election of a new czar.
Persecution of Christians by the Japanese began.
Philip III of Spain wooed Princess Elizabeth of England.
The Protestant Union of German signed a defensive alliance with England.

Jacob Boheme, a German philosopher, published *Aurora,* a work that was to influence the Romantics.
The first important Italian dictionary appeared.
A Spanish Jesuit, Francisco Suarez, published *On Law,* which, in arguing that sovereignty was a contract between ruler and subject, attempted to refute James I's claim to rule by divine right.
The Art of Glass Making was one of many books that helped to spread technological advances in the arts.

John Rolfe introduced tobacco growing to Virginia, leading to the colony's initial prosperity. Captain John Smith's *A Map of Virginia* was issued. The first English settlers arrived in Bermuda.

1613

The War of Kalmar between Sweden and Denmark ended with the Peace of Knärod.
The Turks invaded Hungary.
Michael Romanov was elected Czar of Russia. He became the founder of the House of the Romanovs, which ruled Russia until 1917.
The Protestant Union of German Princes signed a treaty of alliance with the United Provinces.
Francis Bacon became England's Attorney General.

El Greco's last great work, *The Immaculate Conception,* completed at about this time, was criticized for the distorted, elongated forms, a product of Mannerism.

The Globe Theater, Southwark, in London, was burnt down.
Monteverdi was appointed master of music at San Marco, Venice.
Russia's first known theater was built on the orders of Czar Michael III.

Adriaen Block explored the New York and New England coasts for Dutch interests.
Virginia began to make grants to individual tenant farmers.
French outposts on the Bay of Fundy were attacked by the English.

1614

Gustavus Adolphus II of Sweden established a supreme court. After ensuring popular support for his Russian campaign, he went on to capture Novgorod.
The French States-General assembled for the last time until 1789: Richelieu came to the government's attention for the first time.

Fifty-four metrical psalms under the title of *Teares and Lamentations of a Sorrowful Soule* were published by Sir William Leighton.
John Webster completed his best-known play, *The Duchess of Malfi.*

Guide Reni, a graceful colorist of the Bologna school, completed his masterpiece, the *Aurora* ceiling fresco in the Casino Rospigliosi, Rome.

The study of metabolism was founded by Sanctorius, Italian professor of medicine, with his *De Medicina Statica.*
The use of logarithms was discovered by Scottish mathematician John Napier, and described in his *Mirifici Logarithmorum Canonis Descriptio.*

John Rolfe married Pocahontas in April, the month after Virginia's first cargo of tobacco was sent to England.
John Smith's voyage to the New England coast heightened the Plymouth company's interest in the area.

GUSTAVUS ADOLPHUS   **FRANCIS BACON**   **NAPIER'S LOGARITHM RODS**

Civil War broke out in France, with the Prince of Condé in league with the Huguenots.
Louis XIII of France married Anna of Austria.
Emperor Matthias recognized Gábor Bethlen as Prince of Transylvania with the Peace of Tyrnau.
A group of Tungus tribes in Manchuria grew powerful under Nurhachi.
The Dutch seized the Moluccas from Portugal.
Galileo faced the Inquisition for the first time.

The Spanish picaresque novel was introduced to Germany through a translation of *Guzman De Alfarache* by Mateo Aleman.
The collected plays of Cervantes were published.

The Accademia dei Filomusi was founded in Bologna by Adriano Banchieri.
Giovanni Paolo Maggini established a violin-making business in Brescia.

Coin-in-the-slot vending machines for loose tobacco were introduced into English taverns.

Missionary activity by the French started in Quebec with the arrival of four Franciscan friars.

The Treaty of Loudun ended the civil war in France. An amnesty was granted to the Prince of Condé.
War broke out between Venice and Austria.
Manchu Tartars invaded China.
Galileo was threatened with torture and death by the Inquisition unless he stopped teaching the Copernican "heresy". The Catholic Church prohibited him from continuing with his scientific studies.
Cape Horn was rounded for the first time by the Dutch East India Company's mariner, Willem Cornelis Schouten.
English navigator William Baffin discovered and named Baffin Bay while seeking the North-West Passage.

One of France's greatest religious poets, Theodore Agrippa d'Aubigne, finished his epic work, *Les Tragiques*. It dealt with religious wars.

The Flemish-born Dutch artist Frans Hals painted his first version of *The Banquet of the St George Civic Guard*, a huge group portrait which revealed a masterly spontaneity of technique and feeling.

The Collegium Musicum was founded in Prague.

The law of refraction was discovered by Dutch astronomer and mathematician Willebrod Snellius.

George Yeardley succeeded Dale and became Virginia's acting governor.
John Smith's *A Description of New England* stimulated interest in the area.

The Peace of Stolbovo ended the war between Russia and Sweden. Sweden's war with Poland continued unabated. Concino Concini, Marquis d'Ancre, was assassinated by order of Louis XIII.
Ferdinand of Styria, the future Emperor Ferdinand II, was accepted as King of Bohemia.
The Peace of Madrid ended the war between Venice and Austria.

The Blue Mosque in Istanbul was completed. The wall decorations included Venetian glass and ostrich eggshell.

Monteverdi was appointed choirmaster at San Marco.
German composer Heinrich Schütz was made master of music in the Electoral Chapel in Dresden.
The first dance suite, *Banchetto Musicale*, was composed by J H Schein.

The technique of trigonometrical triangulation for cartography was established by Willebrod Snellius.

Settlement in Virginia was encouraged by the introduction of the headright system for land grants.
Pocahontas died in England.
A fort was established by the Dutch at the site of Albany, New York.

The Thirty Years War began after a nationalist and Protestant revolt in Bohemia. In the Defenestration of Prague rebels threw regents Jaroslav von Martinitz and William Slawata from the windows of Hradcany Palace.
Sir Walter Raleigh was beheaded to placate Spain after the failure of his expedition in search of El Dorado.
Ferdinand of Styria was crowned King of Hungary.
Prince Philip William of Orange died and was succeeded by his brother, Maurice of Nassau.
Richelieu was ordered into exile at Avignon for plotting with the Queen Mother, Maria de'Medici.

The most important German court poet of the period, George Rudolph Weckherlin, published a two-volume work, *Oden und Gesange*.
Lope de Vega, a Spanish dramatist, began editing his plays for publication. Tradition puts their number at 2,000.

Figured bass developed in Italian lute songs.

A dredger was patented by English inventor Captain John Gilbert.
The Royal College of Physicians issued *Pharmacopoeia Londinensis*, containing 1,960 remedies.

The Treaty of Angoulême resulted in a truce between Louis XIII and the Queen Mother, Maria de' Medici.
Emperor Matthias died and was succeeded by Ferdinand II. Ferdinand was then deposed as King of Bohemia by the largely Protestant Bohemian Diet, which elected in his place Frederick V, son-in-law of James I of England.
Gábor Bethlen of Transylvania allied himself with Protestant leader Count von Thurn, who had besieged Vienna.
Batavia was founded by Dutch explorer Jan Pieters Coen.

Frei Luis de Sousa's *Vida de Dom Frei Bartolomeu dos Martires* revealed him as a master of Portuguese prose.

Diego Rodriguez de Silva y Velázquez was challenging the divide between "serious" subjects and genre painting: *The Immaculate Conception* and *The Adoration of the Magi* shared the naturalism and immediacy of his secular work.
Inigo Jones' *Banqueting Hall* was begun in the heart of Tudor Whitehall.

A treasury of early English keyboard music titled *Fitzwilliam Virginal Book* was compiled by Francis Tregian.

Harmonice Mundi, by Kepler, contained his third law of planetary motion.

The General Assembly, the first American legislature, was convened in Jamestown.
The first blacks arrived in Virginia. Initially they had the same rights as white indentured servants.

DEFENESTRATION OF PRAGUE　　　RICHELIEU　　　THE BANQUETING HALL

World Events

The Pilgrim Fathers, sailing in the *Mayflower,* left Plymouth, England, and arrived in New Plymouth, Massachusetts, after a 63-day voyage.
In the Battle of the White Mountain, near Prague, Bohemia's Frederick V was defeated by a Catholic League army in support of Ferdinand II and led by the Bavarian general Johan Tserclaes, Count von Tilly. Bohemia was forcibly Catholicized.

Philip III of Spain died and was succeeded by his son, Philip IV.
Livonia was captured by Gustavus Adolphus in the war between Sweden and Poland.
War was resumed between Holland and Spain after a 12-year truce.

Louis XIII recalled Richelieu and made him a cardinal.
Gábor Bethlen and Ferdinand II signed a peace treaty.
A Huguenot rebellion in France ended with the Treaty of Montpellier.
Turkish Sultan Osman II was murdered by rebellious Janissaries, who restored the mentally deficient Mustafa I to the sultanate.
Count Olivares became chief minister of Spain.
Count von Tilly's Catholic army was defeated in the Battle of Wiesloch by Count Peter Ernst Mansfeld II, who led the Protestant forces. Shortly afterward, Tilly won the Battle of Wimpfen and the Battle of Höchst.

Maximilian, Duke of Bavaria, received the Upper Palatinate as a gift from Emperor Ferdinand II during the Thirty Years War.
Shah Abbas I captured Baghdad.
Colonists of the English East India Company were murdered by the Dutch in the Massacre of Amboina, and survivors expelled from the Spice Islands.
Turkish Sultan Mustafa I abdicated in favor of his 14-old nephew Murad IV, who reigned initially under the regency of his mother, Kussem Sultana.
Iemitsu succeeded to the Japanese shogunate when his father, Tokugawa shogun Hidetada, abdicated.
Christian of Brunswick was defeated by Count von Tilly at the Battle of Stadtlohn.

England declared war on Spain.
Cardinal Richelieu became Louis XIII's chief minister.
Spanish traders were banned from Japan, and Japanese trade with the Philippines came to an end.
An Anglo-French treaty was signed providing for the marriage of Charles, Prince of Wales, to Henrietta Maria, daughter of Henry IV and Maria de' Medici.

Literature Religion Philosophy

Francis Bacon published *Novum Organum* (New Logic).
A deaf-and-dumb sign language was described by Spanish author Juan Pablo Bonet in his manual called *The Art of Teaching Dumb People to Speak.*
A vivid history of the unsettled period in Russia before the first Romanov czar was crowned was written by a monk, Avraamy Palitsyn.

A work by Johann Kepler, *The Epitome of the Copernican Astronomer,* was banned by the Roman Catholic Church.
The Anatomy of Melancholy by Robert Burton secured a place in literature as a masterpiece of style and a valuable index to the ideas of the period.
John Donne was made Dean of St Paul's and began to compose his famous sermons.

A mock heroic poem by Alessandro Tassoni, *The Rape of the Bucket,* placed imaginary adventures in the context of historical fact.

The first folio edition of Shakespeare's plays was published by John Heminge and Henry Condell.

Seventeenth-century literary reform in Germany was given impetus by Martin Opitz von Boberfeld's *Book of German Poetry.*
Ideas central to Deism, which attacked the religious establishment, were expressed in *On Truth* by Lord Herbert of Cherbury.

Art and Architecture

Gianlorenzo Bernini began a series of sculptures, including *Apollo and Dapne* and *David,* which established him as the greatest sculptor since Michelangelo. The sense of movement and vitality in his works set them apart from the Mannerist trend.

Potatoes from the New World were planted in Germany for the first time.

Rubens began his highly ambitious *Medici Cycle* in the Luxembourg Palace, Paris (completed 1625).
George Schwanhardt developed the method of engraving on glass with a wheel and diamond.

Inigo Jones built the first English ecclesiastical building in the classical style, *The Queen's Chapel,* St James's Palace, London.

Frans Hals painted his most famous work, *The Laughing Cavalier.*
Bernini was commissioned to design the canopy over the high altar of St Peter's.

Performing Arts

Cantata first appeared as a term for a solo song with continuo in a collection of songs by Alessandro Grandi.
Michael Praetorius, German composer, compiled a music encyclopedia called *Syntagma musicum.*

William Bradford was chosen as Plymouth's governor and served almost continuously until his death in 1657.
Miles Standish was the colony's military leader.
The Dutch West India Company was chartered by Holland.

The first theater in Japan was opened by Saruwaka Kanzaburo.

Science

January 1 was accepted as the beginning of the year (instead of March 25) by the papal chancellery.

A patents law came into force in England to protect inventors.

The term "gas" for compressible fluid was coined by Belgian scientist Johannes Baptista van Helmont.
The first working submarine was built by Dutch physicist Cornelius Drebbel. It traveled under the Thames for two hours, propelled by 12 oarsmen.

America

The Council for New England received a charter for all the territory between 40 and 48 North latitude.

A widespread massacre of Virginia settlers by Indians threatened the colony's stability.

The first settlements were established in Maine following a land grant in 1622 by the Council of New England to Sir Ferdinando Gorges and John Mason.

Virginia's original charter was revoked, and it was reorganized as a crown colony.
Dutch settlers reached North America and made their major settlement in New Amsterdam.

BERNINI'S *DAVID*   POTATOES   PHILIP IV   JAPANESE OPERA

1625

James I died and was succeeded by his 24-year-old son, Charles I. Charles was married by proxy to France's Catholic 16-year-old Henrietta Maria.

England, the United Provinces, Denmark, and France formed an alliance against the Hapsburgs.

An Anglo-Dutch alliance against Spain was formed by the Treaty of Southampton.

Giovanni Lanfranco began his illusionistic *Assumption of the Virgin* in the dome of S Andrea della valle, Rome.
The young Rembrandt Harmenszoon van Rijn, who was to become the dominant figure of Baroque art in northern Europe, began his series of self-portraits, which finally numbered over 100.
Daniel Seghers became the leading flower painter of the Flemish school.

Philip Massinger's comedy *A New Way to Pay Old Debts* was performed for the first time.

Johann Rudolph Glauber, a German chemist, discovered Glauber's salt.

The population of the English colonies exceeded 2,000 for the first time.

1626

Catholic forces under Austrian General Wallenstein routed a Protestant army under Count Mansfeld at the Bridge of Dessau. Wallenstein chased the defeated army through Silesia to Hungary. There Mansfeld received temporary aid from the Transylvanian prince, Gábor Bethlen, but shortly afterwards died.
Hostilities between the Huguenots and the French king came to an end with the signing of the Peace of La Rochelle.
The Chalais conspiracy against Cardinal Richelieu was brutally suppressed.
French colonists settled in Madagascar, expelling its original native inhabitants.

The Dalmatian poet and playwright Ivan Gundulic wrote his masterpiece, *Osman*, which celebrated the Polish victory over the Turks.
Francisco Gomez de Quevedo y Villegas published a parody picaresque novel called *The Life of a Scoundrel*.

William Heather founded a professorship of music at Oxford University.

Human temperature was measured with a thermometer for the first time by Italian physician Sanctorius.

Indians sold Manhattan Island to Peter Minuit and other Dutch colonists for the equivalent of $24 worth of trading goods.

1627

The Catholic armies of Wallenstein and Count von Tilly conquered Silesia, Brunswick, Mecklenburg and Jutland. Christian IV of Denmark withdrew from the Thirty Years War.
The Hapsburgs were confirmed as hereditary rulers by a new Bohemian constitution.
The Tungus Manchus overran Korea, ousting the Ming dynasty from the Liao basin.
Tyrannical Mughal Emperor Jahangir died and was succeeded by his son, Shah Jahan.

Francis Bacon's *The New Atlantis* created a scientific Utopia and foreshadowed developments in mid-century thought.

Claude Lorraine (Claude Gellée) settled permanently in Rome. His emphasis on light and atmosphere was influential on English landscape painting of the 18th and 19th centuries.
Simon Vouet returned to France after 14 years in Italy. His illusionistic techniques influenced decorative painting for the rest of the century.

The first known opera with a German text, *Dafne*, by Heinrich Schütz, was performed.

The places of 1,005 fixed stars were listed in Johann Kepler's *Rudolphine Tables*.

Tobacco exports from Virginia reached 500,000 pounds.

1628

In France, Richelieu rebuilt royal power, attacking the Huguenots.
Wallenstein assumed the title Admiral of the Baltic after obtaining the Duchy of Mecklenburg. He besieged Stralsund but was soon forced to lift the siege.
Java and the Moluccas were occupied by Dutch forces.
Sweden and Denmark concluded a treaty for the defense of Stralsund. Gustavus Adolphus of Sweden entered the Thirty Years War.

Rembrandt made his earliest etchings and saw them, unlike any artist before him, as more than just a second-string to line engravings.
Salzburg Cathedral, a Roman Baroque-styled building, was completed to the design of Santino Solari.

Monteverdi accepted German composer Heinrich Schütz as a pupil in Venice.

William Harvey, the English physician, discovered the circulation of the blood, but this was not confirmed until the microscope was improved.

A colony was established at Salem, Massachusetts, by John Endecott, who served as its first governor (1628–1630).

1629

By the Edict of Restitution the Emperor ordered the restoration of church property in Europe that had been secularized since the Peace of Augsburg in 1555.
The Peace of Lübeck ended the war between Emperor Ferdinand II and King Christian IV of Denmark. All Denmark's hereditary lands were returned, under certain conditions.
The Peace of Susa ended hostilities between England and France.
The Huguenot revolt ended with the Peace of Alais.
Sweden and Poland signed the Truce of Altmark.

The design of San Isidro el Real, Madrid, by Francisco Bautista, had considerable influence on Spanish architecture. Il Gesù in Rome was used as the model.
Scenes from the life of St Bonaventura by José Ribera revealed a new realism in Spanish art.

Brackets ([ ]) were first used in mathematics by the Dutch mathematician Albert Gerard.
The Guild of Spectacle Makers received a charter from Charles I.

The Massachusetts Bay Company received its charter, permitting settlement.
The Dutch in New Amsterdam organized patronships (large land grants) for those who brought 50 colonists.

CHARLES I   THERMOMETER   HARVEY: CIRCULATION OF THE BLOOD

1630

World Events

The Dutch East India Company seized part of Brazil for its sugar and silver.

Gustavus Adolphus invaded the Holy Roman Empire to protect the Protestant cause against ruthless Catholic suppression.

Emperor Ferdinand II dismissed General Albrecht von Wallenstein, his Austrian Commander-in-Chief and replaced him with Count von Tilly.

The Treaty of Madrid ended the Anglo-French war.

Literature

Art and Architecture

The Barberini tapestry workshop was established in Rome at about this time.

Philip IV in Brown and Silver revealed a change in Velázquez' style, away from the chiaroscuro, the use of light and shade, of Caravaggio and toward an even unity of light.

Performing Arts

Rules of classical tragedy that were to cause decades of dispute in the French theater were laid down in Jean Mairet's preface to *Sylvanaire*.

Bel canto, a lyrical and agile style of singing, developed in Italy.

The first use of the story of Don Juan was made in *El Burlador de Savilla* by the Spanish playwright Tirso de Molina.

Science and Technology

Sash windows were first installed, by Inigo Jones at Raynham Hall, Norfolk.

America

The Massachusetts Bay Colony established a foothold north of Plymouth, with 1,000 colonists, and founded Boston. John Winthrop was the elected governor.

1631

General Wallenstein was re-appointed to the imperial command.

German Protestant Princes agreed to form an alliance with Gustavus Adolphus.

Pope Urban VIII annexed Urbino.

Vesuvius erupted and Naples suffered severe earthquakes.

Count von Tilly led Imperial forces on an orgy of destruction, wiping out a Swedish garrison at Neu Brandenburg, laying to waste Magdeburg and Halle, and invading Saxony.

Gustavus Adolphus retaliated by allying himself with John George, Elector of Saxony, routing Tilly at the Battle of Breitenfeld, and occupying Mainz and Würzburg.

S Maria della Salute, dramatically sited at the entrance to the Grand Canal, Venice, was Baldassare Longhena's masterpiece. It was completed in 1687.

The multiplication sign (x) was introduced by English mathematician William Oughtred in his *Clavis Mathematica.*

The vernier scale, for making fine adjustments to measurements, was invented by French mathematician Pierre Vernier.

Massachusetts Bay expanded its list of settlers admitted to freemanship but required church membership.

1632

Gustavus Adolphus deployed his "Model Army" to capture Nuremberg, and defeat and mortally wound Tilly at the Lech. He went on to defeat Wallenstein at the Battle of Lützen, but was killed in action.

The Portuguese were expelled from Bengal.

The infant Queen Christina, daughter of Gustavus Adolphus, ascended the Swedish throne under five regents.

Sigismund III, King of Poland, died and was succeeded by Vladislav IV.

Cardinal Richelieu broke the power of the nobles in France.

Lope Félix de Vega Carpio, a highly versatile Spanish writer, wrote his masterpiece, *La Dorotea.*

Rembrandt's *The Anatomy Lesson of Dr. Tulp* was the first of his great group portraits and established his reputation in Amsterdam.

The Taj Mahal was begun outside Agra in India for Emperor Shah Jahan in memory of his wife Mumtaz Mahal. The complex took 22 years to complete.

Galileo published *Dialogues concerning two World Systems,* in which he presented the evidence for a heliocentric solar system.

The slide rule was invented by William Oughtred.

Jean Ray, French scientist, invented the water thermometer.

England returned Acadia and St. Lawrence region to France by treaty.

The Calvert family received a royal grant north of the Potomac River.

1633

Wallenstein drove the Swedes, demoralized after the death of Gustavus Adolphus, out of Silesia and invaded Brandenburg.

French forces occupied Lorraine.

Roman High Baroque triumphed in Pietro da Cortona's ceiling fresco for the Gran Salone, Palazzo Barberini. Both painter and architect, Cortona was working simultaneously on the designs for his finest building, SS Martina e Luca.

Jacques Callot published his celebrated etchings *The Miseries of War,* his reaction to Richelieu's invasion of Lorraine. They were an inspiration to Goya.

Galileo retracted his earlier scientific views when threatened by the Inquisition.

A wind sawmill was erected in London.

Bananas appeared in London for the first time, in the shop window of Thomas Johnson.

The Dutch founded Hartford, Connecticut.

Champlain became governor of New France, which expanded rapidly.

1634

Emperor Ferdinand II deprived Wallenstein of his command for the second time, accusing him of treachery. Wallenstein was assassinated, and Austrian general Matthias Gallas, who had plotted against Wallenstein, replaced him as Commander-in-Chief. He went on to defeat the Swedes at Nördlingen.

By the Treaty of Polianovska King Vladislav of Poland renounced all claims to Russia but confirmed that Smolensk was Polish.

Dutch forces captured the island of Curaçao.

The Temple: Sacred Poems and Private Ejaculations by George Herbert, English clergyman and metaphysical poet, was published posthumously.

The Passion Play at Oberammergau, Upper Bavaria, was first performed. It is still performed every ten years.

Comus, a masque by the great English poet John Milton, was first performed at Ludlow Castle.

Maryland was first settled, primarily by Roman Catholics.

SASH WINDOW   COUNT VON TILLY   TAJ MAHAL   SLIDE RULE

France declared war on Spain, supplying four armies against the Imperialist forces.
Cardinal Richelieu and Count Axel Oxenstierna, a Swedish statesman, signed a Franco-Swedish treaty of alliance.
The Peace of Prague was signed by Emperor Ferdinand II and the Elector John George of Saxony, which meant that the Thirty Years War was reduced to a conflict between the House of Hapsburg and the French and Swedish alliance.
The Treaty of Stuhmsdorf resulted in a 20-year truce between Poland and Sweden.
Dutch forces occupied the English Virgin Islands, Formosa, and French Martinique.

Velázquez completed *The Surrender of Breda,* one of the greatest of all history paintings.

Frescobaldi published his *Fiori musicali di toccate,* which allegedly had a strong influence on Johann Sebastian Bach.

Tobacco sales in France were restricted to doctors' prescriptions.

Massachusetts banished Roger Williams for questioning civil authority in matters of conscience.

Brandenburg declared war on Sweden.
The imperial armies invaded Burgundy but were repulsed.
Emperor Ferdinand II had his son, Archduke Ferdinand, elected Ferdinand III, King of the Romans.
The Dutch established a settlement in Ceylon.
The Ch'ing Dynasty was proclaimed by the Manchus at Mukden.
Anton Van Diemen, a Dutch statesman, was appointed Governor General of the Dutch East Indies.

French mathematician Marin Mersenne published *Harmonie Universelle,* an important musical work that included detailed descriptions of all contemporary musical instruments.

A hospital for incurables was opened in Paris.

Roger Williams founded Providence, with a democratic form of government.
Colonists and Pequot Indians engaged in their first hostilities.
The Dutch began a settlement on Long Island.

After the Shimbara revolt of the Christian peasantry, in which all Christians were massacred, Japan cut her foreign trade and cultural contacts.
Emperor Ferdinand II died and was succeeded by his son, Ferdinand III.
French forces invaded The Netherlands.
Dutch troops expelled the Portuguese from the Gold Coast.
Richelieu appointed intendants, royal officers charged with the control of French provinces.

René Descartes, French scientist and philosopher, published *Discours de la Méthode,* in which he established the deductive method.

Le Cid by Pierre Corneille, commonly regarded as the most significant play in the history of French drama, made drama the supreme form of classical French literature.
The first opera house, the Teatro San Cassiano in Venice, opened with Manelli's *Andromedie.*

The first waterproof umbrellas were listed among the effects of King Louis XIII of France.

The Pequot War in New England resulted in some deaths among colonists and in destruction of Pequots.
Anne Hutchinson, found guilty of sedition and contempt, was banished by Massachusetts the following year.

The imperial army was defeated by Bernhard of Saxe-Weimar at Rheinfelden.
The Franco-Swedish alliance was renewed for a futher three years.
A Dutch expedition occupied Mauritius.
Murad IV of Turkey recovered Baghdad from Persia.

The Scottish Covenant (a bond entered into by Scottish Presbyterians to defend their religion) was drawn up and signed.

The Flemish master Sir Anthony van Dyck, who had lived permanently in England since 1632, painted his two greatest portraits of Charles I at about this time.
Francesco Borromini, the great and controversial Baroque architect, began his masterpiece of spatial ingenuity, the small church of S Carlo alle Quattro Fontane, Rome.

Dynamic markings, such as *p* (piano) and *f* (forte), were used for the first time by Italian composer Domenico Mazzochi. He was quickly followed by other composers.

Galileo published *Two New Sciences,* in which he dealt with dynamics and established, more than in any other work, experimental science.

The Swedes founded a colony at Fort Christina (now Wilmington, Delaware).
Hutchinson founded the town of Pocasset (now Portsmouth, Rhode Island).

France first entered the Thirty Years War.
Jules Mazarin, French cardinal and statesman, entered the service of Cardinal Richelieu.
Dutch forces captured Trincomalee from the Portuguese.
Georg Jenatsch, a Swiss soldier and leader of the Grisons (a Swiss canton), was assassinated.

Sunday and Holiday Sonnets was written by Andreas Gryphius, considered the most moving German poet of the period.

The first comic opera, *He Who Suffers, Hopes* by Marco Marazzoli and Virgilio Mazzocchi, was produced in Rome.

Milled-edge coins were introduced into France for the first time.
The transit of Venus was accurately predicted and observed by English astronomer Jeremiah Horrocks.
A pioneer book on modern geometry was published by Gérard Desargues, a French mathematician who introduced a method of perspective.

The Exeter Compact marked the beginning of organized New Hampshire settlement.

CH EAST INDIES SETTLEMENT   RENE DESCARTES

World Events

The Portuguese regained their independence under King John IV of Braganza. They siezed their opportunity when Catalonia began a 19-year revolt against Spain.
The Japanese murdered the members of a Portuguese trade delegation to their country, leaving Japan isolated from most of the world.
Sultan Murad IV of Turkey died, and was succeeded by Sultan Ibrahim.

Dutch forces captured Malacca from the Portuguese.
Sweden signed a **two-year treaty** of neutrality with Brandenburg.
The Marquise de Cinq-Mars conspired against Cardinal Richelieu and made a secret pact with Spain. The plot was discovered and the Marquise was executed.

Charles I raised the royal standard at Nottingham and sparked off the English Civil War. Matters had finally come to a head between the king, who adhered to the "Divine Right of Kings," and Parliament; and between high Churchmen and Puritans, favored by the Scots.
Lennart Torstenson, C-in-C of the Swedish army, defeated Imperialist forces at Schweidnitz and at the second Battle of Breitenfeld.
The Portuguese captured the Gold Coast from the Dutch.
Dutch mariner Abel Tasman became the first European to sight Tasmania, which he called Van Diemen's Land, and New Zealand.

Louis XIII of France died and was succeeded by his five-year-old son Louis XIV. Jules Mazarin, who succeeded Richelieu as prime minister, was retained by the Queen Regent, Anna of Austria.
Abel Tasman discovered Tonga and reached New Guinea.

Thomas Browne, a doctor, later knighted by Charles II, published *Religio Medici*, his thoughts on religion, man and nature.

French forces occupied the Rhineland.
The Swedish army under Torstenson, conquered Jutland and subsequently defeated the imperial army.
Parts of coastal Australia (New Holland) were charted by Tasman.
The Manchus set up the Ta Ch'ing dynasty at Mukden, replacing the Ming dynasty.
The imperial armies at Freiburg were defeated by French Marshal Vicomte de Turenne.

Literature Religion Philosophy

The Dutch theologian Cornelius Jansen's *Augustinus*, published posthumously, proclaimed strict predestinarianism.

Jacques Sarrazin, the most important French sculptor of the mid-century, produced his best-known works, the *Caryatids* for the Pavillon de l'Horloge of the Louvre, Paris.

Molière, French dramatist, founded the Illustré Théâtre in Paris, which subsequently became the Comédie Française.

John Milton's *Areopagitica* was a plea for freedom of speech and thought.

Art and Architecture

Jan Davidsz de Heem's *Still Life*, more than six feet wide, shows him at his most opulent.
Just before he died Pietro Tacca completed his statue of Philip IV of Spain.

The first collection of cathedral music was published in England by John Barnard, Canon of St Paul's Cathedral.

Rembrandt painted his *Night Watch*, a group portrait which emphasized light, shade and movement above the equal prominence of all sitters.
Ludwig van Siegen, the self-proclaimed inventor of the mezzotint engraving, published his first print.

Parcel post was established in France.
Evangelista Torricelli, an Italian physicist, produced the first barometer.

The world's heaviest coins were minted. They were Swedish 10 daler coins, weighing 20lb each.

Performing Arts

Science and Technology

The first stagecoach lines, with coaching houses at regular intervals, were opened in England.

The first cotton factories began to function in Manchester.
Arsenic was used medically for the first time.

America

Swedish colonists introduced log cabin construction along the Delaware River.
The Bay Psalm Book, the first colonial hymnal, was printed.

The Dutch increased the number of settlements in New Netherland.
The Body of Liberties code in Massachusetts based the colony's criminal code on the Bible.

The Puritans ordered all theaters in England to be closed.
The first historical opera, *The Coronation of Poppaea* by Monteverdi, was performed in Venice.

The United Colonies of New England allowed Connecticut, Massachusetts, New Haven, and Plymouth colonies to act jointly while retaining their own territory.

An Indian uprising was suppressed in Virginia.
Roger Williams published *The Bloudy Tenent of Persecution* to protest ecclesiastical government in Massachusetts.

Sir William Berkeley became governor of Virginia and initiated reforms.
Montreal was permanently settled by French colonists.
Massachusetts set fines for neglecting education.

CHATEAU DE MAISONS   ENGLISH CIVIL WAR   BAROMETER   MOLIERE

As the Thirty Years War approached its end, peace negotiations began between France and the Empire at Münster, and between Sweden and the Empire at Osnabrück. The imperial army under Count Matthias Gallas was routed by the Swedes under Torstenson at Magdeburg.
Turkey and Venice went to war over Turkish designs on Crete.
Michael Romanov, Czar of Russia, died and was succeeded by his son Alexis Mikhailovich.

Bernini began his most celebrated work of sculpture, *The Ecstasy of St Theresa* in the Cornaro Chapel, S Maria della Vittoria, Rome. It is the archetypal Baroque sculpture.

The polonaise, a dance said to have originated in triumphal marches of Polish warriors, became popular.
French composer Jean Baptiste Lully was appointed violinist at the French court.

Scientists in London began a series of informal meetings that eventually led to the founding of the Royal Society.
Wallpaper began to be used as a cheap substitute for tapestry.

The Dutch arranged peace with Indians after years of war had threatened the future of New Netherland.

The English Civil War came to an end with the surrender of King Charles to the Scots at Newark.
Prague fell to Swedish forces which, together with a French army, invaded Bavaria.
The Great Elector of Brandenburg married Louise, daughter of Frederick Henry of Orange.

Richard Crawshaw published his *Steps to the Temple,* religious and secular poems in Latin and French.

The first magic lantern, a primitive projector, was built by German mathematician Athanasius Kircher.
The first shorthand teacher was Englishman Jeremiah Rich, who started classes in London.

Governor Winthrop and other leaders dismissed criticisms that the Massachusetts government discriminated against non-Puritans.

France and Sweden signed the Treaty of Ulm with the Elector of Bavaria and the Elector of Cologne, by which the Electors agreed to remain neutral until the end of the Thirty Years War. Shortly afterward, the Elector of Mainz and the Landgrave of Hesse opted out of the war, but Bavaria and Cologne renounced the treaty.
A revolt in Naples, led by Amalfi fisherman Masaniello against the Spanish viceroy, resulted in the murder of the rebellious leader by his own mob.
Czar Alexis I was faced with a revolt in Moscow.
Frederick Henry of Orange died and was succeeded by his son, William II of Orange.
French forces were defeated in The Netherlands.

Paulus Potter, Dutch landscape and animal painter, produced his most famous work, *The young bull,* a lifesize, realist portrait of the animal with a cow and a proud cowherd.

Johann Hevel, a Danzig astronomer, charted the lunar surface in his *Selenographia.*

Peter Stuyvesant arrived as governor of New Netherland.
The Rhode Island constitution separated church and state and permitted religious freedom.
Massachusetts set education standards for towns with more than 50 and 100 families.

The Peace of Westphalia ended the Thirty Years War with every participant exhausted.
The Fronde, a series of noble and peasant uprisings in France, tried to substitute government by law for royal power.
The Treaty of Munster recognized the independence of the Dutch United Provinces.
Turkish Sultan Ibrahim failed in his attempt to take Crete. He was deposed and assassinated. Mohammed IV, his seven-year-old son, succeeded him.
King Christian IV of Denmark died and was succeeded by Frederick III.

Robert Herrick, the English poet and clergyman best known for his line "Gather ye rosebuds while ye may," published *Hesperides,* a collection of 1,400 poems.

Nicolas Poussin painted *The burial of Phocion.*
Bernini began his great public monument, the *Fountain of the four Rivers,* in Rome's Piazza Navona, also designed by him.

Czar Alexis ordered the destruction of all theaters in Russia and prohibited all worldly entertainment.
Opera developed recitative and aria as two distinct elements.

Hydrochloric acid was produced by Johann Rudolf Glauber.

Thomas Hooker's *Survey of the Summe of Church Discipline* summarized Congregationalist beliefs.

King Charles I of England was tried, found guilty, and beheaded. The Prince of Wales, in exile, became Charles II, but only in Scotland and parts of Ireland. England became a Commonwealth, with Oliver Cromwell at its head, and a republican constitution.
The Peace of Ruel ended the first Fronde. The second Fronde developed 11 months later with riots in Paris.

Eikon Basilike, said to have been edited by John Gauden, the king's chaplain, from Charles I's papers, presented the king as a saint and martyr. Published while horror at the execution was still fresh, it was one of the most powerful pieces of propaganda in English history.
Richard Lovelace, the prototype Cavalier, prepared his collected works for the press. The title, *Lucasta,* was taken from his most famous poem.

A study of the plague, *De Peste,* was published by Dutch physician Isbrand de Diemerbrock.

The Toleration Act, early religious freedom legislation, was passed by Maryland.
The Society for the Propagation of the Gospel was founded to convert Indians to Christianity.
Virginia pledged loyalty to the Stuarts.

OLIVER CROMWELL   NICOLAS POUSSIN   MAGIC LANTERN   EXECUTION OF CHARLES I

World Events

The Treaty of Nuremberg was concluded between Sweden and the Holy Roman Emperor.
The second Fronde was put down by Mazarin, who joined up with the leaders of the first Fronde.

Charles II was crowned King of Scotland. He invaded England, was defeated by Cromwell at Worcester, and fled to France.
The French *Parlement* voted to release Condé, the Fronde leader, from prison, forcing Mazarin to flee from Paris. The queen joined forces with the new Fronde against Condé.
St Helena was occupied by the Dutch East India Company. The Dutch also began to colonize the Cape of Good Hope.

England declared war on Holland.
The Fronde war raged in France, with the Royal army led by Turenne and the Frondeurs by Condé. The Frondeurs set up a provisional government in Paris, but Louis XIV reestablished his lawful government, recalled Mazarin, and punished the Frondeurs. Condé allied himself with Spain.
A Catalan revolt ended when Barcelona surrendered to Philip IV.
Cape Town was founded by the Dutch.

Ferdinand III was elected Holy Roman Emperor.
Mazarin returned to Paris. The surrender of Bordeaux meant the end of the Fronde.

The Treaty of Westminster ended the Anglo-Dutch War. The Dutch recognized the Navigation Act.
Queen Christina of Sweden became a Roman Catholic and abdicated. She was succeeded by her cousin Charles X.
Louis XIV was crowned at Rheims.
Russia and Poland went to war. Czar Alexis invaded Poland and captured Smolensk.
England and Sweden concluded a treaty of commerce.

Literature Religion Philosophy

Henry Vaughan's collection *Silex Scintillans (The Glittering Flint,* enlarged 1655), shows the religious bent and genius of this metaphysical poet and mystic.

Issak Walton's *The Compleat Angler* was to become an English classic.
Royalties were first paid in France; Philippe Quinault received a percentage of receipts from the production of *Les Rivales,* rather than the customary lump sum.

Art and Architecture

Georges de La Tour, a French painter and perhaps the greatest of the Caravaggesque artists, painted *The new-born child,* a late work, at about this time.

Thomas Hobbes published *Leviathan* in which he developed his political theory.

The great Dutch poet Joost van den Vondel wrote *Lucifer,* the first play of a trilogy which continued with *Adam in Exile* and *Noah.*

Performing Arts

Modulation in music began to develop, with the scales divided into 12 semitones, as did modern harmony.

The first Viennese opera house was opened.
The minuet was popularized by Lully at the French court.

Science and Technology

The air pump, developed by natural philosopher and mayor of Magdeburg Otto von Guericke, was used to show that sound cannot cross a vacuum.
An invalid carriage, consisting of a tricycle wheelchair with hand cranks, was first used by a crippled citizen of Nuremberg.
The first English coffee house opened in London about this date.

William Harvey founded the study of embryology with his *Exercitationes de generatione animalium.*
A lunar map by Italian astronomer Giovanni Riccioli included a number of modern names.

The Dutch built Ft. Casimir (later Newcastle), Delaware, to control access to New Sweden.

The world's first postage stamps were struck on the Billets de Port Payé and were used by a small local postal service in Paris.
Contemporary surgical instruments and procedures were described in *Armamentarium chirurgicum,* by German surgeon Johann Schultes, published posthumously.

Blaise Pascal, French philosopher, mathematician, and physicist, stated the theory of probability.
Otto von Guericke conducted an experiment in which two teams of 30 horses tried and failed to separate two evacuated hemispheres, thus demonstrating the power of air pressure.

America

Connecticut followed Massachusetts' lead and set education standards.
The Dutch and New England colonies agreed on a boundary line, including the division of Long Island.

Governor Berkeley of Virginia was forced to submit to Cromwell's commissioners and Governor Stone of Maryland was ousted by them.
The Massachusetts court declared Maine to be within Massachusetts' boundaries.

Connecticut seized Ft. Good Hope (Hartford) from the Dutch during the first Anglo-Dutch War.
Virginia settlers moved into the Albemarle Sound area of North Carolina.

The First Jewish colonists settled in New Amsterdam.
Maryland's new governor deprived Lord Baltimore of authority and had religious toleration acts repealed.
Forces from Boston took French Acadia, holding it until 1670.

MAZARIN   COFFEE HOUSE   VON GUERICKE'S EXPERIMENT

The First Northern War began when Charles X of Sweden invaded Poland, capturing Cracow and Warsaw. The Polish king, John Casimir V, refused to recognize Charles's kingship.
England captured Jamaica from Spain.

Gerard Terborch, the much-traveled Dutch genre and portrait painter, produced one of his best-known works, *The Parental Admonition*, an 18th-century title to give respectability to a brothel scene.

Lully replaced shawms (medieval oboes) with modern oboes for concerts at the French court.
The koto became the national musical instrument of Japan. Its strings and movable bridge produced various five-note scales.

In *De Corpore*, Thomas Hobbes, the English political philosopher, following Descartes' mathematical method, suggested that the universe comprises material particles moving in a void.

Civil war in Maryland ended with the defeat of the rebels.
The Dutch took and annexed New Sweden, ending Swedish colonization efforts in North America.

A second invasion of Poland was attempted by Charles X, but he was forced to return to Sweden when the Russians invaded Finland.
Spain declared war on England. Robert Blake captured Spanish treasure ships off Cadiz.
King John IV of Portugal died and was succeeded by his son, Alfonso VI.
The Venetians drove the Turks from the Dardanelles following a period of anarchy among the Turks.
In Turkey, Albanian Mohammed Kiuprili became Mohammed IV's Grand Vizier, with absolute power.

Las Meninas, Velázquez' most celebrated work, was remarkable for both its informality as a royal group portrait and for its truth to observed nature.
Bernini began the highly influential piazza before St Peter's, Rome.

London's first opera house opened.

Artificial pearls, consisting of gypsum globules coated with fish scales, were produced in Paris.
The pendulum clock was devised by Christiaan Huygens.

Lord Baltimore's authority was restored in Maryland.
Quakers arriving in Boston were persecuted and expelled; Massachusetts later executed several of them.

Denmark joined Poland, Austria, and Russia in an attack on Sweden.
Portugal and the Dutch Republic went to war.
The Turks, under Kiuprili, routed the Venetians.
Holy Roman Emperor Ferdinand III died. Louis XIV applied to succeed him.
England and France signed the Treaty of Paris against Spain.

The grandest French château, Château de Vaux le Vicomte, was begun. Built at great speed and expense, it was designed by Louis Le Vau for Nicolas Fouquet.
Bernini began the Cathedra Petri, the magnificent gilt-bronze cover for the medieval wooden Papal throne in St Peter's, Rome.

Accademia del Cimento, the first scientific research institute, was founded in Florence.

The Dutch consolidated their hold on Delaware, sending a large group of settlers to Ft. Casimir.

Oliver Cromwell died and was succeeded as Lord Protector by his son Richard.
The first Northern War between Denmark and Sweden ended with the Treaty of Roskild. The Danes gave up territory in Sweden and Norway. But another invasion of Denmark by Sweden initiated the second Northern War within six months. The Great Elector of Brandenburg ranged himself on the Danish side.
The Spaniards were defeated by an Anglo-French force in the Battle of the Dunes, by which England gained Dunkirk.
Leopold I was elected Holy Roman Emperor. A frustrated Louis XIV formed the Rhenish League under the protectorate of the French.
Shah Jahan, the Mughal emperor, was succeeded by his son Aurangzeb, who locked his father away in Agra fort.

Christiaan Huygens, the Dutch mathematician and astronomer, recorded his discovery of the pendulum as a regulator of clocks in his *Horologium*.
The first bank note, designed by Swedish financier Johann Palmstruck, was issued by the Swedish state bank.

The Convention of The Hague, organized by the English, French, and Dutch, enforced the Treaty of Roskild in order to ensure peace between Sweden and Denmark.
The war between France and Spain ended with the Peace of the Pyrenees, emphasizing the Spanish decline and the rise of French power.
The Swedes were driven out of Prussia and Pomerania by the Great Elector.

Pietas Victrix by Nicholas Avancius, professor of Rhetoric at the University of Vienna, was a Jesuit play which was more than an exercise in Latin and represented a challenge to the professional theater.

Typhoid fever was first described by English physician Thomas Willis.
Christiaan Huygens published *Systema Saturnium,* in which he explained the true nature of Saturn's rings and identified its largest moon.

French explorers began an expedition to Lake Superior and the upper Midwest.
A Spanish treasure-hunting expedition explored the Alabama area.

BLAISE PASCAL   THE KOTO   HUYGENS' PENDULUM CLOCK   AURANGZEB

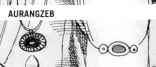

World Events

1660
Charles II was restored to the English throne.
The Treaty of Oliva ended the war between Poland, Brandenburg, Austria, and Sweden.
The Peace of Copenhagen ended the war between Denmark and Sweden, thus allowing foreign warships to enter the Baltic.
Louis XIV of France married Maria Theresa, daughter of Philip IV of Spain.

1661
Cardinal Mazarin died and Louis XIV began his personal rule.
The Treaty of Kardis ended the Northern War between Sweden and Russia.
The Grand Vizier of Turkey, Mohammed Kiuprili, died and was succeeded by his son, Ahmed Kiuprili.
England acquired Bombay and Tangier from Portugal as the dowry of Charles II's queen.

1662
Charles II married Portuguese Princess Catherine da Braganza.
England sold Dunkirk to France for £4000,000.
The first Manchu emperor of China, Shun Chih, was succeeded by his son K'ang-hsi who ushered in an unsurpassed period of cultural splendour.
Louis XIV signed a defense treaty of alliance with the Dutch.

1663
The Turks went to war against Emperor Leopold I. Under Ahmed Kiuprili, they attacked Austria, Transylvania, and Hungary, and took Neuhäusen. They then prepared to invade Germany.
Louis XIV insisted on his right to enlist Swiss mercenaries, in spite of the objection of Protestant cantons.
The Black Death ravaged Amsterdam, killing 10,000 people.

1664
The Battle of St Gotthard resulted in a victory for the Austrian army over the Turks. By the Truce of Vasvar that followed, Turkey kept all its recent gains.
French East and West Indies Companies were founded by French statesman Jean-Baptiste Colbert.

Literature / Religion / Philosophy

1660
German literature entered a golden age: Kaspar Stieler's poems in *Geharnschte Venus* were considered among the best of the century; Andreas Gryphius wrote *The Beloved Sleeping Beauty,* one of the finest comedies of the century; Hans von Grimmelshausen began his *Simplicissimus* series of novels.

1661
During this decade, Sir Peter Lely painted *The Windsor Beauties,* the most admired women at Charles II's court.
Willem Kalf represented the high point in Dutch still life with *Still life with a nautilus cup* of about this date.

1662
Jacob van Ruisdael painted his two versions of *The Jewish Cemetery* at Ouderkerk near Amsterdam at about this time. The tombs are drawn from life, surrounded by fantasatical landscapes of decay.

1663
Christopher Wren began his first building, the Sheldonian Theater, Oxford. The design was adapted from the ancient theater of Marcellus in Rome. University ceremonies continue to be performed there.
The French Academy was reorganized by Jean-Baptiste Colbert with Charles Lebrun as director. Artistic production was completely dictated by court tastes.

1664
The group works *The Regents* and *The Regentesses of the Almshouse* are the finest works of Frans Hals' later career.

Art and Architecture

1660
The Academy of Painting was founded in Seville. Murillo was its first president.

Performing Arts

1660
The Restoration in England saw the return of public theaters after 18 years.
A woman played Desdemona in *Othello,* the first actress in the English theater.

1661
Louis XIV established the Académie Royale de Danse. Its director, Pierre Beauchamp, was the first to define the five basic positions of the feet in classical ballet.
Matthew Locke was appointed court composer by Charles II.
The first London playhouse with a proscenium arch, Lincoln's Inn Fields Theater opened with a performance of *Hamlet.*

1662
The Royal Society received its charter from Charles II.
Robert Boyle, the "Father of Chemistry", announced Boyle's Law: the volume of gas varies inversely as the pressure varies.
The first buses (eight-seater vehicles) appeared in Paris, running a scheduled service at seven- or eight-minute intervals.

1663
The first Drury Lane Theater was built in London.

1664
Jean-Baptiste Lully began composing music for the ballets of Molière.
The first version of *Tartuffe* by Molière (Jean-Baptiste Poquelin) was performed at Versailles.

Science and Technology

1660
A pencil factory was started in Nuremberg by Friedrich Staedtler.

1661
British physicist Robert Boyle's book *The Sceptical Chymist* defined the concepts of element, alkali, and acid.
The manometer was invented by Christiaan Huygens.

1663
The first gold guinea coins were minted in England.
The muscular nature of the heart was described by Danish physician Nicolaus Steno.
The binomial theorem was discovered by English mathematician John Newton.

1664
Jan Swammerdam, Dutch naturalist, discovered the valves of the lymph vessels.
Descartes, in his *Traité de l'homme,* confirmed Harvey's earlier discovery that the blood in the body is in a state of ceaseless circulation.
Springs were fitted to coaches for the first time.

America

1660
A Navigation Act gave English ships exclusive access to colonial imports and exports (some of which could be shipped only to England).
Maryland claimed freedom from the Calvert family, which soon reestablished itself.

1661
The French crown increased its interest in Canada; and reorganized the government of New France (1663).
New England colonies recognized the restoration of English monarchy but protected former Cromwell supporters.

1662
Connecticut received a royal charter; independent towns were brought under its authority by early 1665.
The French made their first settlement in Newfoundland.

1663
A Navigation Act required almost all European exports to colonies to be shipped on English ships.
The first grants to proprietors made in North Carolina.
The Rhode Island charter promised freedom of religion.

1664
The English captured New Amsterdam (renamed New York) and took over all Dutch colonies on East coast after Charles II granted his brother, the Duke of York, lands from Connecticut to Delaware.

CHARLES II   K'ANG-HSI   LOUIS XIV

1665

The Great Plague broke out in London, killing nearly 70,000 between July and October.
The second Anglo-Dutch War broke out. An English fleet defeated the Dutch off Lowestoft.
Philip IV of Spain died.
Louis XIV claimed the Spanish Netherlands.

François VI, duc de la Rochefoucauld, published the first version of his *Maxims.*

Jan Vermeer, at about this time, painted his two masterpieces, *A Woman Weighing Pearls* and *The Artist's Studio.* Both display the artist's keen eye for detail.

Juan Cabanilles, one of the greatest organists in Europe, was appointed to the Cathedral in Valencia.

Isaac Newton began his experiments on gravitation. He also discovered differential calculus.
Robert Hooke discovered living cells in plants and found that plants breathe.
The rotations and periods of Mars, Jupiter, and Venus were determined by French astronomer Jean Dominique Cassini.

New Jersey development began after the Duke of York granted Sir George Carteret and Lord Berkeley proprietorship rights to the region.
England seized the property of the Dutch West India Co.

1666

The Great Fire of London destroyed almost the whole of the city, including St Paul's Cathedral.
France went to war with England in defense of the United Provinces.
The Quadruple Alliance was formed by Holland, Denmark, Brunswick and Brandenburg to secure Dutch independence from French aggression.
Emperor Leopold I was faced with a revolt by Hungarian noblemen.

François Girardon, one of the leading French sculptors of Louis XIV's reign, made *Apollo tended by nymphs* for a niche in the garden of Versailles, a highly classical work. Girardon was the pupil of Jacques Sarrazin.

Antonio Stradivari, still a pupil of Nicolo Amati, began to label his violins.

The Académie Royale des Sciences, in Paris, was founded by Jean-Baptiste Colbert.
Integral calculus was discovered by Isaac Newton. He also separated the colors of the rainbow with a prism and calculated the Moon's orbit.

Philip Carteret became governor of New Jersey.
Massachusetts defied English efforts to force greater allegiance to the crown and to allow religious freedom.

1667

The 13-year war between Russia and Poland was ended by the Treaty of Andrussov, with Russia gaining Kiev and Smolensk.
Charles II agreed in secret not to oppose Louis XIV's invasion of the Spanish Netherlands. The invasion marked the beginning of the War of Devolution.
The Peace of Breda ended the Anglo-Dutch War.
Alfonso VI of Portugal was banished to the Azores by his brother Pedro.
Shah Abbas II of Persia died and was succeeded by his son Shah Suleiman.

John Milton published *Paradise Lost.*

The Louvre Palace, bar 19th-century additions, was completed.

Andromaque by Jean Racine was first performed in Paris.

Robert Hooke's proposals for systematic weather recording marked the beginnings of meteorology.
The first blood transfusion to a human being was carried out at Montpelier University by French philosopher and mathematician Jean-Baptiste Denys. He pumped 9oz of lamb's blood into a 15-year-old boy who had been overbled.
Hand grenades were used in action by the French army.

▸ **The peace** ending the second Anglo-Dutch War recognized England's seizure of New Netherland; English forms of government were adopted.

1668

The War of Devolution ended with the Peace of Aix-la-Chapelle between Spain and France.
With the Treaty of Lisbon, Spain recognized Portuguese independence.
In the Triple Alliance, England, Holland, and Sweden joined to resist Louis XIV's claims to the Spanish Netherlands following the death of Philip IV of Spain.
The Black Death reached Austria after traversing half of Europe.
Emperor Leopold I and Louis XIV signed a secret treaty to partition the Spanish Empire.

Jean de La Fontaine published his first six books of *Fables.*

The Château of Versailles (1624) was enlarged to palatial size. The project took almost 100 years to complete.
The first Russian glass factory, employing Venetian glassblowers, was founded at Izmaylovo.
The architect Guarino Guarini, working in Turin, gave an open lacework of masonry, rather than a solid dome, to the church of S Lorenzo.

Dietrich Buxtehude, Swedish composer and organist, was appointed organist of St Mary's, Lübeck.

The first reflecting telescope was built by Isaac Newton.

Maine gave up its attempt to remain independent and recognized Massachusetts' authority.
The French extended their influence along the Great Lakes to Michigan and Wisconsin.

1669

Venice lost its last colonial possession when Crete was captured by the Turks after a siege that had begun in 1648.
The Hanseatic League met for the last time, with only nine out of the original 166 members present.
France and Brandenburg formed a secret treaty of alliance.
Aurangzeb, Mogul Emperor of India, revoked Hindu toleration, causing unrest in India.

Lettres Portugaises, passionate love-letters supposedly written by a Portuguese nun to a French nobleman, but of doubtful authenticity, was very popular.

The Paris Opéra was initiated by letters patent granted to Pierre Perrin by Louis XIV to establish an academy for the performance of operas in public.

Jan Swammerdam published *History of the Insects.*
Phosphorus was first isolated simultaneously and independently by German alchemist Hennig Brand and English physicist and chemist Robert Boyle.
Street lamp posts first came into use in Amsterdam.
The origin of fossils was accurately described for the first time by Danish anatomist Nicolaus Steno.

The Fundamental Constitutions of North Carolina guaranteed religious freedom (later amended) and envisaged an aristocratic social structure.
South Carolina's first colonists arrived; Charleston was founded.

PLAGUE: PROTECTIVE CLOTHING   **STRADIVARI VIOLIN**   **DENY'S BLOOD TRANSFUSION**   **NEWTON'S TELESCOPE**

	1670	1671	1672	1673	1674

World Events

France and Bavaria concluded an alliance that called for joint action on the death of either Charles II of Spain or Emperor Leopold I.
Ukrainian Cossacks rebelled against their Polish masters but were suppressed by General John Sobieski.
Frederick III of Denmark died. He was succeeded by his son, Christian V.
Lorraine was occupied by French forces.

Turkey declared war on Poland.
Cossack leader Stenka Razin was executed for his part in a huge anti-Russian rebellion.
Spain and the United Provinces formed an alliance against France.
Louis XIV signed treaties with Burnswick, Lüneburg, Hanover, and Osnabrück.
An abortive Hungarian revolt was followed by a reign of terror in that country.

The French again attacked the Dutch. They were opposed by Spain and the Empire, both fearful of French strength in the north.
The third Anglo-Dutch War began because Charles II had to support Louis XIV under the secret provisions of the Treaty of Dover.
The Treaty of Stockholm was signed by France and Sweden.
Poland was invaded by Turks and Cossacks.
The Prince of Orange, appealed to by the Dutch, was made Captain-General of the Union.

William III of Orange opened the sluice gates and flooded huge tracts of The Netherlands to save Amsterdam and the province of Holland from the French invaders.
Holy Roman Emperor Leopold I declared war on France.
King Michael of Poland died. A Polish force defeated the Turks at Khorzim.
The Great Elector made peace with France after his armies had been defeated by the Vicomte de Turenne.

The Treaty of Westminster brought the Anglo-Dutch War to an end.
William III of Orange was made hereditary Stadholder of the United Provinces.
General Sobieski, hero of hostilities against the Turks, was elected King of Poland as John III Sobieski.
French armies under Turenne crushed the Palatinate. The Holy Roman Empire, Spain, and the Dutch formed an alliance against France.

Literature

Art and Architecture

The rebuilding of London's churches began; 87 destroyed in the Great Fire were replaced, after the uniting of parishes, with 51. Christopher Wren, recently appointed the King's Surveyor of Works, was responsible for this ambitious project.

Quirinus Kuhlmann, a religious poet who used the German language with the freedom of the 20th-century expressionists, wrote his best work, *The Divine Embrace.*

The Hôtel des Invalides in Paris was commissioned by Louis XIV to provide for 7,000 old or crippled soldiers. Completed in just five years, the Church of Saint-Louis, designed by Jules Hardouin Mansart, followed directly. This fine Baroque church, with its great gold-plated dome, now houses the remains of Napoleon Bonaparte, his brothers and son.

Juan de Valdes Leal began his masterpiece, a series of paintings on *Death and Judgment* for the Hospital of La Caridad, Seville.
Gerard de Lairesse painted his *Allegory of Amsterdam Trade* for the Peace Palace, The Hague.

One of the finest works of English sculpture of the century was Edward Pierce's bust of Sir Christopher Wren, carved to commemorate the architect's knighthood.

Nicolas Boileau, French poet, satirist and literary critic, published *L'Art poetique,* a didactic treatise, written in vigorous verse, expressing the rules of classical poetry.

Performing Arts

The trio sonata was developed by Germans and Italians, using a quick first movement adapting *aabb* dance form with sections in contrasting moods and keys, and a slow second movement.

The French Académie de Royale Musique (later to become the Paris Opéra) opened with a performance of the opera *Pomone* by Robert Cambert.

The chorale prelude, a free composition based on a hymn tune, exploited the varied capabilities of the organ.

The great French dramatist Molière died a week after his play *Le malade imaginaire* was staged at the Palais-Royal in Paris.
The Country-Wife, William Wycherley's best play, was first performed.
The first Hebrew play, *Asire Hatiqva,* a morality play by Joseph Penco de la Vega, was printed in The Netherlands.

No opera could be performed in France without the permission of Jean-Baptiste Lully, court composer to Louis XIV. He created more than 30 ballets and collaborated with Molière in operatic works.
Jean-Baptiste Lully's opera *Alceste* was performed in Paris, with French set in recitative, a task thought almost impossible.

Science and Technology

The first megaphone was invented by English scientist Sir Samuel Morland and manufactured in London.
Minute hands first appeared on watches.
Symptoms of diabetes were first described by English physician Thomas Willis.

A calculating machine that could multiply and divide was made by Leibniz. He also defined the nature of the ether.

The first flexible fire hose was used by a Dutch fireman. It was 50 feet long and made of leather.

The Royal African Company received a monopoly for the English slave trade.

The first metal dental fillings were fitted by English surgeons.
The Chelsea Physic Garden was established.

The trench mortar was introduced by Dutch inventor Menno von Cochoorn.
The nature of combustion was explored in *Tractatus quinque medio-physici* by English chemist and physicist John Mayow.

America

Virginia passed a code designating as slaves all non-Christian servants who arrived by ship, with children to receive the status of their mother.
England returned Acadia to France.

South Carolina's first assembly met. After defeating local Indians, the colony began enslaving them.
The Quaker founder George Fox visited colonies.

Father Marquette and Louis Joliet began a journey from Lake Michigan to the Mississippi River as far as Arkansas.
The Dutch reoccupation New York, but settlements in eastern Long Island resisted.

New York was restored to the English by treaty and came under the administration of Sir Edmund Andros, while **New Jersey** was governed by Philip Carteret.

FAC

WREN: REBUILDING CHURCHES   GOTTFRIED LEIBNIZ   SOBIESKI

1675

rench forces under Turenne nflicted a heavy defeat on the reat Elector at Turkheim. ut Turenne was killed short- afterward at Sassbach, nd his army retreated across he Rhine.
ouis XIV's Swedish allies in- aded Brandenburg but were efeated by the Great Elector. hristian V of Denmark de- ared war on Sweden. olish forces, under Sobieski, ere defeated at Lemburg.

t Paul's Cathedral was begun n London. Thirty-five years in he making, one architect, Sir hristopher Wren, oversaw he whole project. Its massive valls resemble an Italian aroque palace, the whole urmounted by a great dome.

Matthew Locke composed the nusic for *Psyche*, the earliest urviving English opera.

he speed of light was calcu- ated for the first time by erman astronomer Olavs oemer, and shown to be nite.
reenwich Observatory, in ondon, was founded, princi- ally to improve navigation. It narks the standard meridian f longitude.

ndian raids caused substan- ial loss of life in frontier /irginia, but Governor Ber- eley refused to send a force gainst them.
ing Philip's War began, with ndians terrorizing outlying owns in New England.

1676

The Treaty of Zuravno brought peace between the Poles and the Turks after four years of warfare. The Turks gained the Polish Ukraine and most of Podolia.
Czar Alexis Mikhailovich of Russia died and was suc- ceeded by his oldest surviving son, Fyodor III.
French naval forces defeated a Dutch fleet off Palermo. A combined Dutch and Danish fleet captured Gothland.
Ahmed Kiuprili died and was succeeded by his brother-in- law Kara Mustafa as Grand Vizier of Turkey.
The Battle of Lunden gave Swedish forces a victory over the Danes.

Thomas Otway, the influential Restoration dramatist, wrote *Don Carlos, Prince of Spain*, a play in rhymed verse.

The universal joint was de- vised by Robert Hooke to help maneuver astronomical in- struments.
Thomas Tompion, one of the greatest of all clockmakers, who introduced improve- ments to both flat watches and pendulum clocks, was appointed clockmaker for the new Royal Observatory, then in Greenwich.
A fast-dyeing process for cali- co was developed by William Sherwin.

The Indian threat in New Eng- land was broken, but the war cost settlers 5% of the adult population.
Bacon's Rebellion in Virginia protested against the rule of Berkeley.
New Jersey was divided into East and West Jersey.

1677

A French army, under the Duke of Orleans, defeated William III of Orange at Cassel.
Dutch ports in Africa were cap- tured by the French.
The Swedes were defeated by a combined Danish-Dutch fleet at Oland.
The Great Elector of Branden- burg captured Stettin.

Many of the works of Benedict de Spinoza, including his masterpiece, *Ethica*, were published in Amsterdam fol- lowing his death.

John Dryden wrote *All for Love*, a dignified tragedy based on Shakespeare's *Antony and Cleopatra*. Five years earlier Dryden had written his bril- liant comedy *Marriage A-la- Mode*.
The great French dramatist Jean-Baptiste Racine wrote his most famous tragedy, *Phèdre*, a powerful study of a woman who falls in love with her stepson.

The transit of Venus was observed by English astro- nomer Edmund Halley.
Dutch biologist Anton van Leeuwenhoek discovered pro- tozoa with his single-lens microscope.
The London Pharmacopoeia (third edition) included exotic ingredients such as ipeca- cuanha, cinchona, and jalap.

Culpeper's Rebellion in North Carolina was instigated by opponents of the proprietor and ended in a stalemate.
Massachusetts bought the in- terests in Maine of the heirs of Sir Ferdinando Gorges and retained Maine until 1820.

1678

The "Popish Plot" convulsed England. Before it was ex- posed as an invention by Titus Oates, a renegade Anglican priest, some 35 Catholics were executed and Parlia- ment passed the Papists' Dis- abling Act.
The Franco-Dutch War ended with the Treaty of Nimwegen.
Sweden lost Rügen and Stral- sund to Brandenburg.
Russia and Sweden went to war.
The Hungarians, under Emeric Tökölyi, rebelled against the Hapsburgs.

The Pilgrim's Progress, an im- aginative prose allegory of the journey through life, consi- dered a landmark in English literature, was first published. Its author, John Bunyan, was a Puritan minister and preacher.
La Princesse de Clèves, France's first serious "historic- al" novel, was the master- piece of Marie-Madeleine, Comtesse de La Fayette, known as Madame de La Fayette.

Weekly concerts began in Clerkenwell, London, insti- gated by English patron of music Thomas Britton.
The first German opera house opened in Hamburg.

The first chrysanthemums reached Europe from Japan.
Lorenzo Bellini, Italian ana- tomist, discovered the excre- tory ducts of the kidneys, which were named after him.

Father Louis Hennepin ex- plored (1678—1680) for France the Great Lakes and upper Midwest as far as the site of Minneapolis.

1679

The Treaty of Lund restored peace between Sweden and Denmark.
The Treaty of Nijmegen ended hostilities between France and the Holy Roman Empire.
The war between Sweden and Brandenburg ended with the Peace of St Germain-en-Laye and Sweden gaining almost all Brandenburg's conquests in Pomerania.

The Palazzo Carignano, Turin, was Guarino Guarini's master- piece of palace design.

The pressure cooker was in- vented by French physicist Denis Papin. Papin also ex- perimented with steam en- gines, using both the vacuum made by condensing cylin- ders and the power produced by the expansion of steam as water boils.
Edmund Halley, English astro- nomer, listed the stars of the southern hemisphere in his *Catalogus Stellarum Austyr- alium*.

New York's Governor Andros attempted to extend his au- thority over East Jersey but was resisted by Governor Car- teret.
New Hampshire was separated from Massachusetts and made a crown colony.

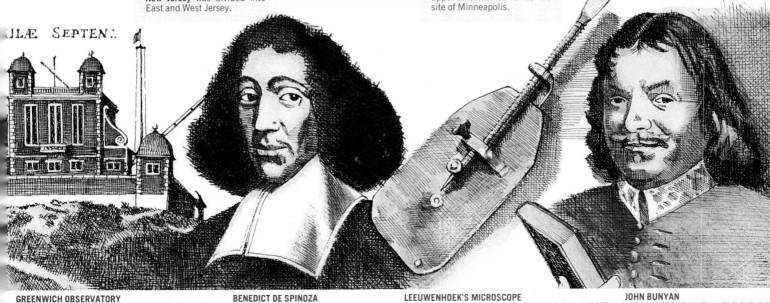

GREENWICH OBSERVATORY   BENEDICT DE SPINOZA   LEEUWENHOEK'S MICROSCOPE   JOHN BUNYAN

1680

World Events

Sweden's King Charles XI confirmed his absolutism by demanding that the properties of all aristocrats revert to the Crown.
Maximilian II Emanuel became Elector of Bavaria.
Brandenburg sent an expedition to West Africa.
Tokugawa shogun Itsuna of Japan died and was succeeded by his brother, Tsunayoshi.

Literature

Art and Architecture

The French Academy published rules for painting which upheld the idealism of Poussin and his emphasis on drawing.

Performing Arts

The Théâtre Française, the world's first national theater, was founded.
English composer Henry Purcell was appointed organist at Westminster Abbey.
Continuo was played on a keyboard instrument — often a harpsichord — filling in the harmony between treble and bass lines, as in the cantatas of Alessandro Scarlatti.
Sadlers Wells in London began to offer musical entertainments.

Science and Technology

The dodo became extinct.
Giovanni Alphonso Borelli, Italian mathematician, wrote *On the Motion of Animals*, a study, published posthumously, of muscles, skeleton, and digestion.

America

New York's Governor Andros successfully and illegally extended his control over both East New Jersey and West New Jersey, where William Penn and other Quakers were active.

1681

Russia gained most of Turkish Ukraine by the Treaty of Radzin. Czar Feodor began a campaign to reduce the status of the boyars.
France excluded Huguenots from all financial posts and trade guilds.
A League was formed to sustain the treaties of Nimwegen and Westphalia.
Frankfurt hosted a meeting of the European Congress.

Andrew Marvell's *Miscellaneous Poems* was published posthumously. His most famous poem, *To His Coy Mistress,* is a work of skillful persuasion.
Absalom and Achitophel was a triumph as both satire and political propaganda. It was Dryden's response, as poet laureate, to the succession crisis, provoked by the Whigs and led by the Earl of Shaftesbury.

Professional female dancers first appeared on the stage in Lully's production of *Le Triomphe de l'Amour.* Their heavy costumes, high heels, tall wigs and masks restricted them to formal court dances.

William Penn was granted a charter and proprietorship for the Pennsylvania region. The charter kept several rights for the crown and required the colony's assembly to approve legislation.

1682

Louis XIV moved his court to a sumptuous palace at Versailles to consolidate his independence from the nobility and the Parisians.
Czar Feodor III of Russia died and was succeeded by his nine-year-old half-brother Peter, who was preferred to the late Czar's imbecile brother Ivan. But Ivan's sister Sophia had Peter's followers assassinated, and made Ivan the new czar, with Peter in support and herself as regent.
Austria and Poland united in a campaign to free Hungary from the Turks. The Turks proclaimed Emeric Tökölyi King of Hungary.
Russia and Turkey signed a peace treaty.
Spain and the Empire formed a defensive league against France.

Claude's *Ascanius and the stag* is evidence of the paramount importance he gave to light and atmosphere in his late work.

"Pirouette" was first mentioned as a dance step by Ménétrier. It was derived from jig dancing and tumbling, which had long since used more adventurous steps than formal ballet.

The comet that bears his name was observed by Edmund Halley.
The "Father of Natural History," English naturalist John Ray, laid the groundwork for modern plant classification in his *Historia generalis plantarum.*

The Frame of Government set out basic laws for Pennsylvania, including religious freedom and a legislature.
Sieur de La Salle reached the Mississippi's mouth, claiming the river basin, named Louisiana, for France.

1683

Spain declared war on France. The Empire joined Spain in the League of the Hague, together with a Dutch-Swedish alliance, all opposed to France.
Afonso VI of Portugal died and was succeeded by his brother Pedro II.
The Chinese conquered Formosa.
Turkish troops under Kara Mustafa besieged Vienna for 58 days.

The hold of classicism on French art was weakened with the death of Jean-Baptiste Colbert.
Pierre Puget produced his dramatic marble statue of the death of *Milo of Croton.*

Henry Purcell's *Sonatas of III Parts* was published.

The relationship between gravitation and the tides was explained by Isaac Newton.
Bacteria, taken off teeth scrapings, were first identified by Dutch scientist Antonie van Leeuwenhoek with his own ×200 microscope.
The last wild boar in Britain was killed.
Gout was first accurately described by English physician Thomas Sydenham.

The autocratic Sir Edmund Andros was replaced as governor of New York.

1684

The Holy League of Linz was formed by the Holy Roman Emperor, Poland, and Venice against Turkey, at the instigation of Pope Innocent XI.
Louis XIV signed the 20-year Truce of Ratisbon with Emperor Leopold after occupying Lorraine, which he retained.
Queen Maria Theresa died and Louis XIV married Mme de Maintenon.
Hotta Masatoshi, Japanese prime minister, was assassinated, thus depriving shogun Sunayoshi of his most able and trusted counsellor.
The Great Elector offered a sanctuary in Brandenburg to Huguenot refugees.

The Galerie des Glaces in the Palace of Versailles was completed at about this time. Both it and the palace were copied throughout Europe.

The heliograph was invented by Robert Hooke.
A working force-pump was invented by French scientist Charles Perrault.

A British court revoked the charter of the Massachusetts Bay colony for failure to observe the Navigation Acts.
La Salle continued his explorations along the Gulf Coast.

THE DODO   PALACE OF VERSAILLES   SIEGE OF VIENNA

The Edict of Nantes, granting freedom of worship to Huguenots, was revoked by Louis XIV.

England's King Charles II died and was succeeded by his Catholic brother, James II (James VII of Scotland).

Charles, the Elector Palatine, died and Louis XIV tried to have his own sister-in-law, Liselotte, succeed him.

Chinese ports were opened to overseas trade.

War broke out between the East India Company and Aurungzeb, Mogul Emperor of Hindustan.

Genoa fell to the French.

Francesco Redi, physician and poet, wrote *Bacchus in Tuscany.*

Three giants of music were born: Johann Sebastian Bach (German), George Frideric Handel (German/English), and Domenico Scarlatti (Italian).

The first English concert hall opened at York Buildings in London.

The Carolina assembly was dissolved by the governor after Charleston area colonists turned down a constitutional revision.

The League of Augsburg provided a formidable line-up of European princes ranged against Louis XIV of France. It included Holy Roman Emperor Leopold I, William of Orange, Carlos II of Spain, Charles XI of Sweden, the Electors of Saxony, the Palatinate, and Bavaria, and the covert support of Pope Innocent XI.

Charles, Duke of Lorraine, commanding the imperial armies, captured the ransacked city of Buda from the Turks.

Madagascar was captured by Louis XIV.

Russia declared war on Turkey.

The Danes were repulsed in their attack on Hamburg.

The first Swedish theater opened in Stockholm.

The first meteorological map was prepared by Edmund Halley, explaining monsoons, trade winds and the salinity of the sea.

Sir Edmund Andros became governor of New England with authority to include New York, New Jersey, and Pennsylvania within Dominion of New England.

The Spanish destroyed the Carolina settlement at Stuart's Town.

The Battle of Mohacs resulted in a victory for the imperial forces under Charles of Lorraine over the Turks under Suleiman Pasha. The Hungarian Diet of Pressburg confirmed that the hereditary succession to the Hungarian throne belonged to the male line of Hapsburgs.

Sultan Mohammed IV of Turkey was deposed after 43 years in power. He was succeeded by his brother, Suleiman III.

Athens and the Greek Peloponessus were taken from the Turks by a Venetian army under Francesco Morosini. The Venetian bombardment badly damaged the Parthenon.

The Age of Louise the Great was an early blow in the "quarrel between the Ancients and the Moderns" which raged within the Académie Française. In this poem, Charles Perrault set modern writers above classical authors.

Isaac Newton published his *Principia,* probably the most important book in science. It dealt with the behavior of moving bodies and enunciated his three laws of motion as well as the principles of gravitation. It also explained the motion of bodies on the Earth and in the universe.

Colonists' resistance to the harsh Andros regime grew; Connecticut tried to evade a government takeover by hiding official documents in the Charter Oak.

La Salle was murdered by his own men.

England's "Glorious Revolution" took place. A son was born to James II, opening up the prospect of a succession of Catholic kings. Seven Whig and Tory leaders invited the king's son-in-law William III of Orange to save England from Roman Catholicism and restore its liberties. William landed on the south coast and James fled to France.

Louis XIV invaded the Palatinate, thus enabling William to cross the Channel undisturbed.

Charles of Lorraine captured Belgrade and Transylvania.

Frederick William, the Great Elector, died and was succeeded by his son Frederick III.

Smyrna was destroyed by an earthquake.

Francesco Redi proved that maggots were produced by egg-laying flies rather than by spontaneous generation. Curiously, he continued to believe that gall flies and intestinal worms generated spontaneously.

Plate glass was cast for the first time by Abraham Thevart.

New Jersey was forced to surrender its charters and was incorporated into the Dominion of New England.

Political unrest in the colonies grew as England approached a crisis over the rule of the Catholic James II.

A Declaration of Rights was issued by the English Convention Parliament. William and his wife Mary were invited to rule jointly as king and queen subject to certain parliamentary restrictions. They accepted.

England and The Netherlands joined the Grand Alliance of the League of Augsburg against France.

Turkey faced an alliance of the Holy Roman Emperor with Russia.

China and Russia signed the Treaty of Nerchinsk.

Peter the Great became Czar of Russia.

The Dutch painter Meindert Hobbema, the most important pupil of Jacob van Ruisdael, painted his celebrated work, *The avenue at Middleharnis.*

An edict decreed that all silver and gold tableware in France was to be melted down. This stimulated the production of ceramic vessels.

Henry Purcell's *Dido and Aeneas,* the first significant English opera, was performed in London.

The first modern trade fair was held in Leyden.

Iroquois massacred 200 French settlers near Montreal.

Governor Andros was forced from office by colonists.

Leisler's Rebellion in New York showed early colonial resistance to English authority.

ISAAC NEWTON **WILLIAM AND MARY** **PLATE GLASS**

World Events

1690
Peter the Great began his policy of Russian expansion toward Azov for an outlet to the Black Sea, and visited western Europe.
Spain and Savoy joined the Grand Alliance against France.
Belgrade was reconquered by the Turks after the Austrians had been driven out of Bulgaria, Serbia, and Transylvania.

1691
The Battle of Szcelankemen saw the defeat of the Turks after they had invaded Hungary. They were routed by Louis of Baden and their leader, Mustafa Kiuprili, was killed in battle.
Suleiman III of Turkey died and was succeeded by his brother, Ahmed II.
Transylvania was conquered by the armies of Emperor Leopold.
French forces captured Nice from Savoy.

1692
An invasion of England was contemplated by Louis XIV and James II until the naval Battle of Cap de La Hogue, in which a large French fleet was destroyed by the English.
On land, the French captured Namur and defeated England's William III in the Battle of Steinkirk.
China issued an Edict of Toleration for Roman Catholics.
An earthquake devastated Jamaica. The pirate city of Port Royal fell into the sea.

1693
An Anglo-Dutch fleet was defeated off Cape St Vincent by French ships under Anne Hilarion de Cotentin, Compte de Tourville, and again in the Battle of Lagos off Portugal. The French commander thus avenged his crushing defeat in the Battle of La Hogue.
Louis XIV, helped by his wife, Mme de Maintenon, began peace overtures by achieving a reconciliation with the Pope.
The Battle of Neerwinden resulted in a victory by French forces (who went on to sack Heidelberg for the second time) over William III's army.

1694
The Royal Navy bombarded L Havre, Dieppe, and Dunkirk but was repulsed at Brest This latter failure was blame on John Churchill (later Duk of Marlborough), who ha been plotting to restore Jame II to the throne and had be trayed military secrets t France.
The French attack on Barce lona was foiled by the Roya Navy.
French lower classes weakened and exhausted b war, were close to famine.
Suleiman, Shah of Persia died and was succeeded b his 19-year-old son Husein.
Augustus the Strong becam Elector of Saxony.

Literature Religion Philosophy

1690
The English philosopher John Locke published his first version of *An Essay Concerning Human Understanding* and *Two Treatises of Government*.
The Accademia dell'Arcadia was founded in Rome to reform Italian poetry, from the decadence of the Baroque to the purity and simplicity of the classical style.

Art & Architecture

1691
The Allegory of the missionary work of the Jesuits on the ceiling of S Ignazio, Rome, represents the climax of Baroque illusionism. Figures and painted architecture surge up to the heavens; this dramatic style spread to Austria and Germany when the artist, a Jesuit lay brother, Fra Andrea Pozzo, settled in Vienna in 1702.

1692
An important botanical work, *The Anatomy of Plants*, was published by English botanist Nehemiah Grew.

1693
José Benito Churrigera painted the altarpiece of S Esteban, Salamanca.
The *romains du roi* typefaces were created by a committee set up by Louis XIV. They were designed for engravers' tools rather than the pen, a revolutionary development.
Grinling Gibbons, raised and trained in The Netherlands, was appointed master carver in England.

Performing Arts

1690
The concerto was developed about this period by Arcangelo Corelli and others as a concerto grosso for a group of instruments and orchestra or for a virtuoso solo performer with orchestra.

1691
English poet and dramatist John Dryden wrote the words and Henry Purcell composed the music for the opera *King Arthur, or the British Worthy*, performed in London's Dorset Garden Theater.

1693
William Congreve, the English master of Restoration comedy, began his brilliant career with *The Old Bachelor* at London's Drury Lane Theater
French composer François Couperin began his prodigious output of chamber music.

Science and Technology

1690
Christiaan Huygens put forward a wave theory of light. Newton proposed a particle theory. Later science would prove them both right.
Calico printing was introduced into Britain from France.

1691
Coal gas as a possible source of lighting was demonstrated by John Clayton.

1694
Rudolf Camerarius, a Germa botanist, explained the sexe of plants in his *De sexu plan tarum epistola*.

America

1690
Schnectady, New York, was burned by a French and Indian force as the Anglo-French conflict of King William's War spread to North America.
Carolina's Albermarle colony overthrew its governor.

1691
Albermarle colony became known as North Carolina. Its former governor took control of Charleston's government but was soon overthrown.
A royal charter brought Plymouth and Maine colonies legally within Massachusetts.

1692
The English crown assumed control of Pennsylvania because of the close connections between the colony and the deposed James II.
Maryland became a royal colony.
The Salem witchcraft trials began.

1693
Maryland, its name honoring England's new rulers, was founded.
Witchcraft hysteria in Massachusetts subsided.

1694
Maryland's capital was move to the Protestant settlemer of Annapolis.

HENRY PURCELL   GRINLING GIBBONS CARVING   PETER THE GREAT

amur was recaptured from
e French by William III.
his was regarded by many as
illiam's finest military
chievement.
eter the Great was foiled in
s attempt to take Azov in
e Russo-Turkish War and
turned to Moscow.
hmad II, Turkish sultan, died
d was succeeded by Musta-
II.

estoration English comedy
ached perfection in the
ork of William Congreve.
ove for Love and, five years
ter, *The Way of the World*
ere his best plays, entertain-
ents which criticized the
anners and behavior of the
ourt circle, his audience.
he **first public concert** was
erformed in Edinburgh.
enry Purcell, the first out-
anding English composer,
ed, his last major work
eing music for the play *In-
an Queen*.

agnesium sulfate (Epsom
alts) was isolated from
rings in the North Downs of
uthern England by botanist
ehemiah Grew.
rown glaze stoneware was
anufactured at Nottingham
y John Morley.
**ngland's first public drinking
untain** was built in Ham-
ersmith, London, by Sir
amuel Morland.

he **first synagogue** in New
ork City was established, de-
onstrating some acceptance
f Jews in the colonies.

The fortress of Azov was finally
captured from the Turks by a
Russian army that also conquered Kamchatka.
Ivan IV of Russia died, leaving
Peter the Great as the only
czar.
France and Savoy concluded
the Treaty of Turin.
Jan Sobieski of Poland died
after several years of defeat
and humiliation.

The death of Marie de Rabu-
tin-Chantal, Marquise de
Sévigné, marked the end of
her extraordinary letter-
writing.

**The Austrian "Versailles" was
begun:** the Palace of Schönbrunn, Vienna, designed by
Johann Fischer von Erlach.

Etienne Loulié invented an instrument for beating time. He
published an engraving and
description of his metronome
in Paris.

The first practical steam engine
was invented by British en-
gineer Thomas Savery.
Peppermint was first described
by English naturalist John
Ray.
**Erection of the first Eddystone
Lighthouse** was begun by
Henry Winstanley.

England created the Board of
Trade to supervise colonial
administration and trade and
to report to the Privy Council.

The Treaty of Ryswick ended
the War of the League of
Augsburg. Louis XIV recognized William III as King of
England. All French con-
quests since the Treaty of
Nijmegen (1679) were res-
tored to Spain.
Charles XI of Sweden died and
was succeeded by his 14-
year-old son, Charles XII.
Frederick Augustus I, Elector
of Saxony, who became a
Roman Catholic, was elected
to succeed John III Sobieski
as King Augustus II of Poland.
Western Mongolia was conquered by the Chinese.
The Battle of Zanta saw the
Turks defeated by Prince
Eugene of Savoy.

The Provok'd Wife was the
most successful play by John
Vanbrugh, English dramatist
and architect.
L'Europe Galante by André
Campra was first performed;
it became the model for all
future ballets.
English composer John Blow
wrote the anthem *I Was Glad
When They Said* for the opening of Christopher Wren's
Choir in St Paul's Cathedral.

The first skating boots were
made in The Netherlands for
Peter the Great, who was
traveling incognito in western
Europe.

Vice-admiralty courts were
established to mediate matters concerning colonial
trade.

**The Empire, France, the United
Provinces, and England** signed
a Treaty of Partition in an
attempt to settle the question
of the Spanish succession.
Carlos II of Spain, who was
childless (thus terminating
the Spanish House of Hapsburg), named the infant
Prince Elector of Bavaria as
his heir.
The Streltsi, Czar Peter's
guard of Russian nobles
established by Ivan the Terrible, were crushed after a rebellion.
The slave trade across the
Atlantic from Africa was
officially sanctioned for British merchants by Parliament.

*A Short view of the Immorality
and Profaneness of the English
Stage* was published by the
Revd Jeremy Collier. A mixture of absurd statement and
valid argument, the author
criticized Shakespeare along-
side contemporary play-
wrights. The maligned Restoration dramatists replied
with speed.

The speed of sound was calculated by Isaac Newton.

The Royal African Company
lost its monopoly of the slave
trade, opening up this lucra-
tive industry to independent
traders.

The Treaty of Karlowitz ended
the war between the Holy
League and Turkey. The Turks
were forced to cede almost all
of Hungary, Translyvania,
Slavonia, and Croatia to Austria; Podolia and Turkish
Ukraine to Poland; and Morea
and the greater part of Dalma-
tia to Venice.
King Christian V of Denmark
died and was succeeded by
his son Frederick IV.
The Treaty of Preobrazhenskoe
outlined the partition of the
Swedish Empire among Rus-
sia, Poland, Denmark, and
Saxony.
**English buccaneer William
Dampier,** with Admiralty backing, explored the western
coast of Australia in his small
ship, the *Roebuck*.

Govind Rai, the tenth Guru of
the Sikhs, led the armed resistance to Mughal persecution, introducing the turban,
uncut hair and possession of
a knife as essentials of male
Sikhism.
**François de Salignac de la
Mothe-Fénelon** wrote *Les
Aventures de Télémaque* for
his pupil Louis, Duc de Bourgogne, grandson and heir to
Louis XIV.

Fugues in organ music during
this period were often paired
with a free composition for
contrast, giving the prelude
and fugue or toccata and
fugue found in many works by
Buxtehude and Bach.

The French established a mission in Illinois and a fort on
the Mississippi coast as part
of their effort to consolidate
their hold on the Mississippi
Valley.
England's Wool Act prohibited
colonial trade in wool.

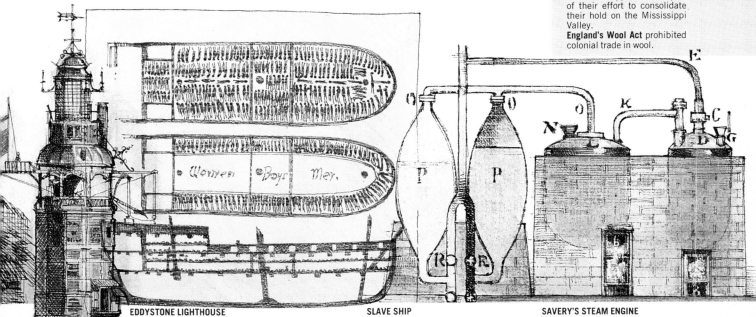

EDDYSTONE LIGHTHOUSE   SLAVE SHIP   SAVERY'S STEAM ENGINE

This was the budget in 1767, in percentages of total income, of a clerk.

Breakfast (Bread and cheese and small beer from the chandler's shop) 6.0%
Dinner (Chuck beef or scrag of mutton or sheep's trotters or pig's ear soused; cabbage or potatoes or parsnips; bread; and small beer with a half pint of porter) 21.2%
Supper (Bread and cheese with radishes or cucumbers or onions; small beer and half a pint of porter) 13.6%

Per week 40.8%
An additional repast on Sunday 1.7%
42.5%

Washing 4.3%
Shaving and combing a wig twice 2.6%
Soap, blacking, pepper, vinegar and salt .... 1.1 %
Rent of furnished room 12.98%
Coal and candles 7.79%

Weekly total 71.3%

Clothes   27.43%

Grand total 98.73%
Available for other expenditure 1.27%

1767   A clerk's budget

Expenditure, in percentages of gross weekly income, by a skilled craftsman with a wife and two children.

Housing 19.95%
Fuel, light & power 4.62%
Food 19.63%
Alcoholic drink 3.79%
Tobacco 2.06%
Clothing & footwear.................................... 7.4%
Durable household goods 8.9%
Other goods 7.16%
Transport & vehicles 14.83%
Services...10.95%
Miscellaneous.. 0.71%
100%

The typical 1986 household budget above assumes income tax has been paid. "Disposable" income, shown below as 26.27 per cent, is distributed among the categories above. For example, alcoholic drink and tobacco have been treated as items on which disposable income is spent, on the grounds that neither is a necessity. Similarly, some expenditure on household goods, other goods and services is treated as being made from disposable income because those categories include such things as video equipment, toys and holidays.

In the breakdowns of both budgets below, "housing" includes rent, food, fuel, light and power.

1986   Household budget

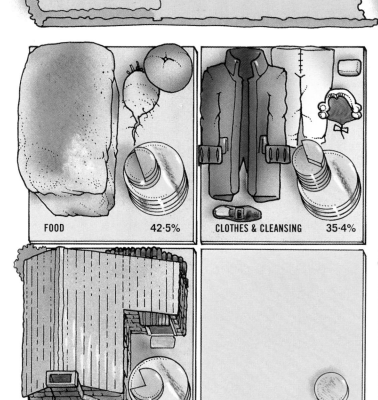

FOOD | 42·5%
CLOTHES & CLEANSING | 35·4%
HOUSING | 20·77%
DISPOSABLE INCOME | 1%

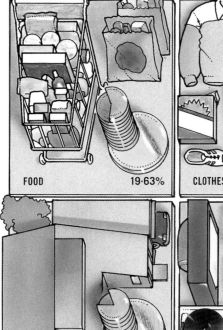

FOOD | 19·63%
CLOTHES & CLEANSING | 8·4%
HOUSING | 45·8%
DISPOSABLE INCOME | 26.27%

Throughout history, the prosperity of ordinary men and women has been at the mercy of events. Plagues, famines, wars, gold strikes, the discovery of new lands and the invention of new forms of transport have all affected work, productivity and trade and hence the standard of life enjoyed by the mass of people. Wars, while in progress, have almost invariably increased the income of those who have stayed at home to feed the war machines; victory (or defeat) has often brought depression in its wake. Gold – whether the wealth the Spaniards discovered in South America or strikes in places such as California and Australia – has also produced booms. So has the introduction of newer, faster forms of transport. And, periodically, natural disasters have had the same effect as wars – the bubonic plague that swept Europe in the 14th century raised wages by creating a scarcity of labour.

In modern times the western world has changed from a predominantly rural economy to an industrial one. Britain's industrial revolution of the mid–18th century pointed the way. It spread to Europe and thence to the United States and within a century had transformed society.

At its base lay the centuries-old putting-out system, whereby light industry was undertaken by cottage workers. This was widespread in Europe by 1762 (when it was legalised in France), but by then Britain had already moved toward a factory system, spurred by the invention of the spinning jenny, the water frame and Crompton's mule. Industrial canals, new roads and the coming of the railway in the 1820s gave Britain its modern shape.

But if Britain, followed by Europe, led the way, they were not to hold the lead. By the end of the 19th century it was already clear that the United States had become the greatest industrial power in the world, passing Britain in steel output in 1890, in coal in 1898, and in the consumption of raw cotton by the end of the century. The other giant, Russia, failed to fulfill its promise because of internal impediments to progress. In Europe, Germany passed Britain in iron and steel manufacture in the 1890s. All these shifts produced corresponding shifts in the balance of political power. By the end of World War I traditional roles had been reversed and, economically at least, Britain had become America's colony.

From the early 1500s until

about 1885, wages had consistently tended to run below prices. The average worker had little left over once he had bought the bare necessities. Life, said Thomas Hobbes, writing in the 17th century, was solitary, poor, nasty, brutish and short; and it remained so until recent times.

The 40 years since World War II have seen a dramatic rise in "disposable" income – income, that is, that can be spent on what earlier generations would have thought of as luxuries. Throughout most of the developed world, wages have increased 30-fold in the last 35 years, while prices have risen only ten times.

The change in lifestyles between the beginning of the industrial revolution and today is exemplified in the two budgets on these pages. One is that of a clerk living in 1767 and one that of an average skilled worker's family of today. There are astonishing differences. Expenditure on housing, fuel, light & power, and personal cleanliness amounts to about the same: the clerk spent 28.77 per cent and the modern family spends 26.46 per cent. But 200 years ago, the clerk spent 42.5 per cent of his income on food; the modern family spends only 19.63 per cent. Most of the rest of the clerk's money (27.43

per cent) went on clothes, whereas the expenditure for two adults and two children today is only 7.4 per cent.

The clerk had less than 1.3 per cent of his income for anything beyond necessities. Today, once necessities have been taken care of, the typical modern family spends almost a quarter of its remaining income (13 per cent of total income) on the family car. Leisure goods and services make up another 12 per cent.

Today's prosperity, which would have seemed incredible to a Victorian chimney sweep – who lived on bread and butter, saveloys and cabbage, fried fish and pudding – is enjoyed by only a part of the world's population. The people who inhabit the great land masses of Africa and Asia, and much of South America, still live as European labourers lived in the late middle ages. History has not passed them by; indeed, the fortunes of what are now the developed nations were largely based on the work and produce of what are now the developing nations; but prosperity has so far eluded them. If it was the industrial revolution that changed the face of the developed world, the next revolution has to bring a similar prosperity to the developing world.

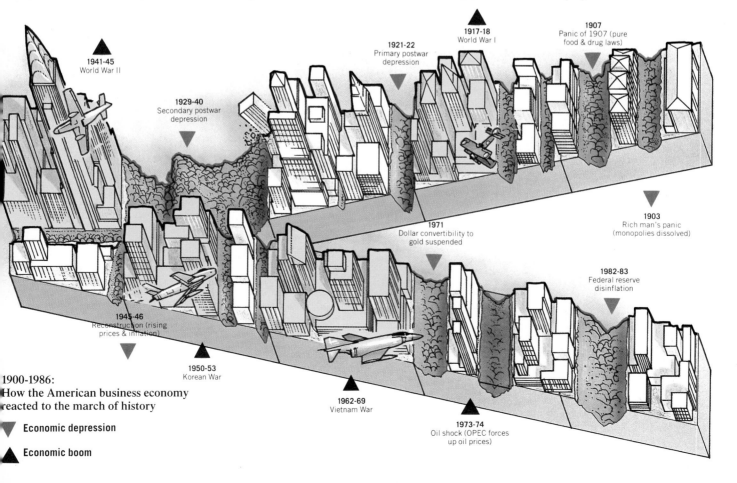

1941-45
World War II

1929-40
Secondary postwar depression

1945-46
Reconstruction (rising prices & inflation)

1950-53
Korean War

1962-69
Vietnam War

1921-22
Primary postwar depression

1917-18
World War I

1971
Dollar convertibility to gold suspended

1973-74
Oil shock (OPEC forces up oil prices)

1907
Panic of 1907 (pure food & drug laws)

1903
Rich man's panic (monopolies dissolved)

1982-83
Federal reserve disinflation

1900-1986:
How the American business economy reacted to the march of history

▼ **Economic depression**

▲ **Economic boom**

The population *BOOM*

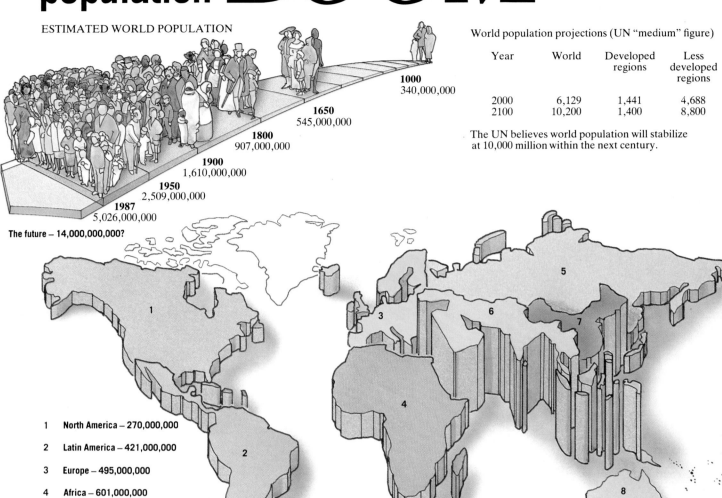

ESTIMATED WORLD POPULATION

1000
340,000,000

1650
545,000,000

1800
907,000,000

1900
1,610,000,000

1950
2,509,000,000

1987
5,026,000,000

The future – 14,000,000,000?

World population projections (UN "medium" figure)

Year	World	Developed regions	Less developed regions
2000	6,129	1,441	4,688
2100	10,200	1,400	8,800

The UN believes world population will stabilize at 10,000 million within the next century.

1   **North America – 270,000,000**

2   **Latin America – 421,000,000**

3   **Europe – 495,000,000**

4   **Africa – 601,000,000**

5   **USSR – 284,000,000**

6   **Asia – 1,868,000,000**

7   **China – 1,062,000,000**

8   **Oceania – 25,000,000**

Ninety per cent of the world's population growth in the next century will take place in less developed regions: Africa alone is expected to pass the 1,000 million mark by 2010. Some European countries, including the United Kingdom, have near-zero or even negative growth rates. The population of the United States is expected to rise by almost 53 million and that of Canada by more than three million.

Current trends suggest that, by the middle of the next century, the world's population will have reached at least 10,000 million, double its present size. So sharp has been the increase that the world's population has grown by about 25 per cent, from 4,000 million to around 5,000 million, since 1975 alone.

For nine-tenths of the time that humans have inhabited the Earth total population probably never exceeded five million. Only with the transition from hunting-gathering to farming, about 10,000 years ago, did it begin to grow significantly, with the result that by 500 BC there were an estimated 100 million people

throughout the world. By 1300, world population stood at about 500 million. A few decades later the ravages of the Black Death claimed as much as two-thirds of the population in parts of Europe.

The disappearance of the plague and the recession of acute famine and epidemics, combined with improvement in medical care, brought about a decline in the deathrate, which became marked by the end of the 19th century. A decline in the birthrate in Europe did not occur until about 100 years later, so that population grew steadily during the 19th century.

The trends changed in both sectors after World War II, with a

rise in the birthrate in the developed nations and a dramatic drop in the deathrate in the rest of the world. Of far greater significance for the future is the latter trend, for 90 per cent of the population growth of the coming century will take place in the Third World, particularly in Africa and Central America.

Various explanations have been advanced for the rapid growth in population of modern times. In the 18th century Malthus held that populations always breed up to the limit of their food supply, so that greater yields lead to an increase in population. Contrary to this principle, however, population has grown fastest in countries

where the food supply available to the poor majority has declined because of export to richer parts of the world.

Another explanation is that improvements in medicine and sanitation have brought about a rise in population by increasing longevity. The theory that currently holds sway is that a major effect of Western-funded development programs is to cause an entrenchment of traditional values, particularly those relating to the extended family. The inhabitants of those countries have, on an enormous scale, sought to counter the socially destructive aspects of development by surrounding themselves with children.

THE

18th

CENTURY

56 1700 1701 1702 1703 1704

World Events

1700: **Charles II** of Spain died, leaving Philip, Duke of Anjou and grandson of Louis XIV, as heir to his lands. This led to the War of the Spanish Succession. Philip acceded to the Spanish throne as Philip V, the first Bourbon king, in contravention of the Second Partition Treaty agreed by William III and Louis XIV.
In the Great Northern War, in which Russia and Denmark fought Sweden for control of the Baltic, the Danes invaded Schleswig, the Poles invaded Riga, and the Russians were defeated by Charles XII of Sweden at the Battle of Narva.
Elector Frederick III of Brandenburg joined Emperor Leopold in a crown treaty against the French during the War of the Spanish Succession.
William Dampier explored New Guinea and was later wrecked off Ascension Island.

1701: **Frederick III,** Elector of Brandenburg, assumed the title King of Prussia with the consent of the emperor and became Frederick I of Prussia.
Charles XII of Sweden invaded Poland.
The Grand Alliance to oppose France was made up of Emperor Leopold, England, Holland, and Savoy.
Prince Eugène of Savoy defeated the French at Carpi.

1702: **In the War of the Spanish Succession,** the Grand Alliance declared war on France.
William III of England died after falling off his horse and was succeeded by his sister-in-law, Queen Anne.
Dutch jurist Cornelius van Bynkershoek established the three-mile territorial sea zone around a nation's shores.

1703: **In the War of the Spanish Succession,** the Grand Alliance proclaimed Austria's Archduke Charles King of Spain. Portugal joined the alliance against France, acting as a base for operations in Spain. The Duke of Marlborough invaded the Spanish Netherlands and captured Bonn, Huy, Limburg and Guelders.
A Bavarian army attempted an abortive invasion of the Tyrol.
In the Great Northern War, Sweden's Charles XII defeated the Russians at Pultusk.
Peter the Great founded St Petersburg as Russia's capital.
An earthquake and fire in Japan destroyed Edo and killed 200,000 people.

1704: **The Battle of Blenheim** in southern Germany resulted in the defeat of combined Franco-Bavarian-Prussian forces by an Allied army commanded by the Duke of Marlborough and supported by Prince Eugène of Savoy. This important victory saved Vienna.
Augustus II of Poland was deposed. With the help of bribes from Sweden's Charles XII, Stanislas Leszczinski was elected King of Poland as Stanislas I.
Peter the Great captured Narva and Dorpat, thus securing Ingria.

Literature

1701: **Hyacinthe Rigaud's** baroque portrait of Louis XIV was one of the most magnificent and influential portraits of royal absolutism.

1702: **Luca Giordano** returned to his native Naples after ten years' service to Charles II in Spain. The frescoes he painted in the Escorial are among his finest paintings.

1703: **Lothario,** the hero of Nicholas Rowe's *The Fair Penitent,* gave the English language a new word for a rake. Rowe was poet laureate and the leading English tragic dramatist of the century.

1704: **Daniel Defoe,** English novelist, journalist and pamphleteer, wrote his periodical, the *Review.* The paper, which survived for almost ten years, was influential on later English essay journals and newspapers.
Jonathan Swift, the Anglo-Irish master of English prose satire, published *A Tale of a Tub* anonymously.

Art and Architecture

1700: **Sir Godfrey Kneller,** had become the leading painter in England and successor to Lely. He is best known for his portrait series, *British Admirals* and *Hampton Court Beauties,* and, above all, his portraits of members of the Whig *Kit-Cat Club.*

1701: **The *entrechat*** was first described in Raoul Auger Feuillet's *Choréographie;* the rapid interchange of the feet during a ballet leap.
Henry Playford, English music publisher, began a series of weekly concerts at Oxford.

1702: **The first scheduled transatlantic mail service** was started. It operated monthly from Falmouth to the West Indies.
The first daily newspaper, *The Daily Courant,* was issued in London.

Performing Arts

1700: **String orchestras** became established.
The French horn appeared in orchestras.

Science

1701: **The first practical seed drill** was invented by English agriculturist Jethro Tull.

1702: **Queen Anne's War,** the American part of the War of the Spanish Succession, began. Carolina forces burned St. Augustine, Florida.
East and West New Jersey were reunited as a royal province.

1703: **Antonio Vivaldi** was appointed violin teacher at the Ospedale della Pietà, Venice, a girls' orphanage. The most famous of his many concertos is *Le quatro stagioni, The Four Seasons.*

1704: **Johann Sebastian Bach** composed his first cantata, *Denn Du wirst meine Seele.*
George Frideric Handel composed his *St John Passion.*
Jeremiah Clarke became the Chapel Royal organist.

1704: **Isaac Newton,** in his *Opticks,* encapsulated his work on light.

America

1700: **The French built** forts at Mackinac and Detroit to ensure control of fur trade.
"The Selling of Joseph", by Samuel Sewall, was the first protest against slavery.

1701: **William Penn's** Charter of Liberties gave Pennsylvania its own constitution.
The Vestry Act made the Church of England the official church of North Carolina.
Yale was founded at Saybrook, Connecticut.

1703: **Jesuits established** a post at the junction of the Kaskaskia and Mississippi Rivers.
The French and the Abenacki Indians raided in Maine.
Delaware became a colony after separation from Pennsylvania.

1704: **The French** and the Abenacki Indians raided Deerfield, Massachusetts, and colonists retaliated in Canada.
Fort Miami was built.

FRENCH HORN   QUEEN ANNE   VIVALDI   BLENHEIM MEDAL

1705

Leopold I, Holy Roman Emperor, died. He was succeeded by his eldest son Joseph I.

A **rebellion in Astrakhan** began in protest at Peter the Great's westernization of Russia.

King Stanislas I of Poland allied himself with Sweden's Charles XII and helped him with his struggle against Peter the Great.

Louis XIV crushed a revolt of the Camisards. Famine became widespread throughout France.

John Vanbrugh designed Blenheim Palace, at Woodstock, Oxfordshire, in collaboration with Nicholas Hawksmoor, Sir Christopher Wren's assistant. Built at the nation's expense for John Churchill, Duke of Marlborough, the palace represents the culmination of the English Baroque style in architecture.

German suites by Bach and others mixed free forms such as prelude and toccata with dance forms such as *allemande, sarabande, minuet, gavotte,* and *gigue.*

Edmund Halley, British Astronomer Royal, correctly predicted the return of the comet that now bears his name.
The ship's wheel replaced the tiller.
The Berlin Royal Observatory was founded.

Colonial exports to Britain expanded to include rice, molasses, pitch and tar.
The Virginia Act made some provisions for public education in the colony.

1706

In the War of the Spanish Succession, Marlborough defeated the French at the Battle of Ramillies. He also conquered the Spanish Netherlands with the surrender of Antwerp, Brussels, Ghent, Ostend, and other cities.
The Portuguese invaded Spain and briefly installed Austrian Archduke Charles as king before being expelled by Philip V.
With the Treaty of Altranstadt, Augustus II of Poland resigned his throne, although he had been deposed some two years earlier.
The French were defeated in Italy by Savoy's Prince Eugène, and were subsequently driven out of Italy altogether.
Portugal's Pedro II died and was succeeded by his son, John V.
Charles XII of Sweden defeated the Russians at Franstadt.

Johann Sebastian Bach, outstanding German organist and harpsichordist and one of the greatest composers ever, wrote his stirring organ *Toccata and Fugue in D Minor* at about this time.

A French and Spanish attack on Charleston, South Carolina, was unsuccessful. **The Church of England** was named the colony's official church.
The Presbyterians organized in Philadelphia and adopted a constitution.

1707

England and Scotland were united as the Kingdom of Great Britain. The Scottish Parliament was abolished, but the two countries retained their own independent legal systems and churches. Scotland sent 45 members to the Commons and 16 peers to the Lords.
Prussia and Sweden signed a Perpetual Alliance, but Prussia declined to take part in the Great Northern War.
In the Battle of Almanza, a French army, commanded by English mercenary the Duke of Berwick, defeated the allied English, Portuguese and Spanish.
A popular insurrection in Switzerland was crushed by Geneva.
Aurungzebe, Emperor of Hindustan and the last of the great Mughal rulers, died and was succeeded by Bahadur Shah. The Mughal empire disintegrated as local princes asserted their autonomy, seeking assistance from European traders.
Fujiyama, the Japanese volcano, erupted.

Gottfried Silbermann, German master organ-builder, built his first organ in Saxony.

Denis Papin invented a steamboat.
The first road tunnel was built on the St Gotthard Road in Switzerland.

The French and Abenackis attacked Winter Harbor.
The British and New Englanders unsuccessfully seized Port Royal, Canada.

1708

The Battle of Oudenarde was a victory for Marlborough and Eugène of Savoy over the French in the War of the Spanish Succession. Marlborough captured Lille after a four-month siege.
Sweden's Charles XII invaded the Ukraine but plague in his ranks forced him to retreat.
Peter the Great divided Russia into eight regions.
The Sikhs became militant and made the Punjab virtually independent of Mughal rule.

Jean-François Regnard, who acknowledged his great debt to his fellow countryman, Molière, wrote one of his best-known comedies, *Le Légataire universel (The Heir).*

Johann Sebastian Bach became court organist at Weimar.
The first permanent German theater was founded in Vienna.

Jesuit missionaries made an accurate map of China.

The French captured British St. Johns, Newfoundland, completing their drive for control of the eastern coast of mainland Canada.
The Act of 1708 expanded the authority in the colonies of vice-admiralty courts.

1709

The Battle of Malplaquet resulted in a victory for Marlborough and Eugène over the French but at the staggering cost of 20,000 Allied lives. Marlborough was branded "butcher" in Parliament.
Peter the Great became dominant in northern Europe after the Battle of Poltava in which Sweden's Charles XII was routed and fled to Anatolia. Charles's defeat encouraged Augustus I, Elector of Saxony, to depose Stanislas I and reclaim his Polish crown.
Tokugawa shogun Sunayoshi of Japan died. He was succeeded by his cousin Ienobu, who promptly freed 9,000 of Sunayoshi's prisoners.

Richard Steele launched *The Tatler,* an English essay periodical which appeared three times a week.

The pianoforte was invented in Florence by Bartolommeo Cristofori, who substituted a hammer action for the harpsichord's plucking action.

High-quality iron was produced by Abraham Darby, a British iron worker, at Coalbrookdale in Shropshire. The iron was smelted with coke and molded in sand, for cheap production.
English scientist Francis Hawksbee made the first accurate observation of capillary action in glass tubes.

A record number of Germans emigrated to America as a result of war in Europe.

FUJIYAMA   BLENHEIM PALACE   J. S. BACH   PIANOFORTE

1710

World Events

Louis XIV initiated peace negotiations with the Allies but these broke down.
Peter the Great annexed Tallin and completed the conquest of Livonia.
Charles XII of Sweden, a refugee in Turkey and virtually powerless without an army, persuaded the Turks to declare war on Peter the Great.

Literature

Art and Architecture

The Meissen porcelain factory was founded in Germany under the directorship of Johann Friedrich Böttger who had discovered, with Ehrenfried Walter von Tschirnhaus, the technique for making true Chinese porcelain.

Performing Arts

Handel visited London and took 14 days to write the opera *Rinaldo*.

Science and Technology

Prussian blue, a colored dye, was first produced.
Leibniz discounted spontaneous generation but suggested that natural science was in accord with the divine will.

America

The colonists took Port Royal, Newfoundland.
The settlement of 3,000 Palatine Germans near Livingston Manor, New York, for the purpose of producing naval stores, was unsuccessful.

1711

Peter the Great, trapped on the River Pruth by the Turks, concluded the Treaty of Pruth with them, ceding Azov and having to destroy all Russian forts on Turkish soil.
Emperor Joseph I died of smallpox and was succeeded as Holy Roman Emperor by his brother, Charles VI, claimant to the Spanish throne.
Afghanistan became an independent state.
The Peace of Szatmar sent Hungarian patriot Francis II Rákóczi into exile in Turkey after his defeat by the Austrians. New Emperor Charles VI agreed to respect the Hungarian constitution.

The Spectator succeeded *The Tatler* as the great English review, produced jointly by Richard Steele and his friend from school days, Joseph Addison. The intention was to entertain and inform, the same aims of the periodical today.

The tuning fork was invented by John Shore, trumpeter at England's Chapel Royal.

War began in North Carolina when the Tuscarora Indians massacred 200 settlers.
The British attack on Quebec was unsuccessful.
The Church of England became the official church of North Carolina.

1712

The Swiss War ended with the Treaty of Aarau.
A war of succession broke out in India between the four sons of Shah Bahadur.
Peter the Great married his mistress, Catharina Alexajovna.
After French victories over British and Dutch forces, the European powers met to try to end the War of the Spanish Succession.
Tokugawa shogun Ienobu died and was succeeded by his three-year-old son Ietsugu.
Philip V of Spain gave up all claims to the French throne.

Arcangelo Corelli's 12 Concerti Grossi gained international recognition for the concerto.

Thomas Newcomen developed the first piston-operated steam engine, worked by atmospheric pressure, at Tipton in England.

New York militia troops suppressed an uprising of blacks. Twenty-one blacks were convicted and executed.
Cotton Mather's 13 letters on natural history and biology were published.

1713

The Treaties of Utrecht, signed 1713–14, effectively settled the War of the Spanish Succession in favor of Philip V. Britain acquired Gibraltar and Minorca.
The Pragmatic Sanction was issued by Holy Roman Emperor Charles VI affirming the female right of succession in Hapsburg kingdoms.
King Frederick I of Prussia died and was succeeded by Frederick William I.
Charles XII was captured by the Turks at Moldavia.
War broke out between Russia and Turkey again but ceased with the Peace of Adrianople.

Joseph Addison's neo-classical tragedy *Cato* was first performed at Drury Lane. There were political overtones to please both Whigs and Tories, and the play had influence for the rest of the century.
Marchesse di Francesco Scipione Maffei introduced classical simplicity to Italian drama in his highly successful verse tragedy *Merope*.
Handel composed a *Te Deum* to celebrate the Treaty of Utrecht.

Newton's *Principia* was revised by English mathematician Roger Cotes.

The Treaty of Utrecht settled Queen Anne's War by giving Newfoundland, Acadia, and Hudson Bay to Britain.
The Tuscarora Indians, defeated in North Carolina, became the sixth Iroquois nation in New York.

1714

The Treaties of Rastatt and **Baden** formally ended the wa**r** between France and the Ho**ly** Roman Empire.
Queen Anne, last monarch o**f** the House of Stuart, died an**d** was succeeded by Germa**n** Prince George Louis of th**e** House of Hanover, who spok**e** no English and reigned a**s** King George I.
Charles XII was deported fro**m** Turkey to Stockholm, but th**e** Great Northern War con****tinued.
The Turks captured Corinth in a new Turkish-Venetian war.

Alexander Pope, complete**d** the final version of the *Rap**e*** *of the Lock,* a mock-epic de****signed to reconcile two fami****lies who had quarreled be****cause a young man took **a** lock of hair without the lady'**s** consent.
Nicholas Rowe published hi**s** nine-volume critical edition o**f** Shakespeare's work.

The most elaborate of all **wooden Russian churches,** th**e** Church of the Transfiguratio**n** in Kishi, was begun.

Italian became the usual op****eratic language in Europe**,** although France still kept it**s** own opera.

The mercury thermometer wa**s** invented by German physicis**t** Gabriel Fahrenheit.
The derrick, a mast-mounte**d** ship's crane, was devised i**n** France.

The Scotch-Irish began large**-**scale emigration to America**,** and first settled extensively i**n** Pennsylvania.

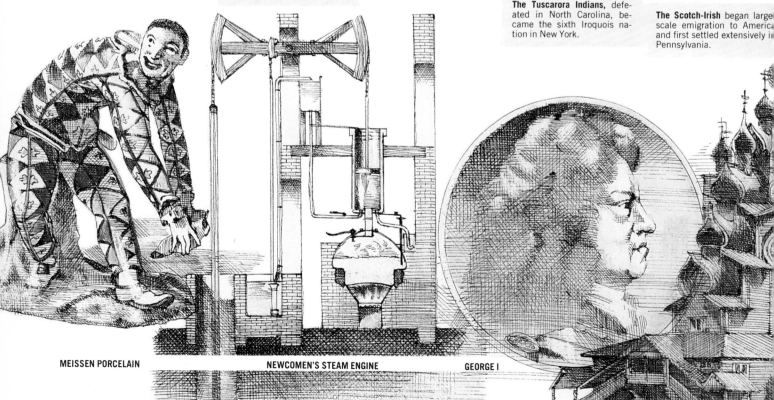

MEISSEN PORCELAIN   NEWCOMEN'S STEAM ENGINE   GEORGE I

Louis XIV died after a 72-year reign with France's economy exhausted. He was succeeded by his five-year-old great-grandson under the regency of the Duke of Orléans.
Charles XII of Sweden attacked Norway.
The Peace of Madrid was negotiated between Spain and Portugal.
Sweden faced an opposing alliance of Poland, Prussia, Denmark, Hanover, and Saxony.

The Karlskirche (Church of St Charles Borromeo) was begun in Vienna by Johann Bernard Fischer von Erlach, who had inaugurated Austrian Baroque in architecture.
The dramatic abbey church of Weingarten, Germany, was begun; it combines native Baroque with the universal influence of Il Gesù, Rome.

Pierre Buffardin, a French flautist who began his 35-year attachment to the court in Dresden, brought flute-playing up to modern standards.

The first practical diving suit was demonstrated in the Thames by its inventor Andrew Becker.

The Yamassee Indians, angered by activities of the settlers, massacred several hundred Carolinians.

The Treaty of Westminster allied England and Austria in a mutual defense pact. England also signed a similar pact with France.
Emperor Charles VI declared war on Turkey. The Turks were routed by Prince Eugène at Peterwardein.
Tokugawa shogun Ietsugu died and was succeeded by Yoshimune, who displayed a more liberal attitude toward Western traders.
Emperor K'ang Hsi of China prohibited Christian teaching.
Peter the Great paid a second visit to Western Europe.

Nicholas Hawksmoor, as one of two architects to the Commission for Fifty New Churches, began St Mary, Woolnoth, perhaps the finest of his six London churches.

François Couperin le Grand, a French harpsichordist whose elegant compositions brought him fame throughout Europe, published *L'Art de Toucher le Clavecin,* one of the most important treatises of the time dealing with the interpretation of French music.

Mineral waters were discovered at Cheltenham, turning the resort into a popular spa.
The first central heating, a hot-water system, was installed in an English greenhouse by Swedish engineer Martin Triewald.

Yamassee Indians were crushed by Carolinian colonists and allied Cherokees.
To encourage western settlement, Virginia's Gov. Alexander Spotswood led an expedition to the Shenandoah Valley.

A triple alliance was concluded between France, England, and the Dutch Republic. The Old Pretender, James III, had to leave France.
Spain seized Sardinia while Prince Eugène was busy capturing Belgrade from the Turks.
The Convention of Amsterdam, signed by Prussia, Russia, and France, insured the honoring of the treaties of Utrecht and Baden.

Antoine Watteau painted the finest of his three versions of *L'Embarquement pour l'Ile de Cythère.* These were supreme examples of *fêtes galantes* which depicted lovers in a pastoral setting.

George Frideric Handel, one of the greatest composers of the late Baroque period, composed his *Water Music* for King George I of England.
The first English attempt at pure ballet was made by John Weaver in *The Loves of Mars and Venus.* Such *ballets d'action* dispensed with spoken words and songs.
Bach's *Orgelbüchlein* contained a collection of his 46 organ chorales.
The Comédie Française in Paris staged *Electra,* by Prosper Jolyot de Crebillon, starring the distinguished French actress Adrienne Lecouvreur.

Britain began to send convicts to the colonies to serve as indentured servants.
John Wise wrote *A Vindication of the Government of New England Churches* to defend the deomocratic structure of the Congregational Church.

Alexis, son and heir of Peter the Great, was tortured and murdered at the instigation of his father.
A Quadruple Alliance was formed by the Holy Roman Emperor, France, England, and Holland against Spain when Spain seized Sicily and raised the specter of a new European war.
The Treaty of Passarowitz ended the four-year war between Austria and Turkey.
Sweden's Charles XII was shot and killed during a skirmish against Norwegian troops. He was succeeded by his sister, Ulrika Eleonora.

Mexico Cathedral, the largest and most impressive church in the country, was designed by Jerónimo Balbas.

Thomas Lombe, an Englishman, patented a machine to make thrown silk.
A machine gun was patented by London lawyer James Puckle. It was not manufactured until 1721.
The iron ramrod was invented by Leopold of Dessau, thereby improving the firepower of Prussian infantry.
Lady Mary Wortley Montagu, wife of the English minister to Constantinople, described a method of inoculation against smallpox.

Forts were built at Columbia and Port Royal in Carolina.
New Orleans was founded by France's Jean Baptiste le Moyne, Sieur de Bienville.
A labor association was established in Philadelphia.

France declared war on Spain.
The Alliance of Vienna was made between the Emperor, England and Hanover, and Poland and Saxony, against Prussia and Russia.
Peace was established between Hanover and Sweden.
Liechtenstein became an independent sovereign state within the Holy Roman Empire.
Mohammed Shah, Mughal Emperor, acceded to the throne as Great Mughal.
The Oriental Company in Vienna was founded by the Holy Roman Emperor to trade with eastern nations.

Daniel Defoe's *Robinson Crusoe* was published. Its author was 59.

Christoph Breitkopf established a printing-press at Leipzig and the music publishing company of Breitkopf and Härtel was founded.

Pathological anatomy was pioneered by Italian physician Giovanni Battista Morgagni.
Full color printing was introduced as a three-color mezzotint process by Jakob Christof le Blon of Frankfurt.

Britain established royal rule in South Carolina.
France accelerated the founding of forts and settlements in the Mississippi Valley.
The American Mercury was published in Philadelphia.

CHURCH IN KISHI GEORGE FRIDERIC HANDEL   THE KARLSKIRCHE MOHAMMED SHAH

World Events

1720

Sweden and Prussia concluded the Treaty of Stockholm. Sweden also signed a Treaty of Fredericksborg with Denmark.
The Quadruple Alliance made peace with Spain.
Tibet became a Chinese dependency.
The Pragmatic Sanction, establishing the indivisibility of Austria-Hungary, was accepted.
France faced national bankruptcy.
The South Sea Bubble burst when the English South Sea Company, which had aimed to restore royal finances, collapsed.

1721

The Great Northern War came to an end with the Treaty of Nystadt between Sweden and Russia. As a result, Russia became a European power.
France occupied Mauritius.
Peter the Great proclaimed Russia an empire and named himself Emperor of all the Russias.
Robert Walpole became Britain's first prime minister. His policy of keeping a permanent national debt brought prosperity.

1722

Hungary agreed to Charles VI's Pragmatic Sanction in favor of Maria Theresa.
Persia lost Baku and Derbent to Russia.
Easter Island was discovered by the Dutch.

1723

The Treaty of Charlottenburg was arranged between Britain and Prussia. By its terms, it was agreed that George I's grandson should eventually marry a Prussian princess, and that Prince Frederick of Prussia should marry the Prince of Wales's daughter.
Turkey attacked Persia.
Yungchen became Emperor of China.
Louis XV of France came of age.
Yellow fever appeared for the first time in Europe.

1724

Philip V of Spain abdicated in favor of Luis. Luis died seven months later so Philip resumed his reign.
The Treaty of Constantin allied Russia and Turkey against Persia. The Shah of Persia went mad and started a reign of terror.
The Austrian Netherlands agreed to the Pragmatic Sanction.
Peter the Great crowned his wife Catherine, Czarina.
The Bourse, a continental stock exchange, opened in Paris.

Literature

Art and Architecture

Rosalba Carriera, a Venetian portraitist who had established a remarkable international reputation, enjoyed her greatest triumph in Paris.
Eszterházy Palace was begun to the designs of Erhard Martinelli. Later extended by Prince Miklós József, the great building came to be known as the Hungarian Versailles.

Fischer von Erlach published his great history of architecture, *A plan of Civil and Historical Architecture.* Covering all times and all nations, it was the first book of its kind.
Monadologia by Gottfried Wilhelm Leibniz, was published posthumously. Philosopher, mathematician and diplomat, he dominated the intellectual life of Germany for decades.

Cadiz Cathedral, designed by Vincente Acero, was begun. It took more than 100 years to finish and is the only completely Baroque cathedral in Spain.

The earliest of all music periodicals, *Music Critica,* by Johann Mattheson, was first published in Germany.
Jean Philippe Rameau, the French composer, published his *Traité de l'harmonie.* It provided the foundation of harmonic thought for two centuries.

The French poet Jean-Baptiste Rousseau published his rhetorical, topical *Odes.*

The French Regence style of furniture design, the fluent, curvilinear manner which bridged Baroque and Rococo, was exemplified in the work of Charles Cressent.

Bach's *St John Passion* was first performed.

Alterations to Toledo Cathedral, Spain, were in progress; the combination of bronze, stucco, multicolored marble and filtered light make this the masterpiece of Narciso Tomé.

The Three Choirs Festival (Gloucester, Hereford, and Worcester) was founded in England.

Performing Arts

The ancestor of the tango, the *tángano,* was introduced to Central America by African slaves around this time.
Handel became director of London's Royal Academy of Music and presented his oratorio *Esther.*

Science and Technology

Zinc was smelted at Swansea, in Wales.

Bach's *Brandenberg Concertos* were given their first performance.

The compensator pendulum for clocks was invented by George Graham.
Smallpox inoculations were first administered in the New World during an epidemic when Zabdiel Boylston inoculated 240 patients, of whom all but six survived.

The Act of 1722 gave jurisdiction over conservation of timber violations to the British vice-admiralty courts.

The meerschaum pipe, made of hydrated magnesium silicate, was designed by Hungarian shoemaker Karol Kowates.

Paul Dudley published a work on North American fruit trees.

America

The French built a fort at Niagara to oversee the Great Lakes trade and to guard against Indian attacks.
Gov. William Burnet of New York extended trade with the Indians.

South Carolina became a royal colony.
Swiss immigrants introduced the rifle in America.

The French continued to expand their influence in the Mississippi Valley and built a fort on the north bank of the Missouri River.
Dunkards, German Baptists who believed in triple immersion, were founded.

SOUTH SEA BUBBLE   ROBERT WALPOLE   JEAN PHILLIPE RAMEAU   EASTER ISLAND

Peter the Great of Russia died, having encouraged industrial growth, centralized the administration, and subdued the nobility.
The Treaty of Vienna was concluded between Austria and Spain. Spain guaranteed the Pragmatic Sanction, and in return Austria agreed to help Spain regain Gibraltar from Britain.
Louis XV of France married Maria Leszczinska, daughter of Poland's former King Stanislas I, who was deposed in 1709.

The Spanish Steps in Rome, an elegant Baroque stairway, was designed by Francesco de Sanctis.
Chiswick House, London, one of the most influential Neo-Palladian buildings in England, was designed by Richard Boyle, 3rd earl of Burlington. ·

Prague opera house was founded.
Johann Joseph Fux, Austrian composer and music theorist, wrote *Gradus ad Parnassum,* an important treatise on counterpoint.

The St Petersburg Academy of Science was founded, run mainly by foreign professors.

The British built Fort Oswego on the eastern banks of Lake Ontario.
The New York Gazette began publication.
Paul Dudley wrote *Natural History of Whales.*

The ministry of Cardinal Fleury in France began to introduce a period of peace and economic growth.
The Treaty of Wusterhausen led to Prussia's guaranteeing the Pragmatic Sanction.
The Holy Roman Empire and Russia formed an alliance against Turkey.
War broke out between England and Spain.

Swift's masterpiece, *Gulliver's Travels,* was published.
Pope completed his translation of Homer with his final books of the *Odyssey;* the *Iliad* had been finished in 1620.

Juste-Aurèle Meissonnier, the most imaginative exponent of French Rococo in the decorative arts, was appointed Dessinateur de la Chambre et du Cabinet du Roi.

Light opera emerged in Germany, where Reinhard Keiser wrote operas with catchy tunes.
Handel became a British citizen.
La Camargo, famous French ballerina, made her debut at the Paris Opéra.

Stephen Hales, an English clergyman physicist, measured blood pressure.
John Harrison, an English clockmaker, invented the gridiron pendulum.

A series of religious revivals, part of The Great Awakening later led by Jonathan Edwards, began to be held from New England down through the South.

George I of Britain died of apoplexy en route to Hanover and was succeeded by his 44-year-old son George II. His wife Caroline, and government ministers, assumed general control.
Empress Catherine I of Russia died and was succeeded by her 12-year-old son Peter II.
Spain blockaded Gibraltar in the Anglo-Spanish War.
The Russian border with China was fixed by the Kiakhta Treaty.
The Austrian East India Company was dissolved.

Plant physiology was founded by the publication of *Vegetable Staticks,* by Stephen Hales. Measuring plant growth and sap production, Hales realized that air is necessary for plants to grow.
Isaac Newton, Britain's most illustrious scientist, died.
The first railroad bridge was the Tanfield Arch, built by Ralph Wood over a colliery railroad at Cawsey Dell.

The Anglo-Spanish War started when Carolina colonists marched to Florida.
The Quakers petitioned for the abolition of slavery in the colonies.

The siege of Gibraltar was lifted by Spain after 14 months. The Anglo-Spanish War ended with the Convention of Prado.
The Treaty of Berlin was concluded between Emperor Charles VI and Frederick William of Prussia.

The Dunciad, Pope's mock-epic response to his numerous critics, appeared. The second edition of 1729 capped the first by including a mock-commentary, a parody of contemporary pedantry.

Jean-Baptiste-Siméon Chardin was elected to the French Académie Royale when he submitted his fine still life, *Skate, cat and kitchen utensils,* which shares the Flemish delight in texture without its opulence.

The Beggar's Opera, written by English poet and playwright John Gay, was first performed. It created a new style of political satire.

Vitus Bering, Danish navigator, discovered the strait and sea between Asia and North America that bears his name.
The first dental drill, worked by hand, was described by Parisian dental surgeon Pierre Fauchard in his work *Le Chirurgien-Dentiste.*

The Carolina forces destroyed a Yamassee Indian village near St. Augustine, Florida.
The first colonial botanical garden was established in Philadelphia by John Bartram.

Corsica became independent of Genoa.
Arabs captured Mombasa from the Portuguese.
Chinese Emperor Yungchen prohibited the smoking of opium throughout his domains.

A Modest Proposal, was one of Swift's brilliant short satires, was published. In it he takes the guise of a public-spirited citizen, suggesting a cure for social and economic hardship — the eating of the children of the poor by the rich.

Bach's great choral masterpiece, *St Matthew Passion,* was first performed.
Handel wrote six oboe concertos.

Stellar aberration, an apparent change in the position of stars caused by the Earth's motion, was detected by English astronomer James Bradley. This was the first absolute confirmation of Copernicus's theory that the Earth moves round the Sun.
An achromatic lens was built by English astronomer Chester Moor Hall.
English scientist Stephen Gray discovered that some bodies conduct electricity and some do not.

North Carolina became a royal colony and began an era of prosperity.
Baltimore was founded.
Chickasaw, Yazoo, and Natchez Indian attacks pushed the French back to what is now the state of Louisiana.

JONATHAN SWIFT   CHISWICK HOUSE   VITUS BERING

World Events

Peter II of Russia died of smallpox at the age of 14 and was succeeded by his cousin, Anna Ivanova (daughter of Ivan V), who organized a coup to become czarina.
Victor Amadeus II of Savoy abdicated and was succeeded by Charles Emmanuel I.
Crown Prince Frederick of Prussia tried to flee to England but was caught and imprisoned by his father.
Denmark's Frederick IV died and was succeeded by his son, Christian VI.
Sultan Ahmad III of Turkey was deposed and succeeded by Mahmoud I.

By the Treaty of Vienna between England, Spain, Austria, and Holland, the Holy Roman Empire dissolved the Ostend East India Company, England's colonial trading rival in cotton and spices.
The Paris Parlement decreed that the clergy should be subservient to the Crown.

The Pragmatic Sanction was guaranteed by the Empire with the exception of the Palatinate, Bavaria, and Saxony.
Genoa regained Corsica from rebel forces.
Western Japanese crops suffered from floods and a plague of grasshoppers. As a result, there was a severe famine.

The Treaty of the Escorial was formed by France and Spain against Britain.
In the War of the Polish Succession, Russia and Austria recognized Augustus III of Saxony, while France and Spain supported Stanislas Leszczinski.
Conscription was introduced in Prussia.
The French occupied Lorraine.

The Russians captured Danzig after an eight-month siege. Poland's Stanislas Leszczynski escaped to Prussia.
Spanish forces in Italy captured Naples, Sicily, and Milan.
France and the Empire were at war once more.
The Turko-Persian War began.

Literature

Manon Lescaut, the final instalment of a seven-volume novel by the French Abbé Antoine-François Prévost, was first published.

Voltaire (Françoise-Marie Arouet), one of the greatest of French authors, wrote his brilliant short work *Lettres philosophiques.* Primarily concerned with religious toleration, it is a landmark in the history of thought.

Art and Architecture

Canaletto (Giovanni Antonio Canal) painted *The Stonemason's Yard* about this time. He rarely again achieved such freedom and subtlety, largely because of the heavy demands made on him for souvenir views of Venice.

The first composition for the modern piano was a sonata by Lodovico Giustini.
English playwright George Lillo staged *The London Merchant, or The History of George Barnwell* at London's Drury Lane Theater. This was the first serious prose play whose leading characters were not all nobles.

The Church of the Carmine, Turin was the masterpiece of the Italian architect Filippo Juvarra. It is one of the finest examples of early Italian Rococo.

The Plaza Mayor in Salamanca, Spain, was completed to the design of Andrés Garcia de Quiñones. A magnificent Baroque square, surrounded by an arcade, it was originally intended to serve on occasion as a bullring.

William Kent, one of the most brilliant exponents of the English Palladian style, began his masterpiece, Holkham Hall, Norfolk, for Thomas Coke, Earl of Leicester.

Performing Arts

La clemenza di Tito was one of the most successful melodrammi written by the celebrated librettist Pietro Metastasio.
The Academy of Ancient Music was founded in London.
Covent Garden Opera House opened in London.

Marie Sallé, French dancer and choreographer, discarded the usual restrictive costume and whig when she played Venus in her ballet *Pygmalion* in London. She wore her hair loose over a Grecian-style muslin dress.
Bach produced his *Christmas Oratorio,* six sacred cantatas linked together under one title.

Science and Technology

French physicist René de Réaumur invented an alcohol thermometer with a graduated scale of 0°-80°.
The reflecting quadrant was invented by English mathematician John Hadley.
Cobalt, a metallic element, was discovered by George Brandt, a Swedish chemist.

Barbers in France were prohibited from practicing surgery.
The first lightship, *The Nore,* was anchored in the Thames Estuary.

A threshing machine was invented by Scottish engineer Michael Menzies.
The first sedative, called "Dover sedative powder," was discovered by Captain Thomas Dover of Warwickshire, England.
Dutch physician Hermann Boerhaave's *Elements of Chemistry* laid the foundations of organic chemistry.

Stephen Hales described his researches into the circulation of the blood in his *Haemostaticks.*
The world's heaviest bell (193 tons), Czar Kolkol, was cast in Moscow.
The flying shuttle, for speeding up cotton weaving, was invented in Lancashire by John Kay.

America

The first Freemason lodge was organized in Philadelphia.
An improved mariner's quadrant was invented by mathematician Thomas Godfrey of Philadelphia.

The French built a fort at Crown Point on Lake Champlain.
The British prohibited taxes from being levied for the import of slaves.
Benjamin Franklin founded a subscription library in Philadelphia.

James Oglethorpe established the colony of Georgia for British debtors.
Benjamin Franklin began publishing *Poor Richard's Almanack.*

The Molasses Act placed high taxes on West Indian sugar, rum, and molasses, and the colonists began smuggling.
Savannah was founded.
John Peter Zenger began publication of the *New York Weekly Journal.*

The French bolstered defenses against the British in the Saskatchewan Valley.
Jonathan Edwards' sermons spur New England's Great Awakening.
The first colonial horserace was run in South Carolina.

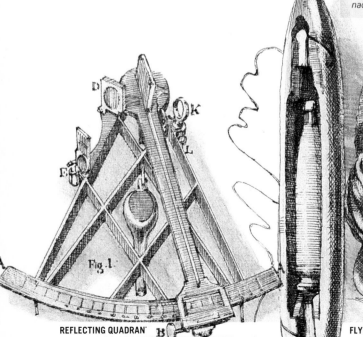

REFLECTING QUADRANT   FLYING SHUTTLE   VOLTAIRE   LINNAEUS' *SYSTEMA NATURA*

CAROLI LINNÆI

SYSTEMA NATURÆ

Per
REGNA TRIA NATURÆ

CLASSES, ORDINES,
GENERA, SPECIES,

The peace of Vienna brought the War of the Polish Succession to an end. The Elector of Saxony was officially recognized as the King of Poland, reigning as Frederick Augustus II.
Russia ceded the last of its Persian conquests and joined Nadir Kuli of Persia in a campaign against the Turks.
The French East India Company became firmly established in India and had set up sugar industries in Réunion and Mauritius.

Alain-René Lesage published the third and final part of his *Histoire de Gil Blas de Santillane,* a French picaresque novel which popularized the form throughout Europe.

The Rake's Progress, William Hogarth's most famous series of morality paintings, was released, delayed by the artist until there was legislation against pirate engravings.

The Imperial Ballet School was founded at St Petersburg.

Carolus Linnaeus, a Swedish botanist, published his *Systema Naturae.* In it he defined the differences between species, and formed the idea of classifying plants and animals into species and genera, classes and orders.
Rubber was found in South America by Charles Marie de la Condamine.

Freedom of the press is established during the trial of John Peter Zenger, who was accused and acquitted of libel in his newspaper.
The French settled Vincennes, Indiana.

Stanislas, King of Poland, died.
Austria and Russia went to war with Turkey. Russia captured Azov and Koslov.
Maria Theresa, daughter of Charles VI, married Francis Stephen of Lorraine.
Prince Eugène, the Austrian general, died.
Kuli Khan, a Turk, became Shah of Persia, reigning as Nadir Khan after the death of six-year-old Shah Abbas III.
Ch'ien Lung became ruler of a Chinese Empire that by now included Tibet and Sinkiang.

The tenor voice first displaced the castrato in a leading operatic part when John Beard first sang at Covent Garden.
Handel successfully set Dryden's ode *Alexander's Feast* to music.
Giovanni Batista Pergolesi, Italian composer of opera and sacred music, completed his finest sacred work, *Stabat Mater,* just weeks before he died.

The ship's chronometer, invented by John Harrison, was accurate to within one-tenth of a second a day.
Leonhard Euler, Swiss physicist, founded analytical mechanics with the publication of his *Mechanica.*

Francis Stephen of Lorraine inherited Tuscany when the last of the Medici, Grand Duke of Tuscany, died.
Austria suffered defeats in its war against the Turks.
The second worst earthquake of all time devastated Calcutta, killing 300,000.

The Radcliffe Camera, a university library in Oxford, was designed by James Gibbs. The building combined Baroque solidity with Mannerist variety of forms.

The Licensing Act in Britain subjected all plays to censorship by the Lord Chamberlain. The number of London theaters was also restricted.
Rameau staged the most notable of his 22 grand operas.

Carolus Linnaeus published his *Genera Plantarum.* This laid the foundation of modern botany, initiating the binomial system of taxonomy, based on the stamens and pistils of a plant.

New York appointed John Peter Zenger as its official printer. New Jersey would do the same the following year.
Richmond, Virginia, was founded by William Byrd.

The Treaty of Vienna (1735) was finally ratified.
France and Sweden began a formal alliance.

The new facade to the al Cathedral of Santiago de Compostela was designed by Fernando Casas y Novoa. It is one of the most imposing in Spain.

Bach produced his *Mass in B Minor,* in the "Kyrie" of which he demonstrated a masterful zenith of contrapuntal writing with music of great power and intricacy.

The first spinning machines were patented in England by Swiss physicist Lewis Paul.
Daniel Bernoulli's kinetic theory of gases, relating fluid flow to pressure, was expounded in his *Hydrodynamics.*
The excavation of the city of Herculaneum, buried by the eruption of Vesuvius in AD79, was begun in Naples.
The first cuckoo clocks appeared in the region of the Black Forest.

British troops were sent to Georgia to prepare for war with Spain.
Evangelist George Whitefield's revival meetings attracted many followers in Georgia.

Walpole yielded to the demand for war with Spain. It became known as the War of Jenkins' Ear, the issue being the maltreatment of British smugglers by the Spaniards after Captain Robert Jenkins had his ear severed by the Spaniards in 1731.
The Treaty of Belgrade ended a three-year war between Austria and Turkey. Austria lost most of its gains from the Treaty of Passorowitz. As the victorious Turks neared Belgrade, Emperor Charles VI abandoned his Russian partners and signed the treaty.
A large Mughal army was routed at Karnal under Nadir Khan, which proceeded to sack Delhi.

Georg Raphael Donner, a sculptor whose work marked the transition from the Baroque to the Neoclassical in Austria, completed his masterpiece, the fountain on the Neuer Markt, Vienna. The original lead figures were replaced by bronze copies in 1873.

Handel had a busy year, completing two oratorios, *Saul* and *Israel in Egypt,* and 12 concerti grossi.

The Swedish Scientific Academy was founded.
Camellias from the Orient were seen in Europe for the first time.

During the Anglo-Spanish War of Jenkin's Ear, Georgians invaded Florida and repulsed Spanish counter-attack.
In the Cato Conspiracy, 30 whites and 44 blacks were killed during a black uprising in South Carolina.

WILLIAM HOGARTH · HARRISON'S CHRONOMETER · CAMELIAS

World Events

1740
Frederick William I died after having molded Prussia into a feared military power. He was succeeded by his son Frederick II (Frederick the Great) who then occupied Silesia, thus striking the first blow in the War of the Austrian Succession.
Emperor Charles VI, the last of the Hapsburgs, died. The War of the Austrian Succession resulted from the disputed accession to the throne by Maria Theresa, daughter of the late emperor.
Russian Czarina Anna Ivanova died, naming her infant great-nephew Ivan VI as her successor under the regency of Count Biron.

1741
Sweden declared war on Russia and was defeated at Vilmanstrad.
France and Prussia concluded a treaty against Austria. Frederick II invaded southern Germany, Austria, and Bohemia. He defeated the Austrians at Mollwitz and conquered Silesia. The French, Bavarians, and Saxons conquered Prague.
Elizabeth Petrovna, daughter of Peter the Great, became Empress of Russia after deposing and imprisoning the infant Ivan VI and banishing his regent, Count Biron, to Siberia on a charge of treason.
Horse artillery was introduced into the Prussian army by Frederick II.
Vitus Bering died of scurvy after discovering Alaska.

1742
England formed an alliance with Prussia.
The French marched out of Prague after their previous year's victory.
Charles Albert, Elector of Bavaria, was elected Holy Roman Emperor as Charles VII.
The Peace of Berlin concluded by Austria and Prussia marked the end of the First Silesian War.

1743
Maria Theresa was crowned in Prague.
George II's Pragmatic Army defeated the French at Dettingen.
The Peace of Abo between Russia and Sweden resulted in Sweden's ceding of southern Finland.
Austria and Saxony formed an alliance.
A pogrom in Russia killed thousands of Jews.
The Turko-Persian War was resumed.
By the Treaty of Worms between Austria and England, and Sardinia, Austria ceded Piacenza and Parma to Sardinia.

1744
Frederick II began the Second Silesian War by invading Saxony and Bohemia.
France declared war on England and Austria. Prussia formed an alliance with France.

Literature Religion Philosophy

1740
Samuel Richardson's novel *Pamela: or, Virtue Rewarded* was quite innovatory in English literature, enormously successful and an inspiration to numerous imitations.

1743
Diego De Torres Villarroel, a Spanish mathematician, began his *Vida,* his memoirs of a very eventful life.

Art and Architecture

1740
Giovanni Battista Piazzetta, one of the outstanding Venetian artists of the century, and one who had evolved from a Baroque artist to a mature master in a Rococo style, painted *Fortune Teller.*

1742
Handel achieved the climax of his popularity when he conducted the first performance of his oratorio *Messiah* in Dublin.
Bach composed the *Goldberg Variations,* a supreme example of harmonic resource and contrapuntal skill.

1741
The bust of William Hogarth, of about this date, is the most famous of many portrait works by the sculptor Louis-François Roubiliac.

1741
Handel composed the first form of his greatest oratorio, *Messiah,* in less than four weeks. *Samson* was written as quickly a month later. Handel made such choral works the most popular musical form in England.
English actor David Garrick made his first appearance on a London stage in Shakespeare's *Richard III.*

1743
Giovanni Paolo Panini's *Piazza del Quirinale* was an excellent example of his views of contemporary Rome, which made him the supreme topographical painter in the city.

1743
Handel scored a magnificent success with his oratorio *Samson.*

1744
The Shrine of Ocotlán, a church near Tlaxcala, Mexico, proved to be unique in the country for the scale and richness of its white towers and the unusual fish-scale effect of the small unglazed bricks, pointed with white mortar, in the side walls.

1744
Equal temperament was worked out in Germany. It made modulation to distant keys possible, as in the *Well-tempered Klavier,* by Bach.

Performing Arts

Science and Technology

1740
The crucible method of making steel by heating scrap iron was founded in England by Benjamin Huntsman.

1742
English cotton factories were set up in Birmingham and Northampton.
Anders Celsius, a Swedish scientist, devised the Celsius (centigrade) scale of temperature, with 0° as the freezing point of water and 100° as the boiling point.

1743
Alex Claude Clairaut, French mathematician, measured the length of a meridian degree in his *Théorie de la figure de la terre.*
Jean d'Alembert, French mathematician, solved problems of mechanics in his *Traité de Dynamique.*

1744
A survey of France by triangulation was begun by French astronomer César François Cassini.

America

1740
Troops under James Oglethorpe invaded Florida and took St. Augustine.
50 blacks were hanged for plotting rebellion in Charleston, South Carolina.
Georgia increased land-holding size limit to 2,000 acres.

1741
In the Negro Plot, 101 blacks were convicted for suspicion of burglary and starting fires in New York City.
Massachusetts farmers attempted unsuccessfully to issue paper money that had been outlawed by Britain.

1742
The Spanish counter-attack to Oglethorpe's Florida invasion, the Battle of Bloody Swamp on St. Simon's Island, resulted in a British victory.
Benjamin Franklin invented the extremely efficient Franklin stove.

1743
The first settlement was established in South Dakota.

1744
During King George's War, the French unsuccessfully attacked Annapolis Royal, Nova Scotia.
Alexander Hamilton published *Itinerarium,* an account of a trip from Annapolis, Maryland, to Portsmouth, New Hampshire.

FREDERICK THE GREAT   GROG FOR THE NAVY   MARIA THERESA

In the Battle of Fontenoy, France and Prussia defeated the Austrians and their allies.
Holy Roman Emperor Charles VII died. He was succeeded as Elector of Bavaria by his son, Maximilian II. The Second Silesian War came to an end.
By the Peace of Füssen between Austria and Bavaria, Bavaria renounced all claims on Hapsburg lands.
Francis Stephen, Maria Theresa's husband, was elected emperor, as Francis I.
Charles Edward Stuart (Bonnie Prince Charlie) landed in Scotland and started a Jacobite rebellion. He was victorious at Prestonpans and advanced into England as far as Derby.

In India the Frenchman Joseph Dupleix took Madras.
Philip V of Spain died insane. He was succeeded by his second son, Ferdinand VI.
Austrian forces briefly occupied Genoa.
The Netherlands were liberated from Austrian rule after the French victory in the Battle of Rocoux, under Marshal Saxe.
Christian VI of Denmark died. He was succeeded by his son, Frederick V.
At the Battle of Culloden Moor the Jacobites were finally defeated by the Duke of Cumberland. Bonnie Prince Charlie escaped to France disguised as a girl.

Britain, Russia, and Holland signed the Convention of St Petersburg.
The Alliance of Stockland was formed by Prussia and Sweden.
The Duke of Cumberland's troops were defeated by a French army at Lauffeld.
William IV of Orange became stadtholder after a revolution in The Netherlands.
Nadir Khan of Persia was assassinated. Ahmad Shah, one of Nadir's generals, took control of the Afghan provinces, asserting Afghanistan's independence from Persia and inaugurating the Barkzai dynasty.

The Peace of Aix-la-Chapelle ended the War of the Austrian Succession. The succession of the House of Hanover was confirmed in its German states and in Britain. Prussia gained Silesia and the Pragmatic Sanction was sustained in Austria. The French gave up territory in The Netherlands, and Madras in India.
The Punjab was invaded by Ahmad Shah.

The Treaty of Aquisgran confirmed British commercial rights in Spain. Spaniards activated their own commercial and administrative reforms.
Drainage began of the Oder moorlands in central Europe.

Emanuel Swedenborg, Swedish scientist, philosopher and theologian, abandoned secular concerns after seeing visions of Christ and angels. His spiritual thinking is summarized in his last work, *Vera Christiana Religio.*

The church of St John Nepomuk, Munich, was completed to the exuberant design of Cosmas Damian and Egid Quirin Asam, Bavarian brother-architects.

Horace Walpole acquired the villa at Twickenham which, with his striking alterations, was to become the stimulus, for the Gothic revival in English domestic architecture.

The Adventures of Roderick Random, Thomas Smollett's masterpiece, was published. For its comic pace and vitality it is unmatched among early English novels.
Charles-Louis de Secondat, Baron de La Brède et de Montesquieu, published his great work *De L'Esprit des Lois.*

Tom Jones, Henry Fielding's epic comic work, was published. It marks a new sophistication in the genre. A traveling barrister and justice of the peace, Fielding had an intimate knowledge of both London and provincial life.

Giambattista Piranesi, whose etchings of Rome were very popular into the next century, began his most famous series, *Carceri d'invenzione (Imaginary Prisons)* at about this time.

In the last years of his life, J.S. Bach completed his *Mass in B Minor,* begun in 1724.
Handel composed a highly successful oratorio, *Judas Maccabaeus,* in tribute to the Duke of Cumberland's victory at Culloden.

David Garrick became part owner and manager of Drury Lane Theater, London: audiences were removed from the stage, the orchestra brought down from the gallery and, in 1765, concealed footlights and sidelights were introduced.

The remains of Pompeii were discovered.

Beyreuth Opera House was opened.

Handel celebrated the Peace of Aix-la-Chapelle with *Music for the Royal Fireworks.*
Bach, nearing the end of his life, became fascinated with fugal composition. His astonishing *The Art of Fugue* is a set of fugues all based on the same subject.

The quadrille, a stately French dance, became fashionable.

John Roebuck, a British inventor, developed a process for manufacturing sulfuric acid, used to bleach textiles, on a large scale.
The duodenal ulcer was first described by German physician George Erhard Hamberger.

Andreas Marggraf, a German chemist, discovered sugar in beetroot.
James Bradley discovered a variation of the Earth's axis.
James Lind, Scottish naval surgeon, pioneered efforts to combat scurvy.

The first silk factory was established in Berlin.
A wool-carding machine, using a revolving cylinder, was invented by Lewis Paul.
The first steel pens were made by Johann Janssen in Aachen, Germany.
Leonhard Euler systemized mathematical analysis in his *Introductio in analysin infinitorum.*
Diphtheria was first described by British physician John Fothergill.

Pellagra was first described by Italian physicians.
Count Buffon (Georges Louis Leclerc), a French naturalist, published the first three volumes of his 36-volume *Histoire naturelle.*
Thomas Chippendale, London cabinet-maker, opened a factory for his world-famous furniture.

The Leyden jar, developed at the University of Leyden, was used in the first investigations into the nature of electricity.
Robert Bakewell, the English agriculturist, produced the Leicester breed of sheep, with twice the amount of meat of earlier breeds.

A British expedition against the Canadians was unsuccessful.
The College of New Jersey (Princeton) was founded by Presbyterians.

The Ohio Company was formed to organize the settling of the Ohio Valley.
Building trade workers organized in New York City.
Benjamin Franklin began experiments with electricity.

The Treaty of Aix-la-Chapelle, the end of King George's War, restored colonial status, except for the return of Louisbourg to France.
The Great Awakening preaching of Samuel Davies reached its peak in Virginia.

Settlers moved into the Ohio Valley with land grants from the Ohio Company and the Loyal Company.
Toronto, Canada, was established as a fort.
Slavery began in Georgia.

The British captured Ft. Louisbourg. The French and the Indians raided Maine border towns and burned Saratoga, New York.

LEICESTER SHEEP   BONNIE PRINCE CHARLIE   DAVID GARRICK   COUNT BUFFON

	1750	1751	1752	1753	1754
World Events	Britain surrendered the *Asiento*, a monopoly of selling black slaves to the Spanish colonies, for £100,000. It had gained the monopoly by the Treaty of Utrecht (1713). John V of Portugal died and was succeeded by Joseph Emanuel, with the Marquess of Pombal as his chief minister. Pombal carried out ruthless internal reforms and destroyed the political influence of Portuguese Jesuits.	Louis XV met united opposition from the nobility and clergy in France when he tried to introduce new taxes on their wealth to pay for his wars. Robert Clive seized Arcot in India, thus establishing English authority over southern India. The Chinese invaded Tibet. William IV of Holland died and was succeeded by his three-year-old son William V, with Anne, daughter of Britain's George II, serving as regent. Frederick I of Sweden died and was succeeded by his brother-in-law Adolphus Frederick.	Robert Clive, after his success at Arcot, went on to relieve the siege of Trichinopoly. A fire devastated Moscow, burning down 18,000 houses.	Frederick the Great expressed hostility toward the Austro-Russian alliance. France faced national bankruptcy for the second time. The Vienna Stock Exchange was founded.	François Dupleix was recalled to France, leaving India to the British. Britain and France went to war in North America.
Literature		Thomas Gray wrote *An Elegy Written in a Country Churchyard,* one of the best known of English lyric poems.			
Art and Architecture	The Prince-Bishop's Palace at Würzburg, Germany, was one of the most spectacular artistic achievements of the century. Stourhead Park, Wiltshire, was created about this time by Henry Hoare.		A final triumph of the Italian Baroque was Luigi Vanvitelli's enormous Royal Palace at Caserta. The palace of Queluz, to the north of Lisbon in Portugal, was completed by Mateus Vicente de Oliveira.		Thomas Chippendale published his *Gentleman and Cabinet Maker's Director,* the first comprehensive collection of English furniture design. The Winter Palace, Leningrad, was begun for the czar. Now the home of the Hermitage Museum, it is one of the largest palaces in Europe.
Performing Arts	Johann Sebastian Bach, the greatest composer of the age, died. He left *The Art of Fugue* unfinished.	One of the most celebrated nudes in the history of art was François Boucher's *Reclining girl,* thought to have been a mistress of Louis XV. Pietro Longhi painted intimate scenes of upper-class and bourgeois life in his native Venice.	The symphony in the hands of Haydn developed greatly from 1750 to 1760, advancing its instrumentation and the form of its contrasting movements, usually four in number.		
Science and Technology	Nicolas de Lacaille, French astronomer, listed 10,000 southern stars. Platinum was analyzed by English engineer William Watson.	Marie Camargo finally retired from the French ballet stage. She was the first *danseuse* to shorten her skirt to calf length and to use flat ballet slippers. The minuet became Europe's most fashionable dance.	Benjamin Franklin, working in America, flew a kite in a thunderstorm to prove that lightning is electrical, and from his results developed a lightning conductor. French naturalist René de Réamur showed that digestion was partly a chemical process.	James Lind, Scottish physician, described his citrus cure in *Treatise on the Scurvy.* The British Museum was founded.	The first iron-rolling mill was established at Fareham, in England. Carbonic gas was discovered by Scottish chemist Joseph Black. The first female doctor of medicine graduated from the German University of Halle.
America	The flatboat and the Conestoga wagon, two means of transportation that helped settle America, first appeared in Pennsylvania. Christopher Gist undertook to explore, for the Ohio Company, its land on the upper Ohio.	Nickel was isolated by German physicist Baron Axel Cronstedt. The institution that would eventually become the University of Pennsylvania (1791) was founded in Philadelphia as Franklin's Academy.	The first general hospital in the colonies opened in Philadelphia, established by Thomas Bond. Benjamin Franklin's experiment of the nature of lightning took place.	George Washington was sent by Virginia's Lt. Gov. Robert Dinwiddie to protest the French occupation of the Ohio Valley. He would report (1754) that only force would expel the French.	The Albany Congress was called by Britain at the outset of the French and Indian War to attempt a treaty between the colonies and the Iroquois Indians. Benjamin Franklin proposed a plan of union among the colonies.

ROBERT CLIVE

FRANKLIN EXPERIMENTS WITH LIGHTNING

LISBON EARTHQUAKE

Lisbon was destroyed by an earthquake that left 30,000 dead.

Genoa faced a Corsican rebellion headed by General Pasquale de Paoli.

The Burmese city of Rangoon was founded by Aloung P'Houra, King of Burma.

Casanova, Venetian alchemist, gambler, preacher, and womanizer, returned to Venice after 14 years of scandalous adventures in Europe, only to be locked up as a spy.

Samuel Johnson completed *A Dictionary of the English Language.* Such precise definitions and range of literary illustrations had not been seen before.

Johann Winckelmann, German archeologist and art historian, wrote *Reflections on the Painting and Sculpture of the Greeks.*

Boucher was made Director of the Gobelins tapestry factory.

Joseph Black demonstrated the difference between magnesium and lime.

Immanuel Kant, in Germany, published his views on the formation of the solar system. He also suggested that galaxies of stars exist and that tides slow the rotation of the Earth.

The Battle of the Wilderness near Ft. Duquesne (now Pittsburgh) was a severe defeat for the British, under Gen. Edward Braddock and the colonials, led by Washington.

6,000 Arcadians were expelled from Nova Scotia for refusing to swear loyalty to the British.

The Treaty of Versailles was a secret agreement by which France, Austria, Russia, Saxony, Sweden, and Poland pledged themselves to partition Prussia.

Frederick the Great of Prussia got to know of the Treaty of Versailles and invaded Saxony with 70,000 men. This was the beginning of the Seven Years' War. The Prussians defeated the Austrians at the Battle of Lowositz and captured Dresden.

Britain declared war on France and formed an alliance with Frederick the Great.

The British island of Minorca capitulated to a large French fleet. Admiral John Byng was sent to the rescue but let discretion get the better of him and retreated to Gibraltar.

The "Black Hole of Calcutta" resulted in the deaths of 123 British prisoners, who were suffocated and crushed in the tiny guardroom at Fort William.

Casanova escaped from his Venetian jail.

Maurice-Quentin de La Tour, the most successful French pastelist of the century, finished his life-size portrait of Mme de Pompadour.

Cotton velvets were first made in Bolton, Lancashire.

Carbon dioxide was discovered by Joseph Black.

As the war spread to Europe as the Seven Years War, the French took Ft. Oswego.

The Marquis de Montcalm arrived in Canada to serve as commander of the French.

Robert Clive recaptured Calcutta. He went on to win the Battle of Plassey, effectively establishing British sovereignty in India.

Louis XV survived an assassination attempt by a French fanatic, Robert François Damiens.

Frederick the Great invaded Bohemia, defeated the Austrians at Prague, but was routed at Kolin and forced to retire from Bohemia. The Duke of Cumberland went to his aid but was defeated by the French at Hastenback and surrounded at Stade. There he agreed to surrender Hanover to the French.

Frederick recovered to capture Silesia by beating the Austrians in the Battle of Leuthen.

The greatest period of the Sèvres porcelain factory near Versailles began with the directorship of Etienne-Maurice Falconet.

The first German acting academy was founded by Konrad Ekhov, advancing a naturalistic style.

John Dollond, an English optician, produced the first achromatic lenses.

Franklin was sent to England to present Pennsylvania's case against the Penn family in a taxation dispute.

In Philadelphia, the first significant colonial magazine, *American Magazine and Monthly Chronicle,* was published.

In the Seven Years' War, Pitt had raised an army, commanded by Prince Ferdinand of Brunswick, to help Frederick the Great. Brunswick defeated the French at Crefeld and drove them from Hanover.

St Malo was attacked by Charles, Duke of Marlborough, and Cherbourg was bombarded and destroyed by General Bligh.

Frederick the Great defeated the Russians at Zorndorf, but was routed by the Austrians at Hochkirch.

French Senegal surrendered to British forces.

The Dutch surrendered to Clive at Chinsura.

The Marathas in India occupied the Punjab.

Voltaire wrote his most famous work, *Candide.*

David Hume, the British empiricist philosopher, published *An Enquiry Concerning Human Understanding.*

Sonata form was advanced by C. P. E. Bach.

Jedediah Strutt, an English cotton spinner, invented a ribbing machine for the manufacture of stockings.

The first blast furnace was installed by John Wilkinson, an English ironmaster, at Bilston in Staffordshire.

The sextant of Englishman John Bird made navigation far more accurate.

The tide began to turn against the French when the British took forts at Duquesne, Frontenac, and Louisbourg.

In Canada the British captured Quebec from the French. The rival commanders, Louis Joseph de Montcalm and General James Wolfe, were mortally wounded.

British naval victories proliferated. Rodney bombarded Le Havre, and French fleets were defeated at Lagos Bay by Boscawen and at Quiberon Bay by Hawke.

Frederick the Great was heavily defeated by the Russians at Kunersdorf, but he was rescued by Prince Ferdinand, who routed the French at Minden.

In Bohemia, 20,000 Prussians surrendered to the Austrians, who captured Dresden.

The Marquess of Pombal expelled the Jesuits from Portugal.

Ferdinand VI of Spain died and was succeeded by his half-brother, Charles III, King of Naples.

Dr. Johnson wrote *The Prince of Abissinia* or *Rasselas.*

Boucher painted one of his many portraits of Mme de Pompadour, the French King's most celebrated mistress.

Handel died and was buried in Poets' Corner, Westminster Abbey, before a congregation of 3,000 people.

Haydn composed the first of more than 100 outstanding symphonies.

The Bavarian Academy of Science was founded.

The British under Jeffrey Amherst took Ft. Carillon, naming it Ft. Ticonderoga.

CASANOVA   IMMANUEL KANT   GENERAL JAMES WOLFE

1760

World Events

Frederick the Great suffered a series of setbacks. His general, Fouque, was captured in Silesia after a defeat by the Austrian commander, Gideon von Laudon. Frederick laid an abortive seige to Dresden, but then defeated the Austrians at Liegnitz. He routed the Austrians at Torgau and recovered Saxony. But by the end of the year he was hard pressed and relying heavily on British financial help.
In India the French commander, Count Lally, was heavily defeated by Sir Eyre Coote at Wandewash. This marked the beginning of the end of hopes for a French Empire in India.
Britain's George II died and was succeeded by his grandson, George III.

Literature Religion Philosophy

Dr. Johnson's final piece for *The Idler* column of the *Universal Chronicle* ended two years of almost weekly contributions.

Art & Architecture

Performing Arts

William Boyce, one of the foremost English composers of church music and Master of the King's Music, began his three-volume work, *Church Music.*

Science and Technology

Joseph Black defined the difference between heat and temperature, and discovered specific and latent heat. His basic work on heat enabled his friend James Watt to build a steam engine.

America

Montreal was captured by the British, and the entire province surrendered. The major ports on the Great Lakes and Detroit were occupied by the British under **Maj. Robert Rogers.**

1761

Belle Isle and Dominica were captured by the British.
France and Spain formed a "Third Family Compact" against Britain.
In India the capture by the British of Pondicherry marked the end of French influence in the subcontinent.
In Europe, Frederick the Great's homelands were invaded by the Austrians and Russians, who burned Berlin.
Ieharu became shogun of Japan.

Louis-François Roubiliac, a French sculptor who worked almost entirely in England, completed his most celebrated work, the monument to Lady Elizabeth Nightingale in Westminster Abbey.
The completion of the *Parnassus* fresco in the Villa Albani, Rome, by Anton Raphael Mengs established the ascendancy of Neoclassical painting.

Haydn was appointed Kapellmeister to Prince Paul Esterházy.

Russian scientist and poet Mikhail Lomonosov was the first man to observe an atmosphere on the planet Venus.
The study of statistics was begun by Johann Peter Süssmilch.

James Otis, argued against enforcing the Molasses Act of 1733.
British colonists moved into western Pennsylvania despite an order banning settlement.

1762

Britain went to war with Spain and captured Havana, Manila, Martinique, St Lucia, St Vincent, Grenada, and a number of Spanish treasure ships. Forces under General John Burgoyne drove the Spaniards out of Portugal.
Czarina Elizabeth of Russia died and was succeeded by Peter III, who was then assassinated. His successor was Catherine II.
Frederick defeated the Austrians at Freiburg and concluded an armistice with them.
The French were defeated at Wilhelmsthal and driven out of Kassel by allied forces under Duke Ferdinand of Brunswick.

Jean-Jacques Rousseau, prophet of the future Romantic generation, published his two great works. *Emilius and Sophia: Or, A New System of Education* and *A Treatise on the Social Compact: Or, The Principles of Political Law.*

Robert Adam began one of his grandest commissions, the redesign and refurbishment of the interior of the Tudor Syon House, London.

Mozart, six years old, toured Europe as a child prodigy.

Cast iron was converted into malleable iron at Carron ironworks in Scotland.

A smelting process, in which iron was extracted from black magnetic sand, was developed by Jared Eliot in Connecticut.

1763

The Treaty of Paris was drawn up between England, and France and Spain. England received Canada, Cape Breton, Nova Scotia, Minorca, Tobago, St Vincent, Grenada, Dominica, Senegal, and Florida. France received back Belle Isle, Guadaloupe, Martinique, St Lucia, and Gorée. Havana and Manila were restored to Spain.
Frederick the Great, deserted by his British allies, made a separate peace with Austria by the Treaty of Hubertsburg. Austria ceded Silesia and Prussia retired from Saxony.

George Stubbs, the great English animal painter, produced one of his most lyrical works at about this time, *Mares and Foals in a River Landscape.*

Wolfgang Amadeus Mozart played before the court of Versailles at the age of seven.

Joseph Gottlieb Kölreuter carried out fertilization experiments on plants by animal pollen carriers.

Pontiac's Rebellion destroyed most British forts in the Great Lakes region.
The Treaty of Paris ended war and French power in North America.
The Proclamation of 1763 barred British settlement west of the Appalachian Mountains.

1764

The Sugar Act, by which Britain aimed to recover revenue from the American colonies, aroused much local opposition.
The constitutions of Sweden and Poland were guaranteed by Russia and Prussia.
Stanislas Poniatowski was elected the last king of independent Poland.
Catherine II confiscated church lands in Russia.
The Falklands were claimed for France by de Bougainville.
Calcutta fell to Indian adventurer Hyder Ali, who also usurped the throne of Mysore.
Ivan VI of Russia, the deposed czar, was murdered.

The Castle of Otranto, by Horace Walpole, was the first "Gothic" novel, a tale of terror and suspense.

Il ventaglio, (The Fan), one of the finest plays of Carlo Goldoni, was first performed.
Counterpoint declined in importance and the continuo disappeared. Contrapuntal forms such as fugue continued to be used, but usually as part of a movement in a larger work.

The spinning jenny was invented in England by James Hargreaves. It could spin several threads at once.
James Watt, Scottish engineer, invented the condenser.

James Otis first addressed the issue of taxation without representation at a Boston town meeting.

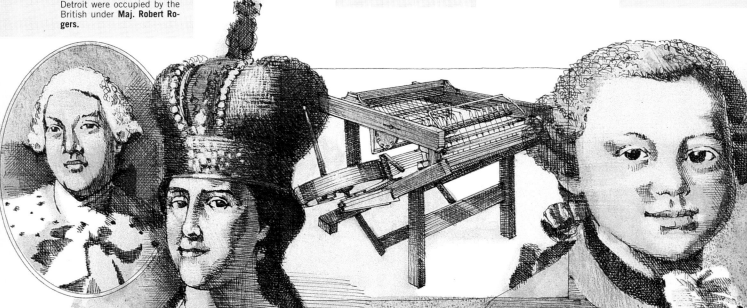

GEORGE III CATHERINE II HARGREAVES' SPINNING JENNY MOZART, A CHILD PRODIGY

Emperor Francis I, husband of Maria Theresa, died. He was succeeded by his son, Joseph II. Joseph's younger brother, Archduke Leopold I, became ruler of Tuscany.
Clive reformed the Indian administration. Britain ruled Bengal and Bihar, maintaining a puppet Mogul emperor.

Dr. Johnson's eight-volume critical edition of Shakespeare's plays appeared after 20 years' gestation.

Josiah Wedgwood, one of the most influential pottery manufacturers of all time, perfected creamware pottery.

Mozart finished his first symphony at the age of nine.

The Lunar Society, an informal society of technologists, was founded in England.
Preserving by hermetic sealing was initiated by an Italian, Lazzaro Spallanzani.

Anti-British feelings developed with the passage of the Stamp Act, a direct tax on legal documents, and newspapers, and the Quartering Act.
The Stamp Act Congress met, and The Sons of Liberty were formed.

Stanislas Leszczynski, Duke of Lorraine and deposed King of Poland, died and the duchy was then transferred to France.
Frederick V of Denmark died and was succeeded by the insane Christian VII.
Nizam Ali of Hyderabad ceded the Northern Sarkars to the East India Company.
Louis de Bougainville set out to explore the Pacific.
The Falklands were taken for England by John Byron, unaware of de Bougainville's earlier claim.

Jean-Honoré Fragonard painted one of his most celebrated works at about this time: *The Swing,* one of the quintessential works of the Rococo.
The first American painting exhibited in England was John Singleton Copley's *Boy with a Squirrel.*

Haydn produced his *Great Mass with Organ.*

Henry Cavendish, English physicist and chemist, discovered that hydrogen is less dense than air. He also made fundamental, unpublished discoveries in electricity.

Parliament repealed the Stamp Act, having been influenced by Benjamin Franklin's testimony, and the colonists dropped their nonimportation policy, but Declaratory Act asserted Parliament's authority over the colonies.

The Jesuits were expelled from Spain by Charles III.
The Burmese invaded Siam.
Catherine II of Russia consulted a convention of all social classes to reform Russian law.

The final volume of *The Life and Opinions of Tristram Shandy, Gentleman,* was written by Laurence Sterne.

Joseph Wright of Derby produced one of the most original English paintings of the period at about this time, *An experiment on a bird in an Air Pump.*
C. P. E. Bach succeeded the late Georg Philipp Telemann as director of church music in Hamburg.

Joseph Priestley published *The History and Present State of Electricity.*
Neville Maskelyne, Astronomer Royal, issued his *Nautical Almanac.*

The Townshend Acts, taxing certain imported items, were passed. The colonies reinstated nonimportation.
Daniel Boone began his first exploration of Kentucky over the Wilderness Road.

The Polish Confederation was formed to counteract Russian intrigue. Plots to kidnap King Stanislas emerged, and eventually civil war broke out in Poland.
Turkey declared war on Russia in support of Poland.
Austria renounced all claims to Silesia.
Pope Clement XIII seized Parma because of the expulsion of the Jesuits. As a result, the King of Naples invaded the Papal States.
The Gurkhas conquered Nepal.
James Cook, in the *Endeavour,* explored the Society Islands and charted the coasts of New Zealand and Western Australia.

The Royal Academy of Arts was founded in England.
Falconet completed his monumental equestrian statue of Peter the Great.

Mozart produced his first opera, *Bastien and Bastienne,* in Vienna.

The water frame was invented by Richard Arkwright, an English cotton manufacturer. Powered by water, it spun cotton into a strong thread.

Samuel Adams' Massachusetts Circular Letter advocated that the colonies write in protest, leading British to dissolve the Massachusetts legislature.
Two regiments of British troops arrived in Boston.

French trade with India increased after the French East India Company lost its monopoly.
Russian troops occupied Moldavia and entered Bucharest.
Pasquale Paoli, the Corsican patriot, was expelled from Corsica by France.
Russia and Denmark signed a treaty to protect the constitution of Sweden.
Mme du Barry became Louis XV's official mistress.
Napoleon Bonaparte was born in Corsica.
Burma was made tributary to China.

The vitality and speed with which Fragonard worked was revealed in *Music, or M de la Bretèche,* a portrait sketch of exuberant spontaneity, painted in an hour.
Josiah Wedgwood opened his famous pottery works in Staffordshire, England.

Christoph Gluck, German-Bohemian composer, reformed opera in Paris, stressing the balance between the musical and the dramatic elements. He expressed his ideals in a preface to his opera *Alceste.*

Venetian blinds were patented in London by Edward Beran.
James Watt, the Scottish engineer, patented his steam engine. It was the first to produce rotary motion and worked quickly and efficiently.

The Virginia Resolves stated that only the governor and the assembly had the right to tax Virginians. The governor then dissolved the assembly.
Colonial imports of British goods dropped sharply.

CAVENDISH'S   EQUIPMENT   JAMES COOK   WATT'S STEAM ENGINE

World Events				

World Events

1770
The Dauphin (direct heir to the French throne) married Marie Antoinette, daughter of Maria Theresa.
The Turkish navy was defeated at Tchesme by a Russian fleet commanded by British officers.
Conflict over the Falklands between Britain and Spain was averted by French intervention.
Count Johann von Struensee, physician to King Christian VII of Denmark, and the king's favorite, persuaded the king to abolish the council of state. He soon became supreme in the country and began to carry out a series of far-reaching reforms.

1771
Spain ceded the uninhabited Falkland Islands to Britain.
Prussia and Russia discussed the proposed partition of Poland.
René Maupeou, the French statesman, overthrew the parlements, replacing them with a less cumbersome system of courts.
The Crimea was completely conquered by Russia.
Turkey and Austria formed an alliance to force Russia to restore all her conquests.
Savoy abolished serfdom.
Adolphus Frederick of Sweden died and was succeeded by Gustavus III.

1772
Johann von Struensee, who had infuriated Danish nobles and clergymen with his crack-down on monopolies, was arrested on spurious charges of "criminal relations with the queen" and beheaded.
Gustavus III suppressed an uprising against the monarchy in Sweden.
Warren Hastings became Governor of Bengal.
The first partition of Poland, organized by Frederick the Great, divided the country between Prussia, Austria, and Russia.
James Cook left England on his second voyage of exploration.

1773
France renewed its alliance with Sweden.
In India, Warren Hastings prepared for his campaign against the Mahrathas by allying with the state of Oudh.
Russia obtained the Duchy of Oldenburg from Denmark. Pretender Emelyan Ivanovich Pugachev led a large Cossack and peasant revolt in southeastern Russia, halting Russia's progress in Turkey. After the revolt, Catherine II reformed Russian provincial administration.
The Papacy received Avignon from France.
The Boston Tea Party occurred when a group of radical colonists in Boston, disguised as Indians, boarded British ships in the harbor and threw their cargoes of tea overboard, in protest at the collection of tax on tea.

1774
Abdul Hamid I became Sultan of Turkey.
Louis XV died and was succeeded by his grandson Louis XVI.
The Turks were heavily defeated by the Russians in the Battle of Shumla.
Pretender Pugachev was handed over to the Russian authorities after the Cossack uprising had been suppressed.
Austria occupied Bukovina, part of the north-eastern Carpathians.
Swiss educator Heinrich Pestalozzi founded his school for orphaned and neglected children in Zurich.

Literature

1774
Die Leiden des jungen Werthers (The Sorrows of Young Werther) brought instant fame to its German author, Johann Wolfgang von Goethe.

Art and Architecture

1770
The Blue Boy, one of Thomas Gainsborough's most famous works, was painted at about this time.
The Royal Crescent, Bath, was completed at about this time. It is one of the longest crescents in Europe.

1771
Pocito Chapel in Guadaloupe was one of very few centrally planned churches in Spanish-America.

1772
The final volumes of plates for the French Encyclopédie were distributed; the first (of 28) had appeared some 20 years earlier. The ambitious project was supervised by Denis Diderot.

1774
The classical Stifsgarden Palace in Trondheim, Norway, built of wood, remains one of the largest buildings in Scandinavia.

Performing Arts

1770
Ludwig van Beethoven was born.

1772
In Haydn's "Farewell" Symphony, the finale allowed the players to leave the platform one by one until only two solo violins were left. This was a hint to Prince Esterházy that his orchestra needed a holiday.

1773
Oliver Goldsmith saw the triumph of his comedy, She Stoops to Conquer, before his early death.
The oldest existing firm of piano manufacturers, John Broadwood and Sons in London, made its first square piano.
The Swedish National Theater was established in Stockholm.
The waltz became fashionable in Vienna.

1774
String quartets were written in large numbers. They were an ideal vehicle for the development of classical designs.

Science and Technology

1770
The first self-propelled road vehicle appeared. It was a steam-driven gun carriage, built by Parisian engineer Nicolas Joseph Cugnot.

1771
Luigi Galvani, an Italian physiologist, found that two metals in contact with a frog's leg caused it to twitch. Unwittingly, he had produced an electric current.
The first spinning mill in England was founded by Richard Arkwright.
The Smeatonian Club for engineers was founded in London.

1772
Daniel Rutherford, Scottish physician, discovered nitrogen.
Oxygen was discovered by the Swedish chemist Carl Scheele. He withheld his findings until after the independent discovery by Joseph Priestley two years later.

1774
Karl Whilhelm Scheele discovered chlorine.
Joseph Priestley discovered oxygen.
English ironmaster John Wilkinson patented a cannon-borer that permitted accurate boring of cylinders for steam engines.

America

1770
A partial repeal of the Townshend Acts left only the duty on tea.
In the Boston Massacre, five were killed in a clash with British troops. Lawyer John Adams helped provide a defense for the British.

1771
2,000 North Carolina "Regulators", protesting inadequate representation in western counties, were defeated by a force of 1,200 British soldiers at Alamance Creek.

1772
The Gaspee, a customs schooner, was burned by a band of colonists near Providence.

1773
Committees of Correspondence appeared throughout the colonies.

1774
Britain's Coercive Acts, in Retaliation for the Boston Tea Party, closed the port of Boston and made drastic changes in Massachusetts government.

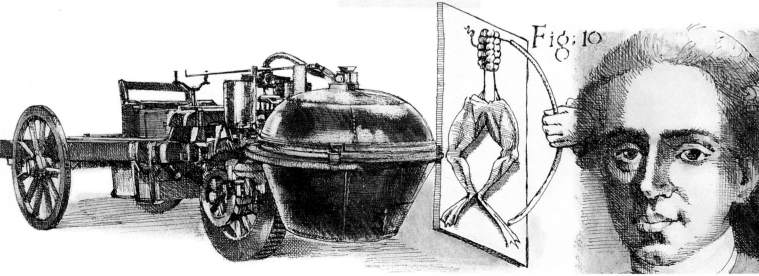

CUGNOT'S STEAM CARRIAGE   GALVANI'S EXPERIMENT   LOUIS XVI

The American War of Independence began with skirmishes at Lexington and Concord, and a sharp battle at Bunker's Hill.
Bohemian peasants rebelled against servitude.
The Portuguese fleet made an abortive attack on Montevideo.
A Spanish expedition sent to eliminate a pirate stronghold in Algiers was repulsed.
Danish language and literature replaced German in Danish schools.

As his eyesight failed, Chardin began to work in pastels rather than oils, producing a series of striking self-portraits.

An Italian, Vincenzo Galeotti, began a 40-year reign as ballet-master at the Royal Danish Ballet.
Pierre Beaumarchais perfected the character of a scheming valet in Figaro of *The Barber of Seville* and, a decade later, *The Marriage of Figaro.*
Yankee Doodle, an old English tune with American words, became the American Army's marching song.

Abraham Gottlob Werner, German geologist and mineralogist, initiated the modern study of geology.
Johan Christian Fabricius, Danish entomologist, classified insects in his *Systema Entomologiae.*

Patrick Henry delivered his "Give me liberty or give me death" speech.
Paul Revere made his dramatic ride to warn Boston residents of the British approach.
Ethan Allen's men took Ft. Ticonderoga.

The American Declaration of Independence, drafted by Thomas Jefferson, was passed by Congress.
A loan of a million francs was granted by France to help the Americans.
Britain recruited 29,000 Hessian mercenaries for the American War.
The Treaty of Copenhagen, concluded by Denmark and Russia, meant that Russia relinquished her claims to Holstein.
Jacques Necker became France's finance minister.
Grigori Potemkin, favorite of Catherine II, built up the Russian Black Sea Fleet.
James Cook began his third voyage of exploration.

Adam Smith, the highly influential English political economist and social philosopher, published his *Wealth of Nations.*

Sir William Chambers began his main work, Somerset House, London, one of the largest buildings in England.

The Bolshoi Theater was founded in Moscow.
Charles Burney wrote his authoritative *History of Music.*

The first submarine to be used in warfare was "Bushnell's Connecticut Turtle," invented by American engineer David Bushnell. With a one-man crew, it was deployed unsuccessfully against British ships in New York harbor.

The British occupied New York, while George Washington retreated. Nathan Hale was executed for spying.

Joseph I of Portugal, insane for his last three years, died. He was succeeded by his daughter, Marie I, who promptly dismissed chief minister Pombal.
French volunteers to oppose the British arrived in America.
Maximilian III of Bavaria died. He was succeeded by Charles Theodore, Elector Palatine, but Austria's Joseph II claimed Lower Bavaria.
The Swiss Cantons allied themselves with France in the face of Austria's hostile attitude.

Richard Brinsley Sheridan, Irish-born English playwright, produced *The School for Scandal,* his most successful satirical comedy.

The torpedo was invented by David Bushnell.
The torsion balance was invented by French physicist Charles August de Coulomb.

Americans under General Gates defeated the British at Saratoga but lost several battles as the British under General Howe took Philadelphia.
Washington wintered at Valley Forge, Pennsylvania.

Austrian claims to Lower Bavaria were acknowledged by the Palatinate.
France signed a military alliance with America: Britain declared war on France.
The War of the Bavarian Succession began with Prussia's declaration of war on Austria.
Holland signed a commercial treaty with America.
Dominica was captured by the French for use as a naval base. The British countered by depriving the French of St Lucia.
Warren Hastings captured Chandernagore from the French and Sir Hector Munro took Pondicherry.

Evelina, published anonymously in London, was a huge success. Its author was Fanny Burney.

The French sculptor Jean-Antoine Houdon made one of his best studies of Voltaire.

La Scala, still one of the greatest opera houses in the world, was opened in Milan.
Machine-produced heads for cellos and double basses were invented by a German, Anton Bachmann.
Beethoven, aged eight, was presented for the first time as an infant prodigy.

Franz Mesmer, Austrian physician, began to practise mesmerism in Paris.

Capt. John Paul Jones in the American privateer *Ranger* took several British ships.
George Rogers Clark won control of the Illinois country.
The British captured Savannah.

Spain declared war on Britain and successfully besieged Gibraltar.
British forces captured Senegal and the French West African port of Gorée.
The Peace of Teschen ended the War of the Bavarian Succession.
French forces captured St Vincent and Grenada in the West Indies from the British.
Captain James Cook was killed by natives in Hawaii.

Claude-Nicolas Ledoux completed his saltworks city at Arc-et-Senans. Part of this project, the first example of large industrial architecture in France, survives.

The Portuguese Royal Academy of Sciences was founded in Lisbon.
The spinning mule was invented in England by Lancashire inventor Samuel Crompton. It was able to spin high-quality thread on many spindles at once and brought about a new era for the British textile industry.

The British controlled most of the south, but were thwarted in their attempt to take the Hudson River, losing at Stony Point.
John Paul Jones in the *Bonhomme Richard* captured the British *Serapis.*

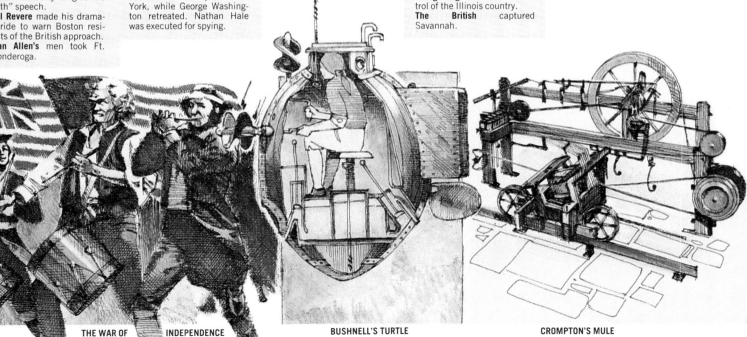

THE WAR OF INDEPENDENCE   BUSHNELL'S TURTLE   CROMPTON'S MULE

1780

World Events

The Battle of Cape St Vincent resulted in a victory over the Spanish fleet by Admiral Rodney, temporarily lifting the siege of Gibraltar.
Serfdom was abolished in Bohemia and Hungary.
Britain declared war on Holland because of that country's support for the American colonists.
Maria Theresa of Austria died and was succeeded by her son, Joseph II.

Literature Religion Philosophy

The first Swedenborgian societies appeared at about this time, devoted to the theology of Swedenborg.

Art and Architecture

Neoclassicism in architecture entered its heyday. The basilica of St Geneviève, later the Panthéon, in Paris, was completed and also the Grand-Théâtre, Bordeaux.

Performing Arts

The waltz first appeared in Germany at about this time.
Haydn composed his *"Toy" Symphony*, in which various toy instruments were introduced into the orchestra parts.

Science and Technology

Cheap soap resulted from the work of French chemist Nicholas Leblanc.

America

In the South, Charleston fell to the British, who also won at Camden but lost badly at King's Mountain.
Benedict Arnold's treason while commanding West Point was discovered, but he escaped to the British.

1781

World Events

Russia and Austria agreed to drive the Turks out of Europe and restore a Greek Empire under Catherine's grandson Constantine.
A British plan to sieze the Cape of Good Hope was thwarted by the French fleet.
Jacques Necker was dismissed by Louis XVI.
Prussia joined the League of Armed Neutrality.
Warren Hastings deposed the Rajah of Benares for refusing to contribute to war expenses. Eyre Coote saved Madras by defeating Hyder Ali at Porto Novo.
American Independence was assured by the surrender of British General Cornwallis at Yorktown with 7,000 men. This virtually marked the end of land operations.

Dr. Johnson wrote *Lives of the English Poets*.

Henry Fuseli, Swiss-born painter and author, completed *The Nightmare*.

German composer Johann Adam Hiller founded the Gewandhaus concerts in Leipzig.
Mozart staged his commissioned opera *Idomeneo* in Munich.

Uranus was discovered by German-born English astronomer Sir William Herschel. It was the first planet to be discovered that was not known to ancient civilizations.

The Articles of Confederation were ratified.

1782

World Events

The British captured Trincomalee from the Dutch but lost Minorca to Spain.
Admiral George Rodney saved Jamaica and recovered most of the lost West Indies by defeating the French in the Battle of the Saints off St Lucia.
Grenville traveled to Paris to negotiate for peace in the American War with Benjamin Franklin and the Count of Vergennes.
The Mahratta War ended with the Treaty of Salbai. Hyder Ali died and was succeeded in Mysore by his son, Tipu.

Les Liaisons Dangereuses by Pierre Choderlos de Laclos, a psychological novel of intrigue and seduction, caused a sensation in France.

Francesco Guardi was commissioned to record the visit of Pope Pius VI to Venice.
George Romney, the English portrait painter, met Emma Hart, later Lady Hamilton, at about this time. His obsession with her inspired some 50 portraits.

Mozart's opera *Die Entführung aus dem Serail* (*The Elopement from the Harem*) was produced in Vienna.

Josiah Wedgwood was the first manufacturer to install a steam engine in his factory.

John Adams, John Jay, and Benjamin Franklin were the principal American peace negotiators in Paris. The terms included independence, the establishment of boundaries, fishing rights, and debt validation.

1783

World Events

Joseph II enforced the teaching and speaking of the German language in Bohemia.
The Russians annexed Kuban. Turkey wanted to declare war on Russia but was dissuaded by Britain and Austria.
The Peace of Versailles included (a) England's treaty with America, which recognized American independence, together with a payment of £10 million by Britain; (b) Britain's treaty with France, which meant Britain's ceding of Tobago, St Lucia, Senegal, Gorée, Pondicherry, Mahé, Chandernagore, and Seurat, in exchange for Grenada, Dominica, St Vincent, Nevis, Montserrat, St Kitts, the River Gambia, and Fort James; and (c) the treaty with Spain by which Britain restored Florida and Minorca to Spain and received Providence, the Bahamas, and Gibraltar. With Holland, conquests were mutually restored.

Moses Mendelssohn, German Jewish philosopher and Bible commentator, published *Jerusalem, or On Religious Power and Judaism*, which upheld the inviolability of thought.

The first manned flight took place in a hot-air balloon made and flown by the French Montgolfier brothers, Joseph and Jacques.

The Treaty of Paris was signed and ratified and the Continental Army was disbanded.
Washington bade his troops farewell and resigned his commission.
A group of 7,000 Loyalists sailed from New York.

1784

World Events

Warren Hastings made an effective peace with the Marathas. Margalore, a strategic shipbuilding base, was ceded to Britain.
Russia's conquest of the Crimea was recognized by Turkey with the Treaty of Constantinople.
Denmark began to enjoy a free press and educational reforms.
William Pitt the Younger became Prime Minister of Great Britain.

The French artist Jacques-Louis David painted the archetypal picture of purist Neoclassicism, *The Oath of the Horatii*.

Sarah Siddons as the *Tragic Muse* exemplified Sir Joshua Reynolds's "grand style."

Shrapnel, invented by Lt. Henry Shrapnel, was first tested at Stirling in Scotland.
James Watt invented the double-acting engine.

Thomas Jefferson developed a plan of government for the Western lands, providing for the future division into new states.
New York City was selected as the country's temporary capital.

SAMUEL JOHNSON   YORKTOWN   BENJAMIN FRANKLIN   MONTGOLFIERS' BALLOON   WILLIAM PITT

Joseph II attempted in vain to exchange his Austrian Netherlands for Bavaria, ruled by Charles Theodore of the Palatinate. The idea was opposed by Frederick the Great, who formed the League of German Princes to frustrate Joseph.

Cardinal Rohan of France was arrested in connection with the Diamond Necklace Affair. The cardinal, infatuated by Marie Antoinette, procured for her (with her forged signature) an £80,000 diamond necklace without paying for it. When the jeweler sued in court, the queen denied all knowledge of it. But her reputation suffered, and the incident contributed to the outbreak of the Revolution.

William Cowper brought a new directness to English poetry. *The Task,* on the virtues of rural life, was an immediate success.

The Morning Walk was one of Gainborough's late works which exhibited a greater freedom of technique.

Mozart dedicated his six string quartets to his teacher, Joseph Haydn.

Chlorine was first used for bleaching cloth by French chemist Claude Berthollet.
The power loom, which mechanized weaving, was invented by English inventor and clergyman Edmund Cartwright.

The new union attempted to regulate foreign commerce but was unable to gain the cooperation of the states.
Thomas Jefferson replaced Benjamin Franklin as minister to France, and John Adams became minister to Britain.

Charles Cornwallis became Governor-General of India. The Rajah of Kedah ceded Penang to Britain.
Frederick the Great died and was succeeded by Frederick William II, brother of the Princess of Orange.
An Anglo-French commercial treaty reduced duty on English clothes, cotton, and iron goods, and on French soap, wines, and olive oil.
William of Orange was deprived of command of the army by the Dutch Patriot Party.

The Prado, Madrid, originally conceived as a natural history museum but later dedicated to art, was under way.

La Fille mal gardée, one of the first comic ballets and one of the first to use realistic rather than idealized characters — and still highly popular — was created by Jean Dauberval in Bordeaux.
Mozart's Marriage of Figaro was staged in Vienna and became his most successful opera.

Coal gas was first used for lighting in England and Germany.
William Herschel published his *Catalogue of Nebulae.*

Shay's Rebellion broke out when Massachusetts refused to help debt-ridden farmers. Led by Daniel Shays, the uprising was put down in 1787.
The Annapolis Convention ended with a call for all the states to meet in Philadelphia.

The Austrian Netherlands were claimed to be part of the Hapsburg monarchy by Joseph II.
In Holland, Princess Wilhelmina was arrested near Gouda by Dutch rebels. Prussia intervened in Dutch affairs to support William V against the Patriotic Party.
The aristocratic parlements in France blocked proposals for financial reform.
A rebellion erupted in Formosa against the Chinese.

The Marquis de Sade, whose erotic writings gave rise to the the term "sadism," wrote his version of his most famous novel, *Justine, or the Misfortunes of Virtue.*
Robert Burns, the national poet of Scotland, published his larger second edition of *Poems, Chiefly in the Scottish Dialect.*

Johann Heinrich Wilhelm Tischbein painted *Goethe in the Campagna.*

Mozart's opera *Don Giovanni,* depicting the life and loves of libertine Don Juan, had a wildly triumphant première in Prague.

Jacques Charles, a French physicist, formulated Charles's Law.

The Constitutional Convention opened in Philadelphia. After disagreements over representation, the Connecticut Compromise satisfied both large and small states, with equal representation in the Senate and proportional in the House.

Britain established convict settlements in Australia.
The French Parlement submitted a list of grievances to the king. National bankruptcy was announced, and Loménie de Brienne was replaced as finance minister by Jacques Necker.
Austria's Joseph II declared war on Turkey.
Britain and Holland concluded an alliance. The Triple Alliance was formed when Prussia joined them to preserve European peace.
Sweden declared war on Russia and invaded Russian Finland. Russia retaliated by sinking a Swedish fleet. Denmark invaded Sweden.
Sierra Leone became the site of a British settlement to serve as a refuge for black waifs and ex-slaves.

Immanuel Kant published his *Critique of Practical Reason.*

The Ecole Militaire was completed in Paris to the design of Jacques Ange Gabriel.

The threshing machine was patented by Andrew Meikle. Andrew Meikle.
James Hutton, a Scottish geologist, wrote *Theory of the Earth.* He became one of the founders of modern geology by viewing all geological change as continuous.

Ratification of the Constitution by the required nine states took place early in 1788. Maryland contributed 10 square miles of land on the Potomac River to be used as a site for a national capital.

The French Revolution began when a group of middle-class radicals took over the administration with the help of the Paris mob and tried to set up a constitutional monarchy.
The Paris mob sacked the Bastille. The French National Assembly adopted the Declaration of the Rights of Man. Louis XVI and his court moved from Versailles to Paris.
George Washington became the first president of the United States.
Gustavus III assumed absolute power in Sweden.
Abdul Hamid I, Sultan of Turkey, died and was succeeded by his nephew, Selim III.
The Austrian Netherlands declared their independence under the name of Belgium.

Jeremy Bentham's *An Introduction to the Principles of Morals and Legislation* brought him instant fame.
William Blake, English poet, painter, engraver and visionary, produced his *Songs of Innocence.*

Thomas Lawrence, when only 20, was summoned to paint Queen Charlotte's portrait.

The first recorded theatrical performance in Australia was George Farquhar's *The Recruiting Officer* (1706), with a cast of convicts.

Antoine Lavoisier, French chemist, founded modern chemistry with his *Traité Eléméntaire du Chimie.*

The first presidential election was won by George Washington, with John Adams as vice president. The cabinet included Jefferson (State) and Hamilton (Treasury).

THE BASTILLE   GEORGE WASHINGTON

World Events

1790

The Treaty of Verela ended the Russo-Swedish War. Russia gained part of Finland.

Emperor Joseph II died and Leopold II, Grand Duke of Tuscany, became Holy Roman Emperor.

The Convention of Berlin was organized by Britain, Prussia, and Holland to coordinate their policy toward Belgium, but Pitt refused to recognize Belgian independence.

At the Reichenbach Conference, Britain and Holland's refusal to support Prussia averted war and led to a treaty between Austria and Prussia.

The Austrians reentered Brussels and suppressed the revolution there.

In India, Britain formed alliances with the Marathas and the Nizam of Hyderabad.

Hungarian nobles defied the Austrian emperor and demanded greater independence for their country.

In France, Jacques Necker resigned. Vast crowds gathered on the Champ de Mars and took an oath of loyalty to the constitution. Louis XVI accepted the revised constitution.

1791

Louis XVI tried to escape from France with his family, in disguise, but was recognized at Varennes and taken back to Paris. The National Assembly, after voting to make France a constitutional monarchy, dissolved and was replaced by the Legislative Assembly.

Honoré Mirabeau was elected President of the French National Assembly but died two months later.

A free constitution for Poland was guaranteed by Austria and Prussia.

Frederick William II of Prussia called on the European powers to support Louis XVI. Austria and Prussia declared their readiness to intervene provided other nations agreed, Britain declared its neutrality.

1792

France declared war on Austria, Prussia, and Sardinia, and was invaded by Austrian and Prussian armies. The Tuileries in Paris was ransacked by a mob and the Swiss Guard massacred. The royal family was imprisoned and Louis XVI put on trial. A French republic was proclaimed.

The Peace of Jassy ended the war between Russia and Turkey.

In India, Britain gained half of Mysore with the defeat of Tipu.

Emperor Leopold II died and was succeeded by his brother Francis II of Austria, the last Holy Roman Emperor.

Gustavus III of Sweden was assassinated and was succeeded by Gustavus IV.

Denmark became the first nation to abolish slavery.

1793

Louis XVI was executed; later, Marie Antoinette followed him to the guillotine.

France went to war with Britain, Holland, Austria, Prussia, Spain, and Sardinia. Belgium was liberated. The Holy Roman Empire declared war on France.

A reign of terror began in France when the Committee on Public Safety came to power, led by Maximilien Robespierre, supported by Georges Jacques Danton and St Just. Jean Marat was murdered by Charlotte Corday.

French Armies were driven from Germany, and the British temporarily occupied Toulon and Corsica. The French defeated a British army in The Netherlands.

Russia and Prussia carried out the second partition of Poland.

1794

Mass executions took place in France, including those of Antoine Lavoisier, Danton, Camille Desmoulins, St Just, and Robespierre. With the latter's death, the reign of terror began to come to an end.

French victories included Tourcoing, Fleurus, Charleroi, and Guadeloupe. French troops invaded Spain, reached the Rhine, and swarmed into Holland. But at sea, French fleets were defeated by the British in the Channel and the West Indies.

The Commune of Paris was abolished. Revolutionary ideas led to the freeing of slaves in the French West Indies, arousing hostility among the European powers.

Polish patriot Tadeusz Kósciuzko led an uprising that was subsequently suppressed by the Russians.

The Alliance of St Petersburg united Britain, Austria, and Russia against France.

The Kajar dynasty in Persia was founded by Aga Mohammed.

Literature Religion Philosophy

1790 — **Edmund Burke,** Irish-born British statesman and political thinker, wrote his *Reflections on the Revolution in France.*

1791 — One of the greatest biographies was published: James Boswell's *The Life of Samuel Johnson, LL.D.*
The most celebrated reply to Burke's *Reflections* was Thomas Paine's *Rights of Man.*

1792 — **Mary Wollstonecraft** published her *Vindication of the Rights of Women.*

1793 — **William Godwin** published his *Enquiry Concerning Political Justice and Its Influence on General Virtue and Happiness.*

1794 — One of the greatest Gothic novels, *The Mysteries of Udolpho,* by Ann Radcliffe, was published.

Art and Architecture

1790 — **Sir Joshua Reynolds** delivered the last of his *Discourses on Art.*

1792 — **The American-born artist Benjamin West** was made President of the Royal Academy, London.

1793 — *The death of Marat* is perhaps David's most famous painting.
Antonio Canova, the Italian Sculptor, produced his most famous work, *Cupid and Psyche.*
The Louvre, Paris, was established as a public art gallery.

Performing Arts

1791 — **Mozart's** *Die Zauberflöte (The Magic Flute)* was first performed in Vienna, shortly before the composer's premature death.
Haydn composed his *"Surprise" Symphony* which, after a *piano* start, embodied a *fortissimo* chord to jolt somnolent listeners.

1792 — **Domenico Cimarosa,** "the Italian Mozart," composed his most celebrated opera, *Il matrimonio segreto* in Vienna.
La Marseillaise, France's national anthem, was composed by C. J. Rouget de Lisle.

1793 — **Niccolò Paganini,** The Italian virtuoso violinist, made his début in Genoa.

1794 — **Haydn's** *"Clock" Symphony* was so-called because of the ticking sound in the slow movement.

Science and Technology

1790 — **James Watt** applied his flyball governor to control the speed of a steam engine.
Free treatment for sexually transmitted diseases was introduced in Denmark.

1791 — **Indiarubber cloth** was patented by Samuel Peel.

1792 — **Scientific institutes** abounded in revolutionary France. They included the Jardin de Plantes and the Ecole Polytechnique.

1793 — **The cotton gin** was invented by the American inventor Eli Whitney.

1794 — **John Hunter's pioneering work** *Treatise on the Blood, Inflamation and Gunshot Wounds* was published.

America

1790 — **Alexander Hamilton** proposed a fiscal program that included the federal government's responsibility for the national debt and for assuming state debts, and a national bank.

1791 — **Vermont** was admitted to the Union as the 14th state.
The First Bank of the United States opened its office in Philadelphia.
The Bill of Rights was ratified and incorporated into the Constitution.

1792 — **Kentucky** became the 15th state to join the Union.
By the Mint Act, a decimal coinage system was set up, with the federal mint located in Philadelphia.
Washington and Adams were reelected.

1793 — **Citizen Genêt,** the French minister to the US, hired US privateers to harrass the British. President Washington asserted American neutrality.

1794 — **At the Battle** of Fallen Timbers, General Anthony Wayne put down Indian resistance in northwest Ohio.

FRANZ JOSEPH HAYDN   WOLFGANG MOZART   MARIE ANTOINETTE   WHITNEY'S COTTON

1795

...ance was ruled by The ...rectory, a five-man execu-...ve established by the Third ...onstitution.

...everal powers made peace ...th France, including Tus-...ny, Prussia, Luxembourg, ...axony, Hanover, the Bava-...an Palatinate, Spain, and ...ustria.

...e French established the ...atavian Republic in The ...etherlands and incorporated ...elgium into France.

...e Third Partition of Poland ...vided the remainder of the ...ountry among Russia, Prus-...a, and Austria.

...eylon was taken from the ...utch by the British.

...e Cape of Good Hope was ...aptured by the British as a ...olony for Prince William V of ...range.

...ing Stanislas II of Poland ...dicated.

...cottish explorer Mungo Park ...aced the River Gambia as ...r as the Niger.

...aydn completed his 12 Lon-...on symphonies.
...alcutta saw the first perma-...ent theater for Bengali ...lays.
...e Conservatoire de Musique ...as established in Paris.
...erman composer Heinrich ...Marschner was born.

...e metric system was ...dopted in France.
...oseph Bramah, British en-...ineer, invented the hydraulic ...ress.

...homas Pinckney negotiated a ...reaty with Spain that estab-...shed US boundaries in the ...outh as the 31st parallel and ...n the west as the Mississippi ...River and gave the US Missis-...ippi navigation rights.

1796

Napoleon Bonaparte married Josephine de Beauharnais. He took command of the French forces in Italy and repeatedly defeated the Austrians in a series of battles.
Sardinia abandoned the Austrian alliance.
The Lombardic Republic was established by the French.
Britain took Elba, Demerara, Essequibo, Berbice, St Lucia, and Grenada but lost Corsica and withdrew the Royal Navy from the Mediterranean.
Spain declared war on Britain.
Catherine II of Russia died and was succeeded by her son, Paul I.
The Aga Muhammad of Persia captured Khorasan.

François-Pascal-Simon Gérard, pupil of David, became the leading society and court portraitist after the triumph of *Jean-Baptiste Isabey and his daughter* at the Paris Salon of this year.

The violin was taken to India by British rulers. Indian musicians absorbed it into their music, utilizing its subtleties of intonation and tone color.

Vaccination, discovered by British physician Edward Jenner, led to the eradication of smallpox.

Washington's Farewell Address urged the nation to be wary of foreign alliances.
John Adams was elected president, with Thomas Jefferson as vice-president.
Tennessee became the 16th state.

1797

Napoleon decisively defeated the Austrians at Rivoli. His triumphant advance in Italy led him eventually to the Tyrol and Vienna.
The French occupied the Ionian Islands and founded the Ligurian, Cisalpine, and Cispadane republics, the last two subsequently merging.
The Peace of Campo Formio ended the war between France and Austria.
Napoleon commanded the forces to invade England. Charles Talleyrand became French foreign minister.
The Peace Conference between France and the Holy Roman Empire opened at Rastadt.
John Jervis and Horatio Nelson destroyed a Franco-Spanish fleet off Cape St Vincent, and Adam Duncan defeated the Dutch off Camperdown.
Frederick William II of Prussia died and was succeeded by his son, Frederick William III.

Francisco de Goya y Lucientes completed the most interesting of his many portraits of the Duchess of Alba.
Thomas Bewick, an English illustrator, published the first part of his most important work, *A History of British Birds; Land Birds.*

The carriage lathe was invented by British engineer Henry Maudslay.
Chromium was discovered by French chemist Louis Nicolas Vauquelin.

The XYZ Affair, a diplomatic crisis, developed when US ministers to France were asked for a bribe and a loan before negotiations to end French interference with US shipping. US outrage led to an undeclared naval war.

1798

French armies occupied Rome and set up the Roman Republic. They also invaded Switzerland and set up the Helvetic Republic.
Napoleon sailed to Egypt. Victory in the Battle of the Pyramids made him master of that country, but Nelson destroyed the French fleet off Aboukir in the Battle of the Nile, leaving Napoleon isolated from Europe.
War broke out between Turkey and France and between Naples and France.
A Second Coalition against France was formed by an Anglo-Russian alliance.

The Romantic movement began: in Germany, the Schlegel brothers, August Wilhelm and Friedrich, started a periodical, *The Athenäum;* in England, William Wordsworth and Samuel Taylor Coleridge published their *Lyrical Ballads.*

Goya painted a fresco in the dome of the Ermita de San Antonio, Madrid, the court chapel of Charles IV.

Haydn's magnificent oratorio *The Creation,* produced in Vienna, was based on Genesis and Milton's *Paradise Lost.*

Henry Cavendish, the British physicist and chemist, determined the mean density of the Earth.
Lithography was invented by Aloys Senefelder, a Bavarian chemist.

Alien and Sedition Acts outlined strict citizenship requirements and outlawed much criticism of the government.
The 11th Amendment to the Constitution was ratified.
The Mississippi Territory was organized.

1799

Napoleon invaded Syria. The French now faced a coalition of Britain, Austria, Portugal, Russia, Naples, and Turkey, and were driven out of Italy. Russia subsequently abandoned the coalition.
When Napoleon returned to France he overthrew The Directory and set up a Consulate, with himself as First Consul.
A peace offer by France was rejected by Britain and Austria.
The Duke of York commanded the British army in Holland. He surrendered ignominiously to the French at Alkmaar.
Britain assumed control of the Carnatic, in India, after Tipu Sahib, last ruler of Mysore, was killed in battle.

Juan Valdés Meléndez, principal Spanish poet of the period, published a collection of his works.

Los Caprichos were published, a series of 80 etchings by Goya which attacked the corruption of the day.

Beethoven dedicated his "Pathétique" piano sonata to Prince Carl von Lichnowsky.

A mammoth, perfectly preserved in ice, was discovered in Siberia.
Discovery of the Rosetta Stone permitted the decipherment of Egyptian hieroglyphics.

Eli Whitney, manufacturing 10,000 muskets under contract for the federal government, developed a system of interchangeable gun parts that simplified weapons production.

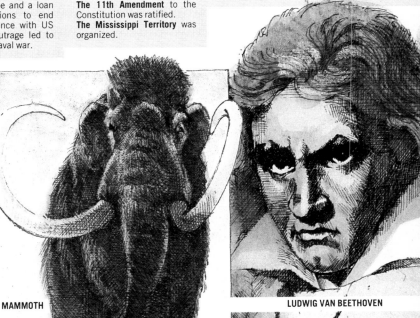

VACCINATION   MAMMOTH   LUDWIG VAN BEETHOVEN

BREAKING the barriers OF SPORT

1954 Roger Bannister (GB) 3min 59.4sec

1945 Gunder Haegg (Sweden) 4min 1.4sec

1944 Arne Andersson (Sweden) 4min 1.6sec

1934 Glen Cunningham (USA) 4min 6.8sec

1937 Sydney Wooderson (GB) 4min 6.4sec

1954 John Landy (Australia) 3min 58.0sec

1957 Derek Ibbotson (GB) 3min 57.2sec

1964 Peter Snell (New Zealand) 3min 54.1sec

1965 Michel Jazy (France) 3min 53.6sec

1967 Jim Ryun (USA) 3min 51.1sec

Walter George, one of the greatest middle-distance runners of all time, was born in Wiltshire, England. He set a world mark of 4min 18.4sec for the mile in 1884 as an amateur, turned professional, and claimed a time of 4min 12.75sec, not bettered until 1915.

Paavo Johannes Nurmi, from Finland, amassed 22 ratified world records: in the 1924 Olympics he won the 1,5000 meters and 5,000 meters, running one only 90 minutes after the other.

Glen Cunningham, known as "the iron man of Kansas", began middle distance running as a therapeutic exercise after a disastrous school fire that killed his brother and left him with legs so badly burned that he was threatened with amputation. He set a new mile record in 1934 and ran his fastest 1,500 meters in 1940, the year he retired.

Jack Lovelock became New Zealand's first Olympic athletics champion when he won the 1,500 meters at the Berlin Games in

1936 in a new Olympic and world record time of 3min 47.8sec. He set his earlier mile record as part of a combined Oxford-Cambridge team challenging a Princeton-Cornell team in the United States. Lovelock later worked as a doctor in New York, and died there in a subway accident.

Roger Gilbert Bannister achieved track and field immortality when, on a cold, wet and windy evening in May 1954, at Oxford, he became the first man in the world to run a mile in less than 4 minutes. His team mates, Chris Brasher and Chris Chataway, were pacemakers, but for the last 230 yards he was on his own. With a final burst of speed, for which he was famous, he hurled himself at the tape as he fell semi-conscious. The 4-minute mile had been known as the "Everest" of athletics.

Herbert James Elliott, born near Perth, Australia, is acknowledged as the greatest mile competitor of them all. From 1954 when, at the age of 16, he ran his first major race, until his retirement in 1962, he won every 1,500–meter and mile race he entered. Trained to maximum fitness on giant sand dunes by his Australian mentor, Percy Cerutty, he seemed almost immunized against fatigue, pain and exhaustion. In addition to his world mile record, he also twice set best times for the 1,500 meters.

Filbert Bayi, born in Kenya, was an uncompromising front runner who blazed away from gun to tape over the middle distances. Besides his mile record, he set a world mark for the 1,500 meters in the 1974 Commonwealth Games of 3min 22.2sec.

Steve Ovett, born in Brighton, England, broke the world mile record on the famed Bislett track in Oslo and two weeks later equalled the world 1,500–meter record on the same track. He caused a sensation in the Moscow Olympics by taking gold in the 800 meters, beating the favourite, his arch-rival Sebastian Coe.

Sebastian Coe, a Londoner, was called "the Nureyev of the track" for the slight build and graceful acceleration that swept him to

world records in the 800 meters, 1,000 meters, 1,500 meters and mile. With his British rivals Steve Ovett and later Steve Cram, he dominated world middle distance running in the early 1980s.

Steve Cram, from the north of England, set new records for the mile and 1,500 meters in 1985. A tall, powerful runner, his combination of stamina with speed enables him to sustain exceptionally long finishing bursts.

1933
...elock (New Zealand)
...min 7.6sec

1923
Paavo Nurmi (Finland)
4min 10.4sec

1931
...adoumègue (France)
...min 9.2sec

1915
Norman Taber (USA)
4min 12.6sec

1895
Thomas Conneff (USA)
4min 15.6sec

1868
Walter Gibbs (GB)
4min 28.8sec

1913
John Paul Jones (USA)
4min 14.4sec

1895
Fred Bacon (GB)
4min 17.0sec

1884
Walter George (GB)
4min 18.4sec

1868
Walter Chinnery (GB)
4min 29.8sec

1958
Herb Elliott (Australia)
3 min 54.5sec

1975
Filbert Bayi (Tanzania)
3min 51.0sec

1975
John Walker (New Zealand)
3min 49.4sec

1980
Steve Ovett (GB)
3min 48.8sec

1981
Sebastian Coe (GB)
3min 47.3sec

1985
Steve Cram (GB)
3min 46.3sec

THE MILE

In running the mile in 3min 46.3sec in 1985 Steve Cram left champions of the past far behind him. The average speed of Walter Chinnery in 1868 would have placed him 283 yards back as Cram reached the tape. Roger Bannister, who broke the 4-minute barrier in 1954, would barely have entered the finishing straight.

Through a combination of physical and psychological factors, improvements in performance by both men and women continue to accelerate in every field of sport, producing records that once seemed impossible.

78 THE POLE VAULT

The world record has been broken more times for the pole vault (a competition for men only) than for any other event. Pole vaulting proper became a recognized sport in England, Germany, and America in the late 1800s. Americans dominated the event for most of the 20th century, winning every Olympic gold medal from 1896 to 1968. Since that time, Eastern European and Soviet athletes have largely taken over.

In the early years of the century, **Robert Gardner** not only made the world's best vault but also twice won the US Amateur Golf Championship. His record vault lasted only a week before **Marcus Wright** (the first man to clear four meters) took over. The greatest bamboo pole vaulter was indisputably **Cornelius Warmerdam**, the first man to clear 15 feet – which he did 43 times. After 15 years his record fell to **Bob "Guts" Gutowski**, the first man to set a world mark with a steel pole.

In 1963 **John Pennel** became the first man to clear 17 feet. He set six new records that year but only two were ratified. In 1970, East German **Wolfgang Nordwig** eclipsed Pennel's best mark of 17ft 10¼in by ¾in, becoming the first European to clear 17ft. Little more than a month later, expert gymnast **Christos Papanicolaou**,

Greece's only world class athlete at that time, became the first man to breach the 18ft barrier.

The 1980s were dominated by the astonishing Russian, **Sergey Bubka**. The first man to vault more than six meters, he broke his own record six times and promised even more.

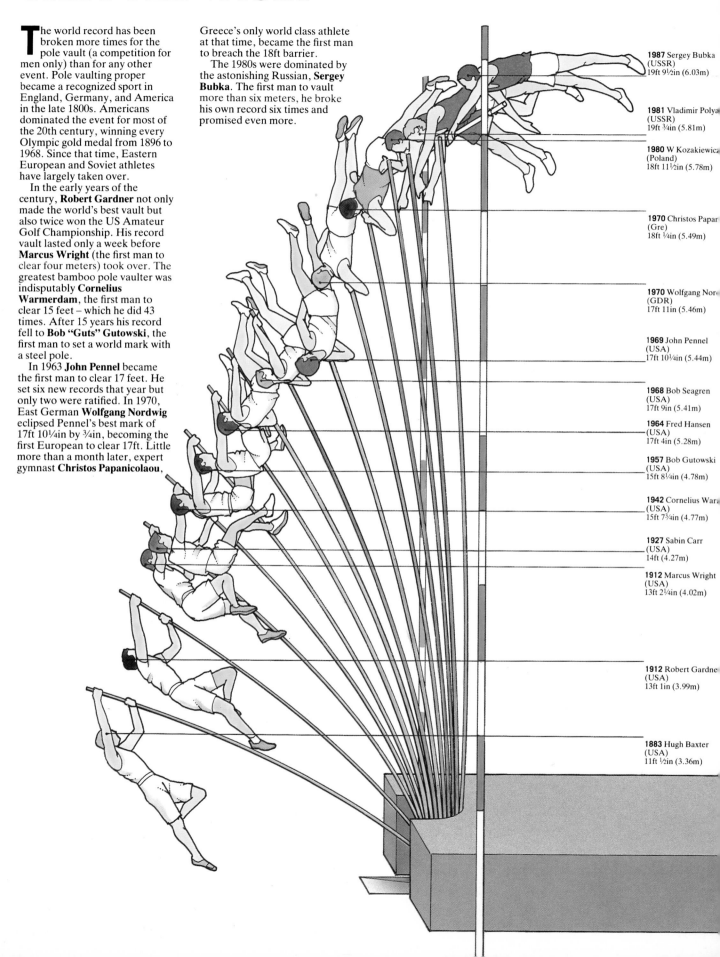

1987 Sergey Bubka (USSR) 19ft 9½in (6.03m)

1981 Vladimir Polya (USSR) 19ft ¾in (5.81m)

1980 W Kozakiewicz (Poland) 18ft 11½in (5.78m)

1970 Christos Papar (Gre) 18ft ¼in (5.49m)

1970 Wolfgang Nor (GDR) 17ft 11in (5.46m)

1969 John Pennel (USA) 17ft 10¼in (5.44m)

1968 Bob Seagren (USA) 17ft 9in (5.41m)

1964 Fred Hansen (USA) 17ft 4in (5.28m)

1957 Bob Gutowski (USA) 15ft 8¼in (4.78m)

1942 Cornelius War (USA) 15ft 7¾in (4.77m)

1927 Sabin Carr (USA) 14ft (4.27m)

1912 Marcus Wright (USA) 13ft 2¼in (4.02m)

1912 Robert Gardne (USA) 13ft 1in (3.99m)

1883 Hugh Baxter (USA) 11ft ½in (3.36m)

THE 19th CENTURY

World Events

1800

General Jean Baptiste Kléber led the French army that defeated the Turks at Heliopolis.
Napoleon defeated the Austrians on the plain of Marengo to recover Italy. A French army under General Moreau smashed the Austrian forces at Hohenlinden and threatened Vienna. The Austrians sued for peace.
Malta was captured by the British.
Louisiana was secretly sold to France by Spain.
The Armed Neutrality of the North consisted of Russia, Denmark, Sweden, and Prussia allied to counter the British right of search on the high seas, and to keep British shipping out of the Baltic.

1801

The Austrians, heavily defeated by the French, signed the Peace of Lunéville.
In Egypt, General Sir Ralph Abercrombie defeated the French army deserted by Napoleon.
The Northern League against Britain was shattered when 18 British ships under Hyde Parker and Nelson sailed into Copenhagen and sank the Danish fleet.
In Russia, Czar Paul was murdered and was succeeded by his son, Alexander I.
Spain declared war on Portugal. Hostilities ended with the Treaty of Badajoz, by which Portugal agreed to close her ports to British shipping.
Cairo was captured by the British, but Turkey later recovered Egypt by treaty with France.

1802

The Treaty of Amiens followed the collapse of the Second Coalition. Britain restored all the conquests she had gained from Holland, France, and Spain, except for Ceylon and Trinidad. France withdrew from Rome, Naples, and Egypt. Malta was returned to the Knights of St John.
Napoleon strengthened his position by making himself Consul for life. But he also put the Revolution on a firm basis. He established the prefecture, improved education and made a compromise with the Church.
Breaking the Treaty of Amiens, Napoleon annexed Piedmont, Parma, and Piacenza.

1803

By the Diet of Ratisbon the German states were reconstructed. Most of the free imperial cities and ecclesiastical princedoms were abolished.
Britain refused to evacuate Malta until Napoleon gave up Piedmont, Parma, Piacenza, and parts of Switzerland.
Napoleon began to assemble a huge fleet at Boulogne and an army of 150,000 at Dunkirk in preparation for the invasion of England. French troops, led by Marshal Mortier, overran Hanover.
British forces captured Tobago and St Lucia from the French, and Berbice, Demerara, and Essequibo from Napoleon's Dutch ally.
Russia and Turkey made peace with France.
France sold Louisiana to the United States.

1804

Napoleon proclaimed himself Emperor, and was subsequently crowned Napoleon I by Pope Pius VII. The *Code Napoléon,* the code of French civil law, drafted by Napoleon, was enforced in all conquered countries.
Britain and Russia united in opposition to France after vain attempts to get Austria and Prussia to join them.
Nationalist feeling brought a Serbian uprising against Turkish rule.
In India, Holkar, Maharajah of Indore, went to war with the East India Company but was vanquished after seven months.
Hobart, Tasmania, was founded.
Haiti gained independence from France.
Spain, urged on by Napoleon, declared war on Britain.

Literature Religion Philosophy

Novalis (Friedrich Leopold von Hardenberg) published *Hymnen an die Nacht,* the archetypal Romantic poem.

What is often regarded as the first modern Italian novel was published, Niccolò (Ugo) Foscolo's *The last letters of Jacopo Ortis.*

Art and Architecture

Goya painted one of the most extraordinary state portraits ever, of *Charles IV and his family.*
Josiah Spode founded a porcelain factory at Stoke-on-Trent at about this time.

English industrialization inspired many Romantic artists: Philippe Jacques de Loutherbourg, a French immigrant, produced *By night,* one of many paintings of Coalbrookdale.

The Palace of Malmaison was restored for Napoleon by Charles Percier and Pierre Fontaine.
The Rococo Twelve Prophets, a life-size statue group, was under way by the remarkable António Francisco Lisboa, Brazilian sculptor and architect.

Thomas Malthus, the English economist produced an enlarged edition of *An Essay on the Principle of Population as it affects the Future Improvement of Society.*

Bertel Thorvaldsen, the Danish artist, impressed Canova with his Neoclassical statue of Jason.

Friedrich Schiller, one of the greatest German dramatists, poets and literary theorists, completed his most popular play, *Wilhelm Tell.*

The ideal city of Chaux, designed but never built by Ledoux, shows his modernist eye in the reduction of buildings to spheres and cylinders.

Performing Arts

Theater censorship was established in France.
Beethoven composed his *First Symphony* and *Third Piano Concerto.*

Niccolò Paganini began composing his 24 *Capricci* for unaccompanied violin.
Ludwig van Beethoven composed his "Moonlight" Sonata.

Beethoven composed his great *Third Symphony,* the "Eroica." The length of the work and size of the orchestra were unprecedented.

Beethoven's "Eroica" Symphony was originally dedicated to Napoleon, but when the composer heard that he had assumed the title of Emperor, he angrily changed his mind and wrote "to celebrate the memory of a great man."

Science and Technology

The battery was invented by Count Volta.
The Royal College of Surgeons was founded in London.
Infrared solar rays were discovered by Sir William Herschel.

The first asteroid, Ceres, was discovered by Italian astronomer Giuseppe Piazzi.

Jean Baptiste Lamarck, French naturalist, coined the term "biology."
American engineer Robert Fulton experimented with a steam-boat on the River Seine.
Johann Wilhelm Ritter, German physicist, built the first accumulator.

English physicist and chemist John Dalton introduced the atomic theory.

English engineer Richard Trevithick built the first successful steam locomotive.
William Hyde Wollaston, the English scientist, isolated palladium from platinum.

America

Land Act set minimum public land purchase at 320 acres.
The US ended its Revolutionary War alliance with France.
Congress met in Washington.

Thomas Jefferson became president and sent ships to blockade Mediterranean ports to protest tribute demanded by Barbary pirates.
The Judiciary Act set Supreme Court justices at five; John Marshall appointed Chief Justice.

The Judiciary Act of 1802 raised the number of Supreme Court Associate Justices to six.
The US Military Academy was established at West Point.

The Louisiana Purchase from France for $15 million gave the US an area from the Mississippi River west to the Rocky Mountains.
Ohio became the 17th state.

Alexander Hamilton was killed in a duel with Aaron Burr.
The Constitution's 12th Amendment provided separate ballots for president and vice-president.
Jefferson was reelected.

NAPOLEON   LOUISIANA PURCHASE   TREVITHICK'S ENGINE

Napoleon proclaimed himself King of Italy, uniting Genoa with France. This provoked the Austrians into becoming the third partner (with Britain and Russia) in the Third Coalition.

The French failed to clear the Channel of the Royal Navy and, as a result, the invasion of England was abandoned. Napoleon turned inland.

Horatio Nelson emphasized Britain's command of the seas off Cape Trafalgar, where, although mortally wounded, he destroyed a Franco-Spanish fleet.

Napoleon inflicted a crushing defeat on a combined Russian and Austrian army at Austerlitz. Emperor Francis II was forced to sue for peace, and by the Treaty of Pressburg had to surrender the Tyrol and all his Dalmatian, Italian and South German possessions.

Napoleon began to distribute European kingdoms and duchies among his relatives.

The marble tomb of the Archduchess Maria Christina in the Augustinerkirche, Vienna, was completed to the design of the Neoclassicist Canova.

The Admiralty in St Petersburg (Leningrad) was begun; designed by Andreyan Zakharov, it is a monument to Neoclassicism.

Niccolò Paganini began to tour Europe as a virtuoso violinist.

Thomas Telford built an iron aqueduct over the Ellesmere Canal.

German chemist Friedrich Sertürner isolated morphine.

Zebulon Pike was sent to explore the upper Mississippi.

The Free School Society was established in New York City.

British forces occupied the Cape of Good Hope.

Joseph Bonaparte became King of Naples and Louis Bonaparte King of Holland.

France and Prussia united against Britain. As a result, Britain declared war on Prussia. France and Prussia quarrelled over Hanover, and Prussia declared war on France. Prussian armies were routed by the French at Jena.

The Confederation of the Rhine was established, uniting a dozen principalities under the protection of France.

The Holy Roman Empire was abolished. Holy Roman Emperor Francis II relinquished his title and became Francis I, Emperor of Austria.

Russia occupied the Danubian Provinces, provoking war with Turkey.

Napoleon began his "Continental System," blockading all British ports and barring continental ports to British shipping.

Wordsworth completed *Ode: Intimations of Immortality from Recollections of Early Childhood.*

The Arc de Triomphe was commissioned by Napoleon but only completed in 1836 under Louis-Philippe to the design of Jean Chalgrin.

Gas lighting was introduced in European cities.

Sir Francis Beaufort, English rear-admiral, designed the scale named after him to measure wind strength.

The Nonimportation Act, banning the importation of certain British goods, was passed in an attempt to force the halt of British attacks on neutral ships and the impressment of US sailors into British service.

The Convention of Bartenstein pledged Russia and Prussia, and subsequently Britain, to expel French forces from Germany.

Turkish Sultan Selim III was deposed by Mustapha IV.

The Treaties of Tilsit were concluded separately between France and Russia and France and Prussia. By the first treaty, the Russians agreed to close their ports to British ships and to force Sweden, Denmark, and Portugal to do the same. By the second, Prussia lost all Polish territories and possessions west of the Elbe and agreed to join the Continental System.

Napoleon invaded Portugal because of its refusal to join the Continental System.

G.W.F. Hegel, German philosopher, published his first great work, *Phenomenology of Mind.*

James Wyatt's extravagant Gothic Revival central tower of Fonthill Abbey, Wiltshire (270 feet), collapsed.

Beethoven straddled the classical and romantic eras, extending the range of sonata form and composing works, such as the *Coriolanus Overture,* inspired by literary ideas.

Robert Fulton's *Clermont* inaugurated the first regular steamboat service along the Hudson River.

The Geological Society of London was founded.

The Embargo Act prohibited trade with any foreign nation.

British ships were ordered from US waters after *Leopard* attacked US *Chesapeake.*

Burr, tried for encouraging the separation of western territory from the US, was acquitted.

The French occupied Rome when Pope Pius VII refused to join the alliance against Britain.

French forces invaded and occupied Spain. King Charles IV and Crown Prince Ferdinand abdicated, and Joseph Bonaparte, King of Naples, became King of Spain. As a result, there was a nationalist revolt. Britain exploited this to attack Napoleon in the Peninsular War.

King Joseph of Spain fled from Madrid because of the threat of Spanish rebels, but Napoleon subsequently captured the city.

A British expedition sent to Portugal defeated the French in the Battle of Vimiero.

Mustapha IV, Sultan of Turkey, was deposed by Mahamed II.

Part I of Faust, Goethe's greatest drama, was published. Part II followed in 1832.

The French Utopian, Charles Fourier, published *The Social Destiny of Man.*

Anne-Louis Girodet de Roucy exemplifies the first phase of the Romantic movement in French art.

Programme music, interpreting the events and moods of a specific story, emerged as a feature of Romanticism, using evocative sounds as in Beethoven's *Pastoral Symphony.*

Joseph Gay-Lussac, a French chemist, announced that gases combine in certain proportions by volume.

Congress prohibited the bringing of African slaves into the US.

James Madison was elected president.

Sir John Moore, in command of a British expedition against the French in Spain, was killed in his retreat to Corunna.

Austria formed an alliance with Britain and declared war on France.

Denmark's victories over Sweden forced Gustavus IV of Sweden to abdicate in favor of Charles XIII.

Arthur Wellesley defeated the French in Spain at Talavera and was rewarded with the title of Duke of Wellington.

Lord Chatham, Pitt's elder brother, commanded the Walcheren Expedition. It failed to capture Antwerp and ended in disaster.

Napoleon defeated the Austrians at Landshut, Eckmühl, and Wagram, and captured Vienna. Austrian Emperor Francis I made huge concessions by the Treaty of Schönbrunn.

The Nazarenes formed a quasi-religious Brotherhood of young German artists.

Orchestral concerts became popular in London, Paris, and Vienna, while the patron and his salon declined in influence.

The polarization of light by reflection was discovered by French engineer and physicist Étienne Malus.

Mounting protests to the embargo resulted in the Non-Intercourse Act, which opened trade with all foreign nations but Britain and France.

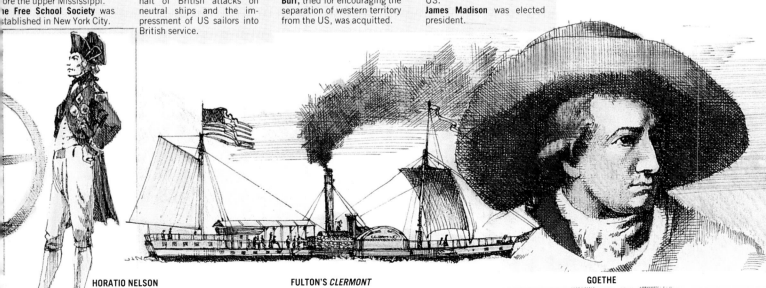

HORATIO NELSON FULTON'S *CLERMONT* GOETHE

World Events

1810

By the Treaty of Paris, Sweden joined Napoleon's Continental System.
In his search for an heir, Napoleon married Marie-Louise of Austria. He continued to tighten his hold on Europe, and by the Rambouillet Decrees ordered the sale of all seized US ships. He annexed Holland after the king had abdicated, and took over Bremen, Lauenburg, Lübeck, Hanover, and Hamburg.
Simón Bolívar, Venezuelan patriot, inspired a number of Latin American states to stage revolutions against their Spanish overlords.
The Duke of Wellington forced into retreat a large French army at Torres Vedras, near Lisbon.
Guadeloupe, the last French colony in the West Indies, was captured by the British.

1811

The Russians captured a Turkish army and entered Belgrade.
The Treaty of Tilsit was again violated by Napoleon. He annexed Oldenburg, thereby alienating Czar Alexander.
François-Charles-Joseph, Napoleon's son and heir, was born and given the title of King of Rome.
British victories over France in the Iberian Peninsula included Wellington's triumph at Fuentes de Oñoro. The French eventually retreated into Spain, leaving Portugal free.
Mamelukes, the ruling family, were murdered in Cairo by Mohammed Alí.
Java was captured by the British.
More Latin American states revolted against Spain, marking the final collapse of Spanish imperial authority.

1812

In Spain, Wellington captured Ciudad Rodrigo and Badajoz, and entered Madrid. He also mauled the French at Salamanca.
After five years of mutual hostility, and resentful of Britain's assumed right to detain its vessels on the high seas, the United States declared war on Britain.
Napoleon forestalled a possible Russo-Swedish alliance by sending his troops once more into Swedish Pomerania and Rügen.
Napoleon assembled an army of 600,000 men drawn from all over Europe for the invasion of Russia. He crushed the Russians at Smolensk and Borodino, and finally entered Moscow, which had been gutted and abandoned. Forced into a disastrous retreat, only 20,000 of his army survived.
In Napoleon's absence, French general Claude François de Malet had conspired to dethrone him and install Louis XVIII as king. The plot was uncovered; Malet was shot.

1813

After revolts against the French, Hamburg was occupied by the Russians. Other European nations began to rise against Napoleon. King Frederick William III of Prussia took the initiative but Napoleon defeated the Prussians and Russians at Lutzen and Bautzen, and captured Dresden.
The Fourth Coalition, formed by Britain, Russia, Prussia, Sweden, and Austria, closed in on Napoleon and forced him back to Leipzig. There, in the "Battle of the Nations," Napoleon was routed.
The French were driven out of Holland and William of Orange returned to his homeland.
Joseph Bonaparte fled from Spain to France after Wellington's victory at Vittoria. Wellington took San Sebastian and Pampeluna, and in France destroyed an army under Marshal Soult and besieged Bayonne.
Mexico declared its independence from Spain.

1814

The Duke of Wellington led the triumphant allied forces into Paris. Napoleon abdicated and was exiled to Elba.
The monarchy was restored under Louis XVIII.
The Congress of Vienna restored monarchs to the Austrian and Prussian thrones and the kingdom of The Netherlands was founded as a buffer against France. Britain won definitive control of the Cape of Good Hope.
The First Peace of Paris was settled mainly by Castlereagh and Austrian chief minister Prince Metternich. France had to renounce all claims to Germany, Italy, The Netherlands, Switzerland and Malta.
Christian Frederick of Denmark was elected King of Norway.
The Treaty of Ghent ended the Anglo-American War.

Literature Religion Philosophy

1810 — **Madame de Staël,** French woman of letters, brilliant conversationalist and friend of Byron, published *De l'Allemagne,* her study of German ways and movements.

1811 — **Die Marquise von O ...** is the most famous work by Heinrich von Kleist.

1814 — **The first of Sir Walter Scott's Waverley novels** was published anonymously.

Art and Architecture

1810 — **Caspar David Friedrich's** *Abbey graveyard under snow* epitomises the mystical quality of his Romantic view.
John Flaxman completed his monument to Nelson in St Paul's Cathedral.

1811 — **James Gillray,** English caricaturist, completed his last work, *Interior of a Barber's Shop in Assize Time.*

1812 — **Thomas Rowlandson,** English caricaturist, began his *Tour of Dr Syntax in search of the Picturesque.*
Joseph Mallord William Turner painted *Snowstorm: Hannibal and his Army crossing the Alps.*

1813 — **Robert Southey** was made English Poet Laureate.
Percy Bysshe Shelley completed and privately printed *Queen Mab,* a long poem which expressed his philosophical ideas.

1812 — **Lord Byron** published the first cantos (parts) of *Childe Harold's Pilgrimage.*

1814 — **John Soane** completed two of his greatest works, the Dulwich College Picture Gallery and his own house at 13 Lincoln's Inn Fields, London. Goya's *May 3rd 1808,* depicting the massacre of Madrid citizens by French troops, is his greatest painting.

Performing Arts

1810 — **The San Carlo Opera House** in Naples was founded.
A greater variety of orchestral instruments allowed richer tonal contrasts.

1811 — **This year saw the establishment of** two new music publishers in London, Novello & Co. and Chapell & Co.

1813 — **The waltz** became the most popular dance in Europe.
The Royal Philharmonic Society was founded in London.

1814 — **Beethoven's only opera,** *Fidelio,* was a triumph.

Science and Technology

1811 — **Avogadro's hypothesis,** about the characteristics of gases, was named after Italian chemist and physicist Amedeo Avogadro.
The Luddite riots involved unemployed English domestic weavers who destroyed new machines, fearing the impact of mechanization.

1810 — **The Krupps works** opened at Essen in Germany.
Samuel Hahnemann, a German physician, founded the practice of homeopathy.

1812 — **The hardness of materials** was classified by German mineralogist Friedrich Mohs.

1813 — **The first practical cartridge** was devised by French inventor Samuel Pauly for the .59 breech-loading rifle.

1814 — **Chemical symbols,** as used today, were introduced by Jöns Berzelius, a Swedish chemist who later made a correct list of atomic weights.

America

1810 — **Macon's Bill No. 2** opened trade with Britain and France, but the US, deceived by Napoleon, renewed the Non-Intercourse act with Britain.

1811 — **US-British** tensions increased after confrontations at sea. War Hawks in Congress urged war with Britain.

1812 — **In naval battles,** the US was victorious, but **Detroit and Ft. Dearborn** were lost to the British.
Louisiana became the 18th state.
Madison was reelected president.

1813 — **New England** ports were left open, but Britain blockaded others. The US burned York (Toronto); the British burned Buffalo.
Oliver Perry won US control of Lake Erie in a naval battle.

1814 — **After US victories** in the north (Lake Champlain) and mid Atlantic (at Baltimore after the British burned Washington), peace was made.
Andrew Jackson's victory at Horseshoe Bend ended the Creek War.

SIMON BOLIVAR

LUDDITES   SHELLEY   WELLINGTON

Ferdinand I regained the Italian throne.
Napoleon escaped from Elba and landed in France. Louis XVIII fled as the "Hundred Days" (of Napoleon's liberty) began. The Fifth Coalition, made up of Britain, Austria, and Prussia, was formed against France.
Napoleon was finally defeated at Waterloo, in Belgium, by Wellington. He was banished to St Helena.
Under the Second Peace of Paris, France was restricted to her 1790 boundaries, looted art treasures had to be returned, a 700-million-franc war indemnity was to be paid, and an allied army of occupation was to be installed.
The Holy Alliance was an agreement signed by the crowned heads of Austria, Russia, and Prussia. They pledged themselves to conduct policy on Christian principles and to uphold order in Europe.

The Vicomte de Chateaubriand began his *Mémoires d'outretombe* for posthumous publication.

Jean-Auguste-Dominique Ingres completed his *Grande Odalisque,* a Classical nude distorted to enhance the body's curve.

The quadrille was danced in England for the first time.

The safety lamp was invented by English chemist Sir Humphry Davy to prevent explosions in mines.

The US under Jackson defeated the British at New Orleans, both sides unaware that the war was over.
Treaties ended Barbary Coast piracy after the US showed force in Algiers.

Brazil became an independent empire under Prince John, Regent of Portugal.
Maria, Queen of Portugal, died insane and was succeeded by her son John VI.
Argentina became independent of Spain.
Bavaria joined the Holy Alliance.
Metternich opened the Diet of German Confederation at Frankfurt.

Coleridge published his great poetic fragment, *Kubla Khan.*

The Regent's Park and Regent Street development was in progress, the lasting monument to John Nash, English architect and city planner.
Lord Elgin sold the Elgin Marbles to the British Museum.

The first genuine German song cycle had its première; *An die Ferne Geliebte* by Beethoven.
The metronome was perfected by German musician Johann Nepomuk Maelzel.
Opera centered on Paris. The light lyricism of *The Barber of Seville* by Gioacchino Rossini was overwhelmingly popular.

The single wire telegraph was erected by English inventor Francis Ronalds.
Photography was born out of the experiments of French physicist Joseph Nicéphore Niepce.
The kaleidoscope was invented by British scientist Sir David Brewster.
The stethoscope was invented by French physician René Laënnec.

Martin v. Hunter's Lessee affirmed the Supreme Court's authority over state courts.
Indiana became a state.
James Monroe was elected president.

The first immigrants settled the Australian grasslands.
Trade with the West Indies was opened up for Britain by an Anglo-Spanish treaty.
The Serbians were granted partial autonomy by Turkey.
Sweden joined the Holy Alliance.
The Third Mahratta War began in India against the British.

Persuasion, the last of Jane Austen's six novels, was published posthumously.
Coleridge, a brilliant prose writer and literary critic as well as poet, wrote *Biographia Literaria.*
David Ricardo, who systematized the science of economics, published *Principles of Political Economy and Taxation in England.*

Thomas Rickman's *An Attempt to Discriminate the Styles of English Architecture* introduced such terms as "decorated" and "perpendicular" Gothic to classify English medieval architecture.

Full gas lighting was introduced at Drury Lane Theatre, London.
Rossini launched two successful operas, *La Cenerentola* (Cinderella) in Rome, and *La Gazza Ladra* (The Thieving Magpie) in La Scala, Milan.

Baron Jöns Berzelius discovered selenium and lithium.

Bonus Bill's federal financing of roads and canals was vetoed by Monroe.
Naval strength on the Great Lakes was limited by the Rush-Bagot Agreement to eight ships each for Britain and US.

The US and Canadian border was defined as the 49th Parallel.
Only Nepal, the Sikh and Sind States, and Afghanistan were independent of British rule in India.
The Bavarian constitution was proclaimed. Prussia was divided into 10 provinces.
Charles XIII of Sweden died and was succeeded by Jean Bernadotte as Charles XIV.
Chile and Venezuela became independent from Spain.
The Congress of Aix-la-Chapelle was held by Britain, Austria, Prussia, Russia, and France to discuss the indemnity paid by France. The withdrawal of allied troops from France was agreed.
The Zulu Empire was founded by military chieftain Chaka.

Shelley began his epic lyrical drama *Prometheus.* His close friend, **Thomas Love Peacock,** published his best-known satirical novel, *Nightmare Abbey,* while his wife, **Mary Wollstonecraft Shelley,** published the most influential tale of terror ever written, *Frankenstein.*

John Crome's masterpiece, *The Poringland Oak,* was painted without Romanticism, in the Dutch realist tradition.
The replanning of Italian cities began with Turin.

The first steamship, the *Savannah,* crossed the Atlantic in 26 days.
Prussian astronomer Friedrich Wilhelm Bessel listed 3,222 stars in his *Fundamenta Astronomiae.*

Jackson marched against Seminole Indians in Spain's East Florida.
Illinois became the 21st state.

Singapore was founded by the East India Company, represented by British administrator Sir Stamford Raffles.
Florida was bought by the US from Spain.
Simón Bolívar became President of Greater Colombia.
Freedom of the press was achieved in France.
Political activity in Germany was suppressed by the Carlsbad Decrees.

John Keats wrote *La Belle Dame sans Merci* and the great odes *On Melancholy, To a Nightingale, On a Grecian Urn* and *To Psyche.*
The first cantos of Byron's picaresque verse satire, *Don Juan,* were published.
The German philosopher Arthur Schopenhauer published his main work, *The World as Will and Idea.*

The White Horse was John Constable's first "six-footer" to be exhibited at the Royal Academy.
Théodore Géricault, the great French Romantic artist, completed his *Raft of the Medusa.*

Beethoven became stone deaf.

The flat-bed cylinder press for printing was built by David Napier.
Electromagnetism was discovered by Danish physicist Hans Christian Oersted.

In **Adams-Onis Treaty,** the US acquired East Florida and gave up Texas claims.
Supreme Court cases *Dartmouth College v. Woodward* and *McCullough v. Maryland* were blows to states' rights.
Alabama became the 22nd state.

NAPOLEON   **DAVY'S LAMP**   **JANE AUSTEN**   **THE SAVANNAH**

World Events

1820

During a revolution in Spain, King Ferdinand VII was captured by liberal rebels. He was forced to restore the constitution of 1812 and abolished the Inquisition.
The Duc de Berry, heir presumptive to the French throne, was assassinated.
French press censorship was reimposed.
Egypt began the conquest of Sudan.
King George III of England died. He was succeeded by the Prince Regent as George IV. The accession was followed by a general election with Tory success.
As a protest against John VI's living in Brazil, a revolution broke out in Portugal with demands for a constitution.

1821

The nationalist Greek war for independence from the Ottoman Empire began after a revolt in Moldavia.
Spain lost Mexico, Peru, Panama, Guatemala, and Santo Domingo.
After a revolution in Piedmont, King Victor Emmanuel abdicated in favor of his brother, Charles Felix.
The Congress of Laibach authorized Austria to suppress uprisings in Piedmont and Naples.
Napoleon died on St Helena.

1822

Brazil achieved independence from Portugal. Colombia and Ecuador also became independent from Spain.
The Greeks proclaimed their independence, whereupon the Turks captured the Greek island of Chios and massacred its Christian inhabitants.
The Congress of Verma, met to discuss the problems of Greece and Spain.
Liberia, in West Africa, was founded as a colony for freed American slaves.

1823

A Spanish liberal revolt was crushed with French help.
The Monroe Doctrine asserted that the American continent could no longer be an arena for European colonial activity.
War between France and Spain broke out. France reestablished Ferdinand VII on the throne.
Mexico became a republic after Augustus de Iturbide was forced to abdicate.
Provincial diets were set up in Prussia.

1824

The Anglo-Burmese Wars began, following Burmese aggression. Britain began the annexation of Burma.
Lord Byron, English poet, died at Missolonghi, helping the Greeks in their struggle against the Turks.
Louis XVIII of France died. He was succeeded by his brother, Charles X, who proceeded to subdue signs of growing liberalism in France.
Simón Bolívar proclaimed himself Emperor of Peru.
Egyptian forces captured Crete.
The Greeks routed the Turks at Mitylene.

Literature Religion Philosophy

1820

Washington Irving, published *The Sketch book of Geoffrey Crayon, Gent.,* a collection of short stories which included *Rip Van Winkle.*
Méditations poétiques by Alphonse de Lamartine influenced the development of the Romantic movement in France.

1821

William Hazlitt, English essayist, published *Table Talk,* one of his most famous collections.
E.T.A. Hoffmann, German writer, composer and caricaturist, published his fourth volume of *Tales* of fantasy and the supernatural.

1822

Thomas de Quincey's *Confessions of an English Opium-Eater* was published.

1823

Charles Lamb, English essayist, critic and fine letter-writer, published *Essays of Elia,* with a second volume ten years later.
Isaac D'Israeli, father of Benjamin Disraeli, completed his 30 year work, *Curiosities of Literature.*
Hymn to Liberty was composed by Count Dhionisios Solomós, first poet of modern Greece.
John Galt completed his fine novel, *The Entail.*

1824

Eugène Delacroix depicted a grisly contemporary event from the Greek War of Liberation, *The Massacre at Chios.*

Art and Architecture

1820

In this year, Constable exhibited *Flatford Mill* at the Royal Academy, in the next, *The Hay-Wain.*

1822

Géricault began a series of portraits of the mentally ill.
Louis-Jacques-Mandé Daguerre and C.M. Bouton opened their Diorama in Paris.
St Pancras Church, London, was completed. It was designed by William Inwood.

1823

Hokusai began his *Thirty-six Views of Mount Fuji.*
Nash completed the fantastical Royal Pavilion in Brighton for the Prince of Wales.

1824

The symphony found new depths of expression, especially with Beethoven, as a personal creation requiring a large orchestra. His *Ninth Symphony* is a fine example.

Performing Arts

1820

Conductors became necessary to marshal the expanded orchestra.

1821

Der Freischutz by Carl Maria Ernst von Weber established German Romantic opera.

1822

Schubert began his "Unfinished Symphony."
Franz Liszt made his debut as a pianist in Vienna at the age of 11.
The Royal Academy of Music was founded in London.

1823

Beethoven completed his *Missa Solemnis,* the Mass in D.

Science and Technology

1820

André Ampère, French physicist and mathematician, founded and named the science of electrodynamics.

1821

The thermocouple, an instrument for measuring temperature as electricity, was invented by Russo-German physicist Thomas Seebeck.
Sound reproduction was demonstrated by British physicist and inventor Sir Charles Wheatstone.
The fundamentals of electromagnetic rotation were discovered by British physicist and chemist Michael Faraday.

1822

The world's first iron railroad bridge was built on the Stockton-to-Darlington line by British engineer George Stephenson.
The first permanent photograph was made by the French inventor Joseph-Nicéphore Niepce.

1823

Michael Faraday succeeded in liquifing chlorine.
A rudimentary calculator was built by British mathematician Charles Babbage.

1824

Sadi Carnot, French army officer and engineer, published *On the Motive Power of Fire,* in which he showed that only a fraction of the heat produced by burning fuel in an engine is converted to motion, which depended only on the temperature difference in the engine. This was the basis of modern thermodynamics.

America

1820

The Missouri Compromise prohibited slavery in the northern Louisiana Purchase, but guaranteed a balance of free and slave states.
Maine, the 23rd state, joined the Union as a free state.

1821

Moses Austin and his son Stephen became the first Americans to settle in Spanish Texas.
Missouri, the 24th state, was admitted as a slave state.
The Santa Fe Trail opened as a trade route in the southwest.

1822

The US recognized Mexico as an independent country.
President Monroe vetoed a bill to establish tolls to pay for repairs to the Cumberland Road.
The first cotton mills began production in Massachusetts.

1823

The Monroe Doctrine; European interference in the Western Hemisphere would be considered interference in US affairs.

1824

A treaty with Russia set the US northwest boundary at 54° 40'.
Texas was annexed by Mexico.
John Quincy Adams was elected president.

ANDRE AMPERE   HOKUSAI: *THE WAVE*   LORD BYRON

1825

Charles X alienated bourgeois support in France by restoring to nobles land lost in the revolution.
Egyptian forces invaded Greece.
Bolivia and Uruguay declared their independence. Brazil and Argentina went to war over Uruguay.
Ferdinand I of Naples died and was succeeded by Francis I.
Maximilian I, King of Bavaria, died and was succeeded by his son Louis I.
Czar Alexander I of Russia died and was succeeded by his younger son, Nicholas I.

Alessandro Manzoni, Italian writer and patriot, began his masterpiece, I promessi sposi (The Betrothed).

João Baptista da Silva Leitão de Almeida Garrett introduced Romanticism to Portugal in his epic poem, Camões.

The first treatise on the art of musical accompaniment was published in Paris by Ferdinando Carulli.

The first public steam railroad opened in England between Stockton and Darlington. The first train was drawn by Locomotion No 1, built by British engineer George Stephenson.
Michael Faraday isolated benzene.
Horse-drawn buses appeared in London.
The Menai Straits suspension bridge was completed in Wales, the crowning achievement of Thomas Telford.

Factionalism grew in the South while Adams's policies got support elsewhere.
The Erie Canal opened.
The US began the removal of Indians to western lands.

1826

The Portuguese Civil War began when John VI of Portugal died and his eldest son, Dom Pedro, elected to stay in Brazil. He resigned Portugal to his daughter, Maria da Gloria, but his brother, Miguel, usurped the throne. This led to civil war, with Britain going to the aid of Maria.
The Turks captured Missolonghi from the Greeks.
War broke out between Persia and Russia because Turkey trespassed into Transcaucasia.
The Burmese War ended with the Treaty of Yandabu.
Dost Mohammed became Amir of Kabul.

The Last of the Mohicans is the most famous of James Fenimore Cooper's five "Leatherstocking" stories, the first truly original American novels.
The Plain Speaker was published. It included some of Hazlitt's best essays.

Felix Mendelssohn produced the incidental music to Shakespeare's play, A Midsummer Night's Dream.

The first German gasworks were erected at Hanover.
Italian physicist Leopoldo Nobili invented the galvanometer.
Otto Unverdorben, a German chemist, obtained aniline from indigo.

Thomas Jefferson and John Adams both died on July 4, the nation's birthday.

1827

The Treaty of London was signed by Britain, France, and Russia to protect the Greeks from Turkish tyranny. A combined British, Russian, and French fleet under Admiral Edward Codrington destroyed a Turko-Egyptian fleet in Navarino Bay.
Count Kapodistrias was elected President of Greece.
The Russians defeated the Persians and captured Erivan, in Armenia.
Dom Miguel of Portugal became engaged to his niece Maria and was made regent.

Delacroix painted The Death of Sardanapalus, inspired by the hero of Byron's drama.
Samuel Palmer, English painter and etcher of visionary landscapes, entered his most productive period.

Franz Schubert composed the Trout Quintet, so-called because the fourth of the five movements is a set of variations on his song, The Trout.
Ludwig van Beethoven died.

English physician Richard Bright described the disease that bears his name.
Joseph Ressel, an Austrian engineer, invented the ship's screw propeller.
Robert Brown, a British botanist, observed the random movement of particles.
Ohm's law, relating current, voltage, and resistance, was laid down by German physicist Georg Ohm.

Proponents of higher tariffs presented a plan to Congress to protect domestic cotton and woollen material and iron industries. Southern states opposed the plan because of their reliance on imported manufactures.

1828

The Miguelite Wars broke out in Portugal. Regent Dom Miguel overthrew the government, deposed Maria, and proclaimed himself King of Portugal after a coup d'état.
Russia declared war on Turkey. This was settled by the Peace of Turkmantchai. Persia ceded part of Armenia to Russia.
The Treaty of Rio de Janeiro established Uruguay as an independent buffer state between Argentina and Brazil.
The London Protocol, concluded by Britain, France, and Russia, recognized Greek independence.

Franz Schubert died, shortly after producing his "Great" C Major Symphony.
Paganini arrived in Vienna and set out to refute rumors that he had been in prison between 1801 and 1804.

The polarimeter, which analyzes the passage of polarized light through matter, was developed by British physicist William Nicol.
Embryology was founded by the German biologist Karl Baer.
Organic chemistry began with the synthesis of urea by German chemist Friedrich Wöhler.

The Tariff of Abominations, which set unreasonable tariffs on raw materials, was passed. The South Carolina legislature refused to recognize.
Andrew Jackson was elected president.

1829

Turkey recognized the independence of Greece after British and Russian intervention.
Greater Colombia was divided into Colombia, Venezuela, Ecuador, and New Granada.
Suttee (the Indian custom of immolating a widow with her dead husband) was declared illegal in British India.
Russia and Turkey signed the Treaty of Adrianople.

Honoré de Balzac, supreme French novelist, began his life work, The Human Comedy, 40 volumes of stories which included his most famous piece, Father Goriot (1834–35).

The redesigned St James's Park was completed in London, to Nash's scheme.

The mouth organ, the Chinese sheng, arrived in Vienna.
Felix Mendelssohn revived Bach's music after a century of eclipse, thereby starting to lend it the status it enjoys today.

Scottish chemist Thomas Graham formulated the law on diffusion of gases.
George Stephensons' locomotive, Rocket, won the Liverpool and Manchester Railway Competition.

Jackson relied heavily on his "Kitchen Cabinet" as unofficial advisors. He was the first president to use the "spoils system", or patronage, extensively.
The Workingmen's Party was formed in Pennsylvania.

STEPHENSON'S LOCOMOTION NO 1   THE PROPELLOR   PAGANINI

1830

World Events

The French liberal opposition expelled Charles X, replacing him with King Louis-Philippe. This sparked off a liberal and nationalist revolt in Belgium, which became independent of The Netherlands.
National risings in Italy and Germany were unsuccessful.
The French established their authority in Algiers.
Greece was formally declared to be independent under the protection of Britain, Russia, and France.
Simón Bolívar abdicated as President of Colombia and died later in the year.
George IV died and William IV, third son of George III, became King of Britain.
Ferdinand II became King of Naples.
A revolution in Poland erupted against Russian rule.

Literature Religion Philosophy

The Church of Jesus Christ of the Latter-day Saints (Mormonism) was founded.
Stendhal (Marie-Henri Beyle) published his most famous novel, *Scarlet and Black*.
The challenge to Classicism represented by Victor Hugo's play *Hernani* provoked clashes between traditionalists and the new Romantics.

Art & Architecture

Performing Arts

Hector Berlioz made inspired use of the orchestra in the "program music" of his *Symphonie fantastique*.

Science and Technology

Non-Euclidean geometry was developed by Russian mathematician Nikolai Lobachevski.
Paraffin was discovered by German naturalist and industrialist Karl von Reichenbach.
The Liverpool to Manchester railroad was formally opened.

America

Daniel Webster (Massachusetts) and Robert Hayne (South Carolina) debated in the Senate over states' rights.
The Cumberland Road Bill was approved by Congress.

1831

The Young Italy group was launched by Italian patriot Giuseppe Mazzini in Italy.
Austria suppressed uprisings in Modena, Parma, and the Papal States.
Dom Pedro I of Brazil abdicated in favor of his son, Pedro II.
The Russians suppressed the Polish revolution and entered Warsaw.
Britain and France guaranteed Belgian independence. Leopold of Saxe-Coburg became Leopold I, King of the Belgians.
Count Kapodistrias, President of Greece, was assassinated.
The East India Company annexed Mysore.

Victor Hugo, one of the most important and prolific French writers, published *The Hunchback of Notre-Dame*.
Aleksandr Pushkin, the greatest Russian poet, completed his verse novel, *Yevgeny* (Eugene) *Onegin*, and published his famous play, *Boris Godunov*.
The first congregation of the Plymouth Brethren was established in Devon, England.

Electromagnetic induction was discovered by British physicist Michael Faraday.
Sir James Clark Ross, Scottish explorer, determined the position of the magnetic North Pole.

Jackson and Vice-President John Calhoun split over the reputation of Secretary of War John Eaton's wife Peggy.
The Nat Turner insurrection against whites in Virginia resulted in execution of 13 blacks.

1832

Egypt and Turkey went to war. The Turks were heavily defeated at the battle of Koniah.
Prince Otto of Bavaria was elected King of Greece as Otto I.
The Polish constitution was abolished.
Holland was forced to recognize Belgian indpendence when the French captured Antwerp.

George Sand, pen name of Amandine Dudevant, found immediate fame with the publication of her first novel *Indiana*.

Ingres' excellence as a portraitist is revealed in his strong image of *Monsieur Louis-François Bertin*.

The Romantic ballet *La Sylphide* was first performed.
Frédéric Chopin, a Polish exile working mostly in Paris at this time, wrote dazzling short pieces for piano in such forms as nocturne, mazurka, and polonaise.

Karl von Reichenbach discovered creosote in wood tar.
Corrugated iron was manufactured by John Walker of Rotherhithe in London.

The Tariff of 1832, which revised the 1828 tariff, failed to appease the South.
The Black Hawk War resulted in defeat of Sac and Fox Indians.
Presidential candidates were nominated at the first party conventions.

1833

British sovereignty was proclaimed over the Falkland Islands.
Prussia established Zollverein (customs union) in Germany. This became the focus of German nationalism.
Turkey recognized the independence of Egypt, ceding Syria and Aden.
The Treaty of Unkiar Skelessi between Turkey and Russia closed the Dardanelles to all but Russian ships.
Ferdinand VII of Spain died. He was succeeded by Queen Isabella II.
Slavery was abolished throughout the British Empire.

The Oxford Movement, which believed in a "catholic," undivided Church, was established.
Jules Michelet began his monumental *History of France*.

The Royal William, a Canadian vessel, was the first steamship to cross the Atlantic wholly under its own power.
The Wheatstone bridge (named after Sir Charles Wheatstone) for the comparison of electrical resistances, capacitances, and inductances, was devised by English mathematician Samuel Hunter Christie.
The electric telegraph was built in Göttingen, Germany, by Wilhelm Eduard Weber and Karl Friedrich Gauss.

Jackson, reelected in 1832, removed funds from the Bank of the US and deposited them among 23 state banks.
The Force Bill authorized military power to enforce tariff laws.
The American Anti-Slavery Society was established.

1834

Regional opposition to the liberal Spanish regime led the Carlist Wars, in support of Don Carlos.
Britain, France, Spain, and Portugal formed the Quadruple Alliance to protect the Spanish and Portuguese governments.
Dom Miguel of Portugal abdicated. Dom Pedro died and was succeeded by Queen Maria da Gloria who had the throne restored to her.
The colony of Victoria, in Australia, was founded.

Frei Luís de Sousa, one of the greatest Portuguese plays of the century, was written by Garrett.
Edward Bulwer Lytton, 1st Baron Lytton, published his most famous historical novel *The Last Days of Pompeii*.

Robert Schumann, German composer, was an arch-Romantic, especially in his evocative piano music such as *Carnaval*. He founded the avant-garde publication *Neue Zeitschrift für Musik* (The New Music Journal).

Electrical self-induction was discovered by Michael Faraday.
Louis Braille, French musician, inventor, and teacher, perfected a system of characters to help the blind to read.

The Whig Party, in opposition to the Jackson administration, was formed by southerners John Calhoun and Henry Clay and northerner Daniel Webster.
Maryland workers, protesting conditions, were put down by federal troops.

HECTOR BERLIOZ MICHAEL FARADAY BRAILLE

King Louis-Philippe of France renounced his radical support and introduced strict censorship. An unsuccessful assassination attempt on him was made by Corsican patriot Giuseppe Fieschi.
British trade with China increased after the East India Company's monopoly ended.
Some 4,000 Boers in South Africa began the Great Trek to find new territory free from British rule.
Francis I of Austria died: Ferdinand I succeeded him.
The dictatorship of Juan Manuel de Rosas, Governor of Buenos Aires, began in Argentina.
English became the official government language in India.

Hans Christian Andersen published the first volume of his *Tales, Told for Children.*
Adolphe Quételet, Belgian statistician, published *A Treatise on Man and the Development of His Faculties* in which the theory of probability was applied to social phenomena in relation to the "average man."

Jean-Baptiste-Camille Corot, French landscape painter who influenced the Impressionists, began a particularly delicate *View of Avray.*

The Colt pistol, the first repeating firearm, was patented by American Samuel Colt.
The first botanical laboratory was established at Kew, near London, by English botanist William Hooker.

The Southern states imposed harsh penalties for circulating antislavery literature.
Loco-Focos, a radical faction of Jacksonian Democrats, formed its own party and platform.

Texas declared itself independent of Mexico, reinforcing its claim with a victory over the Mexicans at the Battle of San Jacinto.
Adolphe Thiers became premier of France but resigned seven months later, after urging the invasion of Spain.
The Federation of Peru and Bolivia was proclaimed. Chile declared war on the federation.
Louis Napoleon was exiled to the United States after failing to take Strasbourg.
Adelaide became the capital of South Australia.

François Rudé completed his sculpture group, *Departure of the volunteers, 1792,* on the Arc de Triomphe in Paris, combining classical detail with Romantic verve.

Mikhail Glinka, in such works as *A Life for the Czar,* heralded the rise of a Russian national school, using folk music and inspired by the Napoleonic Wars.

A great railroad building boom began in Britain.
The needle-gun was invented by German gunsmith Johann Nikolaus von Dreyse.

The Alamo Massacre began Mexican Santa Anna's campaign in Texas. After his capture at San Jacinto, Texas declared itself an independent republic.
Arkansas became the 25th state.

King William IV of Britain died and was succeeded by Queen Victoria. Hanover became separated from England because female succession was forbidden by Salic Law. Hanover's King Ernest Augustus, Duke of Northumberland, suppressed the constitution.
In Spain, a liberal constitution was proclaimed.
The Republic of Natal was proclaimed by Dutch settlers in southern Africa.

Following its triumph in serial form, Charles Dickens published his first major novel, *The Pickwick Papers.* A spokesman for the conscience and sentimentality of his age, Dickens is generally regarded as the greatest English novelist.

Northern Neoclassical architects built in Greece: Friderich von Gärtner's Old Palace was begun in Athens.

Isambard Kingdom Brunel, an engineer of great originality and daring, saw the completion of the Great Western, the first transatlantic steamship.
The Morse code was invented by Samuel Morse.
German educator Friedrich Froebel opened the first kindergarten, near Blankenburg.
Isaac Pitman, English phonographer, invented his system of shorthand.
The electrical telegraph was patented in Britain by Charles Wheatstone and English electrical engineer William Fothergill Cooke.

The Panic of 1837 resulted in unemployment and bank failures.
The Gag Rule was adopted as a way to ignore antislavery petitions in Congress.

The Boers routed the Zulus in the Battle of Blood River in Natal.
The French occupied Vera Cruz and declared war on Mexico.
The first Anglo-Afghan War broke out as Britain attempted to restrict Russian influence.
The first regular steamship communication began between England and the United States with the *Great Western* and the *Sirius.*
Slavery was abolished in India.

George Cruikshank, the renowned English caricaturist, illustrated Charles Dicken's *Oliver Twist* after successfully contributing to the novelist's Sketches by "Boz." These were the most famous of the 850 books he illustrated.

Jenny Lind, the "Swedish Nightingale", coloratura soprano, made her debut in Stockholm in Weber's *Der Freischütz.*

Stellar parallax was detected by Prussian astronomer Friedrich Bessel, showing that the stars lie at immense distances from the Earth.
The science of biochemistry was founded by German chemist Baron Justus von Liebig.

Tension built along Canadian-US border with burning of the American steamer *Caroline,* an American's murder, and the **Aroostook War** over the Maine-New Brunswick boundaries.
Charles Wilkes surveyed Pacific Ocean water routes.

Aden was occupied by British forces.
The Turks invaded Syria but were defeated at the Battle of Nesib.
The Treaty of London established the international status of independent Belgium.
The Peru-Bolivian Federation was dissolved after being defeated by Chile.
Uruguay declared war on Argentina.
Sultan Mahmud II of Turkey died and was succeeded by his son, Abdul Mejid.
The Opium Wars between Britain and China began.
Frederick VI of Denmark died and was succeeded by his nephew, Christian VIII.

One of Turner's finest late works was The *"Fighting Téméraire" Tugged to her Last Berth to be Broken Up, 1838.*

Mendelssohn conducted the first performance of Schubert's *Symphony in C Major.*

Vulcanization was invented by the American inventor Charles Goodyear.
The anatomy of animal and plant cells was first described by German biologists Theodor Schwann and Matthias Schleiden.
Photography was invented (independently) by French painter Louis Daguerre — with his daguerreotype — and British scientist William Fox Talbot.

The antislavery Liberty Party, which pledged loyalty to the Union, was founded. By 1848, it had merged with the Free-Soil Party.

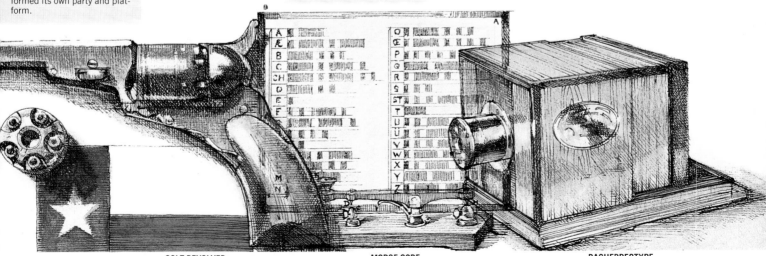

COLT REVOLVER   MORSE CODE   DAGUERREOTYPE

	1840	**1841**	**1842**	**1843**	**1844**
World Events	Frederick William III of Prussia died and was succeeded by Frederick William IV. **By the Treaty of Waitangi,** Maori chiefs ceded sovereignty to Britain and New Zealand became a Crown Colony. **The Carlist Wars** in Spain ended. **By the Treaty of London,** Britain, Russia, Prussia, and Austria agreed to limit Egyptian expansion. **King William I** of Holland resigned in favor of his son, William II. **Louis Napoleon** attempted an unsuccessful coup in France and was imprisoned for life in the fortress of Ham. **The Afghan War ended** with the Afghans surrendering to Britain.	**The Straits Convention** between Russia, Britain, France, Austria, and Prussia closed the Dardanelles and Bosphorus to foreign shipping. **The Convention of Alexandria** confirmed that Mohammed Ali would be the hereditary ruler of Egypt. **Britain proclaimed its sovereignty** over Hong Kong. **Lajos Kossuth** became the Hungarian nationalist leader. **The Second Afghan War** began after the massacre of British officers by Afghans. **Sir James Clark Ross,** Scottish explorer, discovered the Great Southern Continent.	**The Treaty of Nanking** ended the Opium Wars and opened Chinese ports to British trade. **British forces in Afghanistan** surrendered at Kabul and were wiped out during their retreat to India. **The Boers** established the Orange Free State in southern Africa. **The Second Afghan War** ended with a British victory.	**In India,** Charles Napier captured and formally annexed Sind. **General Baldomero Espartero,** regent and virtual dictator of Spain, was overthrown and expelled from the country. Isabella II became Queen. **Maori revolts** against the British broke out in New Zealand. **Hawaii** became independent.	**Utopian socialism** became popular in France among intellectuals and the working classes. **Charles XIV,** King of Sweden and Norway, died and was succeeded by his son, Oscar I. **Weavers** rioted in Bohemia and Silesia. **Karl Marx** met Friedrich Engels in Paris. **An assassination attempt** on Frederick William IV of Prussia failed. **The Treaty of Tangiers** ended the French war in Morocco.
Literature Religion Philosophy	**Pierre-Joseph Proudhon** created a sensation with *What is Property?*: in it he stated "property is theft." **A Hero of Our Time** by Mikhail Lermontov greatly influenced the development of Russian psychological realism. **Edgar Allan Poe,** great American writer of the macabre, published one of his major works, *Tales of the Grotesque and Arabesque.*	**The Essence of Christianity,** by the German philosopher Ludwig Feuerbach, advocating humanistic atheism, influenced Karl Marx.	**Dead Souls,** satirical and a mixture of realism and fantasy, was the masterwork of Nikolai Gogol who was largely responsible for advancing Russian literature to the first world rank. He was also the author of the comedy, *The Government Inspector* (1836). **The final volume** of Auguste Comte's *Course of Positive Philosophy* was published. He founded Positivism and advanced the science of Sociology.	**Soren Kierkegaard,** Danish religious philosopher, published *Either/Or.* The book expressed the basic tenets of Existentialism. **John Stuart Mill,** great Victorian philosopher and political economist, published his first major work, *A System of Logic.*	**Alexandre Dumas père** published *The Three Musketeers* and began *The Count of Monte Cristo,* his two most famous novels. **Ralph Waldo Emerson's** second volume of *Essays* enhanced his international reputation. American poet and lecturer, he was the leading exponent of New England Transcendentalism. **The Babi movement,** which developed into the Bahai religion, was founded in Persia by Ali Muhammed. It emphasized the unity of mankind.
Art and Architecture	**The reconstruction of the Palace of Westminster** (Houses of Parliament), London, was begun to the design of Charles Barry and Augustus Pugin.	**Théodore Chassériau's** painting, *The Toilet of Esther,* shows the influence of his master, Ingres. **Augustus Pugin,** advocate of the English Roman Catholic and Gothic revivals, published a revised edition of *Contrasts,* which suggested an intimate link between the quality of a society and its architecture.		**Modern Painters** was begun by John Ruskin. Its influence on Victorian tastes was enormous.	
Performing Arts		**The supreme Romantic ballet** was first performed; *Giselle* choreographed by Jules Perrot and Jean Coralli. **The saxophone** was invented by Belgian Adolphe Sax.	**The Philharmonic Society of New York** was founded. **The polka,** a dance of Czech origin, became popular.	**Richard Wagner's** opera, *The Flying Dutchman,* was produced in Dresden.	**Brass bands,** especially in Germany, produced a popular music of their own. **Joseph Joachim,** Hungarian violinist and composer, made his London debut playing Beethoven's *Violin Concerto,* with Mendelssohn conducting.
Science and Technology	**Jean-Louis Agassiz,** a Swiss naturalist, showed that an Ice Age had once occurred. **Artificial fertilizer** was first prepared by Baron Justus von Liebig.	**The carbon-zinc battery** was invented by German chemist Robert Wilhelm Bunsen. **The British Pharmaceutical Society** was founded.	**Anaesthesia** had its beginning when American surgeon Crawford Long operated on an etherized patient. **The steam hammer** was invented by Scottish engineer, James Nasmyth.	**Brunel's Great Britain,** the first iron-hulled steamer powered by a screw propeller, crossed the Atlantic. **English physician James Prescott Joule** determined the amount of work required to produce a unit of heat. **Carl Gustav Mosander,** Swedish chemist, discovered the metallic element erbium.	**Samuel Morse's telegraph** transmitted its first messages, between Baltimore and Washington.
America	**President Van Buren** supported the Independent Treasury Act to establish independent depositories for federal funds. **William Henry Harrison** was victorious over incumbent president Van Buren.	**Harrison died,** and Vice President Tyler succeeded him. **Whig attempts** to establish a national bank were vetoed by Tyler. **The Supreme Court** freed black slaves who mutinied in the *Amistad Case.*	**Webster-Ashburton Treaty** set the US-Canadian border between Maine and New Brunswick. **The unofficial election** of Thomas Dorr as Rhode Island governor by a rebel group in favor of universal male suffrage brought about martial law.	**The Anti-Catholic** American Republic party was formed in New York City to oppose demands for voting privileges, funds for parochial schools, and restrictions regarding the use of the Protestant Bible in public schools.	**The dispute** over Oregon's boundaries and Texas annexation were key issues in the presidential campaign won by Democrat dark horse James K. Polk. Opposition to annexation cost Van Buren the Democratic nomination.

PENNY BLACK   POE'S MACABRE VISION   THE SAXOPHONE   RICHARD WAGNER

1845

A new Spanish constitution was proclaimed.
More Maori risings erupted against the British in New Zealand.
The Anglo-Sikh Wars broke out in India. Britain annexed the Punjab.
Texas was annexed by the United States.

A posthumous collection of work by Giacomo Leopardi was published as *Thoughts*. Personal hardship colored all Leopardi's work.
Benjamin Disraeli, twice Prime Minister of England, was also a fine novelist; *Sybil; or, The Two Nations,* published this year, is his most famous.

The St Geneviève Library was begun in Paris. Designed by Henri Labrouste, it was one of the earliest buildings with an iron-based interior.

Richard Wagner's opera *Tannhäuser* showed early promise of the composer's genius for fusing the elements of music and stage drama as one.

The hydraulic crane was invented by Sir William George Armstrong.
American inventor Erastus Brigham Bigelow built a power loom for weaving carpets.
Acetic acid was synthesized for the first time by German chemist Adolf Kolbe.

The Polk Doctrine favored US possession of Oregon Territory as "manifest destiny".
Florida became the 27th state. When **Texas** was admitted to the Union as the 28th state, Mexico broke off relations with the US.

1846

A revolt began in Poland. Austria took Cracow.
A new pope, Pius IX, raised natioanlist hopes in Italy.
The United States declared war on Mexico.
A revolution in Portugal, started by supporters of Dom Miguel, forced dictator Costa Cabral into exile.
In southern Africa, Kaffirs fought against the British. The first signs of segregation were seen when Zulu reserves were set up in Nâtal.
After more victories by Hugh Gough, the Sikhs settled for peace with the Treaty of Lahore.
Louis Napoleon escaped from his Ham fortress to London.

Prosper Mérimée published *Carmen,* a novella which formed the basis of Bizet's greatest opera of 1875.

Eugène-Emmanuel Viollet-le Duc, French Gothic Revival architect and medievalist, began his first restoration project, the Abbey of Saint-Denis.
The Gothic Revivalist Smithsonian Institute, Washington, D.C., was designed by James Renwick.

Mendelssohn presented his second and last great oratorio, *Elijah,* in Birmingham.

Nitroglycerine was discovered by the Italian chemist Ascanio Sobrero.
Neptune was discovered by the German astronomer Johann Galle.
Gun-cotton was invented by German chemist Christian Schönbein.

The Oregon boundary was set at the 49th parallel.
The Independent Treasury Act of 1840 was revived and passed.
A Mexican attack on Ft. Texas forced a US declaration of war.

1847

The United States invaded Mexico and occupied the capital, defeating Mexico after conflict over Texas.
Liberal hopes in Prussia were raised when the Landtag (legislative assembly) was called by the king, who asked for funds to build railroads.
Portuguese rebels were crushed by royal troops. The civil war ended with the Convention of Gramido.
Poland became a Russian province.
The Straits Settlements became a Crown Colony.
Liberia proclaimed its independence.
Gold was discovered in California.

Emily Brontë wrote *Wuthering Heights* and her sister, Charlotte, published *Jane Eyre*. The next year saw the publication of Ann Brontë's *Tenant of Wildfell Hall*.

Turner's painting, *Venice from the Steps of the Europa,* was hung in the National Gallery, London.
Rudé produced perhaps the most remarkable Romantic sculpture, *Bonaparte Awakening to Immortality,* illusionistic, realistic and odd.
The Neoclassical British Museum was completed, the most important work of Sir Robert Smirke.

The rotary printing press was invented by American industrialist Richard Hoe.
Evaporated milk was manufactured for the first time.
Britain's Factory Act ruled that women and young people between 13 and 18 years of age were prohibited from exceeding a 10-hour day.

In the Mexican War, US troops conquered the south-west.

1848

Christian VIII of Denmark died and was succeeded by Frederick VII.
Metternich resigned in Austria after a revolution in Vienna. Emperor Ferdinand I abdicated in favor of his nephew, Franz Joseph.
In a year of revolutions, there were uprisings in Sicily, Milan, Naples, Berlin, Parma, Venice, Rome, Warsaw, Prague and Budapest. Most of them were quickly suppressed but that in Rome forced Pope Pius IX to flee.
The Second Sikh War began.
Prussia invaded Denmark.
An outburst of urban radicalism brought the expulsion of King Louis-Philippe in France and the establishment of a republic. Louis Napoleon was elected president. Slavery was abolished in the French colonies.
Hungary declared itself independent.

The Communist Manifesto was written by Karl Marx and Friedrich Engels.
W.M. Thackeray's masterpiece, *Vanity Fair,* was published.
The Christian Socialism Movement was founded in England.

The Pre-Raphaelite Brotherhood of painters was formed.
Daumier was the first Impressionist: his lithographs of this date have contours dissolved by light.

Franz Liszt toured the capitals of Europe and established the symphonic poem while at Weimar.

Hydrotherapy was introduced at Worrishofen, in Germany, by German priest Sebastian Kniepp.

The Treaty of Guadalupe Hidalgo brought the US territory north of the Rio Grande, California, and New Mexico.
The discovery of gold in California precipitated a rush.

1849

The Sikhs, defeated by British forces, surrendered at Rawalpindi.
Rome was proclaimed a republic under Giuseppe Mazzini.
Charles Albert of Sardinia abdicated in favor of his son, Victor Emmanuel II.
The German National Assembly elected King Frederick William IV of Prussia "Emperor of the Germans," but he declined the invitation.
After Hungary had declared its independence it surrendered to the Austrians at Vilagos.
Sardinia resumed its war with Austria. This ended with the Peace of Milan.
Revolts broke out in Dresden and Baden.
French troops entered Rome and restored Pope Pius IX, in spite of determined resistance from Garibaldi and his followers.

Thomas Macaulay, Whig historian, began his great unfinished work, the *History of England*.

John Ruskin published *The Seven Lamps of Architecture. In this and The Stones of Venice* (1851–53), he upheld the Gothic style for its truth to nature and its moral worth.

Richard Wagner took part in the Dresden revolt and was forced to flee to Zurich.

Reinforced concrete was invented by French engineer Joseph Monier.
Armand Fizeau, French physicist, measured the speed of light.

Zachary Taylor, a Whig and a Mexican War hero, was inaugurated as president.

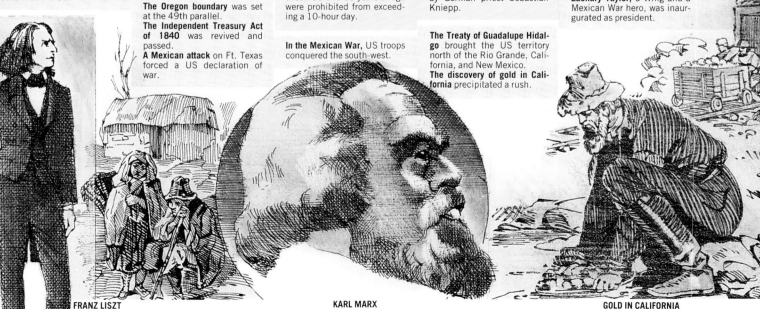

FRANZ LISZT   KARL MARX   GOLD IN CALIFORNIA

	1850	**1851**	**1852**	**1853**	**1854**
World Events	The German Confederation was restored under Austrian leadership by the Treaty of Olmütz. **Pope Pius IX** re-entered Rome. **The Peace of Berlin** was concluded between Denmark and Prussia. **The Eighth Kaffir War** began. **The vastly destructive Taiping Rebellion** broke out in China.	**Gold** was discovered in Australia. Victoria became a separate colony. **Cuba** proclaimed its independence. **Louis Napoleon** staged a *coup d'état* in France. Most French people favored a new constitution. **The Austrian constitution** was abolished.	**The English in India** subdued Burma. **The Sand River Convention** established the South African Republic (Transvaal), recognized by Britain. **General Rosas** was overthrown in Argentina. **A new constitution for New Zealand** provided for representative government. **Louis Napoleon** set up the Second Empire as Napoleon III, Emperor of France.	**Europe** experienced an economic boom. **Russia and Turkey** went to war after a controversey between Greek and Romanist monks over the custody of the holy places in Jerusalem. Russia favored the Greeks, while Turkey, backed by Napoleon III, sided with the Romanists. The Russians destroyed a Turkish fleet off Sinope. **Maria II** of Portugal died and was succeeded by her son Pedro V. **Peace was concluded** between Britain and Burma. **France** annexed New Caledonia.	**The Crimean War** developed into a struggle of an alliance of Britain, France, Turkey, and Sardinia against Russia. Russia invaded Turkish European territory, claiming to protect Christians in Turkish lands and demanding free passage for its warships. But the Russians were defeated in the battles of Balaclava (the scene of the charge of the Light Brigade) and Inkerman, and endured a bitter siege at Sebastopol. **Austria and Prussia** formed a defensive alliance against Russia. **Abbas I,** Viceroy of Egypt, died and was succeeded by Mohammed Said.
Literature Religion Philosophy	**In Memoriam** won Alfred, Lord Tennyson the friendship of Queen Victoria and the position of Poet Laureate. **The Prelude,** Wordsworth's autobiographical epic poem and testament to the Romantic age, was published soon after the poet's death. **Nathaniel Hawthorne,** great allegorical and imaginative American writer, wrote his masterpiece, *The Scarlet Letter.*	**The American novelist, Herman Melville,** completed his masterpiece, *Moby Dick,* which anticipated the obsessive quality of many modern novels. It was not a success. **The French brothers Goncourt** began their fascinating *Journal,* a diary written as a single voice for 45 years.	**Uncle Tom's Cabin,** Harriet Beecher Stowe's anti-slavery novel, is cited as a cause of the American Civil War, such was its impact.		**Henry Thoreau,** influential American writer and practical philosopher, published his account of Transcendentalism in his masterwork, *Walden: or, Life in the Woods.*
Art and Architecture	**Dante Gabriel Rossetti,** Pre-Raphaelite painter and poet, published *The Blessed Damozel* in the first issue of *The Germ,* the Brotherhood's magazine. **John Everett Millais's** *Christ in the House of His Parents* caused outrage when exhibited at the Royal Academy.	**Verdi's opera** *Rigoletto,* based on Victor Hugo's play *Le roi s'amuse,* was staged for the first time in Venice. **The Italian Straw Hat** by Eugène-Marin Labiche, foremost comic French playwright, was performed for the first time.	**The awakening conscience,** begun at this time, is William Holman Hunt's most famous work. It was typical of the Pre-Raphaelite movement. **A group of oaks near Barbizon** epitomies the work of Théodore Rousseau and of the Barbizon School in general. **Robert Schumann's** incidental music for Byron's drama *Manfred* was first performed at Weimar.	**Verdi's** opera, *La Traviata,* was based on *La Dame aux camélias* (Camille), a recent play by Alexandre Dumas fils. **Late Romantic composers** such as Richard Wagner and Anton Bruckner aimed for grandeur by using large forces and a rubato (freer) beat to savor the sound. **Henry Steinway** and his sons began the manufacture of their famous pianos in New York City.	**Gustave Doré,** prolific and highly successful book illustrator, completed an edition of *The Works of Rabelais.* **Robert Schumann** attempted suicide by throwing himself into the Rhine. He was confined in an asylum for the last two years of his life.
Performing Arts	**The work of composers** such as Liszt gave music a mystical aura.	**The first submarine cable** was laid, from Dover to Calais. **The rotation of the Earth** was demonstrated conclusively by French physicist Jean Foucault. **The sewing machine** was developed by American inventor Isaac Singer.	**A new theory of organic compounds** was formulated by French chemist Charles Frédéric Gerhardt. **French engineer Henri Giffard** made the first airship flight.		
Science and Technology	**The second law of thermodynamics** was enunciated by German mathematical physicist Rudolf Clausius. **The Bunsen burner** was invented by the German chemist Wilhelm Bunsen.	**The schooner America** won the first 60-mile race that became known as the **America's Cup.** A US sailboat would win every race until 1983.	**Uncle Tom's Cabin** galvanized Northern antislavery sentiment and was used as abolitionist propaganda.	**By the Gadsden Purchase,** the US agreed to buy nearly 30,000 square miles of territory in present-day New Mexico and Arizona from Mexico for $10 million, to settle the border with Mexico and obtain a railroad route to the Pacific.	**German watchmaker Heinrich Goebel** invented a primitive electric light bulb. **Symbolic logic** was founded by George Boole, a British mathematician, with his *Laws of Thought.*
America	**The Compromise of 1850** was introduced before the Senate by Henry Clay to reduce tensions between slave and free states. Following a bitter debate, it passed.				**Commodore Matthew Perry** concluded a treaty with previously isolated Japan, opening it to US trade. **The Kansas-Nebraska Act** allowed each US territory to choose to be slave or free.

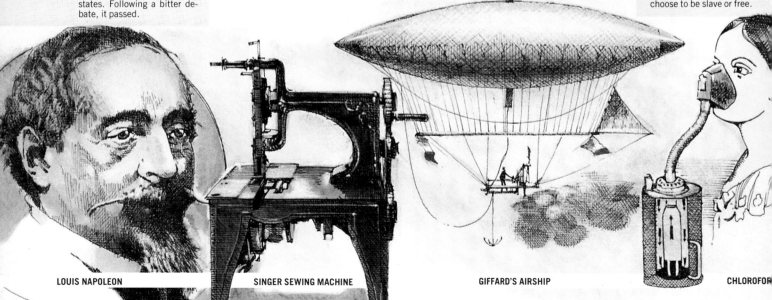

LOUIS NAPOLEON   **SINGER SEWING MACHINE**   **GIFFARD'S AIRSHIP**   **CHLOROFOR**

Czar Nicholas I of Russia died and was succeeded by Alexander II.

The Treaty of Peshawar made allies of Britain and Afghanistan in a war against Persia.

The Russians in Sebastopol finally surrendered to the besieging Allies.

Sweden joined Britain and France against Russia.

The Taiping rebellion was crushed by the Chinese.

The Paris World Exhibition was opened.

Scottish missionary and explorer David Livingstone discovered the Victoria Falls on the River Zambezi.

The first of many revised and enlarged editions of *Leaves of Grass* by Walt Whitman was published.

Ivan Turgenev completed his play *A Month in the Country.*

Westward Ho! is Charles Kingsley's best-known novel. His children's book, *The Water-Babies,* was published in 1863.

Gustave Courbet, founder of the French Realist school, completed (in only six weeks) his enormous masterpiece, *The Artist's Studio.*

The first synthetic plastic material, later named celluloid, was patented by the British chemist Alexander Parkes.

The printing telegraph was invented by London-born American inventor David Edward Hughes.

Conflict between proslavery and free state factions escalated in Kansas.

The consolidation of four Illinois railroad lines connected the Midwest with the East coast.

Lord Dalhousie, Governor-General of India, dethroned the King of Oude because of his tyranny, and annexed his kingdom.

The Crimean War ended with the Treaty of Paris. Britain, France, and Austria guaranteed the independence of Turkey. The Black Sea was declared neutral and the virtual independence of Serbia was recognized by the major European powers.

The Persian capture of Herat in Afghanistan led to war with Britain.

The Arrow War, in which Britain and France sided against China, broke out when the *Arrow,* a ship flying the British flag, was boarded by Chinese forces and the crew arrested.

Natal and Tasmania became self-governing colonies.

The Blind Girl was one of Millais's greatest public successes, its sentiment and technical excellence well attuned to Victorian tastes.

Friedrich Carl Bechstein, German piano-maker, founded his first factory in Germany.

Mauve, the first artificial dye, was derived from aniline by British chemist William Perkin and was soon seen in textiles. Production of the new synthetic substances stimulated the growth of modern organic chemistry.

Steel was produced cheaply in the converter patented by British metallurgist Henry Bessemer.

A virtual civil war between pro- and anti-slavery elements continued to rage in "Bleeding Kansas". John Brown and other abolitionists murdered five proslavery settlers.

Democrat James Buchanan won the presidential election.

The Peace of Paris ended the Anglo-Persian War, with the shah recognizing the independence of Afghanistan.

Garibaldi formed the Italian National Association for unification.

The Indian Mutiny, a series of mutinies by Sepoy troops and scattered popular uprisings against British rule, was ruthlessly suppressed. Before it was over, Sepoys had massacred soldiers and civilians, captured Cawnpore and besieged Lucknow.

A Chinese fleet was destroyed by the Royal Navy; British and French forces took Canton.

The emancipation of Russian serfs began unde Czar Alexander II.

Madame Bovary, a realistic portrayal of bourgeois life, was Gustave Flaubert's masterpiece. The author narrowly missed conviction for the novel's alleged immorality.

Charles Baudelaire was less fortunate, convicted for obscenity and blasphemy when his volume of poetry, *Les Fleurs du mal,* was published.

Charles Hallé founded the Hallé Orchestra in Manchester, England.

The Atlantic cable was completed.

French chemist Louis Pasteur proved that fermentation was caused by living organisms.

Elisha Graves Otis, American engineer, installed the first safety lift.

The Supreme Court ruled in the Dred Scott decision that the Missouri Compromise was unconstitutional and that slaves were not citizens.

Napoleon III escaped an assassination attempt by Italian nationalist Felice Orsini.

By the Government of India Act, British rule in India was transferred to the Crown.

British forces raised the siege of Lucknow, and the Indian Mutiny came to an end.

By the Treaty of Aigun, Russia gained the Amur region from China.

The Treaties of Tientsin resulted in the end of the Anglo-Chinese War and the opening of Chinese ports for trade.

Lake Tanganyika was discovered by British explorers Sir Richard Burton and John Speke.

Turkey and Montenegro went to war.

Nadar (Gaspard-Felix Tournachon) had taken the first aerial photograph by this date, from a balloon.

Edgar Degas, before his technique became Impressionistic, painted the *Bellini family* portrait.

The principles of molecular structure were discovered by Friedrich August Kekulé von Stradonitz, a German chemist.

Atomic weights and chemical formulae were standardized by Italian chemist Stanislao Cannizzaro.

British surgeon Joseph Lister studied coagulation of the blood.

The Great Eastern, the largest ship in the world at that time, at 27,000 tons, was launched.

Senate candidate Abraham Lincoln met his opponent Stephen A. Douglas in a series of debates that established Lincoln's national reputation although he was defeated.

Minnesota became the 32nd state in the union.

France signed a treaty of alliance with Sardinia and declared war on Austria when that country invaded Sardinia. The Austrians defeated French forces at Magenta and Solferino, and the war ended with the Peace of Villafranca.

Piedmont drove the Austrians from northern Italy with French assistance.

Spain declared war on Morocco.

King Oscar I of Sweden died and was succeeded by Charles XV.

Charles Darwin's *On the Origin of Species by Means of Natural Selection ...* revolutionized human knowledge and, in its day, was the subject of much controversy.

La Légende des Siècles, a collection based on history and legend, included Victor Hugo's most impressive poetry.

The Red House, Bexley Heath, was designed by Philip Webb for William Morris, founder of the Arts and Crafts movement.

Jean-François Millet completed his most famous painting, *The Angelus.*

Grand opera carried the Romantic ideal to a peak in the works of Giuseppe Verdi.

Spectrum analysis was discovered by German physicist Gustav Robert Kirchoff and chemist Robert Wilhelm Bunsen.

John Brown led 21 followers on a raid on the arsenal at Harper's Ferry, Virginia, hoping to foment a slave rebellion. Brown and six others were hanged.

FLORENCE NIGHTINGALE   LOUIS PASTEUR   *THE GREAT EASTERN*   CHARLES DARWIN

	1860	**1861**	**1862**	**1863**	**1864**
World Events	In the Italian War of Independence the Italians expelled the Austrians from Parma, Modena, Tuscany, and Romagna, and united with Piedmont. **Garibaldi** and his "1000 Redshirts" conquered Naples and Sicily. Victor Emmanuel II was proclaimed King of Italy. The first Italian Parliament convened at Turin. **British and French troops** entered Peking and brought the Anglo-Chinese War to an end. **The Second Maori War** began in New Zealand. **Spain and Morocco** made peace. **Abraham Lincoln** was elected 16th President of the United States on an anti-slavery platform. As a result, South Carolina seceded from the Union. **Vladivostock** was founded. **The Treaty of Vienna** ended the war between Austria and Italy.	**Italy**, except for Rome and Venice, was united as one kingdom. **Frederick William IV** of Prussia died and was succeeded by William I. **The Confederate states** of America were formed by South Carolina and 10 other states. Civil war broke out between these and the Union. **Serfs in Russia** were freed. **Sultan Abdul Mejid** of Turkey died and was succeeded by his brother, Abdul Aziz. **Pedro V** of Portugal died and was succeeded by Louis I.	**Zanzibar's independence** was recognized by Britain and France. **Cochin-China** became a French protectorate. **Garibaldi** planned to conquer Rome but was captured by Royalist troops. **Otto von Bismarck** became Prime Minister of Prussia.	**Civil war in Afghanistan** followed Dost Mohammed's death. **William, Prince of Denmark,** was recognized as King George I of Greece. **French troops** occupied Mexico City and set up a puppet emperor, Archduke Maximilian. **Ismail** succeeded Mohammed Said as Viceroy of Egypt. **Schleswig** became a Danish province. **A revolution began in Poland** after the National Committee published its manifesto. **Cambodia** became a French protectorate. **The first international postal congress** opened in Paris. **Frederick VII** of Denmark died and was succeeded by Christian IX.	An allied Western expedition participated in a violent civil war in Japan. **Karl Marx** presided over the First International in London. **By the Peace of Vienna,** Austria and Prussia took Schleswig-Holstein and Lauenburg from Denmark. **Italy** renounced all claims to Rome. Florence replaced Turin as the capital. **King Maximilian II** of Bavaria died and was succeeded by Louis II. **Queen Maria Cristina** returned to Spain. **The Geneva Convention for the Protection of Wounded** (the Red Cross) was established. **The most important event of the century in China** reached its dénouement: the Taiping Rebellion, a radical Christian-communist movement, conceived in 1850, was crushed with western aid. Some 20 million people had lost their lives.
Literature Religion Philosophy	*The Mill on the Floss* is George Eliot's greatest novel. Eliot was really Mary Anne Evans; like the Brontë sisters, she chose a male pseudonym.	**Francis Turner Palgrave** compiled the first edition of *The Golden Treasury of English Songs and Lyrics*.	**Hugo's** novel, *Les Misérables,* an epic about the people of Paris, was an international success on publication. **Christina Rossetti,** sister of Dante Gabriel, published her first major collection of poems, *Goblin Market and other poems.* **Fathers and Sons** was Turgenev's greatest novel, the hero, Bazarov, a triumph of objective portraiture.	**Rossetti's** *Beata Beatrix* reflects his admiration for the great Italian poet, Dante Alighieri.	
Art and Architecture	**The imposing St Michel fountain in Paris** combined the skills of the sculptor Duret with those of the architect Gabriel Davioud. **Arthur's Tomb** reflects Rossetti's new direction: an enthusiasm for the legendary past rather than truth to nature was the guiding force in his later paintings.	**Morris, Marshall, Faulkner & Co.,** an association of "fine art workmen," was founded in England, with William Morris at the helm. Their aim was to reform the applied arts.	**The most famous early painting** by James McNeill Whistler was his *Symphony in White No. 1: The White Girl.*	**Edouard Manet** painted his two most controversial works, *Le Déjeuner sur l'Herbe* and *Olympia.* Acceptable forms — a Raphael original for one, the classic Venus for the other — were made acceptable in a contemporary setting.	**Julia Margaret Cameron** took her first photographic portraits at about this time. She was inspired by the Pre-Raphaelite and Romantic movements.
Performing Arts	**The first modern Welsh Eisteddfod** was held.	**The Royal Academy of Music** was founded in London.	**French actress Sarah Bernhardt** made her debut at the Comédie-Française in Racine's *Iphigénie en Aulide.* **The catalog of Mozart's works** was prepared by Austrian music librarian Ludwig von Köchel.	**The opera Faust,** by Charles Gounod, was produced in London, Dublin, and New York.	**Negro spirituals** emerged in the United States as blacks took up the singing school tradition of colonial America, but mixed with it a rhythmic work-song style.
Science and Technology	**The first practical internal-combustion engine** was invented by French engineer Etienne Lenoir.	**Colloids** were distinguished by British chemist Thomas Graham, who also discovered osmosis. **Daily weather forecasts** began in Britain. **The skeleton of an archaeopteryx,** the link between reptiles and birds, was unearthed at Solnhofen in Germany. **HMS Warrior,** the first all-iron warship, was completed in England.	**The open hearth process** for the production of steel was developed in France. **German botanist Julius von Sachs** proved that starch is produced by photosynthesis. **American inventor Richard Jordan Gatling** devised his rapid-fire 10-barrel machine-gun.	**The first underground railroad** opened in London. **English geologist Henry Clifton Sorby** discovered the microstructure of steel, which led to the development of the science of metallurgy. **Ebenezer Butterick,** American inventor and tailor, developed the first paper dress patterns.	**French chemist Louis Pasteur** discovered that microorganisms can be destroyed by heat, a process named after him, now known as pasteurization.
America	**Lincoln** defeated Stephen A. Douglas in the election. **South Carolina** became the first Southern state to secede from the Union.	**Mississippi, Florida,** Alabama, Georgia, Louisiana, Texas, Arkansas, North Carolina, Tennessee, and Virginia followed to form the Confederate States of America. Confederates fired on Fort Sumpter. **Kansas** joined the Union.	**The Confederates** achieved major eastern victories including Bull Run and Fredericksburg. The Union gained in the West, and its *Monitor* met the *Merrimack* in the first ironclad ship battle.	**The Emancipation Proclamation** freed slaves in rebel states. The South lost at Gettysburg.	**Gen. Ulysses S. Grant** became the Union commander. The South retreated, with Atlanta and Savannah falling to General Sherman and Adm. David Farragut breaking the Confederate blockade.

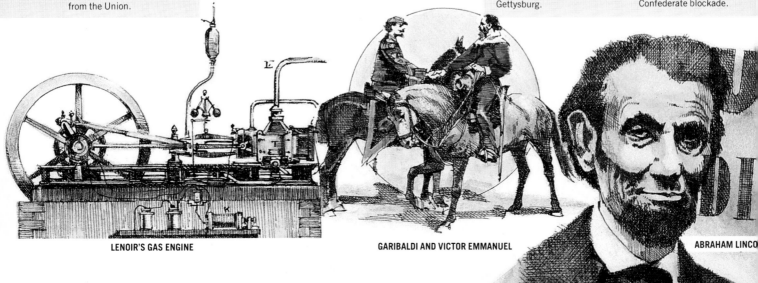

LENOIR'S GAS ENGINE   **GARIBALDI AND VICTOR EMMANUEL**   **ABRAHAM LINCOLN**

The American Civil War came to an end when Confederate General Lee surrendered to Union General Grant at Appomattox, Virginia.
Abraham Lincoln was assassinated by actor John Wilkes Booth while attending a play at Ford's Theater in Washington.
Bismarck and Napoleon III met at Biarritz.
Paraguay declared war on Argentina, Brazil, and Uruguay.
The Second Maori War ended. Wellington was made the capital of New Zealand.
Leopold I of Belgium died and was succeeded by his son, Leopold II.

Ford Maddox Brown, an associate of the Pre-Raphaelite Brotherhood, completed his ambitious "real allegory," *Work.*
George Gilbert Scott, English Gothic Revival architect, designed the grand Midland Hotel attached to St Pancras Station, London. His Albert Memorial was under construction at this time.

Light opera centred on Paris and Vienna, with the theatrical humor of Jacques Offenbach and the lavish settings of the younger Johann Strauss.

The Massachusetts Institute of Technology was founded.
Genetics was founded with the publication of the experiments of Austrian botanist Gregor Mendel.
Joseph Lister pioneered antiseptic surgery by applying carbolic acid to a compound wound.

Lincoln was succeeded by Andrew Johnson.
Slavery was abolished by the 13th Amendment.

Peru declared war on Spain.
An alliance was formed between Italy and Prussia against Austria. Prussia invaded Holstein, Saxony, Hanover, and Hesse.
Prussia defeated the Austrians at Sadowa. Austria ceded Venice to Napoleon III.
The war between Austria and Prussia ended with the former's defeat and the Peace of Prague. The North German Federation was set up.

The first volume of *Le Parnasse Contemporain* was published; objective verse opposed to Romanticism.
Algernon Charles Swinburne, English poet and critic, published his first series of *Poems and Ballads.*

The Palais de Justice, Brussels was begun. Designed by Joseph Poelaert, the gigantic classical building dominates the city.

English actor-manager Sir Henry Irving made his London stage debut.
Richard Wagner revolutionized opera, using a continuously moving harmonic structure over which the *leitmotiv* (short theme) identified dramatic elements.

Dynamite was invented by Swedish chemist and industrialist Alfred Nobel.
The dynamo was invented by William Siemens.
The Aeronautical Society was founded in London.

The 14th Amendment established full national citizenship for blacks.
In Congressional elections, Radical Republicans, bent on punishing the South, achieved power.
The Ku Klux Klan was formed.

The Dominion of Canada was established by the British North America Act.
The dual monarchy of Austria-Hungary was established. Franz Joseph of Austria became also King of Hungary.
Russia sold Alaska to the United States for less than 2 cents an acre.
The London Conference guaranteed the neutrality of Luxembourg.
The Abyssinian War began when Theodore, King of Abyssinia, imprisoned the British Consul and some missionaries.
Garibaldi marched on Rome but was defeated by French troops and captured.
In Japan, Shogun Yoshinobu resigned. This led to the abolition of the shogunate and the restoration of the Meiji dynasty. Edo was renamed Tokyo and became the nation's capital.

Volume I of Marx's *Das Kapital* was published.
Emile Zola the first Realist novelist in France, began his controversial career with *Thérèse Raquin.*

Claude Monet's famous Women in the Garden has all the spontaneity of his later Impressionist work, without the free technique.

Johann Strauss the Younger composed *The Blue Danube* waltz.

French engineer Joseph Monier patented a process for manufacturing reinforced concrete.
A railroad was completed through the Brenner Pass.

The Reconstruction Act divided the South into five districts new state constitutions.
The fee paid for **Alaska** was $7,200,000.
Nebraska became 37th state.

Sir Charles Napier made an epic dash across Abyssinia to rescue the British captives.
Russia occupied Samarkand.
Michael III, King of Serbia, was assassinated and was succeeded by Milan IV.
The Third Maori War began.
A liberal revolt in Spain forced Queen Isabella to flee to France.

Robert Browning, one of the great poets of the Victorian age, began his finest work, *The Ring and the Book.*

Daumier's *Don Quixote* paintings have an eerie realism unmatched by other illustrators of Cervantes.
Paul Cézanne began his controversial portrait of *Achille Empéraire,* a dwarf treated with heroism. Rejected from the Salon, it inspired great animosity.

Richard Wagner's awareness of sounds and mastery of original orchestration found full expression in his opera *The Mastersingers of Nuremberg.*

The skeleton of Cro-Magnon man from the Upper Paleolithic Age was found in France by Louis Lartet.
American inventor and manufacturer George Westinghouse invented the air brake for passenger trains.

The House passed articles of impeachment against President Johnson, but the Senate voted his acquittal.
In the presidential elections former Union commander Grant was elected as a Republican supporting Reconstruction.

The Greeks agreed to withdraw from Crete after a Turkish ultimatum.
A new Spanish Constitution was proclaimed.
Napoleon III once more adopted a parliamentary system for France.
Tunis was bankrupt and accepted control by Britain, France, and Italy.
The German Social Democratic Party was founded.

Leo Tolstoy completed his enormous epic, *War and Peace.*
Matthew Arnold, poet, critic and long-standing inspector of English schools, analyzed the maladies of his age in *Culture and Anarchy.*

Jean-Baptiste Carpeaux completed his lively sculptural group, *The dance,* for the façade of the Paris Opera.

The science of eugenics was founded by English explorer and scientist Sir Francis Galton with his *Hereditary Genius, Its Laws and Consequences.*
The Suez Canal was opened by Empress Eugénie, consort of Napoleon III.
The *Cutty Sark,* record-breaking British clipper, was launched.
Dmitri Mendeleyev, Russian chemist, devised the first form of the periodic table of the elements.

A financial panic occurred on Black Friday (24 September) when speculators James Fisk and Jay Gould attempted to corner the gold market.
The Central Pacific and Union Pacific Railroads were joined.

US CIVIL WAR   BENJAMIN DISRAELI   WILLIAM GLADSTONE   SUEZ CANAL

World Events

The war ended between Paraguay and the allied forces of Brazil, Argentina, and Uruguay.
Queen Isabella of Spain abdicated in favor of her son Alfonso. But Amadeus, Duke of Aosta, was elected king.
The Franco-Prussian War began with France's declaration of war on Prussia. After a series of defeats, the French surrendered at Sedan. Napoleon III was captured.
After a revolution in Paris, the second French Empire came to an end and the third French Republic was established.
Paris was besieged by Prussian armies.
The Papal States were annexed by Italy. Rome became the nation's capital.

Paris surrendered to Prussian forces after a bitter siege.
Prussia's seizure of Alsace-Lorraine completed German unification and a German Empire was proclaimed under William I.
A revolutionary commune was set up in Paris, rejecting the authority of the French government after the surrender to Prussia. It was ruthlessly suppressed.
Louis Thiers was elected first President of the Third French Republic.
The Peace of Frankfurt ended the Franco-Prussian War. France was forced to pay a heavy indemnity.
Britain annexed the Kimberley diamond fields in South Africa.
British journalist Henry Morton Stanley met Livingstone at Ujiji, on the shores of Lake Tanganyika.

The Earl of Mayo, Viceroy of India, was assassinated.
In the Spanish civil war, the Carlists were defeated and Don Carlos fled to France.
Thomas François Burgess was elected President of the Transvaal Republic.
The League of the Three Emperors — William I of Germany, Franz Joseph of Austria-Hungary, and Czar Alexander II of Russia — was established in Berlin.
Compulsory national service was instituted in Japan.
A rebellion against Spain broke out in the Philippines.

Napoleon III died at Chislehurst in England. French President Louis Thiers resigned and was replaced by Marie de MacMahon.
Amadeus I of Spain abdicated and the First Republic was established there with Emilio Castelar as premier.
The Second Ashanti War broke out in West Africa.
German forces evacuated France.
Bengal was ravaged by famine.

French power in Indochina, extended by Napoleon III, was confirmed.
The Ashanti War ended.
The Fiji Islands were annexed by Britain.
Civil marriage became compulsory in Germany.
The Spanish monarchy was restored. Alfonso, son of Queen Isabella, was proclaimed King of Spain.

Literature Religion Philosophy

Papal infallibility was asserted by the first Vatican Council.
Paul Verlaine, lyrical French poet, published some of his most beautiful verse in *La Bonne Chanson.*
Francis Brett Harte found world fame with *The Luck of Roaring Camp, and Other Sketches.*

As Farpas (The Darts) was a satirical review produced by José Duarte Ramalho Ortigão, Portuguese essayist.

Sir John Tenniel illustrated *Through the Looking-Glass,* the sequel to *Alice's Adventures in Wonderland* (1865) by Lewis Carroll.
Ricardo Palma's first series of *Peruvian Traditions* marked a high point in South American literature.
El gaucho Martín Fierro by José Hernández is the best example of gaucho poetry.

Une Saison en Enfer (a Season in Hell) was the masterpiece of the French Symbolist poet Arthur Rimbaud.

Thomas Hardy, great English novelist and poet, published *Far from the Madding Crowd,* one of his finest "Wessex" novels.
Pedro Antonio de Alarcón, Spanish writer, published his most famous novel, *The Three-Cornered Hat.*

Art and Architecture

Hommage à Manet is an important group portrait by Henri Fantin-Latour.
The Viennese furniture firm of Michael Thonet, father of modern bentwood designs, was producing 400,000 pieces annually.

The Opera House, Cairo, saw the first performance of Verdi's *Aida;* commissioned for the opening of the Suez Canal.
"The greatest show on earth" was how American showmen Phineas Taylor Barnum and James Bailey described their circus when they opened for the first time in Brooklyn.

The spirit of Impressionism can be seen in Eugène Boudin's *Women on the Beach of Trouville.*

Boatmen on the Volga established Ilya Efimovich Repin as the leader of the Wanderers, Russian Social Realist painters.
The Cradle is typical of Berthe Morisot and her taste for portraying quiet, domestic scenes. The first woman painter to join the Impressionists, she perhaps encouraged Monet to paint *en plein air,* in the open air.

The "Impressionist" painters first exhibited together.
Whistler's *Nocturne in black and gold: Falling rocket,* painted at about this time, was the cause of a libel action when denounced by Ruskin in 1876.
Sacré-Coeur Church, great Parisian landmark, was begun.

Performing Arts

Coppélia, the most famous ballet by Léo Delibes, was based on one of Hoffmann's *Tales.*

Italian actress Eleonora Duse made her debut in Verona as Juliet at the age of 14.

The Carl Rosa Opera Company was founded in England.

Verdi's magnificent *Requiem* was first performed, dedicated to the great writer and patriot Alessandro Manzoni.

Science and Technology

The Standard Oil Company was founded by American industrialist John D Rockefeller.

A pneumatic rock drill was invented by American engineer Simon Ingersoll.
W.S. Jevon's *Theory of Political Economy,* with its theories of marginal utility and supply and demand, advanced modern economics.

The British náutical expedition that sailed out on HMS *Challenger* to study sea life in the Atlantic, Pacific, and Indian oceans, founded the science of oceanography.
A machine for taking depth soundings at sea was invented by British mathematician and physicist Lord Kelvin.

Intermolecular forces were calculated by Dutch physicist Johannes van der Waals. He accurately described the behavior of real gases, using mathematical equations.
Light was shown to be an electromagnetic radiation by British physicist James Clerk-Maxwell.
E Remington & Sons, American gunsmiths, began to manufacture typewriters.

The leprosy bacillus was discovered by Norwegian physician Gerhard Hansen.
Streptococci and staphylococci were discovered by Albert Billroth.
Osteopathy was founded by American Andrew Taylor Still.

America

The Ku Klux Klan Acts disrupted secret societies.
The Senate rejected President Grant's scheme to annex Santo Domingo.

William Marcy "Boss" Tweed, of New York's Tammany Hall political organization, was indicted for graft.
A disastrous fire destroyed much of Chicago.

Civil rights were restored to all Southerners except Confederate leaders.
The Alabama Claims awarded the US $15.5 million for British damages to shipping.

Gold became the US monetary standard.
The Salary Grab Act greatly increased presidential and congressional salaries.
The Panic of 1873, saw 100 banks fail.

The Carpetbaggers, unscrupulous Northern whites who flocked to the South, were expelled from Arkansas.
Barbed wire was introduced and began to change life in the West.

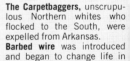

PARIS COMMUNE   STANLEY AND LIVINGSTONE   REMINGTON TYPEWRITER

...wang Hsu became Emperor ...China.

...republican constitution was ...tablished in France.

...n uprising against the Turks ...curred in Bosnia and Her-...govina.

...decisive share in the Suez ...nal was bought by Britain.

...e Universal Postal Union was ...unded.

...rkey was declared bank-...pt.

...rald Manley Hopkins, En-...sh poet and Jesuit priest, ...ote his sonnet *The Wind-...ver.*

...e Paris Opera House, de-...gned by Charles Garnier, ...s completed. Eclectic ...yle, it became a symbol of ...cond Empire taste.

...tterfield's most famous ...cular commission was Ke-...e College, Oxford, largely ...mplete by this year.

...omas Eakins, celebrated ...merican artist, caused a stir ...th *The Gross Clinic,* a por-...yal of dissection.

...tional qualities appeared in ...rious music, heard, for ex-...mple in Czech composer ...edrich Smetana's cycle of ...symphonic poems *Má-...ast* (My Country).

...bert and Sullivan produced ...eir first comic opera, *Trial ...Jury.*

...e London Medical School for ...omen was founded.

...e metallic element gallium ...s discovered by French ...emist Paul Emile Lecoq.

...e Civil Rights Act ensured ...ore rights for blacks.

...ry Baker Eddy published ...ience and Health,* the basis ...Christian science.

Korea's independence was proclaimed by China.

Don Carlos III (self-proclaimed King Charles VII) fled from Spain to end the Carlist Wars.

Abdul Aziz of Turkey was de-posed and was succeeded by his nephew Murad V who was himself deposed within three months because of alleged insanity. Abdul Hamid II be-came sultan.

Serbia and Montenegro de-clared war on Turkey.

Mark Twain, pen name of Samuel Langhorne Clemens, published *The Adventures of Tom Sawyer,* a great Amer-ican tale of boyhood.

A new era in English town planning was opened by Richard Norman Shaw's "Garden Suburb," to the west of London.

Metal spanning arches did away with piers in construc-tion: the central hall of St Pancras station, London, completed in this year, is 240 feet wide.

Alfred Sisley painted a series recording the *Floods at Port-Marly.*

Edgar Degas' *The glass of absinth* captures the seamier side of Parisian life.

The Bayreuth Festival opened with the first complete per-formance of Wagner's *The Ring of the Nibelung.*

The telephone was invented by Scottish-born American in-ventor Alexander Graham Bell.

The phonograph was invented by American inventor Thomas Alva Edison.

Canals on Mars were observed by Italian astronomer Giovan-ni Schiaparelli.

Col. George Custer and 266 cavalrymen were killed by the Sioux at The Little Bighorn.

Colorado achieved statehood.

At the London Protocol the major powers insisted that Turkey carry out reforms. Tur-key refused.

Britain annexed the Transvaal.

Russia declared war on Turkey over the Balkans and invaded Romania. Romania and Ser-bia declared war on Turkey.

The First Kaffir War began.

The Satsuma rebellion, in Japan, failed to halt the tide of reform and new ideas.

Madagascar and Britain signed a treaty of commerce.

Anna Karenina, Tolstoy's second masterpiece, was completed.

August Rodin's *The Age of Bronze* was exhibited at the Paris Salon. The naturalism of the form was Impressionis-tic, yet the heroic quality was akin to Michelangelo.

Red roofs shows Camille Pis-sarro's work at its best; rich colors, impasto (thick ap-plication of paint) and a rural subject.

The Victor-Emmanuel Arcade was completed in Milan to cruciform plan. Housing shops and cafés, it is the largest scheme of its kind.

Swan Lake opened a new era of ballet: the choreography was unequal to Tchaikovsky's great score and the ballet failed.

French composer Camille Saint-Saëns's opera *Samson and Delilah* was staged at Weimar. It was banned from French stages until 1892.

The first shipment of frozen meat was sent from the Argen-tine to Europe.

American astronomer Asaph Hall discovered the two satel-lites of Mars, which he named Deimos and Phobos.

A commission declared Rutherford B. Hayes presi-dent in a disputed election.

King Victor Emmanuel of Italy died and was succeeded by his son Humbert I.

The Treaty of San Stefano be-tween Russia and Turkey fol-lowed Turkey's capitulation.

By the Berlin Congress Russia acquired Bessarabia and part of Armenia from Turkey. Mon-tenegro, Bulgaria, Romania, and Serbia were granted inde-pendence.

In Afghanistan Britain sought to secure her position in India against Russian expansion.

Pope Pius IX died and was succeeded by Leo XIII.

Britain acquired Cyprus from Turkey.

There was an unsuccessful attempt on the life of German Emperor William I.

German socialists were out-lawed.

Flemish became the official language in Flanders.

Art songs were composed all over Europe, after decades of domination by German *Lieder* writers. The form was finely worked by French composers such as Henri Duparc.

Joseph Swan, a British physi-cist, demonstrated the first reliable filament electric lamp.

The Bland-Allison Act allowed the Secretary of the Treasury to purchase silver for coinage.

Congress established a govern-ment for the District of Co-lumbia. It would be governed by Congress until 1967.

Britain declared war on Cete-wayo, Zulu leader, to start the Zulu War. A British army was annihilated at Isandula, but after severe fighting Lord Chelmsford managed to crush the Zulus and capture Cete-wayo.

The frontier between India and Afghanistan was fixed by the Treaty of Gandamak. At Kabul, the British Legation was massacred and, as a re-sult, Britain invaded Afgha-nistan.

Alsace-Lorraine became part of Germany.

Germany and Austria-Hungary formed a Dual Alliance.

Chile began her successful Nitrate War against Bolivia and Peru.

Egypt was controlled once more by Britain and France.

Ismail, Khedive of Egypt, was deposed and succeeded by Tewfik.

The neo-Gothic Votivkirche, by H. von Ferstel, was com-pleted in Vienna.

Henrik Ibsen, Norwegian pioneer of realist drama, wrote *A Doll's House.*

Steele Mackaye, American theatrical innovator, invented the first moving "double stage." He also invented fold-ing theater seats.

English light opera, notably the deft, light creations of W S Gilbert and Arthur Sullivan, became a craze throughout Europe, the USA, and Au-stralia.

Thomas Alva Edison patented his incandescent light bulb.

The Panama Canal Company was founded by Ferdinand de Lesseps.

The first electric railway was shown by W E Siemens at the Berlin Trade Exhibition.

The Exodus of 1879 brought 20—40,000 southern blacks to Kansas.

Frank W. Woolworth and W.H. Moore opened the first five cent store, in Utica, N.Y.

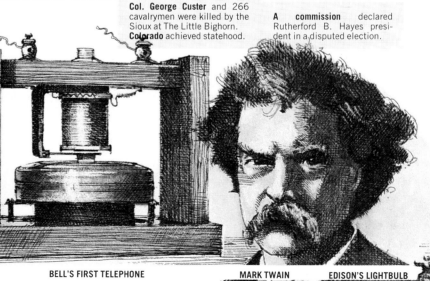

BELL'S FIRST TELEPHONE   MARK TWAIN   EDISON'S LIGHTBULB

CETEWAYO

World Events

Under Bismarck Germany aimed to build a solid European power structure.
France annexed Tahiti.
In the Pacific War, Chile began a struggle against Bolivia and Peru.
The Transvaal declared its independence, the Boers under Kruger proclaiming a republic.

The Boers in South Africa were victorious against the British in the Battle of Majuba Hill. The conflict was resolved by the Treaty of Pretoria.
Tunis became a French protectorate.
A nationalist rising in Egypt was led by Arabi Pasha.
Léon Gambetta became Prime Minister of France.
Alexander II, Czar of Russia, was murdered and succeeded by Alexander III.
James A Garfield, 20th President of the United States, was shot, and died two months later.

The Triple Alliance was formed by Germany, Austria, and Italy.
The Hague Convention fixed a three-mile limit for territorial waters.
British forces bombarded Alexandria and occupied Cairo. The French withdrew from Egypt.
Italy established the colony of Eritrea.

Paul Kruger became President of the South African Republic.
Sickness insurance was introduced into Germany by Bismarck.
Amman and Tonkin became French protectorates.
British forces began evacuating the Sudan.
French forces began the conquest of the Upper Niger.
Austria and Romania formed an alliance.

General Charles Gordon w sent to the Sudan to resc the Egyptian garrisons fr Muslim agitator, the Mah Gordon was besieged at Kh toum.
The Alliance of the Thr Emperors was renewed by G many, Austria, and Russia.
German troops occupied Tog land, the Cameroons, a South West Africa.
The Treaty of Berlin defin the rights of 14 Europe powers in Africa.
France took Indochina.
British protectorates we established over Basutolar the Somali coast, Niger and New Guinea.
As anti-semitism grew, Zionist Movement held first conference, in Prussia.

Literature Religion Philosophy

The Brothers Karamazov, the last and perhaps best novel by Fyodor Dostoyevsky, was published.
Les Soirées de Médan was a collection of war stories by six authors. The best was *Boule de suif (Ball of Fat),* perhaps the finest short story by Guy de Maupassant.

Henry James, one of the most influential American writers, published his masterpeice, *The Portrait of a Lady.*
Giovanni Verga, founder of the Italian verismo (Realist) school, finished his great novel, *I malavoglia.*

The Rime nuove and Odi barbare which appeared during this decade, contained the best poems by Giosuè Carducci, Italian republican and influential poet.

John Singer Sargent, American painter of elegant portraits, was influenced by Velazquez in his informal depiction of *The Boit Children.*
Etienne-Jules Marey brought the motion picture closer with his camera that could take a series of photographs in a second.

Emile Verhaeren, foremost Belgian poet and art critic, published the controversial poems *Les Flamandes.*
Poems by Charles Harpur was published posthumously, a collection by the first significant Australian poet.
Jean-Marie-Mathias Villiers de l'Isle-Adam published *Cruel Tales.*
The Story of an African Farm by the South African novelist Olive Schreiner, was a huge success.

A rebours (Against Natur "the breviary of decadence" was Joris-Karl Huysma masterpiece.

Art and Architecture

The Thinker, originally designed to preside over the two leaves of Rodin's Gates of Hell, is one of the most famous images in art.
The Island of the Dead is the masterpiece of the Swiss artist, Arnold Böcklin.

The bronze casts of Degas' *The little 14-year-old dancer* had gauze tutus and real ribbons in the hair.

Antoni Gaudí, the Spanish architect, began his church of the Sagrada Familia, Barcelona, a quasi-Gothic structure of enormous size, unfinished at his death.
A brilliant feat of engineering was the Brooklyn Suspension Bridge, completed in this year. Designed by John Augustus Roebling, it was the first bridge to use steel for cable wire.

The Salon des Indépenda was established, in oppo tion to the orthodox Pa Salon.
Edward Burne-Jones, paint tales of medieval chival *King Cophetua and the B gar Maid* is the most famo example.
Auguste Renoir complet *Umbrellas,* which has the i mediacy of a photograph.

Performing Arts

The Guildhall School of Music was founded in London.
Skis were first used in mountaineering in Norway.

A performance of Patience, by W S Gilbert and Arthur Sullivan, marked the opening of the Savoy Theatre, London.
Jacques Offenbach's opera *The Tales of Hoffmann* paid homage to the German writer.

The Berlin Philharmonic Orchestra was founded.

Science and Technology

Piezoelectricity — electricity produced by the compression of certain types of crystal — was discovered by French scientist Pierre Curie.

Thomas Alva Edison designed the first hydroelectric plant.
Cell division was described by the German anatomist Walther Flemming.
Viennese physician Joseph Breuer used hypnosis to treat hysteria.

British physicist Sir Joseph Swan produced synthetic fibre.

The tetanus bacillus was di overed by German physic Arthur Nicolaier.
Hiram Maxim, American gu mith, invented the Max machine gun in England.
The steam turbine was ma by British engineer Char Parsons.
The St Gotthard Tunnel, Switzerland, was opened.

America

Republican "dark horse" James A. Garfield won the presidential election.
A treaty with China allowed the US to regulate the immigration of Chinese laborers, reflecting a trend toward Chinese exclusion from US.

The ether was proved not to exist by the experiments of the American physicists Albert Michelson and Edward Morley.
The electric tram first ran in Berlin.
Louis Pasteur, following Koch's work, used attenuated bacteria to confer immunity to anthrax.
The Natural History Museum in London opened.

The US joined other countries in approving the Geneva Convention to ensure humane treatment of wounded soldiers.
German and Chinese immigration reached an all-time high point.

The origins of jazz and blues are found in the work songs that united poor blacks as they toiled in fields, and in their gospel songs.

As a result of the Pendleton Law, the civil service was reformed, with exams as part of employee selection, formerly dependent on patronage.

The Supreme Court ruled in Ku Klux Klan cases that terfering with a citizen's ri to vote in national electio was a federal offense.

Booker T. Washington became the first head of Tuskegee, an Alabama school for blacks.

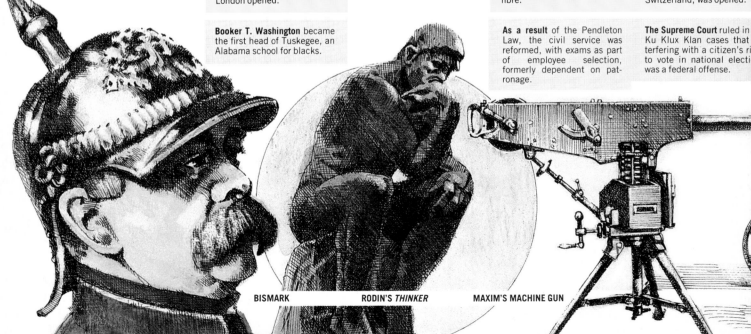

BISMARK   RODIN'S *THINKER*   MAXIM'S MACHINE GUN

Khartoum fell to the Mahdi and General Gordon was killed. The British evacuated the Sudan.
The Congo Free State was established under Leopold II of Belgium.
Tanganyika and Zanzibar were annexed by Germany.
The Niger region and Bechuanaland became British protectorates.
New Guinea was annexed by Britain and Germany.
King Alfonso XII of Spain died and was succeeded by Queen Maria Cristina.
The Third Anglo-Burmese War began.

Jules Laforgue completed *Les Complaintes*. French Symbolist poet, he was one of the first to use free verse.

The Rijksmuseum, Amsterdam, was completed.
Glessner House, Chicago was the last building by American architect Henry Hobson Richardson.
Woman drying her feet is typical of the observational spirit of Degas' work.
The Danaid shows the beautiful line and finish of Rodin's marble works.

The American Academy of Dramatic Art was established by MacKaye.

German engineer Karl Benz invented the automobile and another, Gottlieb Daimler, patented a gasoline engine which he used initially to power a motorcycle.
The Canadian Pacific Railway was completed.

Iron frame construction was employed in the nation's first skyscraper in Chicago.
Silver and lead deposits discovered in Idaho would produce £200 million worth of ore.

The Peace of Bucharest ended the war between Serbia and Bulgaria.
The Bonapartes and Orleans were banished from France.
A coup in Bulgaria dethroned Alexander. He was succeeded by Regent Stephen Stambulov.
King Louis II of Bavaria died and was succeeded by Otto I.
Gold was discovered in South Africa.
The First Indian National Congress met.

Following *Treasure Island* (1881), Robert Louis Stevenson wrote his second masterpiece, *Kidnapped*.

Hope was the most famous work by George Frederic Watts. It was reproduced in its thousands.
The last Impressionist Exhibition in Paris included Georges Seurat's controversial *La Grande Jatte,* the supreme Pointillist work.
Rodin completed *The Burghers of Calais.*

Franz Liszt, the world's greatest pianist, died after catching a chill at the Bayreuth Wagner festival.

Aluminum could be produced economically by the electrolytic process developed independently by American chemist Charles Hall and French chemist Paul Heroult.
Fluorine was produced by French chemist Henri Moissan.
The metalloid element germanium was discovered by German chemist Clemens Winkler.

The Statue of Liberty, a gift from France, was dedicated in New York harbor.
The American Federation of Labor was founded in Columbus, Ohio.

Zululand was annexed by the British.
Prince Ferdinand of Saxe-Coburg was elected King of Bulgaria.
Baluchistan was united with India.
Britian, Italy, and Austria-Hungary agreed to maintain the status quo in the Mediterranean and Near East.

Sherlock Holmes made his first appearance, in Arthur Conan Doyle's *A Study in Scarlet.*
Friedrich Nietzsche, German classical scholar and philosopher, published *The Genealogy of Morals.*

Renoir's famous Bathers is a homage to the traditional nude.
Eadweard Muybridge published *Animal Locomotion,* a collection of photographic motion studies which sold widely.

The Théâtre-Libre was founded in Paris.
Ignacy Jan Paderewski, Polish pianist, composer, and statesman, gave his first major recital in Vienna.
English organist and composer John Stainer produced his memorable oratorio, *The Crucifixion.*

Radio waves were produced by German physicist Heinrich Hertz.
American clergyman Hannibal Williston Goodwin invented celluloid film.
International language Esperanto was invented by Polish philologist Lazarus Ludwig Zamenhof.

The Interstate Commerce Act prohibited railroads from certain discriminatory practices and set up the first federal regulatory agency.
A treaty with Hawaii granted the US the right to build a Pearl Harbor naval base.

Emperor William I of Germany died and was succeeded by his son, Frederick III. His death occurred within the year and he was succeeded by his son William II.
Britain established protectorates over North Borneo, Brunei, and Sarawak.

Miss Julie is the most famous play by Swedish writer August Strindberg.
Blue, a collection of verse and prose, was the first major work by Rubén Darío, leader of the Spanish-American Modernism movement.

Vincent van Gogh painted his series of *Sunflowers.*
The National Library, Athens, was begun in this year.
From Paul Sérusier's painting *The Talisman,* the Nabis group ("Prophet") sprang.
The development of the Kodak camera saw the birth of mass amateur photography.

Symphonic traditions continued in Europe with vast works by Austrian Romantic composers Anton Bruckner and Gustav Mahler, who introduced folk elements.
Gustav Mahler became director of the Budapest Opera.

The pneumatic tyre was invented by British vet John Dunlop.
The first Chinese railroad was built.
The Pasteur Institute was founded in Paris.
An aeronautical exhibition was held in Vienna.

A 36–hour blizzard crippled the northeastern US, killing 400 people.
Benjamin Harrison defeated Grover Cleveland in the presidential elections.
The Department of Labor was created.

Georges Boulanger, former French War Minister, fled from France after plotting against the Third Republic.
The Ivory Coast became a French protectorate.
Abyssinia became an Italian protectorate.
Brazil became a republic after Pedro II abdicated.
Charles I became King of Portugal.
Milan of Serbia abdicated in favor of his son Alexander.
The Treaty of Constantinople internationalized the Suez Canal.

Before Dawn was the first German Realistic play and made Gerhart Hauptmann famous overnight.

The Eiffel Tower was raised in months by the bridge engineer Alexandre-Gustave Eiffel for the Paris Centennial Exposition.
Pont-Aven became the home of Paul Gaugin for a spell; the simplicity of his line and his glorious coloring attracted many followers.
Fernand Khnopff, Belgian Symbolist painter, was working on Memories, a dreamlike composition.
The Heidelberg school of Australian painters held their major *nine-inch-by-five-inch Impression* Exhibition in Melbourne.

The Socialist battle song, *The Red Flag,* was written in London after a dock strike.

English chemist Sir Frederick Abel invented cordite.
A celluloid-roll film was produced by American photographer George Eastman.

The first antitrust law was passed by Kansas, with several other states following.
North Dakota, South Dakota, Washington, and Montana were admitted to the Union.

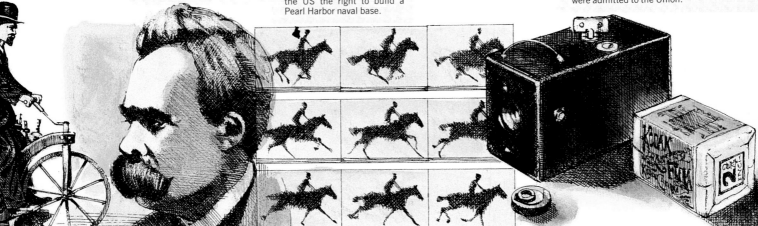

DAIMLER'S MOTORCYCLE   FRIEDRICH NIETZSCHE   MUYBRIDGE'S ANIMAL STUDIES   EASTMAN'S ROLL FILM

World Events

1890

In Germany, **Kaiser Wilhelm II** dismissed Bismarck and let his treaty with Russia lapse.
Spain adopted universal suffrage.
The first Japanese Diet opened.
The Grand Duchy of Luxembourg was separated from The Netherlands as Queen Wilhelmina ascended the throne.

1891

Brazil adopted a federal republican constitution.
The Triple Alliance of Germany, Austria-Hungary, and Italy was renewed. Russia and France made a Dual Alliance.
There was widespread famine in Russia.
An earthquake in Japan killed 10,000 people.

1892

Tewfik died and was succeeded by Abbas II as Khedive of Egypt.
Prince Ito became Prime Minister of Japan.
The Panama Canal fiasco brought Ferdinand de Lesseps to trial in France.
A Pan-Slav Congress met at Cracow.
Portugal was declared bankrupt.

1893

Hawaii became a republic.
The Ivory Coast became a French protectorate.
Belgium was paralyzed by a general strike.
Natal was granted self-government.
France and Siam went to war.
New Zealand extended the franchise to women.
Fridtjof Nansen, Norwegian explorer and statesman, led an expedition to the North Pole.

1894

Uganda became a British protectorate.
Dahomey became a French colony.
Marie François Sadi Carnot, fourth President of France, was assassinated by an Italian anarchist in Lyons.
Alfred Dreyfus, a French officer of Jewish descent, was convicted of treason after a controversial trial and deported to Devil's Island.
Alexander III died and was succeeded by his son, Nicholas II, last of the Czars.
The first organized massacre of Armenians by Turks took place.
In China, Sun Yat-sen formed the first of several revolutionary societies.

Literature Religion Philosophy

1890

The Golden Bough by the Scottish anthropologist, James Frazer, was a landmark in anthropology.

1891

The Picture of Dorian Gray was Oscar Wilde's only novel, a brilliant "decadent" work.

1892

Pelléas et Mélisande, by the Belgian Maurice Maeterlinck, was the masterpiece of Symbolist drama.
The Weavers was Hauptmann's best play, Naturalistic and gripping.

1893

The Second Mrs Tanqueray established Arthur Wing Pinero as an important playwright.

1894

Rudyard Kipling, remembered for his jingoistic stories of British imperialism, wrote his first *Jungle Book.*

Art and Architecture

1890

Dropping the Pilot is Tenniel's most famous cartoon. A comment on Bismarck's resignation, it appeared in *Punch.*
Henri Rousseau, *le douanier,* ("customs officer") painted his famous self-portrait.
Jacob August Riis published *How the Other Half Lives,* a photographic study of New York slum-life.
Shearing the Rams shows Tom Roberts, Australian Impressionist painter, at his best.

1891

The ten-storey Wainright Building in St Louis is the most important skyscraper designed by Louis Sullivan, father of modern American architecture.
The most important landscape painter of the Heidelberg school, Arthur Streeton, painted his heroic *Fire's On.*

1892

Henri de Toulouse-Lautrec, brilliant avant-garde painter of low-life Paris, found fame through his posters, such as *Le Divan japonais.*
Edouard Vuillard became known as an Intimist painter for works such as *Woman Sweeping.*
The Bath is a fine example of Mary Cassatt's mother-and-child compositions. She had exhibited regularly with the French Impressionists.

1893

Eros, in London's Piccadilly Circus, is the most famous public monument by Alfred Gilbert.
Art Nouveau was a rising force. It marked the definitive liberation of modern architecture from the restraints of classicism.
Adolf von Hildebrand, German sculptor, published his influential treatise, *The Problem of Form.*
Medardo Rosso completed his extraordinary Impressionist sculpture, *Conversation in a garden.*
Edvard Munch, forerunner of Expressionism, painted his most famous work, *The Scream.*

1894

Alphonse Mucha, Czech Art Nouveau illustrator, began to design costumes, jewelery, posters, and stage sets for French actress Sarah Bernhardt.
Anatole de Baudot realized his neo-Gothic design for St Jean, Montmartre, in Paris, in reinforced concrete.
Aubrey Beardsley, Art Nouveau illustrator, worked on Oscar Wilde's *Salomé.*

Performing Arts

1890

Italian composer Pietro Mascagni produced *Cavalleria Rusticana* (Rustic Chivalry) in Rome.

1891

Inspired by the Théâtre-Libre in Paris, Jack Thomas Grein founded the Independent Theatre, London.
National styles developed in the works of composers such as Jean Sibelius in Finland and Isaac Albéniz in Spain.

1892

Antonín Dvořák became director of the New York National Conservatory of Music.

1893

Giuseppe Verdi's opera *Falstaff* was first staged at La Scala, Milan.

1894

Claude-Achille Debussy, French composer, brought impressionism to music.
George Bernard Shaw's play *Arms and the Man.*

Science and Technology

1890

The United States overtook Britain in steel production.
Rubber gloves were used for the first time in surgery, in Baltimore.
Principles of Economics, including such new concepts as elasticity of demand, was Alfred Marshall's most important work.

1891

The term "electron" was introduced by Irish scientist Johnstone Stoney.
Thomas Edison patented the Kinetoscope, a motion picture peepshow viewer invented an Englishman, William Dickson.
Java Man (*Pithecanthropus erectus*) was discovered in Java by a Dutch anatomist.

1892

Viscose, leading to the manufacture of rayon, was produced by British chemists Charles Frederick Cross and E J Bevan.
German engineer Rudolf Diesel patented his internal combustion engine.
Auriga, a new star, was discovered in the Milky Way.
Diphtheria antitoxin was isolated by German biologist Paul Ehrlich.

1893

Karl Benz built his first four-wheel car.
The Manchester Ship Canal was completed.

1894

Auguste Lumière and his brother Louis, French inventors, developed good cine equipment.

America

1890

The Sherman Antitrust Act was passed by Congress.
Idaho and Wyoming joined the Union.
The last Indian battle at Wounded Knee, South Dakota, resulted in the death of about 200 Sioux.

1891

The US Circuit Court of Appeals was created to relieve the Supreme Court's hearing all appeals from lower federal courts.
The first three non-military federal prisons were authorized.

1892

Labor unrest brought a violent strike at the Carnegie steel works in Homestead, Pennsylvania.
Grover Cleveland was elected president for the second time.

1893

The World's Columbian Exposition to celebrate the discovery of America opened in Chicago. More than 20,000,000 people attended.
A financial panic resulted from a loss of confidence in US monetary policy.

1894

The Pullman Strike, paralyzed railroads.
Coxey's Army of unemployed men marched on Washington.

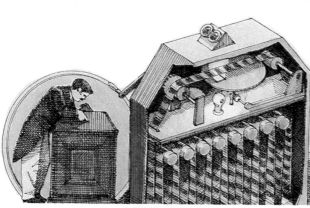

DICKSON'S KINETOSCOPE

WAINWRIGHT BUILDING

G. B. SHAW

War broke out between Italy and Abyssinia.
The Sino-Japanese War ended.
In South Africa, Rhodesia was named after Cecil Rhodes.
The Jameson Raid took place when Sir Leander Starr Jameson, British politician, led an abortive raid against the Boers in South Africa.

The Importance of being Earnest, is Oscar Wilde's most popular work.
H.G. Wells published *The Time Machine.*

Lunch Break at the Lumière Factory, the first film, was made by the Lumière brothers, Auguste and Louis.
Monet exhibited twenty versions of *Rouen Cathedral.*
Otto Wagner, Austrian architect, published his lectures as *Moderne Architektur.*

Russian composer Peter Ilyich Tchaikovsky's ballet *Swan Lake* had its first complete performance at St Petersburg, in Russia.

Italian physicist Guglielmo Marconi invented wireless telegraphy.
X rays were discovered by German physicist Wilhelm Roëntgen.

Silver Democrats called for unlimited silver coinage.
The first meeting of the National Association of Manufacturers took place.
The Contract Labor Act forbade the importation of contract laborers.

Cecil Rhodes relinquished the premiership of Cape Colony.
By the Treaty of Addis Ababa, Italy recognized the independence of Abyssinia.
Madagascar was annexed by the French.
Anglo-Egyptian forces, led by General Horatio Kitchener, began the reconquest of the Sudan.

A.E. Housman published *A Shropshire Lad.*
One of the world's finest printed books was prepared, the Kelmscott Press *Chaucer,* under William Morris.
Anton Chekhov's *The Seagull* had a poor reception.

The Glasgow School of Art was begun at this time by Charles Rennie Mackintosh.
Cézanne painted *The Lake of Annecy.*

Edward Elgar's *Enigma Variations* brought him recognition as a composer.

The first electric submarine was built in France.
Radioactivity was discovered by the French physicist Antoine Becquerel.
Helium was discovered by William Ramsay.

Gold was discovered in Alaska's Klondike.
In Plessy v. Ferguson, the Supreme Court upheld the separate but equal segregation doctrine of facilities.
William McKinley was elected president.

Crete proclaimed union with Greece. Greece declared war on Turkey and was defeated in Thessaly. The major powers intervened and brought about the Peace of Constantinople.
The King of Korea proclaimed himself emperor.
Russia threatened China, where the Powers gained territory and concessions.
Famine devastated India.
Goldfields were discovered in the Klondike, Canada.

Cyrano de Bergerac was an immediate international success for the French playwright, Edmond Rostand.
Emile Durkheim, founder of French sociology, published *Suicide.*
The first six volumes of *Studies in the Psychology of Sex* by Havelock Ellis was published.

The world-famous favrile glass of the American, Louis Comfort Tiffany, had taken on Art Nouveau qualities.

Gustav Mahler was appointed conductor of the Vienna Opera.
John Philip Sousa, American composer, wrote superb marches for marine bands, including *The Stars and Stripes Forever.*

The electron was discovered by British physicist J. J. Thomson.
Malaria was shown to be transmitted by the mosquito by British physician Ronald Ross.

Spain made changes in its Cuban policy in an effort to placate US.

The United States and Spain went to war over Cuba. By the Treaty of Paris, Cuba became independent and the United States gained Puerto Rico, Guam, and the Philippines.
At the Battle of Omdurman Kitchener defeated the Dervishes (Sudanese rebels).
"J'accuse", Zola's open letter in the newspaper *L'Aurore,* denounced the French general al staff in the Dreyfus case.

Henry James's wrote *The Turn of the Screw.*

Rodin finished his colossal statue of *Balzac.*
Gauguin completed his chief Tahitian work, *Where do we come from? What are we? Where are we going?.*
Käthe Kollwitz's etchings *Weavers' Revolt* appeared.

Ragtime was played in the United States by black pianists, notably by Scott Joplin.

The theoretical basis for space travel was provided in the work of Konstantin Tsiolkovsky.
Viruses were discovered by Dutch scientist Martinus Beijerinck.
Radium was discovered by Pierre and Marie Curie.
Count von Zeppelin invented his airship.

The battleship Maine sinking in Havana led to the Spanish-American War.

The Boer War, between the British and the Boers, was sparked off by Paul Kruger's ultimatum to the British. The British were besieged at Mafeking, Kimberley, and Ladysmith.
The first Hague Peace Conference was attended by 26 nations.
After the second Dreyfus trial, Dreyfus was pardoned by presidential decree.
The Baghdad railroad contract was secured by Germany.

The Brazilian Joaquim Maria Machado de Assis, published his masterpiece, *Dom Casmurro.*
Sigmund Freud, founder of psychoanalysis, published *The Interpretation of Dreams.*
The Foundations of the Nineteenth Century advanced H.S. Chamberlain's theories of Aryan racial superiority. It inspired Hitler.

Josef Maria Olbrich completed the Secession Art Gallery, Vienna, headquarters of the Austrian Art Nouveau movement.

Rutherford identified alpha rays and beta rays.
Aspirin was first marketed.
The first magnetic recording of sound was made.

Wake Island was claimed by the US.
The Open Door Policy with China, announced by Secretary of State John Hays, demanded that all nations be allowed equal trade opportunities there.

ART NOUVEAU   ZOLA'S OPEN LETTER   SPAIN AND THE US AT WAR   SIGMUND FREUD

L'AURORE
J'Accuse!
E AU PRESIDENT DE LA R
Par EMILE ZOLA

DEFEATING
illness & disease

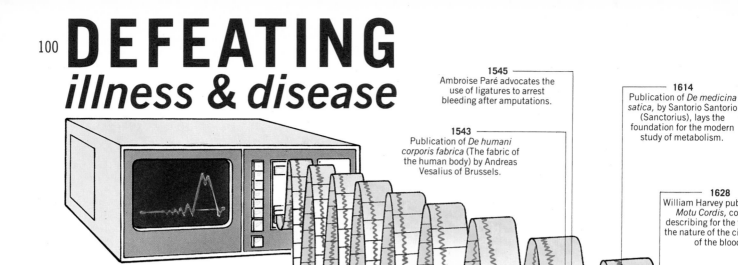

1545
Ambroise Paré advocates the use of ligatures to arrest bleeding after amputations.

1543
Publication of *De humani corporis fabrica* (The fabric of the human body) by Andreas Vesalius of Brussels.

1614
Publication of *De medicina satica,* by Santorio Santorio (Sanctorius), lays the foundation for the modern study of metabolism.

1628
William Harvey publish *Motu Cordis,* correct describing for the first the nature of the circul of the blood.

Humankind seems always to have been a ready victim of disease, whether because of inherited factors, adverse environmental conditions or infection by micro-organisms. It seems likely that many disease-causing organisms may predate humans by millions of years and that it is humans who have had to learn to combat not only those micro-organisms but also their own genetic weaknesses and the problems we create in our environment. Only in the last 50 years or so, with the advent of chemotherapy, have some disease organisms had to evolve to keep pace with our recently-acquired skills.

When modern men and women roamed Neolithic Europe 10,000 years ago, they suffered, as we know from skeletal evidence, from arthritis, sinusitis, rickets, poliomyelitis and spina bifida. Evidence from the better preserved Egyptian mummies shows the prevalence of pneumonia, pleurisy, gallstones, kidney stones, appendicitis, smallpox and so on. The average life expectancy of an Egyptian 3,000 years ago was only 18 years.

Medicine as an art may be as old as humankind, but the first leap forward for medicine based on clinical observation had to wait until classical Greek times and, notably, the thought and observations of Hippocrates (460–379BC). Some advance in anatomy and surgery, and in the philosophy of medicine, took place at this time. The most influential of all Greek physicians following Hippocrates was Galen (AD130–210), whose many treatises were influential not only in his lifetime but later, in the Middle Ages, when his views had a significant effect on the development of modern medicine.

The end of the Dark Ages saw a revival of interest in anatomy and in the 16th century the new knowledge was applied to surgery. Physiology as a science came into its own during the next three centuries.

Those advances in surgery, anatomy, physiology and microbiology were not translated into a significant decrease in mortality on the operating table until the 19th century. It was the discovery of anaesthesia and asepsis – the control of infection – that made this possible.

1683
Antoni van Leeuwenhoek describes and illustrates bacteria.

1753
James Lind publishes *A Treatise of the Scurvy* advocating the use of fresh fruit or lemon juice.

1846
William Thomas Morton gives the first convincing demonstration of ether as an anaesthetic.

Longevity

It took about 2,800 years for life expectancy to climb from 18 to 32 years. In the West today, most people can expect to live into their seventies and by the year 2000 the figure should reach 80. But in countries like Nigeria it is still only 37 years.

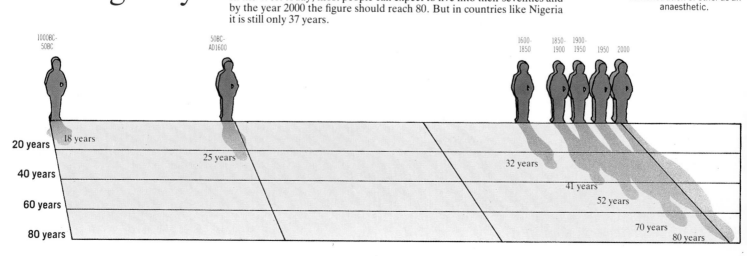

1000BC-50BC	50BC-AD1600	1600-1850	1850-1900	1900-1950	1950	2000

20 years — 18 years

25 years

40 years

32 years

41 years

60 years

52 years

80 years

70 years

80 years

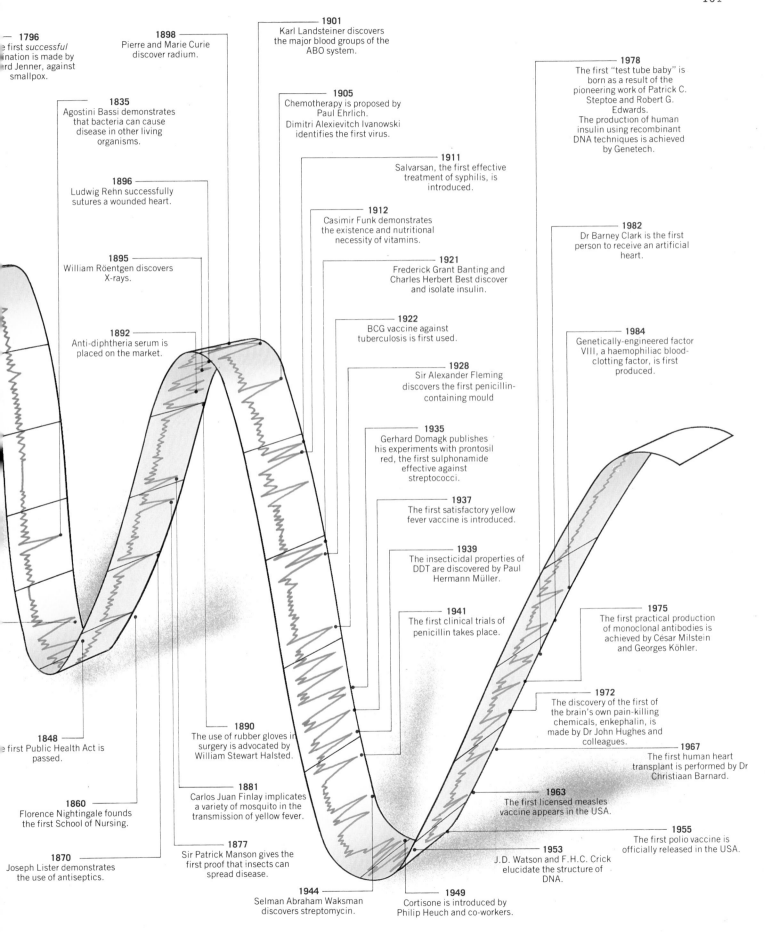

1796
The first *successful* vaccination is made by Edward Jenner, against smallpox.

1898
Pierre and Marie Curie discover radium.

1901
Karl Landsteiner discovers the major blood groups of the ABO system.

1978
The first "test tube baby" is born as a result of the pioneering work of Patrick C. Steptoe and Robert G. Edwards.
The production of human insulin using recombinant DNA techniques is achieved by Genetech.

1835
Agostini Bassi demonstrates that bacteria can cause disease in other living organisms.

1905
Chemotherapy is proposed by Paul Ehrlich.
Dimitri Alexievitch Ivanowski identifies the first virus.

1896
Ludwig Rehn successfully sutures a wounded heart.

1911
Salvarsan, the first effective treatment of syphilis, is introduced.

1982
Dr Barney Clark is the first person to receive an artificial heart.

1912
Casimir Funk demonstrates the existence and nutritional necessity of vitamins.

1895
William Röentgen discovers X-rays.

1921
Frederick Grant Banting and Charles Herbert Best discover and isolate insulin.

1984
Genetically-engineered factor VIII, a haemophiliac blood-clotting factor, is first produced.

1892
Anti-diphtheria serum is placed on the market.

1922
BCG vaccine against tuberculosis is first used.

1928
Sir Alexander Fleming discovers the first penicillin-containing mould

1935
Gerhard Domagk publishes his experiments with prontosil red, the first sulphonamide effective against streptococci.

1937
The first satisfactory yellow fever vaccine is introduced.

1939
The insecticidal properties of DDT are discovered by Paul Hermann Müller.

1975
The first practical production of monoclonal antibodies is achieved by César Milstein and Georges Köhler.

1941
The first clinical trials of penicillin takes place.

1972
The discovery of the first of the brain's own pain-killing chemicals, enkephalin, is made by Dr John Hughes and colleagues.

1967
The first human heart transplant is performed by Dr Christiaan Barnard.

1848
The first Public Health Act is passed.

1890
The use of rubber gloves in surgery is advocated by William Stewart Halsted.

1963
The first licensed measles vaccine appears in the USA.

1955
The first polio vaccine is officially released in the USA.

1860
Florence Nightingale founds the first School of Nursing.

1881
Carlos Juan Finlay implicates a variety of mosquito in the transmission of yellow fever.

1953
J.D. Watson and F.H.C. Crick elucidate the structure of DNA.

1870
Joseph Lister demonstrates the use of antiseptics.

1877
Sir Patrick Manson gives the first proof that insects can spread disease.

1944
Selman Abraham Waksman discovers streptomycin.

1949
Cortisone is introduced by Philip Heuch and co-workers.

c.1492
False teeth Partial dentures, with gold bridge work, were made by the Etruscans in 700BC. The earliest full set for both upper and lower jaws so far discovered was unearthed in Switzerland, and estimated to date from the late 1400s. The teeth were attached to hinged side-pieces and were most probably a cosmetic feature, quite useless for eating with.

c.1498
Toothbrush The Chinese claim to have invented the toothbrush in 1498 and, from its description, it seems to have changed little over the centuries. By 1649 toothbrushes were available in Paris, but were not found in England until the end of the 1600s. The first nylon toothbrush was marketed in America in 1938, with bristles made by du Pont.

c.1509
Wallpaper The earliest surviving fragment of wallpaper was discovered in Cambridge in 1911 and dates from 1509. It was reliably ascribed to Hugo Goes, a well known printer. The black and white design is an imitation of brocade. The first wallpapers were substitutes for earlier very expensive wall hangings such as tapestries.

1596
Water closet The first water closet was installed in a mansion at Kelston, near Bath in 1596. The hygienic recipient was Sir John Harington, an Elizabethan poet. Only two examples of this model were ever made, and they bore a marked resemblance to its 20th century successor. Quantity production of water closets began nearly 200 years later with two main manufacturers – Cummings in 1775 and Bramah in 1778.

1790
Sewing machine A London cabinet-maker called Thomas Saint invented and patented the first sewing machine in 1790. It had many of the basic features later incorporated into the successful domestic machines manufactured by the American, Isaac Meritt Singer. A humble French tailor, called Barthélemy Thimmonier, built the first machine to be distributed commercially.

c.1795
Canned food The process of canning food owes much to a French confectioner, Nicolas Appert who, in the 1790s successfully preserved food for several months in glass bottles sealed with up to five layers of cork. Tinplate for canning was introduced in 1812 by Donkin and Hall, of Bermondsey. The contents were introduced into the can through a small hole in the top, which was then sealed with a soldered disc. Customers were advised to use a hammer and chisel to open their cans.

1805
Lawn mower Thomas Plucknett, in 1805, was the first to produce a machine for cutting grass. A pair of carriage wheels, attached to shafts, drove a big circular blade parallel with the ground. This primitive machine was outmoded by the model invented by Edwin Budding of Stroud, Gloucestershire, in 1830. His was a 19-inch roller mower with grass box, which looked remarkably like today's models. Before the advent of the mower, grass was usually scythed when damp.

1816
Fire extinguisher In 1734 M. Fuches, a German doctor, produced a series of glass balls filled with salt in solution. These were thrown at the flames with variable results, depending on aim and the supply of balls. The first automatic extinguisher was invented by Captain George Manby, of Yarmouth, in 1816. It consisted of a four-gallon copper canister holding three gallons of water and compressed air in the space above. The water was released by turning a stopcock.

Thimmonier's sewing machine

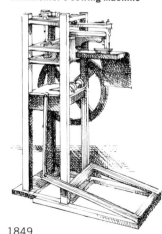

1849
Safety-pin This indispensable device has been in existence for at least 4,000 years, but until 1849 only in rudimentary form. In that year, the American inventor Walter Hunt gave the contemporary pin a circular twist at the bend. This acted as a coil spring and prevented the pin from slipping out of its slot.

1869
Margarine A French chemist named Hippolyte Mège-Mouriez patented the first margarine in 1869 in answer to a demand by Napoleon III for a cheap butter for "the less prosperous classes". After a close study of cows and the butterfat content of milk, Mège-Mouriez came up with an unpalatable mixture of beef tallow, milk, water, and chopped cow's udder. Because it was the color of pearls, he named it margarine, from the Greek word *margarites* (pearl). In England it was called "butterine" until 1887.

Budding's lawnmower

1876
Carpet-sweeper Although clumsy attempts at mechanical carpet-sweeping had been made as early as 1811, nothing proved really practicable until 1876, when Melvile R. Bissell, of Grand Rapids, Michigan, invented a carpet-sweeper with a dust box and a knob to adjust the height of the brushes to different surfaces. Bissell owned a china shop and was allergic to the dusty straw in which his wares were packed. It was to overcome this problem that he invented this boon to the housewives of the world.

1893
Zip-fastener This was the brainchild of Whitcomb L Judson, an engineer from Chicago. His "slide fastener", patented in 1893, consisted of two metal chains that could be joined together with a single movement of a slide fastener. Because of a tendency to frequently come apart, it never caught on. Success had to wait until 1913 when Gideon Sundback, a Swedish engineer from Hoboken, New Jersey, patented his "separable fasteners". Attached to a flexible backing, his metal locks were foolproof. Zips on women's dresses were introduced by Schiaparelli in 1930. Zip flies appeared in 1935.

1901
Vacuum cleaner An English bridge-builder and designer of fair ground big wheels, Hubert Booth, was the inventor in 1901 of the first really foolproof vacuum cleaner. Having seen the disastrous results of a new cleaner's *blowing* the dust around St Pancras Station in London, Booth tried a different approach. He lay on the floor with a handkerchief to his mouth and *sucked*. The visible traces of dirt convinced him that he had solved the filter problem.

Electric hearing aid The first patent was taken out in 1901 by the American inventor Miller Reese Hutchinson, who called his apparatus the Acousticon. With its large batteries and telephone-type receiver, it was a cumbersome affair, weighing

Vacuum cleaner

several pounds. The first wearable hearing aid was the Amplivox, provided by Londoner A Edwin Stevens in 1935. The American firm Sonotone produced the first transistorized and truly miniaturized hearing aid in 1952.

1913
Refrigerator Jacob Perkins, an American working in London, first discovered the principles of refrigeration in 1834. He managed to make a little ice by the evaporation of volatile fluids but did not develop his invention. The first domestic refrigerator was called the Domelre, and first appeared in 1913 in Chicago. It had a wooden cabinet and was electrically powered. In Britain, the Frigidaire was the first to be marketed, in 1924.

THE

20th

CENTURY

World Events

1900
The British garrison at Mafeking, commanded by Baden-Powell, was relieved after seven months. 26,000 women and children died in concentration camps established by the British for Boer civilians.
Young Chinese in the "Society of Harmonious Fists" — popularly called the Boxers — attacked foreigners in Peking, killing the German Minister and besieging the legations. A six-nation expeditionary force restored order two months later.
Italy's King Umburto 1 was assassinated by anarchists.

1901
US President William McKinley was shot by a Polish immigrant named Leon Czolgosz, who proclaimed himself an anarchist. The President survived for seven days before dying of his wounds.
Australia was established as a Commonwealth, with the six colonies federated in equal status.

1902
The Treaty of Vereeniging ended the Boer War. The Transvaal and the Orange Free State accepted British sovereignty. Britain provided £3 million to repair war damage.
Mount Pélee erupted in Martinique, totally destroying the city of St Pierre. More than 40,000 lives were lost.

1903
A separatist movement, aided by the United States, founded the Republic of Panama. The US was granted the lease of a five-mile-wide strip of land in the new republic in order to re-commence work on the Panama Canal.
The Bolsheviks, a revolutionary faction led by Lenin, gained control of the Russian Social Democratic Party newspaper *Iskara* (The Spark) at the Second Party Conference in London.

1904
The Japanese Navy launched a surprise attack on the Russian fleet at Port Arthur, a Chinese seaport. War between the two countries was immediately declared.
The governments of France and Britain signed the Anglo-French Entente, or *Entente Cordiale.* It ended long-standing friction over the countries' territorial claims to parts of Africa.
Theodore Roosevelt was re-elected as President of the United States.

Literature Religion Philosophy

1900
Freud wrote *The Interpretation of Dreams.*
The German philosopher and visionary Friedrich Nietzche died.

1901
William James began a series of public lectures in Edinburgh, entitled *The Varieties of Religious Experience: A Study in Human Nature,* which pointed toward a laboratory technique in studying psychology and established him as a major thinker.

1902
Arthur Conan Doyle published the most enduring of his Sherlock Holmes stories — *The Hound of the Baskervilles.*
André Gide explored the nature of sacrifice and sexuality in *L'Immoraliste.*
Lenin outlined his concept of dedicated revolutionaries, the "vanguard of the proletariat," in his pamphlet *What is to be Done?*

1903
British philosopher George Moore published *A refutation of idealism.*
In France, Henri Bergson's *Introduction to Metaphysics* advocated that intuition was the only means by which universal truths could be discovered.

1904
Henry James published his last novel, *The Golden Bowl.* It had a dense, highly-imagined style and intricate use of metaphor.

Art and Architecture

1900
The Güell Park, Barcelona, was a triumph of Gaudi's "equilibrated" design, based on counterpoise.
Gwen John painted her most familiar work, her subdued *Self-portrait.*

1901
Frank Lloyd Wright first published *The Art and Craft of the Machine,* his most famous lecture.
Aristide Maillol expressed the dignity of classical statuary in a modern idiom with his allegorical *Mediterranean* of about this year.

1902
The Exhibition of Decorative Arts, Turin, saw the end of the floral phase of Art Nouveau.
Louis Majorelle was the leading French designer of Art Nouveau furniture.
Alfred Stieglitz founded the Photo-Secession Group.

1903
The Salon d'Automne was founded in France for annual exhibitions.

1904
Otto Wagner began his most important work, the Post Office Savings Bank, Vienna.
Charles Mackintosh completed the Willow Tea Rooms, Glasgow, the height of Art Nouveau elegance.

Performing Arts

1900
The turkey trot, the first of the ragtime dances evolved.
Isadora Duncan, the American dancer, found success in England.
Sir Edward Elgar's oratorio *The Dream of Gerontius* suffered a disastrous first performance in Birmingham.

1901
The Wigmore Hall opened in London.
Ragtime jazz developed in the United States.
Dvořák's tragic fairy-tale, *Rusalka,* was the only one of his operas to score a success outside his native Czechoslovakia.

1902
Enrico Caruso, the Italian tenor, made his first recording.
French composer Claude Debussy reached the peak of his fame with *Pelléas et Mélisande,* his only completed opera.

1903
Verdi's *Ernani* was the first opera ever to be recorded.
Anton Bruckner's *Symphony No 9 in D Minor,* an unfinished symphonic masterpiece, was posthumously performed in Vienna.

1904
The Abbey Theatre, Dublin, was opened. *On Baile's Strand,* by W.B. Yeats, was on the first programme.
Giacomo Puccini, Italian composer, brought Italian grand opera to a grand finale with such dramatic and melodic works as *Madame Butterfly.*
The London Symphony Orchestra gave its first concert.

Science and Technology

1900
Max Planck formulated a quantum theory of light.
The significance of Mendel's work on plant genetics was realized.
The Anopheles mosquito was identified by Sir Patrick Manson as the carrier of malaria

1901
Gugliemo Marconi sent the first-ever transatlantic radio signal. He tapped out the letter "S" in Morse code from a transmitter in Cornwall. It was picked up by an aerial attached to a kite flown over St John's, Newfoundland.
The effect of adrenalin in speeding up the heart was demonstrated by J N Langley, in experiments at Cambridge University.

1902
Oliver Heaviside expounded the theory that radio transmission around the curved surface of the Earth was possible because of a radio-reflecting layer in the upper atmosphere. This layer is now named after him.
Egypt's first Aswan dam — 6,400ft long and the most ambitious civil engineering project of its time — was completed.

1903
Marie and Pierre Curie were awarded the Nobel Prize in physics for their discovery of radium.
'X' rays were first used by the German surgeon Georg Perthes, to inhibit the growth of malignant tumours.

1904
The first synthetic barbiturate, marketed as "Veronal," was synthesized by Emil Fischer.

America

1900
The Currency Act set gold as standard of currency.
McKinley was reelected president.
Puerto Rico became an unorganized territory of US.
US troops joined an international force in China.

1901
Vice President Theodore Roosevelt succeeded President McKinley.
The Platt Amendment gave the US effective control over Cuban affairs.

1902
President Roosevelt called for a "square deal" for everyone.
The Philippines became US territory.
The Bureau of the Census was established.

1903
The Wright brothers achieved the first-ever powered flight with their Flyer 1, at Kitty Hawk, North Carolina. Flyer 1 flew for 59 seconds.
The Alaska boundary dispute with Britain was settled, giving the US access to the Pacific Ocean.
Muckrackers, began to expose corruption in politics and business.

1904
The Republicans kept control of Congress.
The Roosevelt Corollary to Monroe Doctrine rationalized US intervention in the Western Hemisphere.

ISADORA DUNCAN

GUGLIEMO MARCONI

FLYER 1

1905

The Russian fleet engaged the Japanese Navy at the Battle of Tsushima and was almost totally destroyed. Russia sued for peace.

Russia's defeat brought popular discontents to the surface; Czar Nicholas yielded to demands, established a parliament (the Duma) and appointed the country's first Prime Minister.

Norway gained full independence from Sweden.

The German sociologist Karl Weber analyzed the relationship between religious belief and social structure in *The Protestant Ethic and the Spirit of Capitalism.*

Oscar Wilde's *De Profundis* was published.

Cézanne completed his last great *Bathers* composition.

Die Brücke (The Bridge), a German group which became a springboard for Expressionism, was founded.

The Fauves (wild beasts) earned their name with an exhibition of violently colored paintings.

Michel Fokine, great Russian choreographer, created *The Dying Swan* for **Anna Pavlova.**

"Mata Hari" caused a sensation in Paris with her semi-naked dancing.

The blues grew steadily more popular in the United States.

Albert Einstein revolutionized the scientific world view of physical laws with his *Special Theory of Relativity,* which showed that light has a fixed velocity that can never be exceeded.

British biologist Ernest Starling coined the term hormone.

Eugene V. Debs helped found the Industrial Workers of the World (IWW) labor group.

President Roosevelt mediated peace to end the Russo-Japanese War.

1906

A massive earthquake struck San Francisco on the morning of 18 April. Fires began to rage throughout the heart of the city and continued unchecked for three days.

The launch of HMS *Dreadnought* revolutionized battleship design and marked the begining of the British-German naval arms race. Germany began upgrading her fleet.

A conference held between France, Britain and Germany at Algeciras in southern Spain resulted in a ratification of the Entente Cordiale.

John Galsworthy published *A Man of Property,* the first novel in his Forsyte Saga.

Klimt painted one of his finest portraits, *Frau Fritza Riedler.*

Unity Temple, Oak Park, by Frank Lloyd Wright, exphasized concrete and space.

The Fauve *Landscape with red trees* was Maurice de Vlaminck's best work.

Henri Matisse completed *La Joi de Vivre.*

The Manhattan Opera House was built by opera impressario Oscar Hammerstein.

Elgar's oratorio *The Kingdom* formed part of an uncompleted trilogy.

American inventor Lee de Forest patented the triode valve.

C. S. Sherrington published *The Integrative Action of the Nervous System.* The book remains a classic in neurophysiology.

Damages in earthquake and fires in San Francisco, which killed 700 people, reached $400 million.

Accurate labeling of foods and drugs was required by the Pure Food and Drug Act.

1907

The Franco-Japanese Treaty allowed both countries equal "open door" access to China, though Japanese special interests in Manchuria were given special recognition.

Korea became a Japanese protectorate.

An Anglo-Russian Entente, which defined the two countries' spheres of influence in Persia, Afghanistan and Tibet, marked a further distancing of Germany from the other Great Powers.

Norway became the first independent European country to grant women the vote.

New Zealand became a dominion.

A bubonic plague in India claimed more than 1,250,000 lives and promoted fear of a worldwide epidemic.

Immigration into the United States reached its highest level, with 1 ¼ million being granted citizenship during the year.

Henri Bergson further developed his metaphysics with *Creative Evolution.*

Blue Mountain shows Wassily Kandinsky on the way to pure abstraction.

Augustus John painted *Smiling Woman* at about this time.

The dancing Tiller Girls appeared on a London stage for the first time.

The first helicopter - designed in France by Paul Cornu — attained a height of 6ft for a duration of 20 seconds. The machine broke up on landing.

A team led by Ross Harrington at Johns Hopkins University introduced tissue culture.

The Stock market plunged and businesses failed. Roosevelt temporarily loosened antitrust law enforcement in an effort to prevent further decline.

1908

Leopold II granted the Congo Free State, which had previously been his personal possession, to Belgium.

An earthquake in Sicily completely destroyed the city of Messina. An estimated 75,000 people died.

The first oil reserves were discovered in Persia.

Georges Sorel the French social philosopher published *Reflections on Violence,* a mix of Marxist analysis and Nietzschean romanticism.

Rainer Marie Rilke's *New Poems* were published.

Futurism, an attempt to express mechanics in art, began.

Frank Lloyd Wright's Robie House, in Chicago, became one of the most famous *prairie houses,* inspired by Japanese structures.

Sergey Diaghilev founded the Ballets Russes.

Richard Strauss presented his exotic one-act opera *Elektra.*

Russian composer Nikolai Rimsky-Korsakov's last opera, *The Golden Cockerel,* was staged posthumously.

The Geiger counter was invented by Hans Geiger and Ernest Rutherford.

Ilya Metchnikoff and Paul Ehrlich were awarded the Nobel Prize for the discovery of white blood cells.

The barium meal 'X' ray devised to detect stomach ulcers.

William Howard Taft was elected president.

The National Monetary Commission was formed to investigate and analyze banking systems.

1909

The Ottoman Empire recognized Austria's annexation of Bosnia and Herzegovina. Internal strife within the empire remained unresolved.

Leopold II of Belgium died after a reign of 41 years.

Rabindranath Tagore, who was much admired by W.B. Yeats, published *Gitangali,* a series of poems in Bengali which he later translated into English prose versions as *A Handfull of Songs.*

The office of Peter Behrens included three of the most influential architects of the future: Ludwig Mies van der Rohe, Walter Gropius and, later, Le Corbusier.

Cubism first appeared. **Pablo Picasso** painted his proto-Cubist *Les Demoiselles d'Avignon.*

The first Ziegfeld Follies was staged in new York.

English composer Frederick Delius composed *Brigg Fair,* a rhapsody for orchestra based on a Lincolnshire folk song.

Bakelite was made by Leo Baekeland, a Belgian chemist working in New York.

Louis Bleriot became the first person to fly the English Channel.

The term "gene" was used by Danish researcher Wilhelm Johannsen to describe the material controlling heredity.

Henry Ford instituted assembly line production of the Model T.

The National Association for the Advancement of Colored People (NAACP) was founded to advance integration and education and to abolish Jim Crow laws.

Robert Edwin Peary and Matthew Henson became the first to reach the North Pole.

ALBERT EINSTEIN   HMS *DREADNOUGHT*   WRIGHT'S ROBIE HOUSE   LOUIS BLERIOT

World Events

1910
Japan formally annexed Korea, settling Japanese families in the area around Seoul.
The Republic of South Africa was established. Its constitution granted equal rights to citizens of both British and Boer descent.
A revolution in Portugal caused King Manuel II to flee to England. The republican government introduced anticlerical laws and a liberal constitution.
Halley's Comet made one of its closest-ever approaches to Earth.
Dr Crippen, who had murdered his wife, was apprehended in mid-Atlantic as a result of a radio message sent by Britain's Scotland Yard to the captain of the liner on which Crippen was trying to escape. It was the first time radio had been used in crime detection.

1911
The Manchu dynasty, which had ruled China since 1644, was overthrown by a Kuomintang revolt, led by Sun Yatsen.
President Diaz, dictator of Mexico for 35 years, was forced to resign and flee to France.
Italy annexed Tripoli and Benghazi, in Libya, from the Ottoman Empire.
Norwegian explorer Roald Amundsen became the first man to reach the South Pole.

1912
The First Balkan War began when Bulgaria, Serbia, Montenegro and Greece combined to attack Turkey.
United States marines entered Cuba to protect US interests there.
The SS Titanic, the largest ocean liner ever built, struck an iceberg and sank on its maiden transatlantic voyage. Of 2,200 passengers, only 698 survived.
The African National Congress was founded at Bloemfontein.

1913
The Second Balkan War ended a preliminary truce in the first, organized by the Great Powers. Bulgaria was quickly defeated and the subsequent Treaty of Bucharest divided territories in the area between the interested Balkan States.
Marcus Garvey founded the Universal Negro Improvement Society in Jamaica.
The Lambarene hospital for lepers was founded in French Equatorial Africa by Albert Schweitzer.

1914
A Serbian student, Gavrilo Princip, assassinated the Archduke Ferdinand of Austria and his wife at Sarajevo on 28 June. A month later, Austria declared war on Serbia, and a complex system of alliances soon dragged in the Great Powers. Russia massed troops on the German border, and Germany declared war on Russia and then on her ally France. Germany invaded Belgium and Britain then declared war on Germany, on August 4. On the Western Front, both sides were soon entrenched in lines extending from the Belgian coast to Verdun in north-eastern France.
The Panama Canal opened to shipping on August 15, saving vessels the 6,000 mile trip around South America.

Literature Religion Philosophy

1911
Rupert Brooke became the most popular poet of the pre-war generation with the publication of *Poems*.

1912
Romain Rolland published his most important novel, *Jean-Christophe*.

1913
Miguel de Unamuno expounded his philosophy in *The Tragic Sense of Life*.
The first volume of Marcel Prousts's *Remembrance of Things Past — Swann's Way —* was published.
D.H. Lawrence's *Sons and Lovers* was published.

1910
Leo Tolstoy, perhaps the greatest of all novelists, died.
H.G. Wells published the most successful of his social comedies, *The History of Mr. Polly*.

1911
The City Rises by Umberto Boccioni was an exemplary Futurist painting.
Georges Braque's *Man with a Guitar*, a fine example of Analytic Cubism, emphasized form.
Franz Marc, a founder of the Expressionist group, Der Blaue Reiter (The Blue Rider), painted *Blue Horses*.

1912
Boccioni's *Manifesto of Futurist Sculpture* presaged Surrealist sculpture.
Braque's *Fruit Dish and Glass,* which included three pieces of wallpaper, was the first *papier-collé*.
Marcel Duchamp's *Nude Descending a Staircase, No 2* caused uproar in Paris.

1914
James Joyce published *The Dubliners*, realistic short stories in which each tale is centered on a moment of psychological revelation.
Edgar Rice Burroughs wrote the first of his Tarzan books, *Tarzan of the Apes*.

Art and Architecture

1910
The English critic Roger Fry coined the term "Post-Impressionism."
Emil Nolde, the German Expressionist artist, painted *Dance Around the Golden Calf*.
Constantin Brancusi, the Romanian sculptor, began his *Sleeping Muse* series.

1911
Diaghilev's Ballets Russes commissioned major works, such as Stravinsky's *Petrushka*.
Gustav Mahler died.

1912
Mack Sennett formed the Keystone Company, which produced the "Keystone Kop" comedy shorts.
Nijinsky choreographed and performed in *L'Après-midi d'un faune*.
Daphnis and Chloé was written by French composer Maurice Ravel for Diaghilev.

1913
Bicycle Wheel, Marcel Duchamp's first "ready-made," would lead to Dada and Surrealism.
Walter Richard Sickert, one of the greatest English Impressionist painters, produced *Ennui*.
Jacob Epstein sculpted *Rock Drill*, a supreme example of Vorticism.

1914
With his Horse, Raymond Duchamp-Villon produced one of the finest Cubist sculptures.
Wassily Kandinsky's *Autumn* foreshadowed Abstract Expressionism 30 years later.

Performing Arts

1910
Igor Stravinsky wrote *The Firebird*, his first ballet, for Russian impresario Sergey Diaghilev.
The Argentine tango became popular with European and American dancers.

1913
Nijinsky's *The Rite of Spring* was the first great expressionist ballet.
The Squaw Man was produced in a Hollywood barn by Cecil B. de Mille, Jesse Lasky and Samuel Goldwyn.

1914
Italian tenor Beniamino Gigli made his operatic debut.

Science and Technology

1911
Rutherford demonstrated that the atom had a nuclear structure.
Superconductivity was first observed by Kamerlingh Onnes, a Dutch physicist.
The first cloud chamber photographs of sub-atomic particles were taken by Charles Wilson, a Scottish physicist.

1912
Niels Bohr applied theory to sub-atomic physics.
James Herrick, an American, became the first doctor to diagnose a heart attack in a living patient.

1913
John J. Abel constructed the first artificial kidney.

1910
British chemist Frederick Soddy suggested the idea of chemical isotopes, a term he applied to them three years later.

1914
Edward Kendall isolated thyroxin, a hormone vital for full thyroid gland functioning.

America

1911
Wisconsin's Robert M. La Follette founded the National Progressive Republican League.
Supreme Court rulings in *Standard Oil Company of NJ v. US* and *US v. American Tobacco Co.* upheld the Sherman Antitrust Act.

1912
The Progressive (Bull Moose) Party was formed by disgruntled Republicans. It split the Republican vote, and Democrat Woodrow Wilson was elected president.
New Mexico became the 47th state and Arizona the 48th.

1913
The Federal Reserve banking system was established by Federal Reserve Act.
Federal income tax was provided for in the Constitution's 16th Amendment, while the 17th provided for popular election of senators.

1914
The Clayton Antitrust Act was passed to give teeth to the Sherman Antitrust Act of 1890.
The Fair Trade Commisson was established to ensure open, fair competition in business.

1910
The Mann-Elkins Act was passed to regulate interstate commerce, while the Mann Act made transportation of women across state lines for immoral purposes illegal.

G** SAISON RUSSE

IGOR STRAVINSKY   NIJINSKY   GAVRILO PRINCIP

British and French naval forces failed to force their way up the Dardanelles to take Constantinople after Turkey entered the war, allied to Austria and Germany. British and Australian and New Zealand troops, the latter known as the Anzacs, then launched a land attack on the forts of Gallipoli but met bitter Turkish resistance, and withdrew after eight months.

A bloody stalemate continued on the Western Front. At Ypres poison gas was used by the Germans for the first time. Italy entered the War on the Allied side during May.

The British liner Lusitania was sunk without warning by German submarines, with the loss of 1,153 passengers.

DH Lawrence's novel *The Rainbow,* was suppressed as obscene.

Rupert Brooke, died on a hospital ship on his way to the Dardenelles.

Georges de Chirico founded the Metaphysical school in Italy, the workings of the Unconscious in paintings.

The Birth of a Nation and *Intolerance* (1916) were D.W. Griffith's greatest films.

Einstein extended his theory of relativity to include the motion of accelerating objects and the nature of gravitational force.

Sonar - Sound Navigation and Ranging – was invented.

The first tank, Little Willie, was designed as a "land battleship" to carry troops across battlefields.

The Preparedness Movement signaled the end of total US neutrality.

The sinking of the *Lusitania,* with the loss of 128 Americans, accelerated anti-German feelings.

Marines intervened in Haiti; a treaty gave the US control of the nation.

The Germans launched a massive attack on Verdun in February. The battle lasted until December, with huge losses on both sides. To relieve the French, Britain launched a major Somme offensive on 1 July, gaining only ten miles for the loss of 600,000 men.

At sea, the outcome of the Battle of Jutland on May 31 was indecisive, but the German fleet retreated to port.

Dada was born, the nihilistic, absurdist movement. Its events prefigured the 1960's "Happenings," its techniques, such as **Jean Arp's** *Squares Arranged According to the Laws of Chance,* the methods of Surrealism and Abstract Expressionism.

Harmony reached a peak of complexity with Stravinsky, who worked in several keys simultaneously, and then split asunder in the keyless music of Arnold Schoenberg and Béla Bartók.

Edward Sharpey Schafer, a British physiologist, identified the site of manufacture of a hypothetical hormone he called insulin, which controlled food metabolism.

Tanks were used for the first time on 15 September by British forces in the Battle of the Somme.

General John J. Pershing and his troops crossed into Mexico to pursue Pancho Villa and his raiders during the Mexican Border Campaign.

Wilson was reelected and continued programs to strengthen the armed forces.

Russia was demoralized by food shortages and by the loss of 5 ½ million troops on the Eastern Front. After strikes and rioting Lenín led a Bolshevik force against the Winter Palace in October and established an All-Russian Congress of Soviets. Promising "Peace, Land and Bread," he arranged a ceasefire with Germany in December.

On the Western Front at Passchendale, appalling weather turned the battlefield into a sea of mud. Allied forces gained five miles, lost to a German spring offensive the following year.

T.E. Lawrence led a revolt of the Arabs against the Turks.

America declared war on Germany on 6 April.

T.S. Eliot published *Prufrock and Other Observations,* poems of a strikingly modern idiom that expressed a sense of urban isolation and decay.

The periodical De Stijl set forth the theories of the Dutch group of the same name (The Style). Its desire for harmony found abstract expression in all the arts. Mondrian was the chief guru.

The ballet Parade was performed by Diaghilev's Ballets Russes.

The Original Dixieland Jazz Band made the first ever jazz recordings.

Clarence Birdseye, as a result of a visit to Alaska, experimented with freezing food to keep it fresh.

The US joined the Allied side in World War I, with forces commanded by General Pershing.

The first Selective Service Act covered men aged 18—45.

The US purchased part of the Virgin Islands.

German spring offensives secured some ground at Ypres and crossed the Marne, but were forced back by a vigorous French counter-offensive led by Marshall Foch. By the autumn, with fresh US troops, the Allies were advancing on all fronts and the German army was demoralized. Germany sued for peace and on 11 November an armistice was signed ending the war.

Oswald Spengler's Decline of the West created an immense impact on publication in Germany.

Gerrit Rietveld with his famous red-and-blue armchair — geometrical and in primary colours — realized the principles of Stijl.

Le Corbusier (Charles-Edouard Jeanneret) and Amédée Ozenfant published the Purist manifesto, *After Cubism.*

Béla Bartók began to make his name internationally with his brooding opera *Bluebeard's Castle.*

Anti-tetanus vaccines were used extensively by the British Army. Their success boosted the campaign for general vaccination of civilians in peace time.

Wilson put forth Fourteen Points, a peace plan that included formation of the League of Nations.

US troops played a key role in last offensives against the Germans.

The major allied powers - Britain, France, Italy and the United States – met at the Paris Peace Conference. The subsequent Treaty of Versailles forced Germany, among other conditions, to return Alsace-Lorraine to France, to pay heavy reparations and to radically limit its armed forces.

The League of Nations was founded to preserve peace and to settle disputes between nations by arbitration.

At Amritsar, in the Punjab, British troops opened fire with inadequate warning on rioting Indians, killing 379 and wounding over 1,000.

Prohibition was introduced in the United States.

John Read's Ten Days that Shook the World gave a realistic, if idealistically tinged, account of the birth of the Russian Revolution.

Amedeo Modigliani painted his sensual *Reclining nude* and portrait of *Jeanne Hébuterne:* their elongated forms are typical.

Léonide Massine choreographed his most famous works, *La Boutique fantasque* and *The Three-Cornered Hat.*

The Theatre Guild was formed in America, to produce experimental plays.

Ernest Rutherford bombarded nitrogen atoms with helium nuclei and found that a minute number split into oxygen and hydrogen nucleii. This was the first artificial nuclear transmutation of matter.

Alcock and Brown made the first nonstop flight across the Atlantic.

Wilson campaigned strongly but unsuccessfully for US entrance into the League of Nations.

The Constitution's 18th Amendment, inaugurated the Prohibition era.

WORLD WAR I   LENIN   RIETVELD'S CHAIR

	1920	1921	1922	1923	1924
World Events	**Soviet Russia** was in turmoil, with famine, sporadic peasant risings and concerted anti-Bolshevik campaigns in many areas as well as Nationalist revolts in Latvia, Estonia, Lithuania and Finland. Poland absorbed enough formerly Russian territory to become the largest of the East European states. **Adolf Hitler** became the seventh member of the National Socialist German Workers' Party — nicknamed the "Nazi" Party.	**Germany** reluctantly agreed to an Ultimatum from London to pay £6,600 million in war reparation damages. An extra 50% British duty on German goods, with other measures, inflicted severe strains on Germany's war damaged economy. **Spain** was in crisis with the assassination of the Prime Minister and the loss of 12,000 Spanish troops against irregular Rif forces in the Battle of Anual in Morocco.	**Mussolini** demanded that a fascist government should be formed in Italy to avert civil war. King Victor Emmanuel III agreed to this on 29 October as Fascist supporters congregated in Rome. **Turkey** under Kemal Ataturk wrested the upper hand from Greece after two years of hostilities in the Graeco-Turkish war, driving the Greek army out of Smyrna. Greek civilians were massacred as the city burned. **Germany and Russia** signed the Rapallo Treaty, pledging co-operation and renouncing any war reparation claims. **King Tutanhkhamun's tomb** was opened by Howard Carter.	**Inflation** raged in Germany and the local currency became literally worthless. **In November, Adolf Hitler** led an abortive coup to seize the state government of Bavaria and was sent to prison for five years during which he wrote *Mein Kampf.* **French and Belgian troops** occupied the Ruhr when Germany failed to meet its quota of reparation payments. **The Treaty of Lausanne** formally ended the war between Greece and Turkey. **The worst recorded earthquake** struck Tokyo in September. The city was destroyed and the death toll put at 150,000.	**Lenin** died on 21 January. Joseph Stalin took control of the party machine in Russia. **Mustapha Kemal,** President of the newly-founded Turkish republic, abolished the position of Caliph as religious leader and declared the country a secular state.
Literature Religion Philosophy	**D.H. Lawrence** continued to explore the theme of male and female sexuality and the difficulty of achieving psychological integrity in a decadent society in his *Women in Love.*	**Jung** offered an alternative view of human psychology in *Psychological Types,* suggesting two fundamental types: the extroverted and the introverted. **Agatha Christie** introduced the Belgian detective Hercule Poirot in *The Mysterious Affair at Styles.*	**Wittgenstein** in his *Tractatus Logico-Philisophicus* examined the inextricable links between language and the meaning of philosophical activity. **The Waste Land** by T.S. Eliot was published, establishing a modern poetic idiom. **James Joyce's Ulysses** was published in Paris — a masterly novel about a single day in the life and thoughts of two Dublin men.	**Rainer Maria Rilke** completed the *Duino Elegies* after 10 years' work, but was then suddenly inspired to write *Sonnets to Orpheus.* Both sequences represent the poet's maturest work. **Martin Buber** published his highly influential book *I and Thou,* describing an existentialist spiritualism in which "Thou" is the everyday experience of God in the world and within the soul.	**E.M. Forster** published his finest novel, *A Passage to India.* **The German novelist Thomas Mann** wrote affectionate satire of German culture in *The Magic Mountain.* **André Breton** published the *Surrealist Manifesto,* an expression of the Unconscious which affected all the arts.
Art and Architecture	**Constructivism,** non-representational art, in "modern" materials, was founded in Russia by Naum Gabo, Antoine Peusner and Vladimir Tatlin. **Lalique** established his own glass factory.	**Erich Mendelsohn** completed the Einstein Tower at Potsdam for the great scientist, an Art Deco sculptural feat.	**Man Ray** in Paris and **Moholy-Nagy** in Berlin were at the forefront of experimental art using light effects.	**Le Corbusier** declared "A house is a machine for living" in *Towards a New Architecture.*	**An eighteenth-century ban** on female actors was lifted in China. **Erich von Stroheim's** screen masterpiece was *Greed.* **Sean O'Casey's** *Juno and the Paycock* was first performed at the Abbey Theatre, Dublin. **Twelve-note or serial music,** was created by Austrian composer Arnold Schoenberg.
Performing Arts	**Reinhardt** established the Salzburg Festival in Austria. **Douglas Fairbanks,** the 1920s "King of Hollywood," made *The Mark of Zorro,* one of his most popular films. **The Planets** by British composer Gustav Holst had its first complete performance in London.	**The Sheik** was Rudolph Valentino's most famous film. **The Kid** was Charlie Chaplin's first great feature-length comedy. **Hermann Rorschach** introduced his ink-blot tests as a diagnostic device for psychological states. A series of cards containing differently-shaped ink-blots are presented to the patient for interpretation.	**An early Dracula film** was Friedrich Murnau's expressionist *Nosferatu.* **Nanook of the North,** a romanticised documentary on Eskimo life by Robert Flaherty, pioneered a new film genre.	**Facade** marked the collaboration between the English poet, Edith Sitwell, and composer, William Walton. **George Gershwin** wrote his perennial symphonic jazz composition *Rhapsody in Blue.*	**French physicist de Broglie's theory** of a constant relationship between a particle's mass and velocity and its wavelength laid the foundation of wave mechanics.
Science and Technology	**An X ray method for detecting fingerprints** was developed in France.		**BCG tuberculosis vaccine** was introduced in France.		**An investigation into the Teapot Dome** oil land-leasing scandal of Harding's administration began.
America	**Republican Warren G. Harding** was elected president on a "return to normalcy" platform.	**A severe recession** led to budget reform and creation of the Budget Bureau in the Treasury Department. Charles Dawes was made its first director. **The welfare of veterans** was consolidated under the new Veterans Bureau.	**The Washington Armament Conference** highlighted the US role in postwar international affairs. **The Cooperative Marketing Act** granted farmers exemption from antitrust laws.	**President Harding,** his administration becoming enmeshed in scandal, died. He was succeeded by Vice President Calvin Coolidge. **Ku Klux Klan** activities, at their most violent, began to be exposed in the press.	**The Johnson Act** limited all immigrants but those from western and northern Europe. **Coolidge** was elected president.

RUDOLPH VALENTINO   GERMAN INFLATION   JAMES JOYCE

The Treaty of Locarno guaranteed the inviolability of the French/German and Belgian/German borders and established a demilitarized zone in the Rhineland.
Chiang Kai-shek gained control of the Kuomintang in China after the death of Sun Yat Sen.
Mussolini banned non-fascist parties in Italy.

Kafka in *The Trial* encapsulated the fate of the individual under totalitarianism.
F. Scott Fitzgerland published his most successful novel, *The Great Gatsby*.

Monet completed the two huge mural cycles of his water-lily ponds at Giverny.
The Paris Exhibition was the culmination of Art Deco.
Peter Behrens completed the offices of the I.G. Farben Paint Co., Frankfurt, with its central hall of plunging brickwork.
The headquarters of The Bauhaus, the most important modern school of architecture and the applied arts, was designed by the director, Walter Gropius, in Desau.

The Battleship Potemkin by Sergey Eisenstein was a masterpiece of world cinema.
Chicago-style jazz became popular in Europe.
Austrian composer Alban Berg's revolutionary atonal opera *Wozzeck* was first staged in Berlin.

Teacher John Scopes was prosecuted for breaking state law by teaching Darwin's theories in Tennesse.

The World War I flying ace Billy Mitchell was courtmartialed for criticizing the Navy.

US troops landed in Nicaragua to protect US interests in the face of a popular revolt.
France bombarded Damascus to regain control after a militant Druze uprising.
Germany entered the League of Nations, furthering her diplomatic rehabilitation.

T.E. Lawrence published *The Seven Pillars of Wisdom.*

Joan Miró, great abstract Surrealist, painted his *Dog barking at the moon.*
Le Corbusier built 40 houses at Pessac, near Bordeaux. Their austere modernism offended the authorities who, for six years, withheld a water supply.

Martha Graham, great innovator in modern dance, made her New York debut as an independent artist.
Fritz Lang completed the film *Metropolis,* his Expressionist vision of the future.
Valentino's death caused hysteria, suicides and mob scenes at his funeral.
An English school, including Frederick Delius, Gustav Holst, and Vaughan Williams produced memorable pastoral music.

Scottish inventor John Logie Baird demonstrated a television system to scientists in Soho, London.
American neurologist Wilder Penfield began work on a surgical treatment of epilepsy fundamental in mapping brain functions.

The Revenue Act reduced certain personal, inheritance, and excise taxes.
The Army Air Corps, later to become the US Air Force, was established from the Air Service of World War I.

Chiang Kai-shek extended his control in China after purging the Communist wing of the Kuomintang.
Trotsky was denounced by Stalin and expelled from the Party.
Charles Lindbergh flew the Atlantic in his monoplane, *The Spirit of St Louis,* landing in France after a 33hr 39min flight to international acclaim.

German existentialist philosopher Martin Heidegger published his most important work: *Being and Time.*

The International Style of architecture was born: the Deutscher Werkbund exposition included 33 model housing units designed by 16 modernist architects.

"Talkies" began in feature films with *The Jazz Singer* when Al Jolson spoke a few lines.
Napoléon was completed, a remarkable unfinished epic, shot partly in three-camera "polyvision," by Abel Gance.
Louis Armstrong created a solo style in jazz with his innovative trumpet improvisations.
Duke Ellington began an orchestral style in jazz.
Show Boat, a musical by Jerome Kern and Oscar Hammerstein II, was first staged in New York.

A prototype iron lung was devised by Professor Philip Drinker at Harvard University.

Anarchists Sacco and Vanzetti were executed.

Stalin's first Five Year Plan to develop heavy industry and collectivize agriculture brought with it a "liquidation" of the Russian *kulaks,* peasants who had gained possession of medium-sized farms during Czarist agrarian reforms.

Evelyn Waugh published his first novel, *Decline and Fall,* an energetic black satire on corruption within a minor English prep school.
American anthropologist Margaret Mead published her best selling *Coming of Age in Samoa* contrasting the dignity of that transition with the traumatic experience of American girls.

Harpist by Jacques Lipchitz was one of the first Cubist sculptures.
The House of Glass was completed in Paris. Pierre Chareau's pure *neoplastic* design used steel and glass, even for the partitions.
Otto Dix, Expressionist painter of ugly realism, finished his masterpiece, the triptych *The City.*

Walt Disney created Mickey Mouse.
Luis Buñuel directed the Surrealist *Un Chien andalou* with Salvador Dalí.
Showboat, the classic American musical, was first performed.
Arturo Toscanini, Italian conductor, was appointed conductor of the New York Philharmonic Symphony Orchestra.
Ravel's Bolero, an orchestral work of Spanish character, was first performed in Paris.

Alexander Fleming proposed that a substance coating a dish of bacteria left in his laboratory could help combat disease. He named it penicillin.
British physicist Paul Dirac predicted the existence of the positron in quantum mechanics.

Republican Herbert Hoover won the presidential race with a campaign for "rugged individualism."

A worldwide Depression began on 24 October – "Black Thursday" – when over 13 million shares changed hands as investors lost confidence in the American boom. As panic selling continued, unemployment rose dramatically.
Pope Pius XI concluded an agreement with Mussolini recognizing the independent sovereignty of the Vatican.

Robert Graves published his candid autobiography *Goodbye to All That,* one of the most moving and damning accounts of the World War I.

The first Academy Awards were presented.
George Balanchine choreographed *Prodigal Son* with the great Serge Lifar in the title role.
Broadway Melody was the first film musical.
Noel Coward wrote his highly successful operetta *Bittersweet.*
William Walton, English composer, produced his *Viola Concerto,* widely acknowledged as the finest composition written for that instrument.

American physicist Ernest Lawrence devised the cyclotron to produce high energy atomic collisions by accelerating particles to incredibly high speeds.
American astronomer Edwin Hubble showed that the relationship between the speed of recession of galaxies, indicated by the red "Doppler" shift in their spectra, and their distance, was constant. His work remains a cornerstone of cosmology.

The Federal Farm Board was established to encourage cooperatives through low-interest loans.

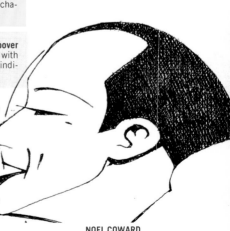

THE BAUHAUS   ALEXANDER FLEMING   NOEL COWARD

1930

World Events

Haile Selassie acceded to the throne as Emperor of Ethiopia.
Right-wing dictatorships were established in Brazil and Argentina after social unrest.
Gandhi began a campaign of civil disobedience in India.
Amy Johnson flew solo to Australia.

Literature Religion Philosophy

Spanish philosopher Ortega y Gasset published his prophetic critique of democracy in *The Revolt of the Masses* warning that importunate majorities could institute tyranny against minorities.

Art and Architecture

The Chrysler Building by William Van Alan in New York was a triumph of Art Deco.
Epstein's *Genesis*, crudely hewn from stone, caused controversy in Britain.

Performing Arts

Jean Harlow began an American craze for platinum-blonde hair following her screen success in *Hell's Angels*.
All Quiet on the Western Front, directed by Lewis Milestone, was one of the greatest war films.
A chamber music trio of unrivalled talent was founded by Jacques Thibaud (violin), Pablo Casals (cello), and Alfred Cortot (piano).

Science and Technology

Swiss chemist Paul Karrer's work led to a clarification of Vitamin A and an understanding of the metabolic relationship between vitamins and enzymes.
Karl Landsteiner won the Nobel Prize for discovering different human blood groups.

America

The Federal Veteran's Administration was formed to oversee benefits for veterans and dependants.
Work programs for the unemployed were initiated by Hoover, but unemployment continued to rise.

1931

In Spain, Republicans gained electoral victories and drove out King Alphonso XIII.
Austrian and German banks closed as the Depression gripped. Reparation payments ceased.
Japanese forces seized the Manchurian city of Mukden, marking the rise of Japanese militarism.

French novelist Saint-Exupéry achieved fame with his book *Night Flight*, a story of the pilots on the air mail service from France to the colonies in N. Africa.

Salvador Dali painted his great fantasy of the unconscious, *The persistence of memory*, with its melting watches.

The Vic-Wells Ballet was established at Sadler's Wells Theatre, London. Later, it became Sadler's Wells Ballet.
Frankenstein made Boris Karloff the king of horror films for over 20 years.
The Star-Spangled Banner, with words by Francis Scott Key, became America's official national anthem.

Deuterium, a heavy isotope of hydrogen was isolated by Harold Urey at Columbia University. Deuterium combines with oxygen to make heavy water, essential for many nuclear reactions.

Crime syndicate boss Al Capone was jailed for income tax evasion.
Veterans' organizations demanded early payment on bonus, or compensation, certificates provided for veterans in 1924.

1932

Franklin D. Roosevelt was elected President of the United States, offering the country a "New Deal" to beat the economic recession.
Unrest in Spain continued, with the Basque country and Catalonia agitating for national autonomy. Churches and monasteries were attacked in a wave of anti-clericalism.
Bolivia and Paraguay started a three-year territorial war which killed over 100,000.

A nightmare vision of a manipulated future humanity was presented by Aldous Huxley in *Brave New World*.

The term International Style was coined for a retrospective exhibition of modern European architecture, held at the Museum of Modern Art, New York.

The Royal Danish Ballet underwent a renaissance when Harald Lander became ballet master.
The Shakespeare Memorial Theatre was opened in Stratford-on-Avon.
English conductor Thomas Beecham founded the London Philharmonic Orchestra.
Arnold Schoenberg, largely self-taught, completed the first two acts of his opera *Moses and Aaron*.

The Bonus Army of veterans, camped in Washington, D.C., demanded payment of bonuses but were violently dispersed by troops under Douglas MacArthur.

1933

On 30 January German President Hindenburg invited Adolf Hitler, leader of the Nazi Party, to become Chancellor of Germany. A month later, the Reichstag (parliament building) in Berlin was destroyed by arson. Hitler used this opportunity to ban opposition and give himself total power. The first concentration camps for "political and racial enemies" were established at Dachau and Oranienburg.
Prohibition ended in the United States.

French novelist André Malraux published *La Condition Humaine*. Set in the Shanghai of Chiang Kai-shek, the book describes the corruption of revolutionary idealism.
George Orwell published an account of his experiences with the destitute in *Down and Out in Paris and London*.

The first issue of Minotaure had a cover by Picasso. He claimed not to be a Surrealist but, an artist of many "periods," he fell under their influence.

The Private Life of Henry VIII directed by Alexander Korda invigorated the British film industry.
The Neoclassic movement reinterpreting classical form in modern sound was initiated by Stravinsky and attracted Sergey Prokofiev and Paul Hindemith.
American composer and songwriter Jerome Kern wrote the musical *Roberta*, which introduced the song *Smoke Gets In Your Eyes*.

The Polish/Swiss chemist Tadeus Reichstein synthesized Vitamin C for the first time.

The 20th Amendment set dates for convening Congress and inaugurating the president.
In 100 Days, Roosevelt initiated dramatic emergency measures to deal with recovery.

1934

Chinese communists under the command of Mao Tse-tung set out on their Long March from the province of Kiangsi (where they were blockaded by Chiang Kai-shek's forces) to the mountains in northwest China.
Stalin began a series of show trials to rid the Party of any possible leadership rivals.
The Australian Chancellor, Engelbert Dollfuss, ordered troops into the working-class districts of Vienna, and there was effective civil war as the socialists fought back. In June Dollfuss was assassinated by Austrian Nazis in an abortive coup.
In the "Night of the Long Knives" SS troops murdered Hitler's rivals within the Nazi party.

British historian Arnold Toynbee published the first volume of his major work, *A Study of History*.
Blood Wedding was the first of a trilogy of folk dramas written by Federico Garcia Lorca.

Victor Vasarély, pioneer of Op art, had begun his illusionistic series of *Zebras*.

It Happened One Night, directed by Frank Capra, began the trend for witty Hollywood comedies.
Bright Eyes, starring Shirley Temple, included her most famous song, *On The Good Ship Lollipop*.
The Glyndebourne Operatic Festival was founded.

Enrico Fermi discovered that a chain reaction of nuclear fission could be achieved with uranium.

New Deal programs set up the Federal Farm Mortgage Corporation and the Federal Housing Administration.

AMY JOHNSON   ECONOMIC RECESSION   FRANKLIN DELANO ROOSEVELT   ADOLF HITLER

Mussolini invaded Abyssinia (now Ethiopia) as part of a plan to establish an East African Empire. Limited sanctions by the League of Nations were ineffective.
The Saar was returned to Germany after a League of Nations referendum.
Hitler passed the Nuremberg Laws, which made Jews second-class citizens and made sex between Jews and non-Jews a capital offence.

Christopher Isherwood gave a witty, episodic account of the decline of German society under the Nazis in *Mr Norris Changes Trains*.

Ben Nicholson and his wife, **Barbara Hepworth** came to the fore with their non-representational sculpture in Britain.
Ansel Adams, great American landscape photographer, won acclaim for his book *Making a Photograph*, illustrated with his own work.

Marie Rambert founded the Ballet Rambert.
Fred Astaire made his famous film *Top Hat*.
US musical theater reached a peak of sophistication with George Gershwin's *Porgy and Bess*.
Hammond electric organs became popular in the United States.
T.S. Eliot's poetic drama *Murder in the Cathedral* appeared.

Radar was developed in secrecy by Britain.
A prototype of the Spitfire was built.

The Works Progress Administration was established to initiate a wide variety of employment programs. Unemployment insurance and other benefits were assured by the Social Security Act.

Civil war broke out in Spain when General Franco led an army revolt against the Republican government. Assisted by Italian troops and German air support, Franco took half the country with Catalonia and the Basque region remaining Republican.
German troops entered the demilitarized zone of the Rhineland, violating the Treaty of Versailles.
Germany and Japan signed an Anti-Comintern Pact. Italy and Germany entered into a loose collaboration of mutual aid.

British economist John Maynard Keynes in *The General Theory of Employment, Interest and Money* advocated government intervention to control investment, employment and consumer consumption.

Frank Lloyd Wright won acclaim for "Falling Water," Bear Run, Pennsylvania, a daring structure built over a waterfall.
Life magazine began, famous for the quality of its photographic content.

Biochemists Dale and Loewi were awarded the Nobel prize for showing that the chemical acetylcholine transmitted nerve signals to muscle cells.

Price fixing to discourage competition was outlawed by the Robinson-Patman Act.
Roosevelt, campaigning on success of his New Deal programs, was triumphantly reelected, defeating Alf Landon.

German dive-bombers razed the Basque city of Guernica as German and Italian military backing for Franco increased.
Japan invaded China, rapidly capturing Peking, Tiensin, Shanghai and Nanking where over 200,000 civilians were massacred.
The German airship *Hindenburg* exploded while landing in New Jersey, ending the airship era.

J.R.R. Tolkein, an Oxford academic, wrote *The Hobbit*, first of his great fantasies.

Picasso painted his famous outcry against war, *Guernica*.
One of the first modern buildings in South America was begun, Lúcio Costa and Oscar Niemeyer's Ministry of Education and Health, Rio.

Walt Disney's *Snow White and the Seven Dwarfs* was the first feature-length cartoon.
Jean Renoir, son of Auguste, directed one of his finest films, *La Grand Illusion*.
Pépé le Moko, directed by Julien Duvivier, initiated the theme of pessimism in the French cinema.

Sir Frank Whittle built the first experimental jet aircraft engine.
Nylon - the first completely synthetic material — was produced commercially.

In attempt to get New Deal legislation upheld, Roosevelt tried to "pack" the conservative Supreme Court with additional justices. His plan failed, but older, reactionary justices soon retired.

The Anschluss united Austria and Germany as the Austrian Nazi Party invited German troops to march in.
As Germany threatened Czechoslovakia with war the Munich Agreement between Germany, France, Britain and Italy acceeded to Germany's demands for the return of the Sudetenland with a guarantee to Czechoslovakia against further aggression. British Prime Minister Chamberlain predicted "peace in our time."
German oppression of the Jews continued with the "Kristalnacht", in which Jewish shops were attacked and 30,000 Jews sent to concentration camps.

Jean-Paul Sartre published his first novel, *Nausea,* an account of his own existential dilemma and disgust at bourgeois values.

Three of Brancusi's greatest abstract works were inaugurated in the Tîrgu Jiu Park, Romania.
The Museum of Modern Art, New York was under way.
Picture Post first appeared.

The Winnipeg Ballet Company was founded in Canada.
Uday Shankar opened a school of dance in Almora, India, to teach in both the Western and local traditions.
Orson Welles' radio production of H G Wells's *War of the Worlds* caused nationwide panic among millions of listeners in the United States.
Black contralto Marian Anderson was awarded an honorary doctorate by Harvard University.

US virologist Wendell Stanley opened up the genetic study of viruses.
Lazlo Biro invented the ballpoint pen.

A minimum wage and a maximum-hour work day were planned for in the Fair Labor Standards Act.

The Spanish Civil War ended in March with Franco's victory.
A Nazi-Soviet non-aggression pact was signed in August.
Germany invaded Poland on 1 September, overrunning it in four weeks. Britain and France declared war on Germany two days later.
The first significant engagement of World War II was the Battle of the River Plate on 13 December. The German pocket battleship Graf Spee was sighted and attacked in the South Atlantic by HMS Ajax, Exeter and Achilles. After putting into Montevideo for repairs, the Graf Spee was scuttled.
Sigmund Freud died in London.

John Steinbeck published his novel *Grapes of Wrath*.

René Magritte brought a meticulous technique to his illusionistic works, such as *Time Transfixed*.

Bernard Shaw won an Academy Award for his screen adaptation of his play *Pygmalion* later adapted as the musical *My Fair Lady*.
Gone with the Wind was completed.
The Wizard of Oz brought Judy Garland international fame.
English pianist Myra Hess organized National Gallery lunchtime concerts in wartime London.

The U-235 isotope of uranium was split for the first time in experiments at Columbia University.

As conditions worsened in Europe, Roosevelt asked for increased defense funds.
The US reasserted neutrality.
The Hatch Act limited the political activity of government employees.

BENITO MUSSOLINI　　　　FRED ASTAIRE　　　　NEVILLE CHAMBERLAIN　　　　WORLD WAR II

World Events

1940

German forces occupied Denmark in April and went on to invade Norway. Holland and Belgium were invaded in the following month, and France fell at the end of June.
The British Expeditionary Force and the First French Army were cut off around Dunkirk. More than 850 vessels from Britain evacuated 350,000 Allied troops from the beaches in a week.
Italy entered the war, on Germany's side, on 10 June.
The Battle of Britain was fought in the skies over southern England.
Marshall Pétain signed an armistice between Germany and France and set up a pro-German government at Vichy.
Leon Trotsky was murdered by a Stalinist agent in Mexico.

1941

Germany opened up a 2,000—mile Russian front. By September, Leningrad was surrounded. It withstood almost 900 days of siege.
Greece fell to Germany. In May, 1,500 German paratroopers took Crete in the first successful airborne invasion in military history.
Japanese carrier-borne aircraft launched a surprise attack on the American fleet at Pearl Harbor. America declared war on Japan the next day, 8 December, and three days later Germany and Italy declared war on America.

1942

Japanese forces advanced towards Singapore, which fell on 15 February, with the surrender of more than 70,000 Allied troops.
The British Eighth Army checked a German advance towards Cairo in the 1st Battle of El-Alamein. Allied forces defeated combined German and Italian forces at the 2nd Battle of El-Alamein, and began a drive to eject them from North Africa.
United States naval forces prevented a Japanese advance into the Pacific at the Battle of Midway Island. The battle was fought almost entirely between opposing naval aircraft, the fleets being some 200 miles apart.

1943

German and Italian troops were forced from North Africa and a combined British and American force under Dwight D. Eisenhower landed in Sicily. Italy officially surrendered. Mussolini was rescued from internment by German airborne troops and set up a fascist republic in German-controlled northern Italy.
On the Eastern Front, the German Sixth Army, supported by the Fourth Panzer Army and Romanian units, advanced to Stalingrad on the lower Volga. In late November a Soviet counter-offensive succeeded in cutting off the German advance from its support, effectively trapping them in Stalingrad. The German divisions were finally defeated in the following January.

1944

American troops landed at Anzio, in Italy, behind German lines. Rome fell on 4 June and German forces retreated northwards.
On 6 June — D-Day — British, American and Canadian troops landed on the beaches of Normandy. Paris was liberated on 25 August and Brussels on 2 September.
The Japanese were forced to retreat from their positions in the Irrawaddy Delta. Singapore was recaptured by British troops on 5 September.
Anti-Nazi elements within the German army failed in an assassination attempt on Hitler on 20 July.
The first wave of German V2 rocket bombs fell on London.

Literature Religion Philosophy

Arthur Koestler's *Darkness at Noon* provided a frightening insight to the inhumanity of Stalin's Soviet regime.

In The Fancy Dress Party, the Italian novelist Alberto Moravia presented a satirical portrait of Mussolini.

Siegfried Giedion, the Swiss art historian, published his most influential book, *Space, Time and Architecture*.
Paul Nash completed his masterpiece of war wreckage, *Totes Meer* (Dead sea).

Albert Camus published the first of his three major novels, *The Outsider*. Set in Algeria, it is a portrait of an alienated sensualist condemned for the murder of an Arab.

Jean-Paul Sartre's existentialist philosophy was expounded in *Being and Nothingness*.

TS Eliot's Four Quartets were published in collected form.

Picasso produced *Man with a Sheep,* his most famous sculpture.

Art and Architecture

Paul Klee painted *Death and fire*.
Sidney Nolan, the Australian painter, caused a stir with his *Boy and the Moon*.

John Huston directed his first great film, *The Maltese Falcon*.
English composer Michael Tippett made his name with the oratorio *A Child of Our Time*.
Noël Coward's *Blithe Spirit* was recognized by audiences as elegant high comedy.

Edward Hopper, American painter of loneliness and silence, painted his most famous work, *Nighthawks*.

Alexander Calder, American master of moving sculpture, exhibited at the Museum of Modern Art, New York.

The first part of Eisenstein's *Ivan the Terrible* was completed.
Appalachian Spring, Martha Graham's ballet to music by Aaron Copland, was performed for the first time.
American composer and conductor Leonard Bernstein wrote the score for the Broadway musical comedy *On the Town*.

Performing Arts

Romeo and Juliet was created by Leonid Lavrosky, to music by Prokofiev.
Peter and the Wolf, Frank Staff's comic ballet, was first performed.
Alfred Hitchcock's film version of *Rebecca* won four Academy Awards.
Duke Ellington began to gain recognition as a composer and jazz pianist.

Antony Tudor, English-born dancer, choreographed his masterpiece, *Pillar of Fire*.
Agnes de Mille created an extended version of *Rodeo,* the first ballet to include tap dancing, for Ballet Russe de Monte Carlo.
Ossessione established Luchino Visconti's reputation as a film director.
Casablanca, a film destined to become a classic, was produced.
Glen Miller entertained troops with his distinctive "big band" saxophone sound.

Battle of the Ukraine was a documentary film, shot with 24 cameras on the war front.
Ralph Vaughan Williams wrote his contemplative *Symphony No 5 in D,* a masterpiece of grave, symphonic composition.

The age of jets began with the introduction of the RAF's Gloster Meteor and Luftwaffe's Messerschmitt Me 262.

Science and Technology

British scientist Howard Florey devised a process for the large-scale production of penicillin, and clinical trials began.

Scientists began work on the Manhattan Project to develop an atomic bomb.
Frank Whittle's jet engine achieved its first test flight.

The Lend-Lease Act authorized the US to aid its allies.
Pearl Harbor resulted in the loss of 19 ships, 140 aircraft and 2,300 lives.

The first operational nuclear reactor produced plutonium for use in the Manhattan Project.
The first portable kidney dialysis machine was developed.
Barnes Wallis invented the bouncing bomb to attack the Mohne and Eder dams in Germany.

After appointment as supreme commander of allied forces in Europe, Eisenhower supervised the D-Day invasion.
The G.I. Bill of Rights provided education and other benefits for veterans.

America

Franklin D. Roosevelt was elected to an unprecedented third term as President.
The Selective Service and Training Act, was passed by Congress.

A team of scientists led by Enrico Fermi achieved the first controlled nuclear chain reaction in an experimental nuclear pile at the University of Chicago.

General MacArthur was appointed Commander of the Southwest Pacific area.
Approximately 110,000 Japanese-Americans were relocated from the West Coast to interior camps.

The "Big Inch", the world's longest oil pipeline, from Texas to Pennsylvania, was dedicated.

THE BATTLE OF BRITAIN   WINSTON CHURCHILL   PEARL HARBOR   V2 ROCKET   CONCENTRATION CAM

Soviet troops entered Berlin on 21 April. Hitler shot himself on 30 April. Germany formally capitulated at Rheims on 7 May.

The concentration camps at Dachau and Auschwitz were liberated. It was estimated that Nazi genocide had claimed more than 14 million lives.

Mussolini was shot by Italian partisans on 28 April.

A US B-29 bomber dropped an atomic bomb on the Japanese city of Hiroshima on 6 August. Three days later a second bomb was dropped on Nagasaki. Japan officially surrendered on 15 August.

The structure of the United Nations Organization was agreed.

Sartre published *The Age of Reason,* the first novel in his Roads to Freedom trilogy.

Evelyn Waugh published *Brideshead Revisited.*

La Belle et la Bête became Jean Cocteau's most famous film.

Roberto Rossellini directed *Rome, Open City,* a neo-realist film.

Be bop emerged as a reaction to swing.

Benjamin Britten's masterpiece, *Peter Grimes,* marked the start of a new era in English opera.

Following the death of President Roosevelt and the successful testing of an atomic bomb in Alamogordo, New Mexico, President Harry S. Truman ordered the bombing of Hiroshima and Nagasaki.

Former Nazi leaders were tried at Nuremberg for war crimes. Ten were executed; Goering committed suicide. Rudolf Hess was sentenced to life imprisonment.

Juan Perón was elected President of Argentina. He instituted a Spanish-style fascist government.

Zionist terrorists blew up the King David Hotel in Jerusalem, where the British administration of Palestine was housed. Ninety-one people died.

William Carlos Williams published the first volume of his ambitious poem *Paterson.*

Germaine Richier completed *The bat-man,* a typical, shocking, mutilated sculptural form.

Sidney Nolan, the Australian painter, began his celebrated *Ned Kelly* series.

David Lean made two of his greatest films, *Brief Encounter* and *Great Expectations.*

The musical comedy *Annie Get Your Gun* produced more hits than any previous show.

British choreographer Frederick Ashton used César Franck's music for his ballet *Symphonic Variations.*

The Electronic Numerical Integrator and Calculator — ENIAC — became the first completely electronic computer, using 18,000 radio valves.

The Atomic Energy Commission was established to regulate peaceful and military uses of nuclear energy.

The United Nations selected New York City as its permanent headquarters.

Nationalist Viet-Minh forces attacked the French at Hanoi, marking the outbreak of the Indo-China war.

The India Independence Act, which created a predominately Hindu India and a Muslim Pakistan, was rushed through Parliament in eight days.

General Marshall, the US Secretary of State, proposed the Marshall Plan, offering US aid for the economic rebuilding of Europe.

King Michael of Romania abdicated and the country became a People's Republic.

Malcolm Lowry's *Under the Volcano* was published.

Jean Genet, French novelist and ex-convict, published his first novel, *Querelle de Brest.*

Man Pointing was a fine example of the work of Alberto Giacometti.

Richard Neutra completed the Kauffmann Desert House and began the Tremaine House, both in California.

Henri Cartier-Bresson, the French photographer who advanced the art of photojournalism, was given a one-man show at the Museum of Modern Art, New York.

The Edinburgh International Festival of Music and Drama was founded.

Italian operatic soprano Maria Callas made her debut at Verona in Ponchielli's *Gioconda.*

Radio carbon dating was suggested by American chemist Willard Libby.

The Truman Doctrine offered aid to countries that resisted totalitarianism.

The Taft-Hartley Act limited the power of US labor unions.

Israel was proclaimed a Jewish state on 14 May. The Arab countries invaded the next day. The War of Independence continued for six months.

The Soviet authorities in Berlin effectively blockaded the city. Britain and America responded with an air-lift of food and fuel.

The National Party of South Africa won a general election and imposed apartheid policies.

Mahatma Gandhi was assassinated by a Hindu extremist on 30 January.

The Lady's Not for Burning, Christopher Fry's most famous play, showed his command of language.

Albert Camus published *The Plague.*

The Equitable Building in Portland Oregon, was designed by Pietro Belluschi.

Barnett Newman, the American Color-Field painter, arrived at his restrained, mature style in *Onement I.*

The film *The Red Shoes* was choreographed by Léonide Massine.

New York City Ballet was formed by George Balanchine.

Eero Saarinen began the huge General Motors Technical Center in Warren, Michigan.

Cole Porter wrote *Kiss Me Kate.*

The first transistor was made at Bell Laboratories by the American physicist John Bardeen.

American sexologist Alfred Kinsey published *Sexual Behavior in the Human Male.*

Astronomer George Garrow proposed a Big Bang theory of the universe.

US participation in the Berlin airlift marked severe escalation of the Cold War.

President Truman upset Republican Thomas Dewey in the presidential election.

The Chinese People's Republic was formally proclaimed on 7 October in Peking.

The North Atlantic Treaty Organization (NATO) became the cornerstone of Western military policy.

The German Democratic Republic, the area of Germany under Soviet control, came into being on 7 October.

The Soviet Union exploded its first atomic bomb.

George Orwell's *1984* was published.

Simone de Beauvoir published her study on the role of women in society, *The Second Sex.*

Philip Johnson found fame for his "Glass House" in New Canaan, Connecticut. Entirely of glass and steel, apart from a cylindrical, brick bathroom, it is a study in purism.

The greatest Ealing Studio comedies appeared in this year: *Passport to Pimlico, Whisky Galore* and *Kind Hearts and Coronets.*

The samba, a dance originating in Brazil, became internationally popular.

Rodgers and Hammerstein's *South Pacific* opened and eventually notched up 1,925 consecutive performances.

Medical researchers at Ohio State University used cobalt-60 to treat cancer patients.

The Senate ratified the North Atlantic Treaty, signed in Washington D.C. by 12 nations.

Eleven US Communist leaders were convicted for advocating overthrow of US government.

ATOMIC BOMB   UNITED NATIONS SYMBOL   TRANSISTOR   MAHATMA GHANDI   ORWELL'S PROPHECY

1950   1951   1952   1953   1954

World Events

The Korean War erupted on June 25 when communist North Korea invaded South Korea. United Nations troops (mainly American and South Korean) under General Douglas MacArthur counterattacked but were thrown back by the entry of Chinese troops.
India, under Jawaharlal Nehru, became an independent democratic republic.
Tibet was occupied by China.
Klaus Fuchs a German communist spy and naturalized Briton, was convicted of passing atomic secrets to the USSR.

The Korean War reached a bloody stalemate after General MacArthur was dismissed by President Truman for advocating the bombing of China.
The Soviet Union tested an atomic bomb.
Winston Churchill's Conservatives returned to power in Britain after six years of Labour government.
The Japanese Peace Treaty recognized Japan's "full sovereignty".

J D Salinger the American novelist, caught a new undercurrent of teenage disillusion in *The Catcher in the Rye.*

Dwight D Eisenhower was elected United States President.
Elizabeth II became Queen of Great Britain and Northern Ireland.
The Bonn Convention ended the occupation of West Germany.
Mau Mau terrorists began a seven-year campaign to drive Europeans out of Kenya.
A military coup in Egypt forced King Farouk I to abdicate.

Dylan Thomas published his *Collected Poems.*

Joseph Stalin died, to be replaced by a collective USSR leadership in which Nikita Khrushchev was soon to emerge as the dominant figure.
The Korean War ended with an armistice signed at Panmunjom.
Dag Hammarskjold became an influential Secretary-General of the United Nations.
Mt Everest was conquered by Edmund Hillary and Tenzing Norgay.
Julius and Ethel Rosenberg were executed for passing atomic secrets to Russia.

In **Indo-China** the Viet Minh defeated the French at Dien Bien Phu. Vietnam was soon partitioned between a communist regime in Hanoi led by Ho Chi Minh and an anticommunist regime in Saigon under Ngo Dinh Diem.
Greek Cypriots seeking *enosis* (union with Greece) caused disturbances throughout the British colony of Cyprus.
Gamal Abdel Nasser became Prime Minister of Egypt, emerging as a key figure in Middle East nationalism.

Literature Religion Philosophy

Pope Pius XII proclaimed the dogma of the bodily assumption of the Virgin Mary.

Ernest Hemingway, who had published *The Old Man and the Sea* in 1952, won the Nobel Prize for Literature.
William Golding published his allegory of human evil, *Lord of the Flies.*
J R R Tolkien introduced a new mythological world for children in the first part of his trilogy, *The Lord of the Rings.*

Art and Architecture

The Secretariat Building of the United Nations was completed, exemplifying monumental styles in glass and concrete.

Japanese films came to the West's attention when *Rashomon,* directed by Akira Kurosawa, won the Venice Grand Prix.

Samuel Beckett's masterly *Waiting for Godot* established Theater of the Absurd as the major trend in avant-garde theater.
Fred Zimmerman directed *High Noon,* his most famous film.
Merce Cunningham formed his own modern dance company in the United States.

Arthur Miller, the American dramatist, dealt a forceful blow against the McCarthy witch hunts in his play *The Crucible.*

Performing Arts

Science and Technology

Radio paging started in the United States with a call to a doctor on a golf course.
Antihistamines arrived on the market as popular remedies for colds and allergies.
Britain and France were linked by TV for the first time.

The first heart-lung machine was invented.
The first transistorized hearing aid was exhibited.

The first sex-change operation was carried out.
The first major nuclear accident occurred at a reactor in Canada.
The ultra-wide screen, was installed in cinemas.
The first pocket-sized transistor radio was marketed.
The first hydrogen bomb was tested by the United States.

The first Soviet hydrogen bomb was exploded.
The double helix structure of the DNA molecule was revealed by Francis Crick and James Watson.
Lung cancer was attributed for the first time by doctors to cigarette smoking.
The first human transplant (a kidney from mother to son) was performed in Paris.

The final version of Under Milk Wood, Dylan Thomas's play for voices, was broadcast by the BBC.
The Annual International Jazz Festival was established at Newport, Rhode Island.

A polio vaccine, was developed by American virologist Jonas Edward Salk.

America

Sen. Joseph McCarthy accused the State Department of employing 205 communists. The Senate found the charges untrue, **but anti-communist feeling** led Congress to pass the McCarran Act restricting communists in the US.

The Constitution's 22nd Amendment limited the president to a maximum of two terms.
US troops in Korea halted north of the 38th parallel as peace talks began.

President Truman seized steel mills to prevent a workers' strike; the move was ruled unconstitutional by the Supreme Court.
Eisenhower and running mate **Richard Nixon** campaigned against Truman's policies on Korea and China.

Eisenhower appointed as Secretary of State the staunch anti-communist John Foster Dulles.
Spies Julius and Ethel Rosenberg were executed for passing atomic secrets to Russia.

The Supreme Court, in *Brown v. Board of Education of Topeka,* found segregation in public schools illegal under the Constitution's 14th Amendment.
Senator McCarthy was censured by the Senate for his conduct.

KOREA   JAWAHARLAL NEHRU   EDMUND HILLARY TENZING NORGAY   NAS

The Warsaw Pact was formed as West Germany joined NATO.
Juan Peron, President of Argentina, was forced into exile.
Allied occupation of Austria ended.

Vladimir Nabokov Russian-born master of English literary form, published his most famous novel, *Lolita.*

Pablo Picasso, the Spanish painter and sculptor, celebrated his 75th birthday with international exhibitions of his work.

Serge Prokofiev's opera, *The Angel of Fire* (1925), which the composer regarded as his finest work, had its first performance.

The hovercraft was invented in Britain.
Optical fibers were invented in London.
Oral contraceptives were successfully tested in the United States.
Electricity generated by atomic energy was first used commercially in the United States.
Albert Einstein the German-born American physicist, died. He developed the general theory of relativity (1916) on mass and energy.

Eisenhower attended the first "summit conference," with UK, French, and Soviet leaders.
The Montgomery (Alabama) bus boycott began; its leader, Martin Luther King, Jr., became prominent in the civil rights movement.

Hungary was invaded by Soviet troops to crush a revolt against the communist regime.
The Suez Canal was nationalized by Nasser. Israel attacked Egypt, joined by Britain and France until United States pressure forced a withdrawal.
A Sino-Soviet split developed along ideological lines.
Nikita Khrushchev denounced Stalinism.
France granted independence to Tunisia and Morocco.
Sudan became independent.

Pop art emerged, pioneered in Britain by artists such as David Hockney, Richard Hamilton, and Peter Blake and in the United States, by Andy Warhol, Roy Lichtenstein, and Robert Rauschenberg.
Sydney Opera House was designed by the Danish architect Joern Utzon.

John Osborne, the English dramatist, introduced the "angry young man" in *Look Back in Anger.*
Maria Callas, American-born Greek operative soprano, made her debut at the Metropolitan Opera House.

The first video recording was demonstrated in the United States.
Atoms became visible in a new ion microscope.
FORTRAN computer language was invented.

Eisenhower was overwhelmingly reelected; Adlai Stevenson won only seven southern states, but Democrats had control of the House and Senate.
Riots prevented the University of Alabama's first black student from enrolling.

The EEC (European Economic Community) was set up by Belgium, France, West Germany, Italy, Luxembourg, and The Netherlands.
Sputnik I, launched by the Soviet Union, became the first manmade satellite.
Israel withdrew from Egypt's Sinai Peninsula and handed the Gaza strip to the United Nations.

Jack Kerouac spoke for America's Beat Generation in *On the Road.*
Boris Pasternak expressed his disillusionment with the Russian Revolution in *Dr Zhivago.*

Leonard Bernstein the American conductor, composed *West Side Story.*

Atlas, the first American intercontinental ballistic missile, was tested.

Violence caused Eisenhower to send federal troops to Little Rock, Arkansas, to enforce school integration of blacks.
The Eisenhower Doctrine allowed the president to aid any Middle Eastern nation requesting it.

Charles de Gaulle became president of France by public demand.
Fidel Castro began total (civil) war in Cuba against the Batista regime.
China's Great Leap Forward began a second five-year plan, which eventually proved disappointing.

Mies van der Rohe finished his perfect work, the Seagram Building, New York.
Kinetic art depended on movement and light for its effects, as in Alexander Calder's *Mobile.*

The Birthday Party was Harold Pinter's first full-length "comedy of menace"

NASA (National Aeronautics and Space Administration) was established.
The first color videotape was transmitted in the US.
Explorer I, the first American satellite, was launched.
High-frequency sound waves were first used to show a clear outline of an unborn child.
Stereophonic records first became available.

Vice President Nixon was confronted by demonstrators in South America.
The Eisenhower Doctrine was invoked to respond to Lebanon's appeal, and up to 15,000 US troops were in the country before withdrawal.

Chinese troops repressed a revolt in Tibet. The Dalai Lama fled to India.
Cuba fell to the leftwing guerilas of Fidel Castro.
The Belgian Congo saw serious anti-European rioting as the Congolese demanded independence.
Archbishop Makarios, exiled Cypriot leader, returned to Cyprus in a Greek-Turkish provisional government.

D H Lawrence's *Lady Chatterley's Lover* was unsuccessfully prosecuted on an obscenity charge.
Pope John XXIII called the first Ecumenical Council since 1870.
The Tin Drum by Günther Grass surveyed German history through the eyes of an insane dwarf.

Frank Lloyd Wright's Guggenheim Museum opened in New York.

Francois Truffaut and Jean-Luc Godard pioneered the New Wave of French cinema.
"Rock 'n roll" began to dominate youth culture, pioneered by Chuck Berry and popularized by Elvis Presley.

Transistors came to the fore in computer and TV technology.
The St Lawrence Seaway, was opened.
Three Luna spacecraft put the USSR ahead in the space race.

Alaska and Hawaii became the 49th and 50th states.
The Soviet leader Khrushchev visited the US, and relations between the superpowers improved.
The Landrum-Griffin Act aimed at ending union corruption.

KITA KHRUSHCHEV   FIDEL CASTRO   CHARLES DE GAULLE   ELVIS PRESLEY

1960

World Events

South African police opened fire on a group of black demonstrators in Sharpeville. Sixty-seven demonstrators were killed and 200 wounded.
An American Lockheed U-2 reconnaissance aircraft was shot down over the Soviet Union.
The Organization of Petroleum-Exporting Countries (OPEC) was formed.
Mrs Bandaranaike became the world's first female head of state, in Ceylon.

Literature Religion Philosophy

John Updike's *Rabbit, Run* was the first of a number of novels in which he portrayed American middle-class guilts and obsessions.

Art and Architecture

Marc Chagall began his *Twelve Tribes of Israel* windows for the Hadassah-Hebrew University Medical Center, Jerusalem.
Aldo van Eyck began his Amsterdam Orphanage. It is an important example of "brutalist" architecture.

Performing Arts

Psycho, Alfred Hitchcock's great thriller, was released.
Federico Fellini directed *La dolce vita*.
British composer Lionel Bart's musical *Oliver!,* based on Charles Dickens's *Oliver Twist,* survived more than 2,600 performances.

Science and Technology

Quasi-stellar objects — quasars — were identified by American astronomers. Sandage and Schmidt.
The laser — light amplification by stimulated emission of radiation — came into use.

America

The Civil Rights Act protected the voting rights of blacks.
John F. Kennedy was elected as the first Roman Catholic president.
In the U-2 Incident, the Soviets downed a US spy plane.

1961

World Events

A US-backed force of 1,500 Cuban exiles landed in the Bay of Pigs, Cuba, in an attempt to overthrow the regime of Fidel Castro. The operation failed.
On the night of 13 August East German forces sealed off 68 of the 80 crossing points between East and West Berlin and erected the Berlin Wall.
Civil War continued in the Congolese province of Katanga.
UN Secretary General Dag Hammarskjöld was killed in an air crash on the Congolese border.

Literature Religion Philosophy

The American psychiatrist Thomas Szasz argued in *The Myth of Mental Illness* that most psychiatric conditions were not illnesses at all.

Art and Architecture

The Convent of Sainte-Marie de la Tourette at Eveux-sur-L'Arbrescle, France, was completed to Le Corbusier's design.
Maekawa Kunio completed the Festival Hall, Tokyo, a building inspired by Le Corbusier's functionalism.
Bill Brandt published *Perspective of Nudes,* his most influential photographic collection.

Performing Arts

François Truffaut released *Jules et Jim,* Alain Resnais, *Last Year at Marienbad,* and Claude Chabrol *Les Godelureaux,* French New Wave films.
Rudolf Nureyev, a dancer with the Kirov Ballet, defected to the West.

Science and Technology

Soviet cosmonaut Yuri Gagarin became the first man to travel in space, completing a single orbit of the Earth on 12 April in the capsule Vostock in a flight lasting 1hr 48mins.
President Kennedy announced the beginning of the Apollo project to put a man on the Moon by the end of the decade.

America

President Kennedy announced the Peace Corps of volunteers to help in underdeveloped countries.

1962

World Events

Confrontation between the super-powers reached a critical point when US intelligence discovered that the Soviet Union was establishing medium-range nuclear missile bases in Cuba. After a week of tension in which nuclear war seemed possible, the USSR agreed to dismantle them.
Nelson Mandela, a member of the banned African National Congress, was jailed in South Africa for five years.
Adolph Eichmann, a former Nazi official, was found guilty of crimes against the Jewish people and hanged in Jerusalem.
The right-wing OAS failed in an assassination attempt on French President De Gaulle.

Literature Religion Philosophy

The Second Vatican Council opened in Rome.
Alexsandr Solzhenitsyn achieved international recognition with his description of life in a Soviet labor camp, *One Day in the Life of Ivan Denisovitch*.

Art and Architecture

Roy Lichtenstein caused a sensation with his first exhibition of giant comic-strip paintings.
Ernst Haas was given the first one-man show of color photographs at the Museum of Modern Art, New York.

Performing Arts

The legendary ballet partnership of Nureyev and Margot Fonteyn began with *Giselle* at Covent Garden.
Benjamin Britten composed his moving *War Requiem* for the opening of the new Coventry Cathedral.
Swiss dramatist Friedrich Dürrenmatt wrote one of his most famous plays, *The Physicist*.

Science and Technology

John Glenn became the first American in space.
The satellite Telstar provided live transatlantic television broadcasts.
Mariner 2 completed the first fly-past of another planet — Venus — after a 109-day flight.

America

The first black student entered the University of Mississippi.

1963

World Events

President Kennedy was shot by a sniper while driving in a motorcade through Dallas, Texas, on 22 November. His assassin, Lee Harvey Oswald, was arrested, but two days later he too was shot dead by Jack Ruby.
Martin Luther King led a peaceful march of 250,000 blacks on Washington to demand equal Civil Rights.
The Soviet Union, the United States and Britain signed a partial Test-Ban Treaty.

Literature Religion Philosophy

Pope John XXIII died after five years in holy office. Cardinal Montini, his successor, took the name Pope Paul VI.
German novelist Günter Grass published *Dog Years,* the second of his novels dealing with Germany and the rise of Fascism.

Art and Architecture

Paul Rudolph's School of Art and Architecture, Yale University, was completed.
Robert Rauschenberg created *Monogram,* a stuffed angora goat, girt with a tyre and dabbed with paint.

Performing Arts

Fielding's *Tom Jones* was adapted for film by John Osborne and directed by Tony Richardson.
Michael Tippett's *Concerto for Orchestra* marked a new phase in the composer's style.

Science and Technology

The British immunologists Elizabeth Press and Robert Porter revealed the chemical structure of antibodies.
American physician J.D. Hardy performed the first human lung transplant.

America

The US presence in Vietnam increased.
Lyndon B. Johnson succeeded Kennedy and appointed The Warren Commission, headed by Chief Justice Earl Warren, to investigate the President's assassination.

1964

World Events

US naval vessels were attacked by North Vietnamese torpedo boats in the Gulf of Tonkin. Congress authorized the President to use force to defend freedom in Southeast Asia.
Nelson Mandela was tried under South Africa's Suppression of Communism Act and given a life sentence.
Nikita Khrushchev was deposed as Prime Minister of the Soviet Union and succeeded by Aleksei Kosygin.
China exploded its first atomic bomb.
Black militancy in the United States led to rioting in the New York district of Harlem.

Literature Religion Philosophy

Roland Barthes published an analytical study of linguistic and social "signs" in *Elements of Semiology*.

Art and Architecture

The New York State Theater was designed by Philip Johnson.
Jasper Johns's *Painted bronze II* depicted two beer cans;
Andy Warhol produced *Brillo*.
Hugh Casson's Elephant House was opened at London Zoo.

Performing Arts

Peter Weiss' *Marat/Sade* was first performed in West Berlin.
Stanley Kubrick's *Dr Strangelove* treated satirically the possibility of a nuclear holocaust.

Science and Technology

The United States Ranger 7 spacecraft sent back detailed close-up photographs of the Moon's surface.

America

The Civil Rights Act guaranteed equal treatment in public accomodation, education, voting, and employment.
Congress passed the Gulf of Tonkin Resolution, allowing action against North Vietnam.

YURI GAGARIN   BERLIN WALL   NELSON MANDELA   JOHN KENNEDY

More than 125,000 American troops were on active service in Vietnam by August.

Mao Tse Tung's Cultural Revolution began in China.

A dispute between India and Pakistan over the status of Kashmir deteriorated into war. The Soviet leader Kosygin arranged a ceasefire.

Rhodesia broke away from Britain.

Winston Churchill died on 24 January, aged 91. He was given a state funeral.

The Thoughts of Chairman Mao was published worldwide by the Chinese authorities.

Ralph Nader drew attention to the rights of the consumer with the publication of *Unsafe at Any Speed,* a study of safety factors in American automobiles.

David Smith, an American sculptor who used welding and surface effects, made his final *Cubi* construction.

Kenneth MacMillan choreographed *Romeo and Juliet* for the Royal Ballet.

Who's Afraid of Virginia Woolf? became a powerful film, with Richard Burton and Elizabeth Taylor.

Bob Dylan launched his hit *Highway 61 Revisited,* a successful fusion of folk and rock.

The space probe Mariner 4 sent back images of Mars showing surface detail with extraordinary clarity.

Alexsei Leonov became the first man to "walk" in space.

Nobel Peace Laureate Martin Luther King led a civil rights march in Selma, Alabama.

Medicare, a federal health insurance program for the aged, was signed into law.

35 died in race riots in the Watts distinct of Los Angeles.

Mrs Gandhi was elected Prime Minister of India.

President Verwoerd, Prime Minister of South Africa, was assassinated by a Portugese East African.

President Nkrumah of Ghana was ousted by a military coup.

TV pictures were transmitted from the surface of the Moon when the Soviet spacecraft Luna 9 made a successful unmanned landing.

The Archbishop of Canterbury, Michael Ramsey, paid an official visit to Rome.

Truman Capote claimed to have invented the "non-fiction novel" with *In Cold Blood.*

Kenneth Noland used stained-canvas technique to produce *Par Transit.*

Robert Venturi published *Complexity and Contradiction in Architecture.*

David Hockney painted *Peter getting out of Nick's pool.*

Liverpool pop stars The Beatles followed their successful invasion of the American market in the early 1960s with *Revolver,* displaying a haunting new development in musical accompaniment.

The new Metropolitan Opera House was opened in the Lincoln Center in New York.

The American physicist Murray Gell-Mann postulated the existence of quarks.

The Model Cities Act offered incentives for the rehabilitation of slums.

Protests mounted as US involvement in Vietnam increased.

Israel launched a pre-emptive strike against neighbouring Arab countries in what became known as the Six-Day War. Israeli forces reached Suez, the west bank of the Jordan river, and the Golan Heights, some 30 miles inside Syria.

In Greece, right-wing colonels in the army staged a coup. King Constantine II was forced into exile eight months later.

Civil war broke out in Nigeria. **"Che" Guevara,** Fidel Castro's trusted aide, was captured and executed by Bolivian authorities while aiding guerrillas in that country.

The British poet Ted Hughes published *Wodwo.*

Twenty Letters to a Friend by Svetlana Alliluyeva, Stalin's daughter, gave a fascinating insight into her childhood.

For Expo 67, a geodesic dome designed by Buckminster Fuller formed the American pavilion.

American popular vocalist Barbra Streisand entertained an audience of 135,000 in Central Park, New York.

Dr Christiaan Barnard, of Cape Town, performed the first human heart transplant.

The British astronomer Anthony Hewish working with a graduate student, Jocelyn Bell, discovered the first pulsar, a rotating neutron star.

Thurgood Marshall became the first black to sit on the US Supreme Court.

Stalin's daughter Svetlana Alliluyeva settled in the US.

Senator Eugene McCarthy became an antiwar candidate for the presidency.

North Vietnamese forces launched the Tet offensive. It led to a review of American policy in Vietnam, and the bombing of North Vietnam was suspended.

Warsaw Pact troops and tanks entered Czechoslovakia "to protect socialism." Reforms instituted by Alexander Dubček, first secretary of the Czechoslovakian Communist Party, were dismantled and Dubček was later replaced.

Student demonstrations in Paris met a violent police response and turned into full-scale riots, followed by a General Strike.

Martin Luther King was assassinated on 4 April.

Senator Robert Kennedy was assassinated on 5 June.

Pope Paul VI re-affirmed the Roman Catholic Church's opposition to any form of artifical birth control.

Columbian novelist Gabriel García Márquez published his masterpiece *A Hundred Years of Solitude.*

The Gallery of the Twentieth Century, by Mies van der Rohe, was dedicated in Berlin.

Edward Kienholz created his *Portable war memorial,* a bizarre tableaux, including a hot dog stand and a coke dispenser.

2001: A Space Odyssey was Stanley Kubrick's sci-fi masterpiece.

Apollo 8, with a crew of three astronauts, made the first manned orbit of the Moon.

The USS Pueblo, an intelligence ship, was seized in North Korean waters.

Racial violence followed Martin Luther King's assassination in Memphis.

Republican Richard Nixon was elected president.

Public opposition to America's role in Vietnam increased when the My Lai massacre of the previous year became known.

Thousands of Biafrans starved as the civil war in Nigeria dragged on.

Mrs Golda Meir was elected Prime Minister of Israel.

Colonel Gadaffi founded the Libyan People's Republic.

Spain sealed its frontier with Gilbraltar.

Philip Roth published *Portnoy's Complaint.*

Kurt Vonnegut published his most successful novel, *Slaughterhouse 5.*

Alexander Calder's *La Grande Vitesse* was set up in Grand Rapids, Michigan.

Buckminster Fuller designed the Samuel Beckett Theatre for St Peter's College, Oxford University.

Monty Python's Flying Circus was first broadcast by the BBC.

Kenneth Clark's *Civilization* brought art to millions via television.

The Woodstock Music and Art Fair attracted an audience of more than 200,000.

On 20 July astronaut Neil Armstrong became the first man to set foot on the Moon.

The first fertilization of a human egg outside the human body was achieved by Dr Robert Edwards in Cambridge.

Warren Burger became the Supreme Court Chief Justice.

The US began reducing the number of troops in Vietnam.

MAO TSE TUNG

MINISKIRT

LAVOIX DE SON MAITRE

PARIS 1968

MARTIN LUTHER KING

ARMSTRONG ON THE MOON

1970

World Events

America recommended heavy bombing of North Vietnam in March.
The Ohio State National Guard was summoned to Kent State University to deal with an anti-war demonstration. Troopers opened fire, killing four students and seriously wounding others.
Salvador Allende was elected President of Chile.
President Nasser of Egypt died and was succeeded by Mohammed Sadat.
There was heavy fighting in Jordan between government forces and Palestinian guerrillas.
President De Gaulle died suddenly at his home in Colombey, aged 90.

Literature Religion Philosophy

Germaine Greer's *The Female Eunuch* became an international best-seller.
The Japanese novelist Yukio Mishima committed *harakiri* after failing to inspire a right-wing coup in Japan.

Art and Architecture

Supermarket lady, a fibreglass figure, illustrated Duane Hanson's Superrealism.

Performing Arts

England's Maggie Smith emerged as an internationally sought after stage and screen actress.
German conductor and composer Otto Klemperer conducted Mahler's *Song of the Earth* at his 85th birthday concert.

Science and Technology

An explosion crippled the Apollo 13 craft 200,000 miles from Earth: the crew transferred to the lunar module.
L-dopa was found to help people suffering from Parkinson's disease.

America

The Occupational Safety and Health Act mandated a hazard-free workplace for employees.

1971

The Ugandan army staged a coup while President Obote was abroad and Idi Amin proclaimed himself head of state. He abolished parliament and instituted a despotic reign of terror.
The state of Bangladesh, formally East Pakistan, was proclaimed by separatists. Civil war followed and the country was plunged into anarchy. Indian intervention to restore order led to a brief war with Pakistan.
"Papa Doc" Duvalier, the despotic President of Haiti, died and was succeeded by his son "Baby Doc."
Switzerland became the last developed Western country to enfranchise women.

Paris honored Picasso on his 90th birthday, displaying eight of his works in the Louvre.

Death in Venice was Visconti's masterpiece.
Losey's *The Go-Between* won the grand prize at the Cannes Film Festival.
Fiddler on the Roof became the longest running musical in Broadway history. It closed the following year after 3,242 performances.

Ivan Illich presented the case for a more libertarian approach to education in his book *Deschooling Society.*

Intel of California produced the first microprocessor, an integrated circuit on a "chip" of silicon.
The Mariner 9 space probe mapped the surface of the planet Mars with over 7,000 photographs.

The 26th Amendment gave 18-year-olds the right to vote.
Defense Department employee Daniel Ellsberg was indicted for leaking the classified Pentagon Papers that detailed the history of US involvement in Vietnam.

1972

Fighting in Vietnam intensified, with more heavy bombing raids.
During the Olympic Games at Munich Palestinian terrorists attacked the Israeli team, killing two athletes outright and taking nine others hostage. The hostages were shot, and five terrorists killed, when German security forces attempted a rescue. Terrorists taken prisoner were released six weeks later when the German authorities capitulated to the hijack of a Lufthansa jet.
The first Strategic Arms Limitation Treaty (SALT 1) was signed.

Solzhenitsyn's novel *August 1914* was published.

Controversy erupted over Carl André's *Equivalent VIII,* known as the Tate Gallery Bricks.
Minoru Yamasaki's award-winning Pruitt-Igoe housing project in St Louis was demolished.

Francis Ford Coppola wrote, directed and produced *The Godfather.*
Play it Again Sam was Woody Allen's film of his 1969 play.
Dmitri Shostakovich's last symphony, his *Symphony No 15 in A,* was a somber musing on death.

Pioneer 10 was launched on a journey to the outer planets.
Computerized axial tomography (CAT) was developed to take X ray images of the brain through any cross-section.

Congress passed the Equal Rights Amendment prohibiting discrimination because of sex.
Despite hints of a Watergate coverup, Nixon was reelected by a landslide.

1973

A ceasefire in Vietnam was signed in Paris and two weeks later the US combat troops withdrew. American military advisers remained to assist the South Vietnamese army.
Egyptian and Syrian forces chose 6 October, Yom Kippur, to launch a surprise attack on Israel. Israel launched a counter-offensive two days later, recovering its positions and advancing to within 60 miles of Cairo. A ceasefire was organized by the United Nations on 24 October.
President Allende of Chile was killed in a military coup. The new regime, headed by General Augusto Pinochet, instituted a regime of severe social and political repression.
Juan Perón returned from exile to become Argentina's President.

Ernst Schumacher argued against the idea of continual economic growth in *Small is Beautiful.*

Sachio Otani completed the extension to the Congress Building, Kyoto, Japan.
Anthony Caro completed *Veduggio Sound,* a metal sculpture of ragged sheets joined at right-angles.
F.E. McWilliam completed his emotional sculpture, *Women of Belfast.*
Pablo Picasso and **Pablo Casals** died.

Perry Como became the most successful American recording artist in Britain.

Nuclear Magnetic Resonance was successfully developed as a new diagnostic technique at Aberdeen University.
A temperature of 59.4° Centigrade (138.9°F) was recorded in Algeria.

Vice President Spiro Agnew resigned after charges of tax evasion and was succeeded by Rep. Gerald Ford.
The widening Watergate scandal resulted in impeachment proceedings against Nixon.

1974

President Nixon resigned on 9 August, admitting complicity in the Watergate affair — a Presidential cover-up of a break-in at the Democratic Party's headquarters in Washington in the run-up to the Presidential election of 1972. Nixon received a pardon from his successor, President Ford.
A UN peace-keeping force was established in the Golan Heights to provide a buffer zone between Israel and Syria.
In Portugal, a group of junior army officers staged a bloodless coup on 25 April.
Turkey invaded Cyprus, seizing almost half the island and establishing a Turkish Federated State.

Cyril Connolly, founder of the influential periodical *Horizon* died.
W.H. Auden's last book of poetry, *Thank You, Fog,* was published.
Joseph Heller, author of *Catch-22,* published *Something Happened.*

The twin towers of the World Trade Center, New York, were completed. At 1,378 feet they are the tallest buildings in Manhatten, Minoru Yamasaki was the designer.
Joseph Beuys, produced *Coyote,* a week-long "dialog" with a live coyote.
Pierre Alechinsky continued working in the CoBrA tradition of strange imagery and rich colouring, as in his *Monsieur Hune.*

Mel Brooks produced *Young Frankenstein.*
ABBA won the Eurovision Song Contest with "Waterloo."

A fourth quark was discovered using the particle accelerator at Stanford.

The Arab oil embargo ended, easing the energy crisis.
Ford offered amnesty to Vietnam War era deserters and draft resisters.

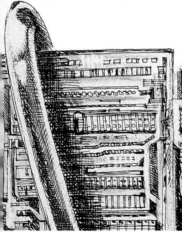

MICROCHIP

VIETNAM

RICHARD NIXON

North Vietnam launched an offensive against the South. Saigon fell on 30 April and was renamed Ho Chih Minh City. The last American advisers and diplomats escaped by helicopter just hours before the city fell.
Portugal granted Angola independence. A confused civil war broke out between rival factions.
Mozambique gained independence from Portugal.
Civil war broke out in Lebanon between Christians and Moslems. Much of Beirut was destroyed in the fighting.
Haile Selassie died while under house detention.
General Franco died.

Saul Bellow published what many critics consider his best novel, *Humboldt's Gift*.

The National Theatre was opened as part of London's South Bank complex.

Soviet and American spacecraft Soyuz 19 and Apollo 18 performed an historic docking in orbit. The craft remained joined for two days.
Monoclonal antibodies were created by genetic engineering at Cambridge. The discovery opened up the possibility of manufacturing antibodies to target on specific diseases.

Several Nixon staff and cabinet members were convicted for criminal activities associated with Watergate.
Supreme Court justice William O. Douglas retired.
President Ford survived two attempts on his life.

An Israeli commando unit made a surprise attack on a hijacked Air France jet at Entebbe Airport, Uganda, freeing 106 hostages. Eleven Ugandan aircraft were destroyed in the raid and 20 Ugandan soldiers and seven PLO terrorists killed. One Israeli officer and three hostages also died.
Riots broke out in the black township of Soweto, South Africa, and lasted for three days. Official figures put the number of dead, almost exclusively black, at 236; other sources at closer to 600.
Syrian troops entered Lebanon and a cease-fire was ordered.
Mao Tse-tung died. His widow and three other leading politicians — the "Gang of Four" — were arrested on charges of conspiracy and sedition.
Official food price rises led to rioting in Polish cities.

"High tech" came of age with the Pompidou Centre, Paris. Renzo Piano and Richard Rogers's great arts complex.
Richard Long, a Land artist, arranged found objects in a pattern, as in *119 stones*.

Hans Werne Henze composed the spectacular war opera *We Came to the River*.

Concorde became the world's first supersonic jet to enter passenger service.

The United States marked the bicentennial of independence with a year-long celebration, cresting on 4 July.
The first women were admitted to US military academies.
Democrat Jimmy Carter defeated Gerald Ford to become President.

The Baader-Meinhof Group hijacked a Lufthansa jet and took it to Mogadishu, Somalia. The 86 hostages were released by a West German anti-terrorist squad and three hijackers killed. News of the rescue caused the group's leader, Andreas Baader, to commit suicide.
Leonid Brezhnev succeeded Kosygin as President of the Soviet Union.
Two jumbo jets collided at Ros Rodeos Airport, Tenerife, killing 575 people.
General Mohammad Zia ousted President Bhutto in Pakistan and arrested him on a charge of conspiracy to murder.
Spain held its first free elections since the civil war. The moderate Democratic Center Party won.
The black South African activist Steve Biko was beaten to death while in police detention.

Sunset at Blandings, P.G. Wodehouse's last, unfinished novel, was published.

Charles Jencks coined the phrase "post-modern". in his essay, *The Language of Post-modern Architecture*.
Heinz Mack's *Light Column* was erected in Munich, tall, slim and vertebrae-like.

Close Encounters of the Third Kind was produced by Steven Spielberg.
George Lucas, writer and director, released *Star Wars*.
Scottish composer Thea Musgrave wrote the opera *Mary Queen of Scots*.

The United States Space Shuttle made its first free-gliding flight.
The United States Defense Department announced the development of a "neutron" bomb.

President Carter established the Department of Energy.

After discussions at Camp David, Maryland, Israel and Egypt agreed to resume normal diplomatic relations. Israel promised to withdraw gradually from Sinai and to establish some form of autonomous Palestinian territory on the West Bank.
The former Prime Minister of Italy, Aldo Moro, was kidnapped by Red Brigade terrorists. The Italian government refused to negotiate, and Moro's body was found in an abandoned car in Rome.
Many "boat people" - Chinese who had left Vietnam or been forcibly expelled — died after drifting for weeks at sea.
The Congolese National Liberation Front massacred more than 200 people in Katanga, Zaire. French and Belgian airborne troops were flown in.
At Jamestown, Guyana, the self-styled Rev. Jim Jones ordered his followers, mostly Americans, to kill themselves by drinking a cocktail laced with cyanide. More than 900 did so.

Polish Cardinal Karol Wojtyla became the first non-Italian Pope since 1522. The new Pope took the name John Paul II.
Graham Green published *The Human Factor,* a story of espionage, loyalty and betrayal.

To celebrate Henry Moore's 80th birthday, an exhibition of his sculptures was held in London's Hyde Park.
John De Andrea's *Seated woman* was nude, made of polyvinyl and utterly realistic.

Evita by Andrew Lloyd Webber and Tim Rice had its first stage performance in London.

The world's first test-tube baby, Louise Brown, was born at Oldham, England, in July.

The US and China agreed to open diplomatic relations.
President Carter hosted successful peace talks between Israeli Premier Begin and Egyptian President Sadat at Camp David, Maryland.

The Ayatollah Khomeini replaced the Shah as head of state in Iran. A committee was formed to govern the country on strict Islamic fundamentalist lines.
Student extremists seized the United States embassy in Teheran and held 63 Americans hostage, demanding the return of the Shah to face trial.
Soviet forces occupied Afghanistan, ostensibly invited in by the socialist Armed Forces Revolutionary Council.
Uganda was invaded by dissident ex-patriot Ugandans and Tanzanian forces. President Amin fled to Libya, accused of crimes ranging from genocide and torture to cannibalism.
Vietnam invaded Kampuchea and captured Phnom-Penh. It was revealed that the Pol Pot regime had killed 3,500,000 people.
In Rhodesia, nationalist guerrilla activity escalated. It was agreed that the country would again be a British dependency controlled by a Governor for a transitional period pending full independence.

William Golding published *Darkness Visible*.

Patrick Caulfield painted *Town and country*, typical of his impersonal, diagramatic interiors.

Sir Laurence Olivier received a special Academy Award for his unrivaled services to theater and cinema.
Abbado Claudio became principal conductor of the London Symphony Orchestra.
Francis Coppola directed *Apocalypse Now*.

Three separate space probes sent back photographs of the planets Jupiter and Saturn.

Following a 1978 treaty, Panama began gradually to take over administration of the Canal Zone.

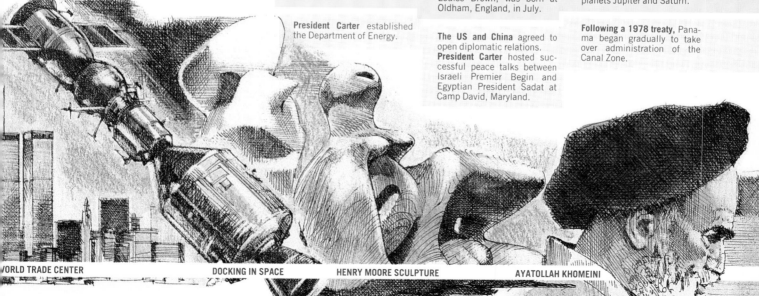

WORLD TRADE CENTER   DOCKING IN SPACE   HENRY MOORE SCULPTURE   AYATOLLAH KHOMEINI

World Events

President Carter tried to resolve the hostage crisis with a helicopter rescue mission in April which failed disastrously – a factor in his decisive defeat by Ronald Reagan in the Presidential elections.
Iraq launched a full-scale war on Iran on 22 September, soon deadlocked.
Civil war raged in El Salvador between left-wing guerrillas and right-wing death squads. Archbishop Oscar Romero, a champion of human rights, was shot while saying Mass.
Rhodesia was proclaimed the independent Republic of Zimbabwe. Robert Mugabe became Prime Minister.
Solidarity, an independent, self-governing union led by Lech Walesa, became the focus of dissent in Poland.

American hostages in Teheran were flown home on 20 January after 444 days in captivity.
President Sadat was assassinated by Moslem fanatics within the Egyptian army during a military review. President Reagan and Pope John Paul II survived assassination attempts after emergency surgery.
Unrest in Poland led to martial law in December and the arrest of Lech Walesa.
Civil Guard Colonel Antonio Tejero spearheaded an attempted coup in Spain by attempting to take over the Cortes at gunpoint. King Juan Carlos ordered the army to remain loyal and the coup failed.
Israeli bombers destroyed a nuclear plant in Iraq.

Britain and Argentina waged an undeclared war over the Falkland Islands. Britain sent out a full task force after Argentina occupied the islands on 2 April. Almost 1,000 lives were lost before Argentinian forces surrendered on 13 June.
Israel invaded the Lebanon to drive out Palestinian forces and laid siege to Palestinian sections of West Beirut for 10 weeks before Palestinian guerrillas were evacuated by sea. Christian Phalangist militia then entered the refugee camps of Chabra and Chatilla and massacred over 800.
Unrest in Sri Lanka, due to a separatist Tamil movement, led to a state of emergency.
Filipe Gonzalez led Spain's socialist party to victory in a general election.

A Cuban-assisted coup in Grenada was overturned when US Marines invaded the island.
In Assam, over 1000 Benghali immigrants were massacred in civil riots over local elections.
The US Marine barracks in Beirut were destroyed when Islamic Jihad terrorists crashed a truck packed with 2,000 lbs of explosives through the gates, killing 239.
MiG Fighters shot down South Korean 747 passenger jet when it strayed into Soviet air space.

Indian troops killed 200 Sikh separatists in an attack on the Golden Temple at Amritsar. Sikh extremists assassinated Mrs Gandhi, the Indian Prime Minister.
Toxic gas from the Union Carbide pesticide plant in Bhopal, India, killed 2,500.
An IRA bomb exploded at the Grand Hotel, Brighton, during the Conservative Party Conference, killing five.
Britain agreed to return Hong Kong to China in 1997.
Ethiopia experienced a disastrous famine.

Literature Religion Philosophy

The Bible was published in China for the first time in 23 years.
Anthony Burgess's monumental novel *Earthly Powers* was published.

Salman Rushdie's *Midnight's Children,* a story of post-Independence India, became a best-seller.

Thomas Keneally published *Schindler's Ark,* a semi-fictional account of a German industrialist who rescued Jews from the concentration camps.

Umberto Eco's *The Name of the Rose,* a detective story set in a medieval monastery, became an international best-seller.

Czech novelist Milan Kundera published *The Unbearable Lightness of Being.*

Art & Architecture

American Photo-Realist painter Ralph Goings continued his depiction of "synthetic America" with *Blue Diner with Figures.*

Hockney Paints the Stage, a touring exhibition of the artist's stage designs, was organized by the Walker Art Center, Minneapolis.

The A.T. & T. Corporation Headquarters in New York was completed, stunningly designed by Philip Johnson and John Burgee.

Performing Arts

Beatle John Lennon was shot dead outside his New York apartment.

Andrew Lloyd-Webber's sensational musical *Cats* opened in London.

Sir Richard Attenborough produced and directed *Ghandhi.*
London's second great arts complex, the Barbican Centre, was opened.

Luis Buñuel, the Spanish film director, died.

Sales of the album *Thriller* by Michael Jackson, topped 45 million copies – a record for pop music.

Science and Technology

Genetic engineering of insulin began clinical trials.

The US Space Shuttle *Columbia* made a three-day maiden flight into Earth orbit.
Voyager II sent back stunning images of Saturn and its system of moons.

The Cray 1 became the world's most powerful computer, able to perform 100 million calculations per second.

The Pioneer 10 space probe passed Neptune and left the Solar System.

The crew of the space shuttle *Challenger* carried out the first retrieval and repair of a satellite in orbit.
The virus causing AIDS was identified.

America

The US boycotted the 1980 Summer Olympic Games to protest the invasion of Afganistan by Soviet forces.
Washington volcano Mount St. Helens erupted violently.

Sandra Day O'Connor became the first woman Supreme Court Justice.

The Equal Rights Amendment, three states short of the 38 needed for ratification, expired on June 30 when the deadline for approval passed.
The Environmental Protection Agency listed 418 dangerous toxic waste sites in the US.

Sally Ride became the first US woman astronaut.
After 132 years, the US lost the America's Cup.

An unidentified Vietnam War casualty was buried in the Tomb of the Unknown Soldier in Arlington, Virginia.
Democrat Geraldine Ferraro was the first woman to be chosen the vice-presidential candidate of a major party.

SOLIDARITY   SPACE SHUTTLE   AIDS

1985

President Reagan started his second term with a "Star Wars" programme, escalating defense expenditure.

Palestinian terrorists hijacked the Italian cruise ship the *Achille Lauro*, killing an American passenger. US jets forced down a plane carrying the escaping terrorists in Sicily but Italy later released them. Terrorists also machine-gunned travelers at Rome and Vienna airports.

French agents sank the Greenpeace ship *Rainbow Warrior* in Auckland to prevent it demonstrating against French nuclear testing in the Pacific.

South Africa declared a State of Emergency as black unrest grew.

Spain re-opened its frontier with Gibraltar after 16 years.

British poet Douglas Dunn was acclaimed for his moving *Elegies*.

Peter Ackroyd published *Hawksmoor*, a brilliant metaphysical mystery story.

Marc Chagall died at 93, longest-lived of the famous School of Paris artists.

French composer/conductor Pierre Boulez completed his *Third Mallarmé Improvisation* celebrating his 60th birthday.

AIDS cases in the United States rose from 8,000 to 14,000 in the course of the year.

President Reagan visited a West German cemetery where Nazi SS troops were buried.

Rock musicians raised funds for African famine victims with Live Aid concert.

Gramm-Rudman Act required a balanced budget by 1991.

1986

The space shuttle *Challenger* exploded just after take-off on 28 January, killing the crew.

At Chernobyl on 26 April the worst-ever accident at a nuclear power station sent radiation fallout drifting across much of Europe.

American aircraft bombed Libyan bases in Tripoli and Benghazi to punish increasing Libyan-inspired terrorist attacks.

President Marcos was ousted in the Philippines by Mrs Corazon Aquino.

President Reagan admitted to a secret "arms for hostages" deal with Iran but denied knowing funds had been illegally diverted to Contra guerrillas in Nicaragua.

German novelist Patrick Susskind published his exotic and experimental *Perfume*.

Sumet Jumsai's design for the Bank of Asia Head Office, Bangkok, combined national and Post-modern styles.

Christopher Hampton's *Les Liaisons Dangereuses*, a Royal Shakespeare production, won a host of prizes.

The European space probe *Giotto* showed the core of Halley's comet to be jet black.

William Rehnquist replaced retiring Chief Justice Burger.

The 100th anniversary of the Statue of Liberty was marked.

1987

Soviet Prime Minister, Mikhail Gorbachev, instituted policies of *glasnost* and *perestroika* — openness and social restructuring to liberalize Soviet society and boost economic productivity. In Washington he and President Reagan agreed to withdraw all land-based intermediate range nuclear missiles.

As the Iran-Iraq war intensified, neutral shipping in the Persian Gulf was attacked by both sides. The US fleet entered the area to protect shipping lanes.

On 19 October – Black Monday – the market on the New York stock exchange collapsed, with over $500 billion being wiped off the value of stocks. The collapse had knock-on effects around the world.

Rudolf Hess, sole Nazi prisoner in Spandau jail, committed suicide.

Iris Murdoch continued her prolific output with *The Book and the Brotherhood*, a philosophic comedy of manners set in Oxford.

Spycatcher made the name of Peter Wright.

David Hockney showed his mastery of stage design in *Tristan and Isolde* directed by Jonathan Miller.

Andrés Segovia, Spanish guitarist who raised the classical guitar to the status of a solo concert instrument, died at 94.

Scientists in Antarctica observed further deterioration in the ozone layer.

The Iran-Contra Affair revealed secret arms sales to Iran, with profits used to arm Contra rebels in Nicaragua.

Reagan and the Soviet leader Mikhail Gorbachev signed a treaty to limit nuclear arms.

1988

Republican Vice-President George Bush was elected US president, beating Democrat, Michael Dukakis.

Tension in the Persian Gulf rose with Iranian attacks on tankers, US naval retaliations and the accidental shooting down of an Iranian airliner.

In a season of natural disasters, flooding in Bangladesh killed thousands and left millions homeless; Hurricane Gilbert swept a trail of destruction through Texas, Haiti, Venezuela and the coast of Mexico; in Armenia entire cities were destroyed by the worst ever earthquake to strike there.

Mikhail Gorbachev was appointed president of the USSR.

A Brief History of Time by severely paralysed author Stephen Hawking became a bestseller in England and the United States.

Prince Charles accused British architects of ruining the appearance of many British towns.

An all-day concert was held at Wembley Stadium in London to mark Nelson Mandela's 70th birthday.

Using sophisticated carbon-dating tests, scientists dated the Turin Shroud to between 1260 and 1390.

A Federal Court charged Panamian leader, General Noriega, of drug-smuggling.

Television evangelist Jimmy Swaggart retired in disgrace after revelations of his affair with a prostitute.

1989

In a year of startling political upheaval the 28-mile long Berlin wall was dismantled allowing free passage between East and West for the first time since 1961. A coalition government was formed in Romania following the abolition of the Communist party, the execution of dictator Nicolae Ceausescu, and the defeat of the *Securitate* by the Romanian army. Anti-government rallies in Prague led to the resignation of the politburo and the end of Communist rule. In Beijing peaceful demonstrations terminated in massacre when the People's Liberation Army advanced on the thousands of students gathered in Tiananmen Square calling for democratic reform.

The Ayatollah Khomeini called on Moslems to kill Salman Rushdie for blasphemy in his novel *The Satanic Verses*.

Surrealist artist Salvador Dali and Nobel prize-winning author Samuel Beckett died.

A new glass pyramid was inaugurated at the Louvre.

Austrian conductor Herbert von Karajan died.

Europe agreed to ban CFCs — industrial gases damaging to the ozone layer.

The oil tanker *Exxon Valdez* ran aground off Alaska, in the worst ever US oil spillage.

The San Francisco Bay area was hit by a quake which measured 6.9 on the Richter scale.

ETHIOPIAN FAMINE   CHERNOBYL   GORBACHEV   THE BERLIN WALL

General History

Boyd, Andrew, *An Atlas of World Affairs* 7th ed., Methuen & Co.Ltd., London, 1983.

Braudel, Fernand, *Capitalism and Material Life 1400-1800*, Harper and Row, London and New York, 1974.

Grun, Bernard, *The Timetables of History*, Simon & Schuster, New York, 1982.

Haig, Christopher, ed., *The Cambridge Historical Encyclopaedia of Great Britain and Ireland*, Cambridge University Press, 1985.

Laudes, David S., *The Unbound Prometheus: Technological Change and Industrial Development in Western Europe from 1750 to the Present*, Cambridge University Press, 1969.

Robertson, Patrick, *The Shell Book of Firsts*, rev. ed., Ebury Press & Michael Joseph, London, 1983.

Steinberg, S. H. and Evans, I. H., *Steinberg's Dictionary of British History*, 2nd ed, Edward Arnold Ltd., London, 1974.

Steinberg, S.H., *Historical Tables*, Macmillan Reference Books, London.

Time Charts from *The Joy of Knowledge Encyclopaedia*, Mitchell Beazley, London, 1977.

Tragers, James, *The People's Chronology*, Heinemann.

Williams, Neville, *Chronology of the Expanding World*, Barrie and Jenkins.

Williams, Neville, *Chronology of the Modern World*, Barrie and Jenkins.

Wright, Esmond, ed., *The Medieval and Renaissance World*, Hamlyn, London, 1979.

Wright, Esmond, ed., *The Expanding World*, Hamlyn, London, 1979.

Wright, Esmond, ed., *The Modern World*, Hamlyn, London, 1979.

Literature, Religion and Philosophy

Drabble, Margaret, ed., *The Oxford Companion to English Literature*, 5th ed., Oxford University Press, Oxford, 1985.

Spiller, Robert et al., *Literary History of The United States*, 4th ed, Vol 1-2, Macmillan, New York, 1975.

Hart, James D., *The Oxford Companion to American Literature*, 5th ed., Oxford University Press, Oxford, 1983.

De Vries, Jan, *The Study of Religion, a Historical Approach*, Harcourt Brace & World, New York, 1967.

Sharpe, E.J., *Comparative Religion: A History*, Duckworth, London, 1976.

Smart, N., *The Phenomenon of Religion*, 2nd rev. ed., Mowbray, Oxford, 1978.

Schneider, Herbert W., *A History of American Philosophy*, Oxford University Press, London, 1946.

Russell, Bertrand, *A History of Western Philosophy*, 2nd ed., Allen & Unwin, London, 1968.

Art and Architecture

Hartt, Frederick, *Art: A History of Painting, Sculpture, Architecture*, Abrams, New York, 1976.

Gombrich, E.H.J., *The Story of Art*, 12th ed., Phaidon, London, 1972.

Janson, H.W., *History of Art: a survey of the major visual arts from the dawn of history to the present day*, rev. ed., Prentice-Hall, New Jersey, 1977.

Pevsner, Nicholas, ed., *The Pelican History of Art*, Harmondsworth; Baltimore, 1953-78.

Green, S.M., *American Art: A Historical Survey*, Ronald, New York, 1966.

Performing Arts

Hartnell, Phyllis, ed., *The Oxford Companion to the Theatre*, 4th ed, Oxford University Press, Oxford, 1983.

Thomson, Peter, and Salgado, Gamini, *The Everyman Companion to the Theatre*, J.M. Dent & Sons, London, 1985.

Arnold, Denis, ed., *The New Oxford Companion to Music*, Oxford University Press, Oxford, 1984.

Earl of Harewood, ed., *Kobbe's Complete Opera Book*, Putnam & Company, London, 1976.

Clarke, May, and Vaughan, David, *The Encyclopedia of Dance and Ballet*, Pitman Publishers, London, 1977.

Lyon, Christopher, ed., *The Macmillan Dictionary of Films and Film makers*, Vol 1-2, The Macmillan Press Ltd, London, 1984.

Bordman, Gerald, *The Oxford Companion to American Theatre*, Oxford University Press, Oxford, 1984.

Medicine, Science and Technology

Sigerist, H.E., *A History of Medicine*, Vol 1-2, Oxford University Press, New York, 1951-61.

Smit, Pieter, *History of the Life Sciences*, A. Asher, Amsterdam, 1974.

Durbin, P.T., ed., *A Guide to the Culture of Science, Technology and Medicine*, Free Press, 1980.

Parkinson, Clare, L., *A Chronology of the Great Achievements in Science and Mathematics*, Mansell Publishing Ltd, London, 1985.

Bynum, W.F., Browne, E.J., Porter, Roy, *Dictionary of the History of Science*, The Macmillan Press Ltd, London, 1981.

Lyons, A.S. & R.J. Petrucelli, *Medicine: An Illustrated History*, Abrams, New York, 1980.

Reference sources for MAKING ENDS MEET (pages 52-3):
The Medieval Economy and Society, M.M. Postan, Pelican, 1975
Reformation to Industrial Revolution, Christopher Hill, Pelican, 1969
Industry and Empire, E.J. Hobsbawm, Pelican, 1969
London Life in the Eighteenth Century, M. Dorothy George, Peregrine Books, 1966
Family Expenditure Survey 1986, HMSO, 1987
Economica, November, 1956 and August, 1955 (London School of Economics & Political Science)
United States economic trends by Ameritrust